SOCIETY FOR NEW TESTAMENT STUDIES

MONOGRAPH SERIES

General Editor: G. N. Stanton

61

WISDOM IN THE Q-TRADITION
THE APHORISTIC TEACHING OF JESUS

Wisdom in the Q-tradition

The Aphoristic Teaching of Jesus

RONALD A. PIPER

Lecturer in New Testament Language and Literature
University of St Andrews

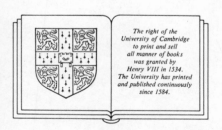

The right of the
University of Cambridge
to print and sell
all manner of books
was granted by
Henry VIII in 1534.
The University has printed
and published continuously
since 1584.

CAMBRIDGE UNIVERSITY PRESS

CAMBRIDGE
NEW YORK   NEW ROCHELLE   MELBOURNE   SYDNEY

Published by the Press Syndicate of the University of Cambridge
The Pitt Building, Trumpington Street, Cambridge CB2 1RP
32 East 57th Street, New York, NY 10022, USA
10 Stamford Road, Oakleigh, Melbourne 3166, Australia

First published 1989

Printed in Great Britain at the University Press, Cambridge

British Library cataloguing in publication data
Piper, Ronald
Wisdom in the Q tradition.
1. Jesus Christ. Teachings
I. Title II. Series
232.9'54

Library of Congress cataloguing in publication data
Piper, Ronald A. (Ronald Allen), 1948–
Wisdom in the Q-tradition: the aphoristic teaching of Jesus
Ronald A. Piper.
        p.   cm. – (Monograph series / Society for New Testament
Studies : 61)
Revision of thesis (doctoral) – University of London, 1986.
Bibliography.
Includes index.
ISBN 0 521 35293 2
1. Jesus Christ – words. 2. Jesus Christ – Teachings. 3. Q
hypothesis (Synoptics criticism) 4. Wisdom literature. 5. Bible.
N.T. Gospels – Criticism, interpretation, etc. I. Title.
II. Series: Monograph series (Society for New Testament Studies):
61.
BT306.P46   1988
226'.066 – dc19   88–10227

ISBN 0 521 35293 2

WS

CONTENTS

PREFACE

One of the characteristics of *logoi sophōn* ('sayings of the wise') is
that they often are viewed less as the creation of individual figures
than as the product of a cumulative tradition of learning. While this
work is hardly to be compared to such *logoi*, it nevertheless shares
the feature that much has been owed to many people during the
process of its composition.

In its present form, this study represents a revision of my doctoral
dissertation, submitted to the University of London in January 1986.
That dissertation was begun under the helpful guidance of Professor
Christopher Evans and his successor, Professor Graham Stanton. As
both supervisor and editor, Professor Stanton has been a continual
encouragement to me, for which I am deeply grateful. The completion
of that dissertation extended into my appointments as temporary
lecturer in New Testament at the University of Aberdeen and as
lecturer at the University of St Andrews. Many of my colleagues at
both of these universities have aided me in important ways of which
they may be only slightly aware.

For perceptive criticisms and helpful suggestions during the period
of revising the thesis for this monograph series, I owe particular
thanks once again to Professor Stanton, and also to Professor David
Catchpole, Professor J. L. Houlden and Dr Christopher Tuckett.
While benefiting from their advice, I am of course solely responsible
for the particular views which are expressed and for any deficiencies
which may be found. I am also grateful to Ulrike Hellen and Dr
Jennifer Fellows of Cambridge University Press for their editorial
advice and to Miss E. A. Gilbertson for her kind help in reading the
proofs.

Finally, I must publicly acknowledge the patience and encouragement offered by my wife during the long, and seemingly unending,
process of 'giving birth' to this work.

ABBREVIATIONS

For periodicals and serials, the abbreviations of the *Theologische Realenzyklopädie* (Berlin/New York, 1976) have been used. Abbreviations for ancient documents, including the Bible, apocryphal and pseudepigraphal works, the early Christian Fathers and rabbinic writings, follow the system in James H. Charlesworth (ed.), *The Old Testament Pseudepigrapha*, I: *Apocalyptic Literature and Testaments* (London, 1982), xliv–l, apart from minor variations which should be self-evident. The system of abbreviation used for the Dead Sea Scrolls follows Joseph A. Fitzmyer, *The Dead Sea Scrolls: Major Publications and Tools for Study* (Missoula, Mont., 1977), pp. 1–53. For Nag Hammadi texts, see C. Tuckett, *Nag Hammadi and the Gospel Tradition* (Edinburgh, 1986), pp. 166–8.

Some abbreviations which are not covered by the above sources include the following:

BDF	Blass, Friedrich, and Debrunner, Albert, *A Greek Grammar of the New Testament and Other Early Christian Literature*, trans. & ed. Robert W. Funk (Chicago/London, 1961)
ET	English Translation
Hennecke–Schneemelcher	Hennecke, Edgar, *New Testament Apocrypha*, I: *Gospels and Related Writings*; II: *Writings Related to the Apostles, Apocalypses and Related Subjects*, ed. W. Schneemelcher, ET by R. McL. Wilson (London, 1963–5)
JSNT	*Journal for the Study of the New Testament*
JSOT	*Journal for the Study of the Old Testament*
log.	logion
NIGTC	The New International Greek Testament Commentary (Exeter)
n.s.	new series

SBL	The Society of Biblical Literature (USA)
Strack–Billerbeck	Strack, Hermann L. and Billerbeck, Paul, *Kommentar zum Neuen Testament aus Talmud und Midrasch* 4 vols. (Munich, 1922–8)
TRE	*Theologische Realenzyklopädie* (Berlin/New York)

INTRODUCTION

Few of the recorded sayings of Jesus can have attracted such a wide popular interest and yet such a limited scholarly interest as his aphorisms. These pithy proverbial sayings are found in abundance in the synoptic tradition. Amongst them are sayings such as:

> 'The labourer is worthy of his hire' (Mt 10:10b)
> 'The measure you give will be the measure you receive'
> (Mt 7:2b)
> 'The tree is known by its fruit' (Mt 12:33b).

Such aphorisms are indeed far more numerous than the parables of Jesus, those figurative sayings with a narrative element. Yet, while the parables have been subjected to intense scholarly study and have been related to the major themes of Jesus' preaching about God's kingdom, very few scholars have known quite what to do with the aphoristic sayings. Therefore, as late as 1983, J.D. Crossan could pointedly write in the introduction to his book, *In Fragments: The Aphorisms of Jesus*, that 'while very many books have been written on the parabolic or narrative tradition of Jesus' sayings, none has ever been written on the non-narrative or aphoristic tradition alone' (p. viii).

Of course it has long been recognized that sayings of a 'proverbial' or 'aphoristic' kind are to be found amongst the sayings of Jesus recorded in the synoptic gospels. Early form-critical studies inevitably had to classify and analyse such sayings. M. Dibelius distinguished the 'gnome' from the Greek 'chria' by indicating that the gnome, unlike the chria, was unconnected with any particular person.[1] However gnomes received little further attention from Dibelius, except to be set in the larger category of apophthegmata.[2] R. Bultmann, on the other hand, chose to differentiate these gnomic sayings from the apophthegmata. He considered the gnomic sayings to be independent units of tradition, not comprising part of a story, and he classified them under the general heading of 'Dominical Sayings' (*Herrenworte*), and more precisely as 'Logia (Jesus as Teacher of Wisdom)'.[3] The close relationship between these sayings and Oriental wisdom was emphasized, and the sayings were described as

> 'proverbs' in the narrower sense, i.e. words of wisdom, aphorisms such as circulated in Israel and in Judaism and throughout the Orient generally, not only among the people but chiefly among the teachers of wisdom – in Judaism the rabbis.[4]

Bultmann further classified the sayings according to their constitutive forms into 'Principles', 'Exhortations', 'Questions' and 'Longer Compositions'.[5] In general, Bultmann's interest lay more in the tendencies which suggest how these sayings may have been modified in the course of transmission than in the way in which the sayings are used, *viz.* the functions which they serve, in the synoptic tradition.

Subsequent studies of the aphoristic sayings in the synoptic gospels have been rather limited. R. W. Funk noted in 1970 the general lack of form-critical analysis of these sayings, declaring that 'form critics threw in the sponge on questions of this order'.[6] Nevertheless some progress has been made in studies by W. Beardslee[7] and N. Perrin,[8] who argue that proverbial wisdom had become intensified eschatologically in the gospels; in D. Zeller's excellent study of wisdom admonitions;[9] and, recently, in J. Crossan's attempt to 'establish a transmissional analysis for each of those 133 sayings'.[10]

The reasons for this relative neglect may be several. The vast quantity of the material is certainly a factor. J. Crossan identifies 133 aphorisms in the synoptic gospels;[11] C.E. Carlston 102;[12] M. Küchler 108.[13] When one also considers the variations in form and context within the synoptic gospels, any task of analysis becomes intimidating. In addition, the importance of these sayings has often been open to question. It may well be that they have suffered from the general reaction in NT studies against the nineteenth-century liberal Protestant theories which all too easily put Jesus' teaching in terms of universal ethical ideals. Bultmann's own conclusion, that most of these sayings (apart from four specific types) cannot be guaranteed to be authentic sayings of Jesus because they lack anything 'characteristic, new, reaching out beyond popular wisdom and piety',[14] must also be a factor.

Another problem has been posed by the very definition of 'proverb'. A. Taylor, in his study of the proverb, consciously avoided even offering a definition of 'proverb'.[15] Other scholars suggest 'proverb' should be distinguished from 'aphorism'.[16] There is also the difficulty of knowing whether a proper distinction can be made between literary and popular proverbs.[17] The very ambiguity of the Hebrew terms *māšāl* and *ḥîḏâ* and of the Greek terms παραβολή, παροιμία and γνώμη only adds to the confusion.[18]

While all of these factors may contribute to the difficulty of analysing aphoristic sayings in the gospels, the task is nonetheless an important one. The sheer quantity of such sayings in the synoptic tradition testifies to its importance. Further, an increasing recognition of other sapiential concepts, such as divine Sophia, in the synoptic tradition[19] makes it all the more pressing that one should develop an understanding of how the various sapiential traditions may be related. It is the desire to make a start towards such an understanding that is the motivation for the present study.

1

APHORISTIC WISDOM AND THE NEW TESTAMENT ERA

A definition of 'aphoristic saying'

It is necessary to begin with at least a working definition of the kind of saying in which we are interested, the 'aphoristic saying'. The following considerations will apply.

1. In form, aphoristic sayings are short, pithy sayings, arresting in their succinctness of expression. They may be either a declarative statement or a question. The special class which are imperative in form will be considered 'wisdom admonitions', and these will be more precisely defined in Chapter 3.2. J. M. Thompson notes: 'Beyond this, however, we find the frequent use of rhyme, meter, repetition, alliteration, assonance, simile, and metaphor.'[1] Yet the presence of simile or metaphor does not in itself constitute an aphoristic saying.[2]

2. Despite their brevity, aphoristic sayings are self-contained and require no specific narrative context. They express thoughts which are general and complete in themselves. Possible fragments of such sayings will receive only slight attention.[3]

3. Partly because they are self-contained, aphoristic sayings can be applied to a variety of contexts and situations. The degree of openness may vary and may be related to the extent of metaphorical imagery which exists for a given saying, but it is questionable how far this may be quantified. It does not seem helpful therefore to distinguish between proverbs and 'non-proverbial wisdom sentences' on the basis of degree of hermeneutical openness.[4] But aphoristic sayings will not be restricted primarily to a single specific setting or situation.

4. The observations set forth in aphoristic sayings are in fact mostly presented as true to the realm of the collective experience of man in this world. Of course, as J. M. Thompson

observes, they 'do not emerge full-blown out of the collective mouth of "the people"',[5] but they are expressed as though they are true to aspects of general experience. They are communicated in language which is vividly concrete and grounded in this world.

5. Accordingly, aphoristic sayings are most frequently expressed in impersonal terms, since they are ostensibly not limited to a particular situation or context.[6] Frequently they are expressed in the third person, although a generalized use of the second or even first person is possible (cf. Lk 11:23). Because they are true to aspects of the collective experience of man, and because they are phrased as generalizations, aphoristic sayings possess a universality which powerfully promotes the acceptance of their truthfulness.

Not included in the considerations above are judgements either concerning the actual popular usage of the sayings or concerning the presence or absence of didactic intent in such sayings. Evidence of wide or popular usage may help to confirm that a saying is aphoristic in accordance with the suggested criteria above, but the absence of such evidence should not be used to deny the possibility of a saying meeting these criteria. The judgement to be made is primarily one of form and content rather than origin or usage. Evidence for origin or earlier usage is difficult to obtain in any case, and Bultmann may be correct in assigning the circulation in Israel of most aphoristic sayings to teachers rather than to the populace.[7] This type of circulation is especially likely for collections of sayings.

How far an aphoristic saying may be didactic has frequently been a point of debate. H.-J. Hermisson defined the proverb (*Sprichwort*) as a saying which must draw a conclusion out of the sum of experience without giving advice as to what one should do. On this basis, he discovered relatively few *Sprichwörter* in the Book of Proverbs, and classified most sayings instead as 'didactic maxims' (*die lehrhaften Sprüche*) or wisdom admonitions.[8] While there is a clear formal differentiation between indicative and imperative sayings of the aphoristic kind, there are serious difficulties in a clear distinction between proverbs and didactic maxims. It is not primarily a matter of form and content that results in a statement being didactic, but rather that statement's use or application. Metaphorical sayings are especially open to a wide range of uses, and it is conceivable that a given saying, such as 'The tree is known by its fruit' (Mt 12:33), could in one context be a conclusion from experience and in another context set forth advice as to how one should act. The suitability for didactic use of a saying, therefore, is hardly to be used for determining whether a saying is 'aphoristic', or even for distinguishing between types of aphoristic statement.[9]

The development of aphoristic traditions

Aphoristic sayings could be used by anyone, but they also comprised part of a wider tradition known as 'wisdom'. The concept of 'wisdom' is a broad one, however, and it is itself not easy to define.

In OT research, some attempts have been made to define 'wisdom' in terms of the 'intellectual tradition' of Israel,[10] but the danger of such a definition is to make the concept of wisdom so intangible as to be of very limited usefulness.[11] Thus it has been argued that it is necessary to introduce narrower distinctions with respect to the term. J. L. Crenshaw[12] has suggested that a distinction must be made between wisdom literature, wisdom traditions (the educational curriculum and pedagogy of the 'wisdom movement' itself) and wisdom thinking (its particular approach to reality). Following the conclusions of H. H. Schmid,[13] Crenshaw suggests even that forms of speech traditionally found in wisdom literature do not necessarily always indicate or constitute wisdom thinking. What in fact does constitute wisdom thinking is less clear, but Crenshaw ventures to define 'wisdom' (wisdom thinking?) as 'the quest for self-understanding in terms of relationships with things, people, and the Creator'. This search moves on three levels: (1) nature wisdom; (2) juridical and practical wisdom (*Erfahrungsweisheit*), including attention to human relationships in an ordered society or state; and (3) theological wisdom, affirming God as ultimate meaning and grappling with the question of theodicy. He further indicates at least four *Sitze im Leben* for this search: the family/clan (with the goal of mastering life), the court (with the goal of educating a select group), the scribes (with the goal of dogmatic-religious education for all), and the self-critical sages (such as Job and Qoheleth).[14]

This attempt to describe the types and limits of wisdom represents a useful counter-balance to the broad general definitions. The classifications which Crenshaw presents may indeed be useful, but even they cannot be considered exhaustive. In the intertestamental period one encounters a cosmological, apocalyptic variety of 'wisdom' expression, such as the revelations to the seer in 1 Enoch, which is not to be identified with the nature wisdom of 1 Ki 4:29−34 or the earlier 'theological wisdom'.[15] Further, in the intertestamental and early Christian periods, other *Sitze im Leben* may have to be sought for the exercise of sapiential thinking than those which Crenshaw enumerates.[16]

The main interest of the present study will be in aphoristic traditions, characteristic of 'experiential wisdom'. But a particular problem arises in this respect. How can one distinguish the occasional use of a popular proverb, by virtually anyone, from evidence of more conscious 'sapiential thinking'? Surely this is when *collections* of aphorisms become significant. The collection of aphoristic sayings is an important indication of a more deliberate sapiential interest. In such collections one has to reckon not only with popular proverbs but also with the possibility of aphorisms coined in literary circles.

This recognition has been forcefully presented by H.-J. Hermission. He has emphasized the role of the wisdom school (in ancient Israel associated with the training of state officials) for both the composition and the collection of most of the aphorisms found in Proverbs.[17] Hermisson admits that in fact it is difficult to devise criteria to differentiate clearly between those individual proverbs owing their origin to folk circles and those composed by 'wise men';[18] but, whatever the origin and usage of isolated proverbs, the compilation into written collections of such sayings clearly owed much to the 'wise men' of Israel. By the time of Sirach, collecting maxims was certainly part of the task of the wise man. The preservation of aphorisms (39:1), investigation of their hidden meaning and intent (39:2–3, 3:29, 13:26), study of maxims of the 'learned' (8:8, 47:14–17) and the correct use of aphorisms in speech (18:24; 20:20; cf. Prov 26:7) are all attested in Sirach.

The collection of aphoristic sayings was not limited in Jewish tradition to Proverbs, Sirach and Qoheleth.[19] M. Küchler traces several further examples of such *logoi sophōn*, including Philo, *Hypothetica* 7:1–9; Josephus, *Contra Apionem* 2:190–219; the Mishnah tractate *Aboth* 1:1–15; 2:4b–7, 8–14; Pseudo-Phocylides and Pseudo-Menander. From the early Christian tradition, Küchler adds Q; PapOxy 1, 654, 655; James; the Gospel of Thomas; the Sentences of Sextus; and the Teaching of Silvanus.[20] It will not be possible in the present study to trace this large field of literature, but three observations may be briefly made.

Firstly, while interest in the collection of aphoristic sayings persisted over several centuries in Jewish and Christian circles, as well as in Greco-Roman education, the nature of these collections was subject to change and to contact with other varied theological and sapiential concepts. For example, it has been noted how the arrangement of maxims in Sirach is more thematic and integrated than in Prov 10ff.[21] Further, while both Sirach and Proverbs contain traditions about divine Wisdom in addition to aphoristic sayings, the reflection on divine Wisdom in Sirach goes beyond that of Prov 1–9 (and Job 28) in the association, but probably not yet complete identification, of divine Wisdom with the Torah (cf. Sir 24).[22] The precise reasons for such developments are much debated,[23] but the aphoristic wisdom was clearly not divorced from other theological and sapiential influences, despite its seemingly profane character.

Secondly, it is nonetheless striking that the collections of aphoristic sayings listed by Küchler tend not to be associated with apocalyptic literature or even with works dominated by strongly eschatological motifs, despite the presence of other sapiential concepts in such works.[24] Sirach, for example, continues to work largely within a framework of this-worldly existence, even despite the prophetic tone which at times emerges.[25] R. Otto did suggest that in 1 En 94–105 and in 2 Enoch many of the exhortations are 'wisdom exhortations', which also he claimed to have parallels in the teaching of Jesus. But Otto himself admitted that the aphoristic forms characteristic of experiential wisdom are largely lacking in 1 Enoch. It is the polemical form of the 'woe' and the consolatory form of beatitude, both of which are more appropriate for a message characterized by eschatological crisis, that predominates among the 'wisdom exhortations'.[26] In a detailed study of 1 En 92–105, G.W.E. Nickelsburg[27] acknowledges that the woe is the most dominant form in these chapters, and he considers the use of the woe here to be more indebted to prophetic traditions than to wisdom.[28] The ethical admonition which exists in these chapters is an encouragement to persevere with good deeds in light of the coming days of destruction for all sinners and oppressors (cf. 1 En 94:1, 6–11; 96:1–2; 97:1; 101:1ff.).[29] Experiential wisdom had little place, and there is hardly a single saying which might be classified as a 'proverb' or 'aphorism' in these chapters of 1 Enoch.[30]

These observations for 1 Enoch can be extended further. In the documents produced by the Qumran community, there is also little evidence of collections of aphorisms or of experiential wisdom such as is found in Proverbs, Qoheleth and Sirach. The concept of 'wisdom' was treated more often at Qumran in relation to mysteries made known to the elect by special divine revelation and inspiration.[31] This wisdom was not only related to eschatological secrets, but to a right understanding of the Torah and of the works of God.[32] Yet the Qumran community did preserve a few examples of earlier experiential wisdom, such as fragments of Sirach and Qoheleth.[33] Sapiential works of a still different character may include, among others, 11QPs[a]18, 4Q184 (the Wiles of the Wicked Woman)[34] and 4Q185. 'Wisdom' as a theme does find a significant place in the community, but the presence of aphoristic sapiential traditions is quite limited, and even the preservation of previous Jewish wisdom literature comprises a relatively small proportion of the Qumran texts that have been published thus far.

Even the Testaments of the Twelve Patriarchs provide little in the way of collections of aphoristic sayings. Proverbial statements can occasionally be isolated,[35] but they are seldom found in even small clusters. As Hollander observes, the parenesis in the Testaments 'is not just a collection of sayings and maxims, but clearly a parenetic composition'.[36] For example, in TDan a vice (anger) is chosen, then elaborated to show how it psychologically works within man and how it can be related to other vices, and finally followed by reference in general terms to the commandment of God.[37] Thus little can be found from 1 Enoch, Qumran or the Testaments of the Twelve Patriarchs to add significantly to Küchler's list of collections of aphoristic sayings or to challenge the observed tendency for such collections to be relatively free of domination by strongly eschatological motifs.

Thirdly, the class responsible for the propagation of aphoristic wisdom is shrouded in darkness in the early Christian era. Direct evidence during this period for the general existence of 'wisdom schools' in Palestine is lacking.[38] The existence of 'schools' of disciples around pre-rabbinic Pharisaic leaders such as Hillel and Shammai is likely, but how far these would be considered to have been based on the study of sapiential concepts is open to question. D. Georgi has argued that there were in fact such schools, the objective of which was to train pupils for the role of 'wise men'. The Jewish Scriptures were a major treasure of wisdom for these men, especially of moral wisdom, but the importance of experiential wisdom was never completely undermined. Georgi argued that these schools were modelled upon the Hellenistic philosophical schools and that they were not so concerned with legal casuistry as with popular religion. Paul is alleged to have been trained in just this sort of school, and he accordingly provides some of the earliest literary evidence for the encounter of 'wisdom school' and Pharisaism. Similarly, it is alleged that the Hillel-tradition also represents Hillel as this union of the truly wise and truly godly man.[39]

Georgi's main evidence for this last contention is the collection of Hillel sayings in Mishnah *Aboth*, but he therefore finds it necessary to differ with J. Neusner's argument that the Hillel collection in Mishnah *Aboth* (2:5ff.) is late.[40] Neusner's careful study of early rabbinic Pharisaism shows that there is little actual evidence of sapiential sayings preserved from the period before AD 70. The parallelism, artful contrasts, rhythm and formal unity of proverbial sentences are not reproduced in the moral sayings attributable to early Pharisees.[41] While it is not possible to deny Georgi's conjecture about the existence of Jewish 'wisdom schools' in Palestine, it is at least clear from Neusner's findings that little has been preserved from such schools that shows much formal affinity with the previously attested genre of aphoristic wisdom. Even where correspondences can be identified (cf. M. *Aboth* 1:1−18) they pertain to a very small proportion of material. Paul, one of Georgi's examples of a Pharisee trained in such a wisdom school, does indeed show some interest in a variety of aspects of identifiable wisdom thought. The speculative types of wisdom, possibly related to the problem of gnosis at Corinth and to concepts parallel to Hellenistic philosophy, have drawn most attention in studies of Paul and wisdom.[42] But of course here one is referring to a very different kind of wisdom from the moral wisdom found in Georgi's other example, Hillel. Pauline correspondences with Jewish moral and experiential wisdom are not lacking, but a clearer definition of the various sapiential influences in Paul's writings may need to be set forth before specific origins can be assigned to them.[43]

The theory of the existence of 'Jewish wisdom schools' also suffers from the difficulty of finding evidence for a distinct system of Jewish education at all in the first century AD. Any Jewish schools might have confined themselves to instruction in the law and religious duty, leaving other necessary forms of knowledge to a Greco-Roman educational system in Palestine.[44] The impact of Greco-Roman rhetoric on Tannaitic rabbinic literature has been argued by H. A. Fischel.[45] The use of proverbs and moral sayings is itself an element in such rhetoric, and Fischel observes that 'the skillful employment of the proverb is recommended by Aristotle, whose view is followed for centuries in the Greco-Roman *rhetorica*, handbooks, *progymnasmata*, and literary tracts on style and grammar, including Christian works'.[46] From the fourth century BC onwards, many collections of poetic epigrams would appear to have been made by individuals, although most of these have been lost.[47] One large critical anthology of such sayings was the *Garland*, collected in *c.* 80 BC by Meleager of Syria. Another came from *c.* 40 AD by Philippus of Thessalonica.[48] Latin *sententiae* are found in the works of Quintilian, Seneca, Tacitus, Juvenal and Martial, and were apparently used for training in rhetoric.[49]

One thus finds a wealth and variety of sapiential traditions in the early Christian era. The collection of aphoristic sayings represents one branch of these traditions, but even so there is only limited information about the actual contexts within which such collections were made and used in first-century Palestine. Yet it seems valid to expect that a conscious interest in aphoristic wisdom is to be found more in relation to *collections* of aphorisms than in the employment of isolated aphorisms in various contexts. It is for these collections, as in Proverbs, Sirach and Qoheleth, that the question of 'sapiential influence' of the experiential and aphoristic kind is least contested and where one may find oneself closest to the activity of a 'wisdom school', although it is probably better to be more cautious and refer only to the 'circle' of those responsible for the collections. For this reason, our method will be to approach the study of aphorisms in the synoptic tradition by first identifying and examining small collections or clusters of aphorisms. Only when certain conclusions have been reached concerning these will we seek further confirmation of our results from the use of isolated aphorisms.

Wisdom and the double tradition

When one turns to the synoptic tradition, special attention must be given to those sayings identified as 'double-tradition' sayings, which have been associated by many scholars with the sayings source 'Q'.[50] The influence of 'wisdom' upon this material has been strongly argued in recent studies of Q, and this points to it as fertile ground for our study. It is all the more significant, however, that *aphoristic* wisdom has not usually been the focal point of studies of wisdom in Q, despite the presence of numerous aphorisms in this material.

J. M. Robinson presented the thesis that the *Gattung* of Q could be designated *logoi sophōn*, a genre whose trajectory he traced from the Jewish wisdom literature to gnostic writings.[51] Prophetic and eschatological forms of expression must be recognized as present in Q-material as well as those forms traditionally associated with the wisdom literature; yet clear affinities have been demonstrated with the earlier Jewish wisdom literature.[52] From another angle, Dieter Lührmann[53] draws attention to the use of OT figures in the Q-material and has been followed by S. Schulz[54] in his suggestion that this reflects a method quite different from rabbinic style, or the controversy saying or the prophecy-fulfilment portrayal.[55] Lührmann considers that the method of citation in Q is related to the tradition of later Jewish wisdom, wherein the use of OT figures illustrates what should have been learned from the experience of the past (i.e. from Israel's preceding history) and is frequently linked to a warning.[56]

Even more interest has been shown in the passages in the double tradition which seem to refer to the figure of divine Wisdom (Sophia). Of the five passages examined by F. Christ[57] in his study of Sophia christology in the synoptic tradition, only Mt 11:28−30 is not generally considered double-tradition material. Subsequent studies of divine Wisdom in Q have been made by a number of scholars, whose work will be considered below (pp. 162−70).

R. A. Edwards[58] has sought to draw all the diverse sapiential elements in Q together and to portray wisdom as one of three main themes running throughout the Q-collection. S. Schulz takes a less simple approach and does not devote a detailed discussion to 'wisdom' as such.[59] But he allows for sapiential motifs in both his 'earlier' and 'later' Q-communities, with the divine Sophia sayings assigned to the 'later' Syrian community, and with the 'earlier' Palestinian community presenting sayings of aphoristic or moral wisdom imbued with prophetic authority.[60]

These studies[61] demonstrate how the material of the double tradition has often inspired interest in sapiential themes. It is therefore all the more imperative that an investigation of aphoristic material within the double tradition be undertaken.

As indicated in the previous section, the first stage of such a study will be to examine *collections* of aphoristic sayings within the double-tradition material, because it is in these collections that one has the greatest expectation of detecting an intentional manipulation of aphoristic material. From that basis one can then compare one's results with other collections in the synoptic tradition and with aphorisms which appear in isolated usage. This will comprise the bulk of our study. But once the aphoristic material has been examined, we shall then return to the question of how this aphoristic wisdom may be related to other sapiential themes in the double-tradition material, such as have been indicated above. A tentative setting for such sapiential activity will finally be considered.

Although the attention of this study will be devoted largely to the sayings of the double tradition (and it will be argued that the sapiential activity behind the collection and use of many of these sayings is distinctive within the synoptic tradition), this study is not primarily a study of Q in the sense of a final collection of sayings or document. No attempt is made to examine a document as such, as for example in A. Jacobson's study of 'Wisdom Christology in Q'.[62] If a study is to be made of the document Q as such, one must look beyond the individual sayings which comprise it to the composition as a whole, or at least to its larger units. Otherwise one has little basis for talking about the redaction(s) of Q, as distinct from the tradition-history of the logia. However, such a compositional perspective cannot be successfully achieved without some previous study of the tradition-history of the logia and of smaller units. Only then can one hope to build up a composite picture which will make possible correlations between stages of development and some kind of effective control over tracing the inevitably complex stages of development of 'pre-Q' traditions and of Q itself.[63] This conviction lies behind the present study, which seeks less to define the 'theology of Q' than to identify an important sphere of sapiential activity behind the traditions which may ultimately feed into Q and which may continue to develop in the history of the Jesus-tradition.

2

COLLECTIONS OF APHORISTIC SAYINGS IN THE DOUBLE TRADITION

1. Introduction

In the synoptic tradition aphoristic sayings can be found either in 'clusters' (small collections) or in more isolated usage. It has been argued that if one is looking for evidence of a sapiential activity within the synoptic tradition, then the small collections are the obvious place to begin. It is with these that one is most likely to be able to investigate compositional activity, because one has a sustained employment of aphoristic sayings. Much more difficult to analyse and synthesize are isolated instances of an aphorism introducing or serving as a climax to an anecdote, such as one finds in the rabbinic literature. H. A. Fischel observes that in the rabbinic literature proverbs no longer generally appear in extensive collections for instruction, in contrast to the Book of Proverbs or Sirach. Fischel traces these shorter aphoristic formulations to Western influences, as distinct from the more traditional Eastern accumulations of aphoristic sayings.[1] But where one does still find small collections, as in the double tradition particularly, there one may well have evidence also of a 'collector' guided by particular motives and interests.

The predilection of form criticism for the study of individual pericopes has frequently been at the cost of the study of collections of Jesus' sayings. Even the recognition of small and early collections of sayings has seldom been matched by much progress in explaining how these collections came into being and what functions they originally served. Such explanations have been still less forthcoming for collections which are predominantly composed of aphoristic sayings, for the well-defined, self-contained nature of such sayings can all too easily lead to the assumption that their collection is simply the result of a loose conjunction of 'variations on a theme'. Catch-word connections or topical associations may explain how some of these sayings have been brought together into larger units, but these considerations may obscure other, more important, motives of compilation. The search for such motives is as important for these collections as for others with more obvious theological interests.

There are five clear examples of small collections of aphoristic sayings in double-tradition material of the synoptic gospels.[2] These include (i) Mt 7:7–11/Lk 11:9–13; (ii) Mt 6:25–33/Lk 12:22–31; (iii) Mt 7:16–20, 12:33–5/Lk 6:43–5; (iv) Mt 7:1–5/Lk 6:37–42; and (v) Mt 10:26–33/Lk 12:2–9. These are each composed of multiple aphoristic sayings, and the formulation of each collection is reasonably similar in both Matthew and Luke.[3] It will be our contention that in each instance the collection of aphoristic sayings is far from haphazard in its structure and that it presents a carefully designed argument. The structure of argument betrays a similar pattern or design in each of the five cases. Once this is established, then an effort will be made to compare this structure of argument with other collections of aphorisms in the synoptic tradition, in order to determine whether any other collections of this kind exist and thus how distinctive the pattern is.

2. Five double-tradition aphoristic collections with similar structure

Mt 7:7–11/Lk 11:9–13

The following reconstruction closely follows that of A. Polag:[4]

(i) αἰτεῖτε καὶ δοθήσεται ὑμῖν,
  ζητεῖτε καὶ εὑρήσετε,
  κρούετε καὶ ἀνοιγήσεται ὑμῖν.

(ii) πᾶς γὰρ ὁ αἰτῶν λαμβάνει
  καὶ ὁ ζητῶν εὑρίσκει
  καὶ τῷ κρούοντι ἀνοιγ[ήσ]εται.

(iii) [ἢ] τίς ἐστιν ἐξ ὑμῶν ἄνθρωπος, ὃν αἰτήσει ὁ υἱὸς·αὐτοῦ
  ἄρτον, μὴ λίθον ἐπιδώσει αὐτῷ;
  ἢ καὶ ἰχθὺν αἰτήσει, μὴ ὄφιν ἐπιδώσει αὐτῷ;

(iv) εἰ οὖν ὑμεῖς πονηροὶ ὄντες οἴδατε δόματα ἀγαθὰ διδόναι
  τοῖς τέκνοις ὑμῶν, πόσῳ μᾶλλον ὁ πατὴρ ὁ ἐξ οὐρανοῦ
  δώσει ἀγαθὰ τοῖς αἰτοῦσιν αὐτόν.

R. Bultmann observed that one can no longer trace with confidence the stages by which the individual sayings in Mt 7:7–11 par were elaborated and joined together, although there is little doubt that some elaboration and uniting of material did occur.[5] The close parallelism between the threefold exhortations and promises in Mt 7:7 par ('Ask, and it will be given you; seek, and you will find; knock, and it will be opened for you') and the threefold aphoristic statements in Mt 7:8 par ('For everyone who asks receives, and he who seeks finds, and to him who knocks it will be opened') suggests that one unit has been modelled on the other, although it is not possible to decide with certainty which preceded.[6] It is also possible that the sayings on 'seeking' and 'knocking' are elaborations of the sayings on 'asking', for it is clear that in the context of the present collection the theme of asking—receiving is dominant. It is this theme alone that holds Mt 7:7—8 par and 7:9—10 par together. The original independence of these two units is confirmed by the self-contained nature of each and the presence of formal and thematic differences between the two.[7] Whereas the opening admonitions and maxims encourage the hearer to 'ask', 'seek', and 'knock' and emphasize the accompanying promises of receiving and finding, the rhetorical questions which follow in Mt 7:9—10 par show concern for whether what is received will meet what is needed. The latter sayings also lack any reference to the images of 'seeking' and 'knocking' and introduce the new imagery of a father—son relationship. Finally, the concluding saying in Mt 7:11 par ('If you then, who are evil, know how to give good gifts to your children, how much more …') must either have been already united in the tradition with Mt 7:9—10 par or added at the time of the collection's compilation. It is doubtful that it could have existed as an independent unit, since it required something to precede the *a minore ad maius* comparison.

Common to these varied sayings, however, is the high suitability of each for persuasive argument and popular appeal through the use of wisdom admonition, maxim, rhetorical question and *a minore ad maius* comparison. Despite the imperatival opening, all these sayings are suited to convince, not simply to demand or announce.[8] This becomes evident not only as one looks at the individual forms, but also as one examines the development of the argument in the context of the collection.

I

The following steps in the argument can be discerned:

1. The first step comprises the admonitions and promises in Mt 7:7 par, which at face value are almost embarrassing in the scope of what is encouraged and promised.[9] There is no limitation on what is to be asked for or sought, and the

threefold illustration accentuates the breadth of the admonition. It is also not immediately clear that petitionary prayer is how 'asking' is to be interpreted. While the verbs δοθήσεται and ἀνοιγήσεται are capable of being considered divine passives,[10] and while ζητεῖτε and κρούετε can be used figuratively of prayer,[11] no such specific interpretation is at first demanded.[12] One must not lose sight of the initial generality of these sayings by reading them too quickly in terms of what follows.[13] Initially the appeal is wide and general.

2. The second unit consists of the three aphorisms (Mt 7:8 par) which run parallel to one another and to the opening admonitions. The sole function of these aphorisms is ostensibly to provide additional support for the preceding promises of receiving, finding and opening. Significantly, the promises are now expressed in the form of general rules. Everyone (πᾶς) who asks receives.[14] What is striking in these sayings is the seemingly universal and categorical quality of the promises, demonstrated by the unqualified πᾶς, the predominance of habitual present rather than future tenses (λαμβάνει, εὑρίσκει) and the continuing absence of clear reference to divine agency. Indeed the change from δοθήσεται (verse 7) to λαμβάνει (verse 8) actually diminishes any theological significance for the passive.

The optimism of these maxims is remarkable. The promise of receiving, which is the main point of contention, may draw support however from its conjunction with the more familiar promise of 'finding' for the one who seeks[15] or the less contentious promise of the 'opening' to the one who knocks.

3. The third unit of the collection, the rhetorical questions found in Mt 7:9–10 par, marks a new departure in the argument, as indicated earlier. The preceding images of asking, seeking and knocking are now confined simply to asking. The context for the asking also comes into clearer focus as it is now expressed within a father–son relationship. The note of assurance struck in the preceding verses is continued, since such rhetorical questions permit no substantial doubt as to their answer; but the assurance has now become that of not receiving something detrimental or useless. What is received will meet one's needs, here expressed in terms of requests for food. These new features provide the essential link between

Mt 7:7–8 par and the final argument in Mt 7:11 par, and maintain the appeal to experiential evidence.[16]

The actual details of the rhetorical questions are of course confused by the differences between Matthew and Luke at this point.[17] Luke may well be responsible for the substitution of πατέρα for ἄνθρωπος (cf. Lk 11:11) so as to improve the connection with the concluding saying. But it serves only to make explicit what is already implied in the common reference to υἱός.[18]

The other differences between Matthew and Luke are not critical to the structure of the argument.[19] The double rhetorical questions effectively indicate that a multiplicity of illustrations from daily life could have been drawn upon for support. Yet the actual questions which are posed are not without significance in terms of the application of the sayings. Matthew and Luke agree on the request of the son for a fish and the incredibility of his receiving a serpent. The paired question in Matthew is for a loaf, and this may well be more original than Luke's 'egg'. W. Ott[20] argues in favour of the Matthean pair on the grounds that Luke strengthened the potentially useful 'stone' to a positively harmful 'scorpion'. D. Catchpole prefers to use other supporting arguments for Matthew's version: that 'bread and fish together constitute basic ordinary food' and that 'ὄφις and σκορπίος is a combination used shortly beforehand in Lucan material (x.19)'.[21] These arguments are compelling, but it is worth noting that in any case all three questions have in common a request for an item of food.[22] One is concerned here with the basic necessities of life.

It is our contention that these questions are aphoristic in style, building up the terms of an argument and drawing carefully on experience. However S. Schulz has argued that even in these rhetorical questions one can detect a 'prophetic' authority. The basis for this argument is the belief that the formula τίς ἐξ ὑμῶν is a typical prophetic introduction. Schulz relies upon Greeven's analysis of this formula, maintaining that it originated not from Pharisaic rabbinism nor from Jewish apocalyptic, but from the OT prophetic tradition. Rabbinic and other parallels are difficult to find.[23] Yet, despite a possible prophetic *origin*,[24] within the synoptic tradition the formula occurs frequently as the introduction to parabolic argument rather than prophetic accusation.[25] It serves often simply to produce an emphatic question. In Mt 7:9 par, the function of the formula is to strengthen the force of the argument, which seeks to portray in exaggerated form what is contrary to expectations in everyday life. The force of the saying lies not in any accusation against the hearers, for they hardly are condemned for giving their sons serpents instead of fish(!), but rather in its presentation of an admittedly hyperbolic and ridiculous situation.[26] This contrasts with the direct accusing function observed in the OT prophets' use of the formula. In Mt 7:9 par, an opposition is not established between 'you' hearers and the authority of the prophetic 'I', but rather both hearer and speaker together testify to collective human experience and commonsense. There is little evidence therefore that the forms of experiential wisdom must be subordinated to the outlook of prophetic enthusiasm in these sayings.[27]

4. The final saying (Mt 7:11; cf. Lk 11:13) provides the interpretative key to all that has preceded, switching from an appeal to experience to an appeal to reason.[28] The preceding example of a father's response to his son's requests is made the basis for an *a minore ad maius* application to the heavenly Father.[29] This is the first direct reference in the compilation to God and therefore also the first clear reference to 'asking' in terms of petitionary prayer. What has previously been phrased in the most general terms is at last made specific.[30] *Assent to the general argument is carefully won before the specific application is made.*

A major difficulty of interpretation, though, is the question of what is to be sought and received of God. First is the problem of the difference between Matthew's ἀγαθά and Luke's πνεῦμα ἅγιον. W. Ott[31] has persuasively argued that Luke's version is the more likely to be secondary because the ambiguous reference to ἀγαθά and its openness to abuse would be incompatible with Luke's general outlook towards material possessions. H.-Th. Wrege,[32] in contrast, has argued that the giving of the Spirit to the disciples prior to Easter would have been an unlikely Lukan introduction. Luke, however, may be pointing forward in this passage to a post-Easter period by the use of the future tense δώσει. Just as the preceding Lord's Prayer in Lk 11:1−4 is a prayer for the church, so also may the Holy Spirit here be a promise for the church.[33] Not only is the Holy Spirit of particular interest to Luke,[34] but Luke elsewhere links the receiving of the Spirit with a request or prayer (cf. Lk 3:21; 10:21; Acts 1:14). Jülicher also noted that in Luke's version both the subject and the object are involved in the *a minore ad maius* argument. The subject is elevated from ὑμεῖς πονηροὶ ὄντες to ὁ πατὴρ [ὁ] ἐξ οὐρανοῦ and the object is elevated from ἀγαθά to the Holy Spirit. In Matthew's version only the subjects are involved. It would seem more likely that Luke has extended the intensification than that Matthew has retracted part of it.[35]

If the wording in Matthew, ἀγαθά, is accepted as earlier than Luke's 'Holy Spirit', then the *a minore ad maius* argument functions with respect to the subjects. It develops the caring father−son relationship. There is no reason to expect that the two uses of ἀγαθά should represent different things. The first use is clearly related in the context of Mt 7:9−10 par to food. In the absence of any other interpretative clues for ἀγαθά one seems compelled to allow at least for the meeting of physical needs in this promise.[36] Indeed if one has here only a vague promise of 'spiritual blessings',[37] it would hardly require the extensive and persuasive argument which has been presented. The impression is that the persuasion is employed to counter doubts about very real problems of need facing followers. Since human fathers, who are evil, know how to meet the physical needs of their sons, how much more will the heavenly Father be able to meet these requirements.

II

From these observations it is increasingly clear that these sayings are so formulated and joined together as to provide exhortation and encouragement to early Christian adherents in the face of genuine concern over material support, and especially food. Although the addressees are called 'evil' (πονηροί), in the context of the passage this amounts to no more than a reflection on the general condition of mankind.[38] There is no sustained attack here on opponents or outsiders: it is followers, not opponents, who are being encouraged to make their petitions to their Father. The instruction is positive, without polemic.[39] That segments of the early church, especially in

Palestine, actually had cause to doubt this provision is clearly indicated in Acts and the letters of Paul (cf. Acts 11:17–30; Rom 15:26; Gal 2:10).[40] The style of argument is therefore suggestive of its purpose, and possibly of a *Sitz im Leben*.

The argument proceeds through four clear steps. The first consists of the general wisdom admonition in Mt 7:7 par, which is set forth in the most general terms. No limitation on the exhortation to ask or on the promise of receiving is presented. No content for the petitions or identification of the person of whom one should ask is specified. This opening step is amplified with the same set of images in the next, the aphorisms in Mt 7:8 par. They add little to narrow the sense of the opening sayings, but their universal formulation gives the impression of a strengthening of the *promises*. The third step is particularly significant. It is characterized by a new set of images and an important focusing of the argument on the requests for food and on a father–son relationship. Formally it is characterized by paired rhetorical questions, which argumentatively are a powerful means of persuasion. The fourth and final step brings the argument to its intended application. Petitions are now addressed to the Father for ἀγαθά. This is the application towards which the whole of the argument has been proceeding, from general to more specific terms. This precise pattern of argument is one which will be encountered again in the remaining passages to be considered in this chapter.

This emphasis on persuasive forms, appeal to experience and use of *a minore ad maius* argument shows great skill on the part of the composer. It is not a haphazard collection of aphorisms; nor can much support be found for the contention of S. Schulz that, despite the artistry of the collection, it is to be classified as *prophetische Aufforderung*. Such a view runs contrary to the tone and positive promises of the entire presentation.[41]

Yet how far can one expect the opening admonitions and promises about asking and receiving to be accepted simply as reflections of experience? Can the readers have been expected to believe that 'everyone who asks receives' is a statement derived wholly from experience?

On the one hand, it must be recognized that the universal and categorical form of the saying (cf. πᾶς) is not unusual for proverbial speech. One can compare such sayings as

'In all toil there is profit' (Prov 14:23a)

'Many seek the favour of a generous man, and everyone is a friend to a man who gives gifts. All a poor man's brothers hate him' (Prov 19:6–7)

'If a ruler listens to falsehood, all his officials will be wicked'
(Prov 29:12)

'In all your works be industrious, and no sickness will over-
take you' (Sir 31:22)

'Whoever glorifies his father will have long life' (Sir 3:6)

As has often been recognized, proverbs can never be and never are
comprehensive generalizations about life.[42] They always express
insights true to aspects of experience rather than to human experience
as a whole. Further, J. Crossan writes that the 'aphorism is often
deliberately exaggerated and overstated'. He further cites K. Kraus
that 'an aphorism never coincides with the truth; it is either a half-
truth or one-and-a-half truths'.[43] Hyperbole and exaggeration often
contribute towards the success that aphorisms have in drawing the
interest and response of the hearers. In this respect the use of πᾶς
in Mt 7:8 par should not give rise unduly to claims that it is no longer
'experiential' or 'aphoristic'; aphorisms frequently function in
precisely this way.

On the other hand, however, if we are correct that these sayings
are primarily addressed to Christians in their present formulation as
a collection, then the promises in the opening sayings inevitably carry
an authority beyond that which experience alone offers. This becomes
clear as one reaches the concluding saying of the collection. Thus
Christian beliefs may be implicit in these promises and encourage-
ments, although it must still be recognized that no explicit moral or
religious virtue is made the condition for obtaining the promises.
Indeed, whatever the underlying presuppositions, this unqualified
formulation does contrast significantly with comparable sayings in
Mt 21:22; Mk 11:24; Jn 14:13−14, 15:7, 16, 16:23−6; 1 Jn 3:22,
5:14−16; ApocJas 10:32−4; ShepHerm *Mand.* 9.4; *Sim.* 6.3.6b.
Thus even if a special authority implicitly bolsters the promises, the
general formulation which is used must be given full weight.

III

One is left with the question of how this collection may have been
joined with other sayings-material prior to its inclusion in Matthew
and Luke. This can only be tentatively indicated. In the Lukan
ordering, this collection immediately follows the Lord's Prayer (Lk
11:1−4; cf. Mt 6:9−13) and the parable of the friend at midnight
(Lk 11:5−8; not in Mt). In Matthew the Lord's Prayer more distant-
ly precedes the collection. The immediate conjunction is with the

collection of sayings on judging one's brother (Mt 7:1−5 par; see pp. 36−44 below) and the isolated saying about casting pearls before swine.[44] The Lukan sequence certainly flows more easily on the theme of prayer, and the reference to food in the double rhetorical questions (Lk 11:11−12 par) may not be unrelated to the important clause in the Lord's Prayer in which followers are to ask for τὸν ἄρτον ἡμῶν τὸν ἐπιούσιον. If Matthew's rendering of ἄρτον in Mt 7:9 is original, then a significant correspondence is produced.[45] Thus in their reconstructions of the sequence of Q, A. Polag,[46] V. Taylor[47] and W. Schenk[48] are inclined to accept the sequence of Lk 11:2−4, 9−13 as most original.[49]

Non-canonical parallels shed only limited additional light on the question. The non-canonical parallels to the 'seeking' sayings in Mt 7:7−8 par are numerous (cf. OxyP 654:2; GThom 2, 92, 94; GTr 17:3−4; GMary 8:20−1; DialSav 126:7−10, 129:15−16; GHeb 4).[50] Crossan distinguishes the 'seeking' sayings, however, from the 'asking' trajectory.[51] He follows Koester in suggesting that Q was not the source for the 'seeking−finding' sayings and that these were not originally directed towards general assurance about one's prayerful requests. Originally the 'seeking' sayings were along the lines of the saying about 'seeking the kingdom' in Mt 6:31−3/Lk 12:29−31.[52] A further association for the 'seeking' sayings is suggested by GThom 92:

> Seek and you will find.
> But those things about which you asked me during those days,
> I did not tell you on that day.
> Now I am willing to tell them,
> and you do not inquire about them.

The themes in this logion recall the close proximity which is also found in Luke's sequence of double-tradition material between Lk 11:9ff. and Lk 10:21−4 (cf. Mt 11:25−7, 13:16−17). In the latter sayings, secrets which have been hidden from the wise and from earlier prophets and kings are now revealed to followers of the Son, who alone knows the Father. It is doubtful, however, whether the parallels are sufficiently strong or the history of the tradition sufficiently clear to be certain that this reflects an early context for the 'seeking' sayings. The parallels with Lk 10:21−4 par in any case apply mainly to part of Mt 7:7−8 par and not at all to Mt 7:9−11 par,[53] so the theme of 'revelation' is hardly dominant in Mt 7:7−11 par. As the collection in Mt 7:7–11 par now stands, 'asking' is the most prominent theme, and 'seeking' is clearly subsidiary.

In Luke the parable of the friend at midnight intervenes between the Lord's Prayer and Lk 11:9–13 par, and this parable does reflect both the theme of 'asking God' and the concern for 'bread'. D. Catchpole has recently argued that this parable belonged to Q at this point on account of the remarkable parallelism between Lk 11:5–8 and Lk 11:9–13.[54] He further argues that this 'cares tradition' leads next in Q to Lk 12:22–31 (Mt 6:25–33),[55] which will be the next aphoristic sayings collection which we shall consider (cf. below). The parallelism between Lk 11:5–8 and Lk 11:9–13 is indeed a striking one in both form and content. It will be our contention however that the structure of the aphoristic sayings collection in Lk 11:9–13 par is self-contained and that this is demonstrated in part by comparison with other similar collections and in part by its own progression of argument. This would imply that the formulation of the collection either preceded any connection with the parable in Lk 11:5–8, even if the latter is attributed to Q and was subsequently attached to the collection in a pre-Lukan version, or took a place in response to an existing parable, but probably still prior to the formation of a 'cares' section of sayings which included Lk 12:22–31 par. Either possibility will be consistent with our findings, but only the second requires a necessary connection with Lk 11:5–8 in the pre-Lukan and presumably pre-Matthean tradition.[56]

     Mt 6:25–33/Lk 12:22–31

     διὰ τοῦτο λέγω ὑμῖν·

(i) μὴ μεριμνᾶτε τῇ ψυχῇ [ὑμῶν] τί φάγητε,
μηδὲ τῷ σώματι [ὑμῶν] τί ἐνδύσησθε.

(ii) οὐχὶ ἡ ψυχὴ πλεῖόν ἐστιν τῆς τροφῆς
καὶ τὸ σῶμα τοῦ ἐνδύματος;

(iii) ἐμβλέψατε εἰς τοὺς κόρακας ὅτι οὐ σπείρουσιν οὐδὲ
θερίζουσιν οὐδὲ συνάγουσιν εἰς ἀποθήκας, καὶ ὁ θεὸς
τρέφει αὐτούς·
οὐχ ὑμεῖς μᾶλλον διαφέρετε αὐτῶν;

τίς δὲ ἐξ ὑμῶν μεριμνῶν δύναται προσθεῖναι ἐπὶ τὴν
ἡλικίαν αὐτοῦ πῆχυν [ἕνα];

καὶ περὶ ἐνδύματος τί μεριμνᾶτε;

καταμάθετε τὰ κρίνα [τοῦ ἀγροῦ] πῶς αὐξάνουσιν· οὐ
κοπιῶσιν οὐδὲ νήθουσιν· λέγω δὲ ὑμῖν ὅτι οὐδὲ Σολομὼν
ἐν πάσῃ τῇ δόξῃ αὐτοῦ περιεβάλετο ὡς ἓν τούτων.
εἰ δὲ τὸν χόρτον ἐν ἀγρῷ σήμερον ὄντα καὶ αὔριον εἰς
κλίβανον βαλλόμενον ὁ θεὸς οὕτως ἀμφιέννυσιν, οὐ
πολλῷ μᾶλλον ὑμᾶς, ὀλιγόπιστοι;

(iv) μὴ [οὖν] μεριμνήσητε λέγοντες· τί φάγωμεν; ἤ· τί πίωμεν;
πάντα γὰρ ταῦτα τὰ ἔθνη ἐπιζητοῦσιν· οἶδεν γὰρ ὁ
πατὴρ ὑμῶν ὅτι χρῄζετε τούτων.
ζητεῖτε δὲ [πρῶτον] τὴν βασιλείαν αὐτοῦ, καὶ ταῦτα
[πάντα] προστεθήσεται ὑμῖν.

A second collection of sayings with the theme of cares and anxieties
about basic material needs is found in Mt 6:25−33 par.[57] This collection presents an overall design of argument similar to that of Mt
7:7−11 par. It contains fewer formal aphorisms, but retains a wide
appeal to experiential wisdom and to some of the precise kinds of
argument (e.g., *a minore ad maius*) found in the preceding collection
of sayings.

The precise boundaries of this collection are slightly blurred
by the different endings in Matthew and Luke. Matthew concludes
in 6:34 with a saying peculiar to that gospel about not being anxious
for tomorrow. Lk 12:32 is a very different saying, found only
in Luke: 'Fear not, little flock, for it is your Father's good pleasure
to give you the kingdom'.[58] A reconstruction of the underlying
tradition therefore best concludes with Mt 6:33/Lk 12:31, which
is itself an entirely appropriate conclusion to the passage.[59]

The sequence of the sayings in Mt 6:25−33/Lk 12:22−31 is exactly
matching, so that it is matters of wording rather than order that
require discussion. The sequence falls naturally into the four divisions
suggested for Mt 7:7−11 par.

I

1. First is a general exhortation in Mt 6:25a/Lk 12:22.[60] This
opening saying is a wide-ranging appeal against anxiety for
one's 'life' (ψυχή − σῶμα), which is then elaborated in terms
of food and clothing. Matthew's formulation of the admonition closely agrees with that in Luke, except for a double
occurrence of ὑμῶν[61] and Matthew's probable inclusion of

a reference to drinking: ἢ τί πίητε (uncertain textually, but cf. Mt 6:31 par). Due to the general nature of the exhortation, it is not initially clear who is being addressed. Anxiety could apply to rich and poor alike, but the fact that the *basic* necessities of food and clothing are emphasized suggests that this is the anxiety of the needy rather than the concern of the rich with an accumulation of 'wealth'.

2. Following the opening admonition comes a supporting aphorism about one's 'life' (ψυχή – σῶμα) consisting of more than simply food or clothing (Mt 6:25b/Lk 12:23). This saying is closely parallel to the opening admonition in theme, and sets forth a principle which superficially argues in support of the admonition (cf. Mt 7:7 and 8 par).[62] This holds true whether the form of the saying was originally a statement (introduced by γάρ), as in Luke, or a rhetorical question, as in Matthew. Luke's tendency to reformulate rhetorical questions on occasion may be responsible for this variation.[63] Strictly, the saying adds little new to the opening admonition, though it is important in affirming a principle which applies behind the exhortation.[64] Catchpole argues on form-critical grounds that it may have been a secondary development, and 'cannot adequately secure v. 25a'.[65] But the exhortation will be further secured later in the sequence of sayings, where the principle of Mt 6:25b par itself receives greater elaboration (cf. Mt 6:33 par).

3. A new line of argument is introduced in Mt 6:26, 28b–30 par. It will be seen to be typical of the formulation of the aphoristic collections that a fresh line of argument is presented at this point. It consists of a double illustration from nature: a call to consider the 'ravens' (Lk; πετεινὰ τοῦ οὐρανοῦ in Mt)[66] with respect to food, and the 'lilies' with respect to clothing. The double illustration is developed as an argument consisting in each case of (1) a command to 'consider' the example from nature,[67] and (2) a rhetorical question suggesting that the hearer is worth more than the natural object. Implicit in those questions is an *a minore ad maius* argument, not dissimilar to that found in Mt 7:11 par. Yet, while in Mt 7:7–11 par the *a minore ad maius* argument followed on from the double rhetorical questions to mark the final interpretative stage of the argument, in this present case it is more closely linked to the double

rhetorical questions themselves. Thus it is used twice and forms only the penultimate step in the argument. The double illustration, the double rhetorical questions, are nonetheless fundamental to this step.

The double rhetorical questions are more obvious in Matthew than in Luke, for Luke seems to record 'exclamations' (πόσῳ μᾶλλον ...) rather than questions in verses 24 and 28. The use of rhetorical questions in Matthew, however, is again taken by Schulz[68] and Wrege[69] to be more original in view of Luke's tendency to recast rhetorical questions.[70] One must allow therefore for the probability that the underlying tradition consisted of double rhetorical questions here.

The nature of the argument presented by each illustration is closely parallel, but the second is elaborated slightly by the reference to the figure of Solomon (Mt 6:29/Lk 12:27) and by the address of the hearers as ὀλιγόπιστοι. The latter will be discussed below, but the reference to the historical figure of Solomon is interesting because of its rare use in the NT. The only other references in the NT are found in the Matthean genealogy (Mt 1:6–7), in Stephen's speech (Acts 7:47) and in the double-tradition saying in Mt 12:42–3 par.[71] In the last instance, Solomon's σοφία is noted as surpassed, but in the present passage it is the magnificence of his wealth that is the point of comparison. Implicit in the use of this figure, though, may be a hint that even great human wisdom cannot surpass the providential provision of the Creator for meeting material needs.

The double illustration in Mt 6:26, 28b–30 par introduces a new element into the argument thus far. The first supporting argument (Mt 6:25b par) emphasized how life consisted of more than one's basic needs. It was an attempt to lessen the sense of need by applying to one's life a different perspective in which such matters are of lesser importance. There is no suggestion initially that the needs will be met. The new line of argument in Mt 6:26, 28b–30 par, however, does now argue that the needs will be met, by illustrating how the Creator cares for the needs of all his creation and *particularly* (the *a minore ad maius* argument) of men, even the ὀλιγόπιστοι. It will be left to the final stage of the collection (Mt 6:31–3 par) to draw these two lines of argument together. It is there that *both* a greater priority is stressed ('seek first...')

and an assurance is given that the needs themselves will actually be met ('and these things will be given to you in addition'). Thus, while Mt 6:25b may seem to be a secondary addition to Mt 6:25a, it becomes an essential element in the argument which is recapitulated in Mt 6:33 par and which is there united with the argument of 6:26, 28b–30.

How far, though, do the double rhetorical questions make their point on the basis of experiential evidence? Strictly, these sayings are not self-contained aphorisms which can be isolated and stand on their own. Yet the sayings are compatible with the perspective of experiential wisdom. The divine care is portrayed as providential, appealing to the order of the natural world. Even if it should be presupposed by the Christian community, it is striking that there is no *direct* appeal to any covenant relationship or to any conditions of faith or moral obedience. The most explicit hint that something more than a Creator–creature relationship may be involved is the title used for God. But here the two gospels differ. The phrase ὁ πατὴρ ὑμῶν ὁ οὐράνιος (Mt 6: 26) is certainly characteristic of Matthew,[72] but the presence of ὁ θεός in the second question (Mt 6:30) and the consistent use of ὁ θεός in Lk 12:24 and 28 are also important indications that ὁ θεός should probably be read throughout, as in Luke.[73] If this is so, as seems probable, then the reference to God as ὁ πατὴρ ὑμῶν only appears in the final verses of the collection (Mt 6:32/Lk 12:30), where a special relationship between God and those addressed has already been indicated by the contrast between the hearers and τὰ ἔθνη.

There is, however, a disruption in the double rhetorical question sequence. This is the saying, itself set as a question, in Mt 6:27/Lk 12:25: 'Which one of you by worrying can add a measure to his time of life?' Not only does it formally interrupt the double illustration which has been discussed, but the content of the question also has little to do with food or clothing or basic material needs. A reference to the measure of one's life is hardly expected, even in spite of the destruction of the grass in Mt 6:30 par.[74] The pessimism of the saying also sits uneasily with the argument thus far. For these reasons this saying is widely recognized as an intrusion into the argument,[75] and its awkwardness has probably led to differing attempts by Matthew and Luke to tie it more closely to the context (cf. Mt 6:28a and Lk 12:26).[76] Yet the close verbal correspondence and matching locations of the aphoristic saying in Matthew and Luke leave no doubt that the maxim had a place eventually in the formulation of the collection itself. How, then, is one to explain its presence?

Certainly it is most easily viewed as a later insertion into the collection. As such it may provide important evidence of a secondary modification of the collection prior to either gospel. A catchword link with the theme of anxiety is clear (μεριμνῶν). More importantly, an aphoristic saying (cf. Ps 39:5; Job 14:5), and one formulated appropriately as a rhetorical question amongst other rhetorical questions, is employed. This shows remarkable sensitivity to the design of the collection, despite the insistence on the intruding saying. Perhaps one is not that far removed from the hands of the earlier compiler(s). Thematically, Fitzmyer suggests that at least in Luke the saying may help to press the argument further. 'Worry cannot add an extra moment to one's life; so if this "tiny little thing" cannot be achieved by human concern, why worry about the rest?'[77] But the concern about the measure of one's life adds a significant new dimension. It is no longer a matter of the basic necessities of life, but of the very future of one's life itself. In this way, it also differs significantly from the question posed in Mt 6:25b. A concern for one's life would reflect a situation of either extreme deprivation or possibly physical threats against one, as in Mt 10:28ff./ Lk 12:4ff., where a very similar appeal to God's providential care of nature is employed (cf. below, pp. 51–61). There is insufficient evidence at this point to judge between these alternatives, but further evidence for the latter possibility will be found in the further analysis of the collections.[78]

4. The concluding sayings are again highly significant for the interpretation of the collection as a whole. As indicated earlier, it is these sayings in Mt 6:31–3/Lk 12:29–31 that draw together the two lines of argument offered previously.[79] It is these sayings that also may be the first to draw specifically on the concept of God not only as the Sustainer of the world but as ὁ πατὴρ ὑμῶν and that express for the first time the priority of 'seeking the kingdom of God'. It is here therefore that the argument comes to its climax and its most specific interpretation.

There are, however, a number of differences between Matthew and Luke in the precise wording of these verses. In both Matthew and Luke the conclusion is marked by a resumption of the opening exhortation (Mt 6:31/Lk 12:29) prior to the final argument and interpretative sayings in Mt 6:32–3 par. The multiple-question formulation in Mt 6:31 is again likely to be more original than the indirect-question formulation in Luke on the grounds of the previously noted Lukan tendency, and because it is difficult to account for Matthew having introduced this formulation here.[80]

Whether Luke was also responsible for the ζητεῖν – instead of μεριμνᾶν as in Matthew – is more problematic. The fact that Luke has introduced ζητεῖν redactionally elsewhere and has used the verb frequently in his gospel and Acts suggests that it is a Lukan substitution.[81] Luke may have changed the wording in Lk 12:29 to highlight the wording in Lk 12:31. W. Ott[82] persuasively argues that the special concerns of Luke are very much in evidence in the ways in which his version of this passage differs from the version in Matthew. Lukan opposition to seeking riches is emphasized by a wording which indicates that one should not 'seek' earthly goods at all (cf. Lk 12:29), while the version in Matthew indicates nothing wrong with such goods so long as one is not over-'anxious' about them and is willing to trust God for them (cf. Mt 6:31). Therefore Luke emphasizes μὴ ζητεῖτε, and Matthew has μὴ μεριμνήσητε. Ott further argues that Matthew uses the saying in Mt 6:32 as a grounding for what is presented in Mt 6:31, which reassures those addressed that they need not worry about these things since God knows they need them, while Luke appears to use the parallel saying in Lk 12:30 to reassert the prohibition against seeking these things like τὰ ἔθνη τοῦ κόσμου.[83] Hence the contrast of seeking the kingdom is heightened again in Lk 12:31 by the use of πλήν, while Matthew stresses not so much contrast as relative priorities (cf. πρῶτον in Mt 6:33). Although it is questionable whether the πρῶτον and πάντα in Mt 6:33 are original,[84] it is quite likely that the πλήν is a Lukan addition,[85] so that the strength of contrast found in Luke is due to Luke himself.[86] In the tradition it appears that it is not seeking after riches that is opposed, but anxiety about earthly needs. The hearers need not be anxious because their Father knows their need (cf. Mt 6:32 par). They are encouraged therefore to accept the vulnerability implicit in trusting the Father and to seek his kingdom (Mt 6:33 par).

Two further points should be mentioned concerning Mt 6:31–3 par. First, both Mt 6:31 and Lk 12:29 resume the opening exhortation by referring to eating and drinking, but only Matthew refers to clothing. The reference to drink is simply an extension of the concept of 'food', but Luke's absence of reference to clothing is surprising in views of the preceding verses. Indeed it is easier to explain Matthew's inserting the reference to clothing than Luke's omitting it. This may therefore be an important hint that in the final interpretation concern about food is nearer the heart of the matter than concern about clothing, which serves simply as an initial illustration of another basic necessity.[87]

Secondly, while this first observation suggests an even closer kinship of theme between Mt 6:25–33 par and Mt 7:7–11 par, there is a sense in which the final call to 'seek the kingdom of God' in Mt 6:33 par goes beyond the call to rely on the Father for material provision in Mt 7:11 par.[88] Yet, although Mt 6:33 par constitutes a new sphere of concern and a more active stance, it is still left very unclear as to what constitutes 'seeking the kingdom'. There is certainly no programme set forth here. Indeed, it is difficult to define what is meant. 'Seeking the kingdom' appears to be concerned here fundamentally with an attitude or orientation which acknowledges a trust in God's coming *kingly* rule as well as in his general providence. Both represent trust in God's ultimate control. Although this attitude of trust inevitably leaves the hearers vulnerable in terms of material provision, the promise that their need will be met is still the final promise: καὶ ταῦτα [πάντα] προστεθήσεται ὑμῖν.

II

How much warrant is there in this reference to God's kingdom, or elsewhere in the collection, for postulating an *intense* or *imminent* sense of eschatological crisis? Bultmann rightly drew attention to the absence of direct eschatological motivation in this passage.[89] Seccombe similarly rejects the attempt of E. G. Selwyn to read additional eschatological themes into the images of food (Messianic banquet) and clothing (garments of glory).[90] Even the reference to the grass of the field being thrown into the oven (Mt 6:30 par) allows only slight possibilities for demonstrating an *intense* eschatological expectation.

But if this is so, then it contrasts sharply with Schulz's assessment of the instruction as a whole as a radical prophetic command for poverty in the face of the imminent End-time.[91] Schulz draws a comparison with the situation at Qumran.[92] Yet it is far from clear even that a radical call for poverty is made in the synoptic collection. Schulz is not unaware of the difficulties, but attempts to deal with them in three ways. First, he suggests that it is in the prophetic introductory formulas (λέγω ὑμῖν: Mt 6:25a, 29 par; τίς ἐξ ὑμῶν: Mt 6:27 par) that an End-time announcement is indicated.[93] However, even if the prophetic nature of these formulas is acknowledged (and it is itself disputable),[94] there is nothing to indicate the particular type of intense eschatological outlook that Schulz requires. Secondly, Schulz notes that the usual apocalyptic interpretation of the kingdom of God in Q is modified here. Here is found a Pharisaic kingdom-understanding which presents the kingdom as present and where men submit voluntarily to the will of God. In Pharisaic thought the kingdom of God was closely related to the Sinaitic Torah. In apocalyptic thought, this Pharisaic view of the kingdom was interpreted as doing the original will of Yahweh through a radicalized Torah. Yet even Schulz admits that there is no hint in this section of a direct grounding in Torah and no indication of legal formulations.[95] Therefore, thirdly, Schulz suggests that the unity of ethic, cosmology and apocalyptic in this era permits basing this view of the kingdom on a direct relationship of man with the Creator God, rather than only through Torah. He alleges that early Christian prophecy has taken up a prominent theme of Hasidic apocalyptic in which the basis for such instructions is found in the work of the Creator God, as in 1 En 2:1−5:4.[96]

Yet an analysis of 1 En 2−5 calls the supposed analogy into question. Here, the stable order of the cosmos is portrayed in detail and then contrasted with the unsteadfastness of God's people. Man is the only unstable element in the cosmos, and this brings upon him a prophetic indictment and direct appeal to the commandments of the Lord (cf. 1 En 5:4; also 5:3). The aphoristic sayings collection in Mt 6:25−33 par, however, presents quite a different picture. There is no prophetic indictment, but rather continuous persuasion. Aphoristic sayings are part of the argument in this collection, while none exists in the 1 Enoch passage. There is no appeal in the synoptic sayings to man's being out of step with the order established for him by God through the commandments. Torah is explicit in 1 Enoch, but absent in the synoptic sayings. There is no threat of future judgement in the sayings collection, by contrast to 1 En 5:5. The differences, therefore, are at least as significant as the similarities. The main parallel between the two passages rests in the belief that the created order allows the work of the Creator to be observed. But in 1 Enoch these works are such that God's ordered pattern for the cosmos may be fixedly followed, while in the sayings collection of Mt 6:25ff. par his care for the needs of his creatures is stressed. 1 Enoch sets forth a basis for indictment; the sayings collection produces examples to persuade one of God's care.

Of course the reference to God's kingly rule does presuppose *some kind* of eschatological expectation, so the question really concerns of what kind it is and how it functions. Clearly it adds another dimension to simple trust in the providential care of the Creator, but it is not sufficiently intense to overpower the sapiential features of the argument. It serves as another recognition of God's control over men's lives. 'Seeking the kingdom' is another demonstration of trust in that control.[97]

It is true that the lack of anxiety which is encouraged contrasts with the practical 'work ethic' found in some sapiential literature. Is this evidence, though, that the eschatological perspective is colliding with the wisdom tradition?[98] Certainly the sapiential literature itself includes proverbial sayings against anxiety (cf. Sir 30:24–31:2; WisSol 6:15; 7:23), and such advice is not limited to biblical literature.[99] Further, it is clear from the content and design of the collection in Mt 6:25–33 par itself that it attempts to *win* agreement. It does not simply authoritatively declare 'God will care for you' or explicitly refer to the need for denial in view of an End-time crisis. It tries to create a sense of conviction, from experience and argument, that God's care is available.

III

But why try to provide a 'reasonable' basis at all for this kind of demand? Is it simply a fondness for sapiential expression? Is it a reaction against more authoritative demands? Or does it suggest a situation in which the issues are so sensitive that an attitude of trust needs to be 'won' and not simply 'required'? These are matters which bear on the *Sitz im Leben* of the collected sayings.

It has not been uncommon to associate these instructions with the missionary activity of the early church in particular. J. Jeremias considered the sayings as prohibiting the involvement of missionaries in paid labour. He claimed that it was incorrect to interpret the instruction in general terms (cf. 1 Cor 9:14), since a sense of eschatological urgency provides the background for these commands.[100] However, there is little to support the view that this teaching must be restricted to such a *Sitz im Leben*. First, there is no reference to mission or missionaries in the sayings themselves. Secondly, it is far from clear that paid labour is being prohibited, as Jeremias suggested. Thirdly, the call to 'seek' the kingdom is not necessarily a call to 'proclaim' the kingdom in a missionary sense. Fourthly, neither Luke nor Matthew associates this instruction with missionary activity.[101] Finally, there is no reason to suppose that anxieties about basic material needs were not present more widely in the early Christian communities, as were anxieties about opposition and persecution. The poverty of Christian communities in Palestine is attested in Acts (6:1ff., 11:27−30, both referring to need of food) and Paul (cf. Rom 15:25−7; 1 Cor 16:1−4; 2 Cor 8:1−9:15; Gal 2:10). These examples show that problems of genuine concern faced *communities*, and not just wandering missionaries.[102] Within double-tradition material, the concern with poverty and hunger is also expressed in the opening beatitudes (Lk 6:20b, 21a par) and in the Lord's Prayer (Lk 11:3). The missionary charge in Lk 10:4−8 par does refer to a lack of material provision, but A. Jacobson has persuasively argued that 'the intent of the account is not to provide information about a past mission or instructions for an ongoing mission but to make a theological point about the unbelief encountered in Israel'.[103] He views the vulnerability of the missionary (Lk 10:3, 4, 7−8 par) as 'appropriate for a mission to a demonic world'.[104] This understanding, and the recognition of the wider concern with the themes of poverty and hunger in double-tradition material (cf. also Mt 7:7−11 par), suggest that such anxieties must not be limited simply to missionaries.

It is likely, however, that those addressed are disciples. This holds true despite the reference to ὀλιγόπιστοι in Mt 6:30 par[105] (cf. ὑμεῖς πονηροί in Mt 7:11 par). This deprecatory reference to those being addressed is not an indication that unbelievers are in view, but rather that the instruction which is being given is apparently difficult to accept. The extensive employment of argument testifies to this. It is also clear that disciples are addressed from the general absence of polemic, the reference to ὁ πατὴρ ὑμῶν (Mt 6:32 par) and the way in which those addressed are contrasted with τὰ ἔθνη (Mt 6:32a par). The reference to τὰ ἔθνη in Mt 6:32a does at first seem odd and out of place,[106] but it is important in drawing out the status of the addressees. At the point where the application becomes most explicit, it is perhaps not surprising that the specific relationship of the hearers to God is established. The contrast with τὰ ἔθνη may imply a Jewish−Christian orientation,[107] although M. Black argues that the term could mean simply 'the rest of men', as opposed to the disciples.[108] It does serve in any case to indicate the status of the disciple, who can view God as ὁ πατὴρ ὑμῶν.

IV

Both Mt 7:7–11 par and Mt 6:25–33 par therefore portray a thematic concern with material needs amongst Christian followers. This common concern also extends to a common pattern of argument. By experiential observations and reasoned arguments, particularly favouring the *a minore ad maius* reasoning, two carefully constructed collections have been formulated to lead followers towards the conviction of God's care in this area and towards an attitude of trust, active petition and 'seeking the kingdom'. It is remarkable that such a careful and persuasive medium of instruction was considered necessary. It may be that this betrays the sensitivity and concern which conditions such as material need and hunger might have raised in some early Christian settings.

D. Catchpole has raised the possibility that the connection between these two collections might have been closer in Q than is often suggested. The introduction to the 'anxiety' sayings in Mt 6:25a par begins διὰ τοῦτο λέγω ὑμῖν in both Matthew and Luke. This appears to be a secondary transition, and Catchpole argues that 'in Q Luke xi. 2–13 led immediately into Luke xii. 22–31'.[109] Lk 11:2–13 alone, he argues, permits a διὰ τοῦτο continuation, for the immediately preceding double-tradition material in Lk 12:2–12 par concerns a different theme: persecution and the threat of death.[110] Although a hint of this persecution theme may emerge in the intruding saying in Lk 12:25 par, and although the argument in Lk 12:4–7 is remarkably similar to Lk 12:22ff. par, this may not in itself be sufficient to overcome the abrupt change of theme caused by an immediate conjunction. Catchpole therefore sees Lk 11:2–13 par and Lk 12:22–31 par together in a Q 'cares' section.[111]

The final arrangement of these collections into a larger sequence of material, however, is not our immediate concern. One must begin by recognizing how these collections and others are so similar in their design as to suggest a common compilational activity. We have made the first step in this direction by showing how Mt 7:7–11 par and Mt 6:25–33 par share a common structure and pattern of argument. This has consisted of (i) a very general opening exhortation, (ii) an initial supporting argument, (iii) a further, new set of supporting arguments using two parallel rhetorical questions and (iv) a final application which provides the interpretative key to the collection. It will be our intention to show that this pattern is found also in a number of other aphoristic collections of the double tradition.

Mt 7:1−5 (15:14; 10:24−5)/Lk 6:37−42

(i) μὴ κρίνετε, ἵνα μὴ κριθῆτε·

(ii) ἐν ᾧ γὰρ κρίματι κρίνετε κριθήσεσθε,
καὶ ἐν ᾧ μέτρῳ μετρεῖτε μετρηθήσεται ὑμῖν.

(iii) μήτι [?οὐχὶ] δύναται τυφλὸς τυφλὸν ὁδηγεῖν;
οὐχὶ ἀμφότεροι εἰς βόθυνον πεσοῦνται;

(iv) τί δὲ βλέπεις τὸ κάρφος τὸ ἐν τῷ ὀφθαλμῷ τοῦ ἀδελφοῦ
σου, τὴν δὲ δοκὸν τὴν ἐν τῷ σῷ ὀφθαλμῷ οὐ κατανοεῖς;
ἢ πῶς ἐρεῖς τῷ ἀδελφῷ σου, Ἄφες ἐκβάλω τὸ κάρφος ἐκ
τοῦ ὀφθαλμοῦ σου, καὶ ἰδοὺ ἡ δοκὸς ἐν τῷ ὀφθαλμῷ
σοῦ;
ὑποκριτά, ἔκβαλε πρῶτον ἐκ τοῦ ὀφθαλμοῦ σοῦ τὴν
δοκόν, καὶ τότε διαβλέψεις ἐκβαλεῖν τὸ κάρφος ἐκ τοῦ
ὀφθαλμοῦ τοῦ ἀδελφοῦ σου.

I

The theme of judging one's ἀδελφός is the subject of a third double-tradition aphoristic sayings collection. The boundaries of this collection are marked by the opening instruction not to judge (Mt 7:1/Lk 6:37a) and by the closing sayings on the hypocrisy of judging (Mt 7:3−5/Lk 6:41−2). Thematically, both the opening and the closing sayings condemn the passing of judgment on others. In the opening admonition this is supported by appeal to the law of retribution. In the closing sayings, the hypocrisy of making judgements on others is highlighted. In Matthew the demarcation of this set of sayings as a 'collection' is clear.[112] The main difference between Matthew and Luke however, concerns the inclusion of other sayings, particularly Lk 6:39 (Mt 15:14) and 6:40 (Mt 10:24−5), in the central portion of the collection. To determine how far Luke's sequence of sayings may be the more original, it will be necessary to work through the longer version in Luke, examining each saying as one proceeds.

1. The opening prohibition, μὴ κρίνετε, in both Mt 7:1 and Lk 6:37a conforms formally to the style of a wisdom admonition, for the general exhortation is immediately followed by a

reason in support of it: καὶ οὐ μὴ/ἵνα μὴ κριθῆτε.[113] Once again one finds at the outset a remarkably simple and very general and unqualified exhortation. No particular subject, object or situation is specified. J. Fitzmyer remarks: '"Judging" does not refer here to the judicial decision of a constituted judge, but to the human tendency to criticize and find fault with one's neighbour.'[114] The subsequent development of the argument will show that this is indeed correct, but one must not overlook the very open-ended way in which the argument begins.[115] This tendency to work from very general principles to more specific application by carefully graduated steps is an important feature of the collections that are being examined.

The initial support for the prohibition raises the idea of retribution. Again no agency is specified for the aorist passive subjunctive verbs.[116] No direct appeal to the Law or word of God or coming judgement of God strengthens or validates this statement of retribution.[117] This absence of elaboration heightens the impression that this principle could apply to many aspects of human experience (cf. Sir 7:1−2; 28:1). This impression will be strengthened by appeal later to the commercial metaphor of 'measures'.

Yet, while Matthew has simply a single opening wisdom admonition, Lk 6:37, 38a testifies to a fourfold opening admonition consisting of two negative and two positive commands in parallel. J. Crossan shows how the later tradition of 1 Clem 13:2 contains six terms prior to the 'measures' saying (only two of which are strictly imperatives) and Polycarp's Phil. 2:3 sets out three parallel exhortations prior to the 'measures' saying.[118] In Crossan's view, Luke best represents the Q-version. He believes that Matthew has truncated this, cutting also the saying referring to the 'good measure' (Lk 6:38b, not found in either 1 Clem 13 or Polycarp's Phil. 2). His grounds for supporting the version in Luke are apparently the good transitions created around the concepts of 'measure' (Lk 6:38b and c) and of διδόναι (Lk 6:38a and b).[119] Yet such transitions are not unambiguous arguments for primitiveness. Luke may have added the sayings in Lk 6:37b, c, 38a, and especially 38b, to provide an improved transition of thought.[120] The admonition to 'give' (Lk 6:38a) is particularly suggestive of Lukan interests in charity, even if the vocabulary does not suggest Lukan free composition.[121] Furthermore, there is evidence that Luke shows some interest in 'lists of four', such as in the Lukan version of the sayings in Lk 6:22, 6:24–6, and 6:27–8, all of which are in the immediate context of the Sermon.[122] These arguments seem slightly to favour Matthew as representing the earlier version.[123] This would suggest that the other forms of tradition are all elaborations of the short Matthean version. The effect of the added clauses in Luke is to present forgiveness as the positive converse of judging and condemning and to add an interest in 'giving'.[124] None of these points is developed in the subsequent argument of the collection,[125] except possibly for the μέτρον saying in Lk 6:38c/Mt 7:2b.

2. Matthew and Luke are agreed in following the opening admonition(s) with an aphorism about 'measures' (Lk 6:38c/Mt 7:2b). In Matthew this is more sharply a change in imagery than in Luke and it could easily have stood once as an independent aphoristic saying, as Mk 4:24 illustrates.[126] But in Matthew the change in imagery is lessened by its parallelism with Mt 7:2a (not in Luke), which is also formulated as an aphorism about retribution.

Although Mt 7:2a may be a secondary expansion patterned upon Mt 7:2b, sharpening Mt 7:1 and serving as a transition to Mt 7:2b, it is not clear whether it was pre-Matthean and known to Luke. S. Schulz argues that it must have existed in Q because Mt 7:2b can hardly follow directly on Mt 7:1.[127] However, Klostermann[128] and Zeller[129] do not find this abruptness insuperable. Ultimately one cannot be certain. It is possible that Matthew and Luke independently found ways to ease the transition between Mt 7:1 par and Mt 7:2b par. Yet some transition seems desirable, so that the primitiveness of Mt 7:2a will be tentatively assumed, and Luke's deletion will be explained as due to his expansion of the parallel exhortations in Lk 6:37bc, 38ab, which more closely reflect his interests.

The function of the aphorism about 'measures' in the argument is to illustrate further from human experience the retributive relationship indicated in the opening prohibition on judging.[130] This was the principle of *jus talionis*. It is discernible in rabbinic thought and was viewed as active in this life and not merely in the hereafter.[131] But it also draws on images of commercial life, as Lk 6:38b makes clear.[132] To refer directly here to an apocalyptic law of End-time judgement fails to allow for the wider applications of the saying in its aphoristic formulation.[133] 'Not judging' is therefore initially supported by appeal to the principle of retribution, in which one is vulnerable to the same judgements.

3. The most vexing problem for the reconstruction of this collection of sayings is whether the sayings in Lk 6:39 and 40 were part of the collection known to Matthew. The two sayings should be considered separately, for in Matthew they are employed independently in Mt 15:14 and 10:24–5. The former saying, about the blind leading the blind, also occurs on its own in GThom 34;[134] and the latter saying, about disciples and teachers, servants and masters, may be partly attested also in Jn 13:16 and 15:20 and in DialSav 139:11.[135]

Regarding the saying about the blind leading the blind, there is a sufficiently close correspondence in wording between the aphoristic saying in Lk 6:39 and Mt 15:14 to lead many scholars to hold that the formulations can be attributed to the same underlying saying.[136] On form-critical grounds Bultmann prefers the double-question form in Luke as the more primitive of the two synoptic versions.[137] This can be maintained while still recognizing some slight Lukan touches to the vocabulary such as ἐμπεσοῦνται for πεσοῦνται and perhaps the use of μήτι in Luke for οὐχί.[138] The formulation of the saying as a statement in Mt 15:14 is explicable by the fact that Matthew has had to adapt the saying into an apophthegm directed against the Pharisees, who are specifically called 'blind guides'. The double-question formulation is manifestly unsuited to the Matthean setting, whereas the statement formulation could have been easily incorporated into the context in Luke. Matthew's context for the saying also appears to be secondary, on account of its interruption of the Markan sequence of thought between Mt 15:11–12 and 15:15ff. (cf. Mk 7:14–20).[139] Thus it is likely that both the form and the context of the saying in Matthew are secondary. The form of the saying in Luke is quite likely to have been near to that of his source, but it need not follow that this context for the saying is also traditional. The saying does appear to be somewhat awkward in its context in Luke. Setting aside Lk 6:40, however, Lk 6:39 appears as an intrusion into this context more because of its question form and its abrupt change of metaphor than because of the inappropriateness of its content. The theme of blindness and the absurdity of the blind leading the blind will prove a very apt transition to Lk 6:41–2 par.[140] It is therefore quite reasonable to suppose that Luke has preserved an earlier setting for this saying, which Matthew then altered because the idea of 'leading' seemed to him less appropriate here than for pointed polemic against the Pharisees.[141] Luke's own attempt to deal with the *stylistic* abruptness of Lk 6:39 following Lk 6:38 is found in the phrase εἶπεν δὲ καὶ παραβολὴν αὐτοῖς, which is almost certainly due to Lukan redaction.[142]

An abrupt change of imagery and the introduction of a new line of argument at precisely this point of the double rhetorical questions is perhaps less surprising in view of the similar phenomenon in Mt 7:9–10 par and even Mt 6:26, 28b–30 par. These rhetorical questions reinforce the prohibition on 'judging' by subtly introducing the idea that the one who passes judgement (here 'leads') may himself have the same fault. This suggestion is then explicitly developed in the concluding sayings of the collection about the eye and the beam (cf. Lk 6:41–2 par), which are also introduced by two further rhetorical questions posing a ridiculous situation. While one cannot be certain that Lk 6:39 was part of this context in the earlier pre-Lukan tradition, it is a possibility which gains credence from the flow of the argument, as well as on other grounds.

In this interpretation, the reference to 'leading' is primarily parallel in thought to 'judging': that is, putting oneself in a position of superiority. It need not in itself refer simply to the recognized leadership in a community, whether Jewish or Christian.[143] But how then is one to evaluate Lk 6:40 (cf. Mt 10:24–5)? In the first place, the theme of leadership in this saying receives separate elaboration. This is achieved through the μαθητής – διδάσκαλος (and possibly the δοῦλος – κύριος)[144] terminology. Secondly, much of the usefulness of Lk 6:39 as a transition to the thought expressed in Lk 6:41–2 par is lost by the intrusion of Lk 6:40 into the sequence. A. Jacobson goes so far as to argue that Lk 6:40

'has no discernible connection with 6:39'.[145] Did Luke himself insert this saying in order to make the section apply to leadership in the early Christian community?[146] Or was it added for a similar purpose in pre-Lukan tradition?[147] Or was it added for some other purpose in pre-Lukan tradition, as when A. Polag suggests that all of Lk 6:39–45 was a Q-polemic against Pharisees and their teaching?[148]

It is instructive to look briefly at Matthew's context for the saying. In Mt 10:24–5, the saying refers to the fate to be expected for disciples, a fate which would be no better than that which awaited their master (κύριος). The δοῦλος – κύριος clause, which is not in Lk 6:40, is not necessarily Matthean. It is attested in Jn 13:16 and 15:20. It is also inappropriate for Luke's context, and in any case Luke has a tendency to destroy or recast such parallelism.[149] S. Schulz and A. Polag rightly note that this theme fits well with other double-tradition sayings in which the rejection both of Jesus (cf. Lk 7:33–4 par) and of his followers (cf. Lk 6:22–3 par; possibly 11:49–50 par) is envisaged.[150] Schulz therefore accepts Matthew's context as the correct *conceptual* context for the saying in Q.[151] If this is so, and if the formulation in Matthew is more original, then Luke has at the very least reapplied the saying and perhaps emphasized the issue of (Christian) leadership by his deletion of the δοῦλος – κύριος clause.[152] As Grundmann argued, for Luke it was necessary for a leader to be a 'seeing' leader, and this could only come through his teacher, Jesus.[153] Luke may have indeed inserted the saying himself after 6:39. The presence of the reference to blind leaders in his source could well have prompted him to include the shortened version of the saying in 6:40. There is evidence elsewhere in Luke of the evangelist following the theme of blindness or lack of understanding by the theme of recognition and instruction (cf. Lk 4:18, 7:21).[154] The saying in Lk 6:40, particularly in the formulation using κατηρτισμένος, looks forward also in a curiously prophetic way to the narrative account of the disciples on the road to Emmaus (Lk 24:13ff.). Is a veiled allusion to an Emmaus-like theme a further explanation of his interesting introduction in 6:39a, εἶπεν δὲ καὶ παραβολὴν αὐτοῖς?

It is not possible to make a decision with confidence about Lk 6:40. The above reasons have inclined us to consider it a

Lukan insertion, prompted partly by Lk 6:39, already in Luke's source. However, if Lk 6:40 was inserted into this context prior to Luke, it most probably reflected an early secondary intrusion on the theme of a problem in Christian leadership or even (in Matthew's formulation) an awkward allusion to the fate of disciples, perhaps not dissimilar to Mt 6:27 par (cf. also Mt 10:30 par below).

4. If Lk 6:39 comprises the 'middle section' with its double rhetorical questions, then the final unit of this collection consists of Lk 6:41–2/Mt 7:3–5.[155] This too begins with double rhetorical questions (Lk 6:41, 42a/Mt 7:3–4), followed by a concluding rejoinder in Lk 6:42b/Mt 7:5. The questions and rejoinder, however, are closely integrated (cf. also Mt 6:31 par), and with some justice A. Jacobson notes that 'Lk 6:41f par is clearly a self-enclosed unit'.[156] Thus, the conclusion to the collection is not simply the command 'Hypocrite, first cast the beam out of your own eye …' (Lk 6:42b/Mt 7:5), but rather the entire group of sayings about the beam in one's eye (Lk 6:41–2 par).

These sayings return to the opening prohibition of 'judging' after the intervening metaphors on measures and the blind leading the blind. It is therefore an apt way to conclude the collection of sayings.[157] The earlier argument citing the principle of retribution may also not be entirely absent from Lk 6:41, 42a. Yet here at the climax 'judging' receives a more specific application in terms of critical attitudes towards one's ἀδελφός. The initial general reference to judging now achieves a focal point.

II

The reference to ἀδελφός would most naturally imply an intracommunity problem. A less specific, and perhaps preparatory, hint along these lines was already suggested in Lk 6:39 in the metaphor of the blind leading the blind. There is no suggestion of 'leadership' in the final sayings, however.[158] The often-noted parallel to Lk 6:42a par in the saying of Rabbi Tarphon (*c.* AD 100), in which implicit in the context is a rejected offer to give *instruction*, cannot be determinative for the context here.[159] This rabbinic formulation is one of accusation and counter-accusation,[160] while the question formulation here focuses on individual self-evaluation. The rabbinic example simply shows that these ideas were not foreign to Jewish thought.[161]

Thus the interpretative significance of these final sayings is (1) to resume the theme of 'judging', (2) to apply it to critical attitudes in particular, and (3) to locate it in an inner-community setting (cf. ἀδελφός). If it represents a problem of divisions within a fellowship, this may also explain the careful and multi-faceted style of argument which is employed in this collection of sayings, which ultimately turns to individual self-evaluation rather than to the divisions themselves. The most natural explanation for such an extensive use of illustrations and arguments in support of a single instruction is that it was a matter of particular difficulty or sensitivity for those addressed.

One apparent exception to the non-polemical and persuasive tone of these sayings is the vocative ὑποκριτά in the final saying (Mt 7:5/Lk 6:42b). But, in the context of Mt 7:3−4/Lk 6:41, 42a, hypocrisy is indeed the issue. This is not simply a random invective. It is fundamental to the argument. In addition, it has been previously argued (cf. p. 20 on Mt 7:11 par; p. 34 on Mt 6:30 par) that such apparently critical designations need not imply an attack on 'outsiders', but are perfectly compatible with instruction for Christian followers.[162]

III

Once again there is also no explicit appeal to End-time reward or punishment in order to reinforce the instruction. This is perhaps all the more significant since the theme of judgement lay so readily at hand. There may be indirect allusions to eschatological judgement in the retributive maxims[163] or even in the metaphor of falling into a pit, but these remain little more than hints, which receive no elaboration and certainly no application to *imminent* events. On the contrary, argument rather than eschatological threat dominates the tone of the passage.

Despite this, and despite his own acknowledgement that the formal nature of the sayings reflects experientially orientated wisdom, S. Schulz tries to emphasize the prophetic enthusiasm of the sayings (at least of Mt 7:1−5/Lk 6:37−8, 41−2).[164] He assigns them to his earlier, enthusiastic and eschatologically orientated Q-setting. For Schulz, experiential wisdom is made the servant of both prophecy and Torah. The *Weisheitsworte* (sayings of wisdom) are often held to be identical with the original intention of the Mosaic Law, expressing as it were the original will of Yahweh. It was the early Christian prophet who discovered that these sayings were in fact the intention of God underlying the Torah and who then authoritatively proclaimed them as a sharpened and radical announcement in the face of the imminent End.[165] In this section, the command about not judging is apparently one aspect of the command to love, which is in turn the radical essence of the Mosaic Law.[166] The prophetic authority with which this is then proclaimed is not undermined by the 'artistic' form of the saying used, although Schulz does at times admit the desire to appeal to the experience of the hearers to show that the command is not absurd.[167]

While Schulz does make a serious attempt to reconcile wisdom and eschatological pronouncement, his approach in this instance is not wholly convincing.[168] Apart from his methodological approach to Q generally,[169] it is not clear why experiential wisdom should be employed at all as the middle term between Torah and eschatological pronouncement. Would not appeal to the commandment directly at least somewhere in this collection of sayings have been more effective, and possibly even less suspect for the early Jewish Christians whom Schulz describes, than appeal to 'worldly' wisdom? Should one also not be suspicious when Schulz has to claim that immediately before the instruction 'Judge not' there was originally a prophetic introduction (λέγω ὑμῖν) which unfortunately had fallen out before being included in the two gospels?[170] And, even if the future passive verbs in Mt 7:2 par should be accepted as referring to an eschatological future event, there is no indication of the enthusiastic urgency or imminence of judgement which Schulz requires.

Therefore, one must take seriously the fact that experiential wisdom itself dominates the thought of this collection of sayings. The direct threat of final judgement is avoided in favour of an approach which is less polemical and less potentially divisive. It seeks to win assent, to encourage an attitude of self-examination, not to specify an offending party.

Mt 7:16–20, 12:33–5/Lk 6:43–5

(i) οὐ γάρ ἐστιν δένδρον καλὸν ποιοῦν καρπὸν σαπρόν,
οὐδὲ δένδρον σαπρὸν ποιοῦν καρπὸν καλόν.

(ii) ἐκ γὰρ τοῦ καρποῦ τὸ δένδρον γινώσκεται.

(iii) μήτι συλλέγουσιν ἀπὸ ἀκανθῶν σῦκα [Mt: σταφυλάς],
ἢ ἀπὸ βάτου [Mt: τριβόλων] σταφυλήν [Mt: σῦκα];

(iv) ὁ ἀγαθὸς ἄνθρωπος ἐκ τοῦ ἀγαθοῦ θησαυροῦ προφέρει
ἀγαθά,
καὶ ὁ πονηρὸς ἐκ τοῦ πονηροῦ προφέρει πονηρά·
ἐκ γὰρ περισσεύματος καρδίας τὸ στόμα λαλεῖ.

Immediately following the aphoristic sayings collection on critical attitudes in Luke and closely following it in Matthew is another important sayings collection. Its dominant theme is 'being recognized by one's fruits'. It will be argued that this too encourages an attitude of self-examination and may also apply to the issue of critical speech in particular.

I

This is the first of the examined collections in which the actual arrangement of the sayings differs markedly in Matthew and Luke. It is in fact an excellent example of an aphoristic collection which has been used in very different ways by the two evangelists. Most of the sayings are also preserved, in an order similar to that of Luke, in GThom 43b, 45.[171]

Following Crossan,[172] the order of the aphorisms in this collection may be helpfully set out as follows:

	Matthew 7	Matthew 12	Luke
Tree and fruit	7:17–18	12:33a	6:43
By its fruit	7:16a = 20	12:33b	6:44a
Grapes and figs	7:16b		6:44b
From one's treasure		12:34b–35	6:45a, b
Heart and mouth		12:34c	6:45c

It is widely accepted that Mt 7:15, about watching out for false prophets, is the product of Matthean editorship, not an early tradition excluded from this context by Luke.[173] The imagery of sheep and wolves is quite distinct from that which follows. Yet by this exhortation Matthew makes clear how he wishes the 'tree–fruit' sayings to be interpreted in Mt 7:16–20. The application to false prophets also explains the introduction of the 'judgement' motif in Mt 7:19 (cf. Mt 3:10 par).[174] An even stronger polemical adaptation of the sayings (against the Pharisees) is found in Mt 12:33–5, but the general correspondence with the order of sayings in Lk 6:43–5 increases the impression that Lk 6:43–5 does in fact preserve the most original sequence of the collection.[175]

If this is so, then it is likely that the repetition of Mt 7:16a in 7:20 is also due to Matthew. His use of *inclusio* is well known,[176] and in Mt 7 the presence only of sayings with tree–fruit imagery makes the use of Mt 7:16a = 20 in an *inclusio* more appropriate in Mt 7 than for a source which contained all the sayings in Lk 6:43–5; Mt 12:33–5.

And, as Mt 12:33−5 suggests, the union of the aphorisms in Lk 6:45 (treasure, heart and mouth) with those in 6:43−4 (trees, fruit, grapes and thorns) was already present in early tradition.

The actual wording of Mt 7:16a and 20 suggests considerable Matthean redaction in an effort to apply this maxim to the themes introduced by Matthew in 7:15. The use of the second person plural to match the warning in Mt 7:15 and the reference to 'them' (false prophets?) instead of 'tree' in these two Matthean counterparts to Lk 6:44a are most likely due to Matthew. A comparison of Mt 12:33b with Lk 6:44a indicates, however, that ἕκαστον and ἰδίου might well have been due to Lukan redaction, possibly in an effort to link the sayings in Lk 6:43−4 to the preceding declaration on the hypocrisy of judging others. Luke may have wished to make clear that examination is of oneself.[177] This suggests that the wording of Mt 12:33b is the formulation of the saying which is most likely to have been earliest, namely the maxim ἐκ γὰρ τοῦ καρποῦ τὸ δένδρον γινώσκεται.[178]

But where does this saying come in the sequence of sayings? The sequence of Lk 6:43, 44a is reproduced in Mt 12:33a, b, which lends considerable support to its primitiveness. The maxim 'By its fruit' follows the description of the good and bad trees−fruit. Despite Schulz's objection to the originality of the sequence in Mt 12 on the grounds that there is strong redactional activity in Mt 12,[179] the same objection could be applied to Mt 7. The correspondence in order between Lk 6:43, 44a and Mt 12:33a, b must not be lightly set aside.

Not unrelated is the question of the placement of the sayings about grapes and figs (Lk 6:44b; Mt 7:16b). In Matthew these rhetorical questions precede the sayings about trees and fruit (7:17−18), while in Luke they follow and are formulated as statements, not questions. The Lukan tendency to recast rhetorical questions supports the greater originality of the question formulation in Matthew.[180] But the placement in Luke seems more appropriate, because it does not interrupt the δένδρον − καρπός imagery. The interruption has occurred in Mt 7:16−20 because Matthew has brought forward the general rule about 'By its fruit' to Mt 7:16a. If the grapes−figs sayings followed this general rule in the earlier tradition (as in Lk 6:44a, b), then Matthew may preserve a reminiscence of this by this placement of the questions in 7:16b immediately after 7:16a. It is therefore likely that the illustrations drawn from grapes and figs did follow immediately the general rule 'By its fruit' and that the Lukan order generally best represents the earlier tradition once again.[181]

Finally, the union of Lk 6:45 with the preceding verses, Lk 6:43−4, was undoubtedly present in the early tradition, as Mt 12:33−5 demon-strates.[182] The sequence in Luke is again probably more original than that of Matthew, since, as Schulz observes,[183] Matthew may have altered the sequence to provide an immediate answer to the question posed in Mt 12:34a, which itself is certainly the product of Matthean redaction applying the sayings directly against the Pharisees. If Luke's order is more primitive, then there is a formal parallel between the structure of the two sayings in Lk 6:45 and that of the two sayings in Lk 6:43, 44a, which are respectively the closing and the opening of this short collection of sayings.[184]

The explanation for why the two sayings in Lk 6:45 par about the treasure of one's heart and about speaking from the heart are joined with the preceding sayings in Lk 6:43−4 raises the question of the purpose of this section generally. The view that Lk 6:43−4 is a 'parable' has been revived partially by Schulz.[185] Schulz considers the 'tree' sayings in Lk 6:43−4 to constitute a *Gleichnis*, followed by its application in Lk 6:45a, b. The original metaphor and the subsequent application are in antithetical parallelism.[186] Lk 6:45c did not originally belong to this parable and application, but was placed here at a pre-redactional stage of Q on account of its content, showing that what is true of deeds is also true of words. The point of the parable is to reverse the tradition of Pharisaic Judaism whereby the man is declared good or bad according to what he does. The man and his works form a unity. In the context of Q, Schulz considers the parable to describe the good man as the Israelite who follows the radically sharpened Mosaic Torah in obedience to Jesus and with uncompromising loyalty in the face of the imminent End.[187]

Formally, there are weighty objections to viewing Lk 6:43−4, 45a, b as a parabolic unit of this kind. Bultmann rightly argued that one is dealing here with several independent sayings.[188] Lk 6:44a, Mt 7:16b, and Lk 6:45c are all likely to have been originally indepen-dent aphorisms. The change in metaphor as one progresses from Lk 6:43, 44a to 6:44b to 6:45a, b and finally to 6:45c is more suggestive of a combination of independent sayings than of a parable and ap-plication(s). Certainly Matthew seems to have treated these sayings as independent units, which could be rearranged at will, rather than as comprising a fixed 'parable'. The passage also has none of the narrative which often characterizes parables in the synoptic tradition. It is therefore best to consider this section as a group of sayings and to investigate its meaning on this basis. Schulz's main contribution is to emphasize the fact that the concluding sayings serve to clarify and limit the rather open-ended range of meanings possible for the opening sayings. The structure of this section therefore deserves closer attention.

II

Once again a pattern of argument emerges in which one moves from general aphorisms to more specific application through several distinct steps. In accordance with the preceding arguments, the order of Luke will be taken to represent that of the tradition.

1. The opening saying, Lk 6:43 (cf. Mt 7:17–18,[189] 12:33[190]), is presented as a general rule expressed in the negative: 'No good tree bears bad fruit, nor does a bad tree bear good fruit.' The saying is clearly metaphorical and an aphorism of the pattern which expresses an impossibility or contrast. But no interpretation of the imagery is given at this point, so that it remains entirely general and open to application. The negative formulation may imply that the intention is to warn or correct a false understanding, rather than simply to make an observation, but whether opponents or companions are addressed is also not initially clear. The aphorism is carefully presented, portraying not only antithetical parallelism, but also a chiastic construction with καλός and σαπρός.[191]

2. The saying in Lk 6:44a, accepting the order in Luke as the most original, is a summary of and support for the preceding aphorism. It is set forth in a more concise, general and positively formulated way. This saying also presents a subtle change of emphasis, which further develops the argument of the collection. The opening aphorism portrayed a general correlation between a tree and its fruit. This next aphorism explains that a means to *identify* (γινώσκειν) the type of tree which one has is to look at its fruit. The concept of a method of testing is introduced,[192] which is why it is so appropriately applied in Matthew to the question of false prophets in the community (Mt 7) and to the teaching of the Pharisees (Mt 12). The emphasis on testing in Matthew may also explain Matthew's use of this particular saying to open and close the entire section in Mt 7:16–20.

3. The following sayings in Lk 6:44b par provide further support for the preceding maxims by drawing on various specific examples from nature to support the thesis. The double

rhetorical questions (so Mt 7:16b: cf. above) mockingly indicate what is clearly contrary to nature and right order. They are reminiscent of proverbs such as 'Do horses run upon rocks? Can the sea be ploughed with oxen?' (Amos 6:12) or 'Can the Ethiopian change his skin, or the leopard his spots?' (Jer 13:23).[193] Although the relation between the type of plant and its fruit is again portrayed, the types here are not expressed in terms of καλός and σαπρός, but in terms of different varieties.[194] New imagery is introduced. Since in Lk 6:45 one immediately returns to the good–bad imagery (ἀγαθός – πονηρός), the rhetorical questions here are probably included entirely for their persuasive and illustrative value. They seek to remove any doubt, as their mocking tone suggests, and are not intended to supply any additional moral insight.

4. Additional insight appears in the 'treasures' saying in Lk 6: 45a, b. Unlike Lk 6:43, this aphorism is positively formulated, its instructional content thereby being emphasized. The range of meanings possible for δένδρον καλόν and δένδρον σαπρόν has been narrowed in this aphorism to refer specifically to ὁ ἀγαθὸς ἄνθρωπος and ὁ πονηρός. Yet what is produced (προφέρειν) remains as unclear as, earlier, ἀγαθά and πονηρά. The decisive interpretation of what is meant has to await the final aphorism in Lk 6:45c.[195] This is the final clue for interpreting the meaning of the sayings in the entire collection. The 'treasury' has now become the περίσσευμα καρδίας, and what it yields (that is, what is meant to be understood by good and bad fruit, or simply by ἀγαθά and πονηρά) is what the mouth speaks.[196] This final saying not only supports and summarizes the preceding sayings through a perceptive observation about life (cf. Prov 13:2, 15:7, 28, 16:23, 27, 18:4, 26:24); it also provides the final clue that what precedes is to refer to one's speech.[197]

III

If the fruit borne by the trees in the opening saying is to refer ultimately to speech, what kind of speech is in view? A. Polag argues that this section of Q opposes the legal teaching of the Pharisees.[198] H. Schürmann has presented a similar view.[199] Schürmann and Polag, though, both base their view on the separation of Lk 6:37–8 from 6:39–45 in Q.[200] A comparison of the sequence of sayings in

Matthew and Luke demonstrates on the contrary that it is more natural to consider the units divided as Lk 6:37–42/Mt 7:1–5 and Lk 6:43–5/Mt 7:16–20, 12:33–5. Our analysis of the structure of these two units also supports the unity of each, and it is very unsatisfactory to view Mt 7:1–2/Lk 6:37–8 as separate from Mt 7:3–5/Lk 6:41–2 (cf. below pp. 36–44). Further, if in Lk 6:43–5 par the compilation of sayings is directed against Pharisaic teaching, then why is there none of the polemic which is directed openly against the Pharisees elsewhere in the Q-sayings? The Pharisees are not even mentioned in the collection, and no saying in the collection refers to judgement or to contradiction of their teaching. The polemical additions of Matthew are absent in the Q-collection of sayings, as even Schürmann concedes.[201] The carefully reasoned, non-polemical formulation of this section is much more suited to instruction of followers. The wealth of support drawn from experience, and the reasoned development,[202] again suggest that the teaching of this section is a matter of concern and probably an issue of sensitivity. A likely alternative to the theory of Schürmann and Polag is that the speech referred to in this section is related to the critical, judgemental speech warned against in the previous collection of aphoristic sayings (Lk 6:37–42 par). Whereas the previous collection admonished followers to beware of such critical attitudes towards their brethren, in the present collection critical or evil speech is shown to be representative of a basic orientation of the heart. This is argued out from general principles. Throughout Lk 6:43–5 par there is no reference to God, judgement, Law or false teaching.[203]

This collection of sayings, however, is not wholly typical of general sapiential teaching on speech. The usual warnings against carelessness in speech are not set forth here (cf. Prov 15:1ff.; Sir 28:13ff.). The emphasis lies not so much on the harmful results of careless speech as upon the source of one's speech, the correspondence between what is brought forth in speech and what underlies it in one's heart or attitudes. The aphoristic sayings which are employed portray not consequences but correspondences. The effect is to expose what lies behind one's speech. The implication is that here lies a test for assessing what is not openly visible for external assessment, one's heart. But why should aphoristic sayings be exclusively used here for this purpose? Apart from wider issues of the importance of wisdom for those who formulated and preserved these traditions, one can note that experiential wisdom is especially suitable for making exposures of this type convincing and inescapable. The generality of the sayings also permits each individual ultimately to apply the test to himself. No particular individual or group is singled out. The test applies to all, and its logic is convincing for all, for the only presupposition upon which the teaching is based is the wide common ground of human experience. It might apply to opponents of the early Christians as well as to followers themselves, but it certainly does not constitute a polemic against opponents.[204] This suggests a situation which demanded tact and skilful persuasion and which is more likely to have been characterized by difficulties within the community of followers than by opponents outside. The application of the sayings to critical attitudes in the community fits well both the tone of this section and the previous concerns about not judging one's brother. The exposure of the source of critical speech is aimed to encourage a change of heart. The harmful results of speech are not in view because they have been referred to in a limited way earlier (cf. Mt 7:1−2 par), and because it is mistaken to view this teaching as merely typical Jewish parenetic material about speech included for the general edification of the early church.

Mt 10:26−33/Lk 12:2−9

(i) οὐδὲν κεκαλυμμένον ἐστὶν ὃ οὐκ ἀποκαλυφθήσεται,
καὶ κρυπτὸν ὃ οὐ γνωσθήσεται.

ὃ ἐν τῇ σκοτίᾳ εἴπατε ἐν τῷ φωτὶ ἀκουσθήσεται,
καὶ ὃ εἰς τὸ οὖς ἐλαλήσατε κηρυχθήσεται ἐπὶ τῶν δωμάτων.

(ii) [i] καὶ μὴ φοβεῖσθε ἀπὸ τῶν ἀποκτεννόντων τὸ σῶμα, τὴν
δὲ ψυχὴν μὴ δυναμένων ἀποκτεῖναι·
[ii?] φοβεῖσθε δὲ μᾶλλον τὸν δυνάμενον καὶ ψυχὴν καὶ σῶμα
ἀπολέσαι ἐν γεέννῃ.

(iii) [iii] οὐχὶ πέντε στρουθία πωλοῦνται ἀσσαρίων δύο;
καὶ ἓν ἐξ αὐτῶν οὐ πεσεῖται ἐπὶ τὴν γῆν ἄνευ τοῦ θεοῦ
[Mt: πατρὸς ὑμῶν].

ὑμῶν δὲ καὶ αἱ τρίχες τῆς κεφαλῆς πᾶσαι ἠριθμημέναι εἰσίν.

[iv] μὴ [οὖν] φοβεῖσθε· πολλῶν στρουθίων διαφέρετε ὑμεῖς.

(iv) πᾶς ὃς ἂν ὁμολογήσῃ ἐν ἐμοὶ ἔμπροσθεν τῶν ἀνθρώπων,
καὶ ὁ υἱὸς τοῦ ἀνθρώπου ὁμολογήσει ἐν αὐτῷ
ἔμπροσθεν τῶν ἀγγέλων τοῦ θεοῦ·
ὃς δ' ἂν ἀρνήσηταί με ἔμπροσθεν τῶν ἀνθρώπων,
ἀρνηθήσεται ἔμπροσθεν τῶν ἀγγέλων τοῦ θεοῦ.

I

This collection of sayings is one of the most interesting of those analysed. The differences between Matthew and Luke are not critical to the argument, so that the main difficulties do not lie with a reconstruction of the tradition. However, the collection is noteworthy because it would appear to have been constructed in at least two stages. First, there is a small collection of sayings comprising Mt 10: 28−31/Lk 12:4−7, which is marked at the beginning and end with exhortations not to fear.[205] The style of argument in these verses is very reminiscent of Mt 6:25−33 par (see above, pp. 24−36), in which the opening exhortation about anxiety was followed by consolation deriving from God's general providential care of nature and from the relatively high worth of the hearers (ὑμεῖς) within the natural world.[206] A repetition of the initial exhortation at the end of the collection can be found in both cases (μὴ φοβεῖσθε; μὴ μεριμνᾶτε). Yet the present collection is generally briefer and less developed than Mt 6:25−33 par. However, at a later stage it would appear that the collection received an additional set of opening (Mt 10:26−7/Lk 12:2−3) and closing sayings (Mt 10:32−3/Lk 12:8−9), which give a new emphasis to the collection but without completely disrupting its structure of argument. It will be suggested that this new emphasis is dictated in part by the theme of the collection: anxiety for one's life in view of external threats and opposition. This concern is more pressing and more fundamentally threatening to the community than anxieties about material needs, and this is revealed in the eschatological promise and warning of Mt 10:32−3/Lk 12:8−9.

II

We will begin with a closer look at Mt 10:28−31/Lk 12:4−7, and consider the sayings in Mt 10:26−7 par and 10:32−3 par subsequently.

1. The collection of sayings in Mt 10:28−31 par opens with the admonition not to fear (Mt 10:28a/Lk 12:4). The introduction to this is simply the conjunction καί in Mt 10:28a, but λέγω δὲ ὑμῖν τοῖς φίλοις μου in Lk 12:4. Schulz observes that λέγω δὲ ὑμῖν is probably Lukan here, and that τοῖς φίλοις μου is almost certainly so.[207] Schulz indicates also that the wording of Lk 12:4−5 generally is secondary to Mt 10:28.[208] The presence of characteristic Lukan vocabulary,[209] the absence of characteristic Matthean vocabulary, the known tendency of Luke to recast strict parallelism[210] and

the Lukan preference for graphic description[211] all support this judgement.

This general admonition not to fear men, who can kill the body but not the ψυχή, goes well beyond anxiety about material needs (cf. Mt 6:25ff. par). A situation of opposition or even persecution seems presupposed, where martyrdom is seen as at least a possible subject of concern. But the admonition remains general, and there is no indication of the context in which such opposition is being met. The effect of the subsequent sayings will be to build up through persuasive argument a sense of reassurance in the face of such fears.[212]

2. It is not clear whether the corresponding exhortation to fear him who can destroy also the ψυχή in Gehenna (Mt 10:28b/Lk 12:5) is an extension of the opening command or whether implicitly it is also the first supporting line of argument against the fear of one's human oppressors. As the negative command *not* to fear is alone repeated in Mt 10:31/Lk 12:7, the positive command 'to fear' in Mt 10:28b/Lk 12:5 seems part of the argumentation rather than the basic exhortation. It sets forth the appeal to a greater power, which will be pursued in relation to God's control of nature in Mt 10:29−30 par.[213] Initially, however, this 'being' is simply presented as commanding a greater threat, namely Gehenna. Yet if men and God are considered opposed, this suggests not only that opposition is being faced, but that fear of it is in some way resulting in a diminished loyalty to God.[214] These observations hold even if the formal parallelism of Mt 10:28a and 28b par (especially strong in Matthew) suggests that they should be considered together as the opening sayings.

3. Mt 10:29a/Lk 12:6a introduces a new set of images in the form of a rhetorical question. It is hardly possible to know which of the two versions of the rhetorical question is more original: Luke's five sparrows for two pennies, or Matthew's two sparrows for a penny. The sense is not, however, affected. It is an allusion to everyday life, but the point of it is then elaborated in Mt 10:29b/Lk 12:6b. Despite the relative insignificance of the sparrows, they are within God's care (cf. Mt 6:26 par).[215] God's providential care of the natural world is invoked.

The form of the reply in Mt 10:29b is usually held to be

more original than that of Luke. In particular, the use of ἐνώπιον is frequently Lukan,[216] and Harnack argued that the periphrastic οὐκ ἔστιν ἐπιλελησμένον is the language of literature.[217] The imagery of a bird falling to earth in Matthew is certainly more concrete and graphic, but this is not in itself a necessary indication of originality, especially since Luke might have been expected to be attracted by graphic expression.[218] Nevertheless, Luke may have altered the form found in Matthew for other reasons. Whether or not he recognized the parallel with Amos 3:5, which refers to a bird falling into a snare, the argument that calamity occurs only with God's consent may not have been seen by Luke as especially reassuring. The purpose of these arguments is to emphasize the trustworthiness of God's care. Thus the Lukan form avoids any reference to calamity under God's control and presents the less difficult and more reassuring observation that 'not one of them is forgotten before God'.[219]

Another significant difference between Matthew and Luke is the name used for God. The specific reference to God is important in any case for interpreting the somewhat ambiguous 'greater being' introduced in Mt 10:28b par. But Matthew refers to ὁ πατὴρ ὑμῶν while Luke uses ὁ θεός. The parallel discussion for Mt 6:26 par (cf. above, p. 28) inclines one towards the wording in Luke. But Schulz[220] here argues against many[221] that Matthew's version is more original, because the use of ὁ πατὴρ ὑμῶν without further predication is not characteristically Matthean, and because the reference to God's 'fatherhood' with respect to the care of birds is somewhat strained. The latter is hardly conclusive, but one must allow for the possibility that the special relationship to the Father of those addressed comes earlier in the argument in this collection than in Mt 6:25ff. par, for their responsibility before God has already been implied in Mt 10:28b par. If a wavering of commitment under persecution is a theme of this collection, then the earlier reference is hardly surprising.

Just as the abrupt change in imagery introduced in Mt 10:29a par about the price of sparrows confirms that one finds in Mt 10:28−31 par a collection of distinct and probably originally independent units,[222] so also another distinct unit is indicated by the new set of images in Mt 10:30 par, about the hairs on one's head being numbered.[223] This is a second illustration of God's control over the fate of those in this world. It is even more clearly aphoristic than the previous sayings (cf. 1 Sam 14:45; 2 Sam 14:11; 1 Ki 1:52; Lk 21:18; Acts 27:34). But, in contrast to the preceding collections which have been examined, this second illustration is not phrased as a second rhetorical question in either Matthew or Luke. A second illustration is not unexpected, but the statement formulation of the aphorism is a departure from what has been observed previously. A further difficulty is that it interrupts the development of thought about the sparrows in Mt 10:29/Lk 12:6 and Mt 10:31/Lk 12:7b. By doing so, it forces a double illustration where a single illustration would be less awkward. A conscious effort to create a double illustration at precisely this point in the argument is at least consistent with our previous findings.

4. By creating a break between Mt 10:29/Lk 12:6 and Mt 10:31/ Lk 12:7b, the 'numbered hairs' aphorism has effectively made Mt 10:31/Lk 12:7b the conclusion for the entire section. This has also been indicated in a second way: namely, by the repetition of the opening command μὴ φοβεῖσθε. The collection therefore ends with an *a minore ad maius* argument: 'you are worth far more than many sparrows'.[224] This is the most precise affirmation of God's care for those being addressed. It is a statement which shows that the divine control over nature applies all the more to those being addressed.

The sayings-collection in Mt 10:28−31 par therefore ultimately bases the command not to fear men in an assurance of God's care. The development of thought moves from God's control over the world to his specific care for those being addressed. The argument is more concise than in many of the previous collections, and more limited in its use of aphorisms, but it betrays close parallels to the kinds of argument employed in Mt 6:25−33 par and in Mt 7:7−11 par. This is particularly evident for Mt 10:29−31 par, which gleans from the natural world examples of God's providential care. It is significant that this divine concern is not directly linked in these sayings with any moral or pietistic considerations. There is also no further appeal to eschatological sanctions beyond Mt 10:28b par. The main thrust of the collection, therefore, is to present persuasive arguments from ordinary life and an appeal to reason in an effort to allay fears of opposition or even persecution. There is little indication, however, that the opposition itself will be eliminated. The collection attempts to foster an attitude of trust in the presence of the adversity. Even the admonition to fear God in Mt 10:28b par argues a reasonable case.[225] It establishes a reasonable basis for deciding whom to fear.[226] This assertion of *greater power* is then coupled with the argument of Mt 10:29–30 par concerning God's *control* over nature, and finally leads to an assertion of his *care* for the addressees (Mt 10:31 par). The appeal to future judgement in Mt 10:28b is not the final decisive warning, but another aspect of the heaping-up of reasons for recognizing God's control over one's fate. It is, therefore, doubtful that the entire section can be considered fundamentally a *prophetische Warnung* to fear God, the apocalyptic judge, as Schulz maintains despite the recognized sapiential structure.[227] The eschatological appeal is only one example among others of the reality of God's power, and the compilation of the sayings-collection, with such a predominance of sapiential forms and argument, requires greater recognition.

III

The force of the eschatological warning, however, is strengthened with the addition of Mt 10:26–7 par and especially of 10:32–3 par. Schulz considers Mt 10:28–31 par in isolation from these other sayings.[228] This does recognize how Mt 10:28–31 par stands as a self-contained set of sayings enveloped by the exhortations μὴ φοβεῖσθε. Yet both Matthew and Luke show knowledge of a more extended collection which included Mt 10:26–7 par and 10:32–3 par in this context. Their precise agreement in the arrangement of double-tradition material does not extend beyond the inclusion of these sayings,[229] but the addition of these sayings does make an intelligible and well-defined larger unit for consideration.[230]

There are a number of indications that Mt 10:26–7 par and 10:32–3 par may have been attached to Mt 10:28–31 par to extend the smaller collection rather than simply to create transitions to other sayings in a larger compilation (e.g., possibly, Lk 12:10,11–12 par). First, Mt 10:26–7 par and 32–3 par are both carefully balanced sayings marked by antithetical parallelism and a future reference. Thus a formal correspondence between the opening and closing sayings of the larger collection is maintained, achieving a rough symmetrical balance for the collection as a whole. Secondly, unlike the sayings in Mt 10:28–31 par, the two additional sayings (both with

Markan parallels: Mk 4:22, 8:38) share a concern with the theme of open 'confession'.[231] Thus the question of fearlessness before men (Mt 10:28–31 par) is extended and applied to the open confession of Jesus. Thirdly, the previously observed tendency of double-tradition aphoristic collections to proceed from general principles towards specific applications is again observed. Mt 10:26–7 par opens with the aphoristic sayings about nothing being hidden that will not be revealed.[232] From these rather general maxims one moves in Mt 10:32–3 par to the specific confession of Jesus and judgement before the Son of Man. This takes even the sayings on fearlessness to a new and much more specific application. Significantly, though, this only comes at the end of the collection. The opening sayings are even more general than Mt 10:28 par. Therefore there are several indications that the short aphoristic collection in Mt 10:28–31 par was extended in the early tradition to include a new opening and conclusion, with a correspondingly new emphasis on open confession of Jesus. Yet this was accomplished with sensitivity to the structure of the aphoristic sayings-collections which we have previously observed.

A closer look at the additional sayings reinforces this impression. So far as Mt 10:26–7 par is concerned, the opening aphorism in Mt 10:26 par about nothing being covered up that will be not uncovered and nothing secret that will not be made known is a maxim with several applications in the gospels,[233] but which is found here with little variation in wording in the two gospels.[234] The two forms of the following saying (Mt 10:27 par), however, vary significantly. Matthew's gospel presents the saying as a double command, and it is openly related to the context of the mission charge. The use of the first person in Matthew sets the disciples' mission in clear relation to Jesus' own instructions.[235] In Luke, the formulation of the saying is a *statement* of synonymous parallelism, rather than an exhortation. The indefinite reference of the second person plural strengthens the aphoristic character of the saying, and Bultmann rightly noted that the saying could derive from a popular observation that secrets are best entrusted to no one.[236] J. Fitzmyer remarks: 'The meaning of Jesus' proverb-like words in vv. 2–3 can be summed up thus: "Truth will out".'[237] The meaning of this in Luke is less clear than in Matthew, but it appears to warn disciples against adopting the hypocritical tendencies of the Pharisees (cf. Lk 12:1), on the grounds that what is said in secret will be brought to light, which in turn is made the basis for fear of God rather than of man.[238] On purely formal grounds it is easier to see the more general form of statement in Luke being altered to the more specific formulation of Matthew, despite some introductions of Lukan vocabulary in this verse.[239] The fact that both versions of the collection of sayings are interpreted in very different contexts in the two gospels suggests that the original form was sufficiently general to permit such adaptation. In addition, Luke's interest in mission might well have inclined him to accept the Matthean formulation if he had known it.[240] If, as is likely, the more general form of the saying in Luke is the more original, then the aphoristic saying in Lk 12:3 is a second maxim, following the first negatively formulated maxim in Lk 12:2 par. The maxim in Lk 12:3 is not only illustrative of that in 12:2 par by portraying specific examples which show how secrets will be revealed, but it also introduces more specifically the theme of 'open proclamation', which sets the theme for the closing sayings.[241]

When one turns to these closing sayings, Mt 10:32−3/Lk 12:8−9 the application does become much more specific. Not only does it now refer clearly to Jesus in the first person, but also to the Son of Man. 'Confession' is also clearly in view. These have been critical sayings in the 'Son of Man' debate (cf. also Mk 8:38),[242] but our interest will be mainly in how the sayings relate to the argument of Mt 10:26−33 par.

Yet one cannot ignore that the most important difference between Matthew's and Luke's version of these sayings is that Mt 10:32 consistently employs the first person to refer to Jesus where Lk 12:8 includes reference to the 'Son of Man'. It is widely accepted that Luke preserves the more original wording here,[243] since it is more likely that the Son of Man was identified with Jesus than that Luke consciously sought to introduce a distinction between Jesus and the Son of Man (cf. also Mk 8:38).[244] Matthew's likely alteration also creates a more balanced *jus talionis*. Attempts at counter-arguments are carefully dispelled in D. Catchpole's recent analysis, which reaffirms that 'a christological amalgamation is more likely to be secondary than a christological differentiation'.[245]

A further important variation in wording is τοῦ πατρός μου τοῦ ἐν τοῖς οὐρανοῖς (Mt 10:33) diff τῶν ἀγγέλων τοῦ θεοῦ (Lk 12:9). Once again Matthean redaction is generally considered most likely in view of Matthew's fondness for the phrase 'my Father in heaven' and the difficulty of explaining Luke's complete replacement of a reference to God with angels.[246]

In whatever way one relates the *person* of Jesus to the Son of Man in this saying, the 'confession' (ὁμολογεῖν) and denial (ἀρνεῖσθαι) of Jesus on earth are intractably bound up with the future acknow-ledgement by the Son of Man. The stress throughout the saying is not so much on christology *per se* as on the one addressed − the relation between his confession and his fate.[247] The very structure of the saying highlights this correspondence and reiterates it through antithetical parallelism.

The saying in Lk 12:8−9 was probably an independent logion originally,[248] but how does it fit into its present context? As we have seen, the fears expressed for one's life in Mt 10:28−31 par suggest the persecution of followers. The temptation of some followers in such a situation to keep silent about their adherence to Jesus or even to have second thoughts about their position in view of strong opposition makes these final sayings in Lk 12:8−9 par quite understandable. The balance of promise and warning in Lk 12:8−9 par encourages those facing opposition to hold fast by relying on God's care, while at the same time leaving no doubt as to the consequences for those who fail to do so. This careful balance between warning and promise is preserved throughout the collection of sayings as a whole. Both positive and negative formulations of logia appear together in Lk 12: 2−3, 4−5, and 8−9 par. But while the sayings in Lk 12:4−7 par were used primarily to persuade the hearers to recognize God's control over his creation and his care for them, the sayings in Lk 12:2−3 par and 12:8−9 par are designed to depict consequences of the hearers' confession, although significantly still presenting these as general principles.

The general principle of a 'reciprocal' acknowledgement in Lk 12:8−9 par has been recognized by E. Käsemann, who identifies this as one of the *Sätze heiligen Rechts* ('sentences of holy law').[249] According to Käsemann, the Christian community is addressed in such sayings by Christian prophets. These prophets proclaimed judge-ment via an eschatological *jus talionis*. Schulz has followed Käsemann's view and argues that the introductory phrase in Lk 12:8, λέγω δὲ ὑμῖν, is original, since it is appropriate to introduce a prophetic sentence of holy law and since it is an important formula in Q generally.[250] Neither argument in itself is compelling, however; and because this formula is seldom eliminated in Matthew's gospel and is popular in Luke, it is likely that the phrase is a Lukan addition of the same sort as in Lk 12:4.[251] The importance of Käsemann's observation is that it would affirm a prophetically directed setting for the use of the saying which also embraces a consciousness of 'eschatological law'. It makes the saying originally the product of the

Palestinian Christian prophet rather than allowing a sapiential interest in the use of the sayings.

Käsemann's analysis of these sentences has in fact been subject to challenges on several fronts, including the question of the setting which he postulates.[252] Kümmel has doubted that Lk 12:8−9 par conforms to the rest of Käsemann's examples of *Sätze heiligen Rechts*, because the relation between the earthly Jesus and the coming Son of Man has no parallel in the other examples.[253] Yet even if Käsemann should be correct in specifying the *origin* of Lk 12:8−9 par, the incorporation of the saying into the context of Lk 12:2−9 par represents a later stage of tradition. In its present context it appears to be dissociated from any direct or obvious prophetic proclamation and set in the context of a reasoned argument with strong sapiential features, to which its form is in any case well suited.[254] As even A. J. B. Higgins concedes, 'there are undeniable resemblances of form between Käsemann's "sentences" and sayings from Wisdom literature'; it is mainly the eschatological content that is distinctive of the former.[255]

It is the union with Lk 12:4−7 par that makes clear that the question of opposition and threat to life is part of the setting within which the promises and warnings of judgement occur. It is for this reason also that Schulz's suggestion of a missionary setting for the opening sayings, Lk 12:2−3 par, seems unnecessarily limited. Schulz considers Lk 12:2−3 par in isolation and argues that it was meant to provide a promise to missionaries that their presently unnoticed preaching would in the imminent End-time be heard before the entire world. They need not worry about the publicity of the kingdom proclamation. In Schulz's view, Lk 12:2−3 par shows how a secular proverb about secrets has been transformed into a prophetic encouragement to End-time Christian missionaries.[256] But Schulz does not specify a missionary *Sitz im Leben* for Lk 12:4−7 par or 12:8−9 par.[257] Indeed, when Lk 12:2−9 par is taken as a whole, the emphasis would seem to lie more on fearlessness in one's adherence to the Christian proclamation in the face of opposition than on missionary proclamation in particular.[258]

It is quite possible for Lk 12:2−3 par to be reconciled with Lk 12:4−7, 8−9 par. Rather than necessarily applying to 'missionary proclamation', the aphoristic form of sayings in Lk 12:2−3 is sufficiently open-ended to permit application to the more general question of individual confession. In the face of opposition, doubts and secret misgivings cannot remain hidden. One's position will be exposed, as it will in future judgement (Lk 12:8−9 par).

Such an interpretation gains indirect support in two further ways. First, the opposition to be faced by followers of Jesus is a theme of other double-tradition sayings. The beatitude in Lk 6:22—3 par[259] seeks to console followers at a time when men hate them and persecute them on account of the Son of Man. Followers here suffer a fate similar to the prophets of old. Even the double-tradition sayings immediately preceding Lk 12:2ff. par in Luke, the 'Wisdom' sayings in Lk 11:49—51/Mt 23:34—6,[260] introduce the theme of the persecution of prophets and 'others' sent by 'Wisdom'.[261] An awareness of opposition is not foreign to the double-tradition material. But while in Lk 11:49—51 par it comprises part of a polemic against Jewish leaders, in Lk 12:2—9 par the attention turns to those who suffer this opposition and to its effect on their confession.

Secondly, if apostasy was the probable concern of Lk 12:2—9 par, then it is perhaps less surprising that eschatological promise and warning emerge far more prominently in this collection, and especially in the added sayings (Lk 12:2—3, 8—9 par), than in the previously studied aphoristic collections. It is here alone that one is dealing with the critical question of adherence to Jesus. It is here, therefore, that the stakes are highest. Critical attitudes among followers and anxieties about material needs may be approached through reasonably gentle persuasion. But the temptation to deny Jesus in the face of external opposition requires warning as well, however reasonably it is set forth. Thus, precisely where the denial of Jesus is most explicitly contemplated — in Lk 12:8—9, at the end of the collection — there also the eschatological warning is present in its most explicit form.

Summary

1. Several formal and structural characteristics have repeatedly been observed in the five aphoristic collections which have been examined.

   (i) Each collection begins with a rather general aphoristic saying. This saying is either a maxim in statement form (cf. Lk 6:43 par, 12:2 par) or a wisdom admonition (cf. Lk 6:37 par, 11:9 par, 12:22 par (and also 12:4 par)). In each case where an admonition introduces a collection, it is an exhortation or prohibition of a very broad nature, concisely stated.

   (ii) The opening saying is then usually followed by a general maxim in statement form which provides ostensible support for whatever is being encouraged. This was observed in

Mt 7:1–2 par, where two aphoristic statements about retributive judgement and 'measure for measure' are set forth in synonymous parallelism introduced by the conjunction γάρ; in Lk 11:10 par, where a threefold general aphorism is set forth in parallelism with the initial command and is again introduced by the conjunction γάρ; and in Mt 6:25b par, where a rhetorical question about the meaning of life presents the first of several supporting arguments after the instruction.[262] Even where the collection starts with a general aphoristic sentence, another maxim immediately follows which supports or illustrates it. Lk 6:44a par follows the initial aphorism with a restatement of it as a more concise general principle, which itself could stand as an independent proverb.

Usually these opening sayings are of wide applicability. The remainder of the collection of sayings is then devoted to specifying the application of the initial sayings and providing support for the instruction or perspective expressed in them.

(iii) The third stage of the aphoristic sayings-collections is frequently marked by a complete change of imagery and the presentation of two sayings which are similar in theme but different in illustration. The hallmark of this section is the rhetorical question formulation.[263] Two parallel rhetorical questions at this point in the collection were observed in Lk 6:39 par, 6:44b par and 11:11–12 par. One rhetorical question and one general aphorism in statement form fulfilled this role in Lk 12:6–7 par. The collection of Mt 6:25–33 par is slightly more complex, however. Here two parallel arguments from nature are set forth in Mt 6:26 par and 6:28b–30 par, and each makes use of the rhetorical question form, but they are significantly interrupted in Mt 6:27 par by a further independent aphoristic saying in the form of a rhetorical question. In effect three arguments of different imagery are presented in this collection, although two are closely related. Mt 6:27 is clearly an intrusion, perhaps added subsequently to the collection.

In general, the rhetorical questions which occur at this point in the collections draw upon examples of concrete human situations or aspects of the natural world which illustrate the more general statements which have preceded.

The use of rhetorical questions here is significant, for it emphasizes the attempt to persuade by argument. The use of such concrete illustrations also conveys the impression of a conscious piling-up of support to demonstrate the reasonableness of what is being presented in the collection. Frequently, however, the examples are also chosen to narrow the application of the argument and to act as a transition to the concluding part of the collection.

(iv) The final unit of the aphoristic collections always provides the key for interpreting the meaning. Here lies the application for each collection of sayings, usually so constructed as to leave little doubt as to the end of the collection, because it is set in structural balance with the opening of the collection. This balance, however, is established in a variety of ways.

In Lk 6:41−2 par, there is a return to the theme of judgement (after Lk 6:38b, 39 par) and to the form of exhortation, which is present only in the very opening and closing phrases of the collection. The interpretative role of these sayings is to narrow the general admonition 'Judge not' to refer particularly to the matter of the hypocrisy of being critical of one's brother. These final sayings employ hyperbole to make their point[264] but still employ no explicit appeal to God or final judgement to interpret or reinforce the instruction.

In Lk 6:43−5 par, the balance of opening and closing focuses thematically on good producing good and bad producing bad. Formally, there is a close parallel in the structure of the two opening sayings (Lk 6:43, 44a par) and the two closing sayings (Lk 6:45 par). In both cases a double-stranded parallel saying about good and bad is followed by a concluding general rule. The interpretative role of the concluding sayings is found in the switch from the earlier plant imagery to the human situation and finally to human speech. Again, there is no direct appeal to 'God' or eschatological concepts anywhere in this collection.

For Mt 7:7−11 par, the concluding saying (Mt 7:11 par) is once again highly important for the application of the preceding sayings, but rather than ending with some kind of formal *inclusio*, the final saying presents an *a minore ad maius* type of argument which takes the argument of the collection to its climax. It is only in this final saying that any explicit reference to God is made.

The collection of sayings in Mt 10:26–33 par portrays a double instance of concluding sayings. The central sub-collection, Mt 10:28–31 par, ends in Mt 10:31 par with a short repetition of the initial admonition in 10:28 par (μὴ φοβεῖσθε) and a short *a minore ad maius* argument which takes one from the preceding examples of God's care for nature to his care for the hearers. The larger collection, Mt 10:26–33 par, is concluded by a double-stranded saying in antithetical parallelism in Mt 10:32–3/Lk 12:8–9. Formally, this concluding saying balances the double-stranded parallel aphoristic statements at the opening of the collection (Mt 10: 26–7/Lk 12:2–3). Thematically, the closing sayings return to the question of future consequences and to the issue of open confession. It is only these closing verses, however, that provide the indication that confession of Jesus and final judgement on this basis are in view. As such, the final verses provide the interpretative key for the rest of the collection.

In the fifth collection, Mt 6:25–33 par, a formal *inclusio* with the opening admonition is presented in Mt 6:31 par. This is extended, however, with a positive alternative command to the preceding negative admonition (cf. Mt 6:33 par). Although God's general providential care for man is indicated in the preceding sayings,[265] only in the final verses of the collection is reference made to the more specific concept of seeking his kingdom. Thus the crucial interpretative function of the concluding sayings is clear in each instance. This is true despite the formal variety of these sayings.

In view of the variety of theme and presentation of these five aphoristic collections, it is remarkable that a common structural pattern can be discerned at all. This pattern suggests that these small collections of aphoristic sayings did not simply grow at random from wide-ranging oral or written traditions into the form in which they now appear. *These are not haphazard collections of aphoristic sayings; they display a design and argument unique in the synoptic tradition.* This rather suggests that the material has been formulated into units so as to conform consciously to a general pattern of argument. This in turn argues strongly in favour of an unique 'compositional activity' responsible for the formulation of these collections. The fact that the correspondences are not extended to every detail of the collections and slavishly adhered to does suggest also that the concern is not with simply perpetuating an artificial structure, but rather with employing it as a helpful and powerful general pattern for pursuing an argument. It is the persuasive drive within a general structure that seems most characteristic of these collections.

It is here that one must differ from the conclusion of D. Zeller. His helpful study of wisdom admonitions led him also to note briefly a correspondence in the structure of some of the extended admonitions which he analysed.[266] Zeller refers to three rather than four steps for the compositions, and his concentration on wisdom admonitions results in a failure to include Lk 6:43–5 par and the sayings in Lk 12:2–3, 8–9 par. Details of parts of Zeller's analysis are also open to question, such as the apparent assignment of Mt 7:11 par, to 'das Mittelstück' of the compilation. Fundamentally, however, Zeller seems to understand these regularities in structure simply as the way in which *various* traditions *grew*: 'Diese Einheiten wachsen nun auf verschiedenen Überlieferungs- ebenen – nur die Abfolge Mt 7,7.9–11 erwies sich als relativ stabil – durch Erweiterung und Verschmelzung zu grösseren Kompositionen an, die auch wieder gewisse Regelmässig- keiten zeigen.'[267] This fails to recognize the strong features of design and argument in these sayings collections and the predominance of such collections in double-tradition material alone, which suggests intentional and unique composition. The uniqueness of this pattern of argument using aphoristic sayings will be explored further below.

2. If it is appropriate to think in terms of a deliberate com- pilational activity, then one must also ask about *stages* of such activity. The analysis of the collection in Mt 10:26–33 par particularly posed this question. In this case it was argued that the formulation of Mt 10:28–31 par may have been expanded at some later stage to form the larger collection of Mt 10:26–33 par.[268] Yet even this enlargement maintained the peculiar development from general opening sayings to interpretative final sayings and the formal balance in opening and closing. This suggests that the expansion may be at- tributed to a similar compilational activity to that responsible for the smaller unit, even if it occurred at a later point in time. A later revision need not imply a great gulf in time or

situation between the two versions. It is doubtful, therefore, whether this instance alone provides sufficient evidence for distinguishing significantly different stages of *theological* interests.

It is interesting, however, that a concern for one's physical life is also evident in the intruding saying in Mt 6:27 par, which seems to be a secondary intrusion into the collection of sayings about anxiety over food and clothing. This addition may provide evidence for a growing concern about actual threats to one's life, also apparent in Mt 10:26−33/Lk 12: 2−9. Anxiety over food and clothing now is heightened to anxiety for one's continuing life. This later concern *could* reflect new external threats and opposition, but this must remain a conjecture.

3. It will not have escaped notice that each of these five collections consists of double-tradition material. This source-critical coherence is another important indication that these collections derive from an unique compilational activity. Little attempt however has been made to relate these collections to a wider theory of the compilation of Q as a whole. It has long been suggested that Q was particularly influenced by a perspective which showed a strong interest in sapiential traditions, including wisdom of an aphoristic kind, as indicated in Chapter 1. The present analysis, however, is more limited in scope. It has been primarily intended to establish the evidence for how aphoristic wisdom has proved attractive as a powerful and persuasive means of developing an argument at the hands of those skilled in its use. This skill has been shown in several instances of a similar pattern of argument, with an emphasis on the outlook of practical wisdom. It will be shown in Chapter 3 how the themes of these collections also overlap with other sayings of double-tradition material, but it is beyond the scope of this present analysis to develop any comprehensive theory of Q.

4. The question of possible parallels to the pattern of argument found in these double-tradition aphoristic sayings collections must be pursued further, however. It is significant that relatively little can be found in the way of parallels to this structure in the Jewish wisdom literature. The closest example in Proverbs is the exhortation against adultery:

Do not desire her beauty in your heart,
and do not let her capture you with her eyelashes;
for a harlot may be hired for a loaf of bread,
but an adulteress stalks a man's very life.
Can a man carry fire in his bosom and his clothes not be
  burned?
Or can one walk upon hot coals and his feet not be
  scorched?[269]
So is he who goes in to his neighbour's wife;
none who touches her will go unpunished. (Prov 6:25–9)

The main point of difference between this example and the
pattern of the double-tradition collections is that this example
is not easily isolated as a unit from its preceding verses.[270]
It is difficult to maintain, therefore, that it is self-contained
or that the structure is deliberate for the collection.[271] While
the concluding verses of this example provide a more specific
application of the instruction which precedes, they do not
provide either a formal balance with the opening or a clear
climax to the section.

In Qoheleth there is no clear example of a similar structure
to that of the double-tradition collections, but some examples
can be discovered in Sirach. Especially notable is the section
which begins with the experiential observation about 'like
consorting with like' and ends by applying this principle to
the rich and the poor:

Every creature loves its like,
and every person his neighbour;
all living beings associate by species,
and a man clings to one like himself.
What fellowship has a wolf with a lamb?
No more has a sinner with a godly man.
What peace is there between a hyena and a dog?
And what peace between a rich man and a poor man?
Wild asses in the wilderness are the prey of lions;
likewise the poor are pastures for the rich.
Humility is an abomination to a proud man;
likewise a poor man is an abomination to a rich man.

(Sir 13:15–20)[272]

Again extensive use of simile is evident in this collection, which is wholly lacking in the synoptic examples.[273] No comparably constructed sections are evident in the instruction of Wisdom of Solomon, Tobit, the Testaments of the XII Patriarchs or 1 En 91ff. It would appear, therefore, that the examples above are sufficient to confirm that it is not erroneous to associate this pattern of argument with sapiential activity, but it is hardly a sufficiently prominent pattern to support claims either that it was common for aphoristic traditions to 'grow together' into such a pattern or even that it would be an obvious model for later 'wise men' to imitate.

Within the synoptic tradition, two further possibilities will be discussed later in this chapter (and see also Appendix). These instances are few, however, and appear to be confined to material which has some contact with double-tradition material. Other aphoristic collections, such as the string of sayings connected by catchwords in Mk 9:42−50, provide no parallel at all, since there is hardly any evidence of a unity of theme or progressive argument and there are no rhetorical questions.[274] No comparable structures are found either in the collections of sayings in the Epistle of James or in the Didache or the Epistle of Barnabas 19−20.

Thus, examples of this type of collection are only rarely discovered. The structure does not correspond to the style of catechetical parenesis, at least as represented in James, the Didache or the Epistle of Barnabas, nor is it a structure of any prominence in Jewish wisdom literature. Where correspondences are found which approximate the structure of the double-tradition collections, they are mainly in the earlier sapiential literature where aphoristic collections are found, Proverbs and Sirach. All of this serves to support the view that one is dealing with a highly individual style of argument, rather than one which can claim to have many parallels in tradition.

5. Not only does the structure for these collections appear to be confined largely to the double-tradition material in Matthew and Luke; it is also clear that neither Matthew nor Luke can be considered the originators of the pattern of argument. This has important implications for the Q-hypothesis, or more strictly for the common pre-Lukan and pre-Matthean origin of these collections. This may be briefly indicated as follows:

(i) Against the theory of simple Lukan dependence upon Matthew, there are at least two important examples where the greater originality of the version of a passage in Luke and the secondary nature of the parallel Matthean version appear quite clear. First, the inclusions of Mt 7:15 and 19 in the Matthean form of the collection of sayings about fruits are widely accepted as secondary additions to a unit resembling Lk 6:43—5.[275] In a second case one faces the problem of why Luke should have separated Lk 12:2—9 from the missionary charge, in which context it is found in Matthew, and why he should have changed Lk 12:3 in particular from the Matthean form. Drury appeals to Luke's interest in the 'inwardness of true religion' as accounting for the changes,[276] but this argument has several weaknesses. First, it cannot account for a change of Mt 10:27 to Lk 12:3, since the proclamation asserted in Mt 10:27 is not significantly different from what is envisaged in Lk 12:8—9, 10, and 12:11—12, where followers are also told that they must disclose their faith before men and at the last day. Secondly, an appeal to Luke's interest in the inwardness of true religion as accounting for his departure from the Matthean context here is not terribly convincing because it ignores Luke's equally strong interest in the mission of the church, so that, had Luke known a context for the material as in Matthew, his alteration is not easily explained.

(ii) Neither Matthew nor Luke shows any deliberate interest in promulgating or even preserving the common structure of the double-tradition aphoristic collections. These are not Matthean constructions, because Matthew has at several points broken the structure. This is observed particularly in Mt 7:16—20, 12:33—5 which appears to be a Matthean duplication of what was originally a single set of sayings and is a highly disrupted version of the collection that is found in Lk 6:43—5 (which in turn matches the structure of the other double-tradition collections).

Yet nor are the five collections wholly Lukan constructions, for they are found clearly in Mt 7:7—11, 6:25—33, 10:26—33. It could be argued that Luke recognized the form in Matthew and created the collections in Lk 6:37—42 and 43—5 according to the pattern which he found in Matthew. Yet this also is unlikely, because Luke then apparently missed the rather obvious basis for such a collection in Mt 6:19–24 (cf. below, pp. 95–99), and he frequently presents alterations in the collections which cast doubt upon whether he recognized and appreciated the structure sufficiently to create collections like Lk 6:37–42 and 43–5 from what is found in Matthew. For example, Luke at times has attached no importance to double rhetorical questions at the centre of the collection and has changed rhetorical questions to statements. If Luke had understood the practice of a change in imagery for the central sayings in the collection, why did he find it necessary to include his own introductory formula in Lk 6:39a? And why did he allow Lk 6:40 to detract from the double question in 6:39? If Luke had been eager to copy the reasonable and non-polemical character of these collections for the instruction of his readers, and able to create a non-polemical collection like Lk 6:43–5 from the polemical material in Mt 7 and 12, why did he discard the reasonable tone of Mt 10:28–9 in favour of the more polemical Lk 12:4–5.[277]

These considerations strongly suggest that both Matthew and Luke found the collections and modified them to their purposes, but neither sufficiently understood or was sufficiently committed to the structure of argument of these collections to be responsible for their compilation. The only acceptable explanation for the composition of this material is to attribute the collections to a common early tradition.

6. So far as the addressees for the collections are concerned, it has been argued that each of the five collections is best understood as directed toward Christian followers rather than toward opponents or those outside the community of faith. In Mt 10:26–33 par, the denial of Jesus is an issue, but the problem appears to be the temptation of some believers to withdraw or apostatize in the face of strong human opposition towards them.

Frequently in these collections those addressed are criticized despite the fact that they are almost certainly followers. In Mt 7:5 par they are addressed as ὑποκριταί, in Mt 7:11 par as ὑμεῖς πονηροί and in Mt 6:30 par as ὀλιγόπιστοι. This suggests that these collections are intended for the instruction and correction of wrong attitudes among followers. Only in the collection in Lk 6:43–5 par is there neither a negative reference to those addressed nor the use of an imperative form anywhere in the collection.

7. With respect to the content of the instruction offered in these collections, a fairly limited range of topics is covered. Each collection tends to concentrate upon a single issue, which is supported and clarified. Yet even these issues are not widely varying. The collection in Lk 6:37−42 par shows the hypocrisy of judging others and encourages self-examination. The sayings in Lk 6:43−5 par closely follow this in theme by discussing the relation between one's speech and the orientation of one's heart. In both collections it is possible to understand the instruction directed at the problem of critical speech.

The second major theme of instruction concerns anxiety, especially for basic material needs. In Mt 7:7−11 par, one is encouraged to petition God for one's needs. The only examples of the things to be expected from God (ἀγαθά) are examples of food. This theme recurs in different form in Mt 6:25−33 par. The anxiety about basic necessities is extended to fear for one's life in the sayings in Mt 10:26−33 par. Interestingly, a similar conjunction of concerns for basic needs, food and persecution is expressed in the opening double-tradition beatitudes (Lk 6:20b−23 par).[278] The narrow range of themes covered in these sayings is somewhat surprising. Many themes popular in sapiential instruction are completely absent, such as the dangers of lust and harmfulness of anger, attitudes towards oaths and lies, choice of friends, the value of moderation, and many others. Even the attitude towards earthly goods and anxiety in these collections presents only one aspect of a theme which often received very different treatment in Jewish wisdom instruction. One frequently finds reference in Jewish instruction, for example, to the prudence of providing for the future oneself, like the industrious ant in Prov 6:6ff.

Parallels to this set of concerns are not easily identified in other NT writings. In the Epistle of James, considerable attention is devoted to the matter of divisiveness in the Christian communities stemming from slanderous speech, jealousy and distinctions between rich and poor. These concerns correspond to some extent to the themes found in the double-tradition collections, although the attitude towards material goods in the Epistle takes the form of a forceful attack against riches (cf. 5:1–6). This polemical tone is quite evident generally in the Epistle, and the instruction of James also touches upon a wider range of topics, including jealous lusts or ambitions (4:1–3), patience (5:7–11), adherence to the teaching of the Law (2:10ff., 4:11–12), anger (1:19–20), and oaths (5:12).

In the picture of the early Palestinian church in Acts there are a few hints of the range of themes found in the double-tradition collections, but no comparable instruction. In the only chapters in Acts in which 'wisdom' receives any mention at all, Acts 6–7 (see Acts 6:3, 10; 7:10, 22), there is an interesting combination of concerns. These include (i) complaints among followers in the community (Acts 6:1); (ii) concern over the daily distribution of food as the ostensible cause of the complaints (Acts 6:1–2); (iii) a situation of opposition and persecution (Acts 6:8ff.). These themes demonstrate a remarkable correspondence to the themes of the five aphoristic collections. The restricted range of topics covered and the correspondence to the situation portrayed in Acts 6–7 at least lend credibility to the view that the collections were intended to confront particular topics of special concern for Christians in the early fellowships, for which persuasion and reasonable argument might have been especially necessary (cf. further below, pp. 184–92).

8. Attempt has been made in the analysis of the collections of sayings not only to show how aphoristic sayings are used in these collections, but also to explain why experiential wisdom is employed at all as the medium for instruction. Part of the reason must lie in the very nature of these sayings. Unlike prophetic pronouncements, this form of instruction does not claim its authority primarily as a revealed word of God, and the tone is not polemical. Specific reference to divine reward or judgement is not the usual sanction for these instructions. The phrasing of the instruction is also not to a particular audience, but is presented as advice which appeals to the reason of every man. Such generality and wide applicability are features of the aphoristic sayings. Where appeal to divine judgement or to God's kingdom becomes explicit in these collections is usually in the concluding sayings. The collections are designed to lead one from general instruction to a

more specific application to concerns of the community of faith.

Undoubtedly part of the appeal of these aphoristic sayings is purely rhetorical. Whether the individual sayings were of popular origin or not, they would have popular appeal. The technique of gradually clarifying a rather sweeping command and gradually unveiling a rather mysterious maxim would also have maintained interest. The primary reason for using this type of instruction, however, appears to have been to convince or persuade those addressed of the importance of the instructions given. The presentation of the teaching as being consistent with general human experience not only makes it memorable, but also makes it compelling. The piling-up of aphoristic sayings in support of an instruction frequently occurs, even when it breaks the line of argument (cf. Mt 10:30 par, 6:27 par). This rather unusual technique suggests that an effort is being made to present a multitude of evidence from observation of the world to corroborate the instruction. Instructions receive extended motivations. The frequent use of rhetorical questions places emphasis on the power of persuasion. It is reasonable to assume that these persuasive techniques were not accidental but deliberate.

Several factors may account for such a deliberate use of aphoristic sayings and other persuasive forms of reasoning, such as the *a minore ad maius* arguments. In the first place, some of the issues may have presented real difficulties for the hearers. Problems over food and clothing and the threats of opponents would have hit at the basis of their existence. To engender an attitude which relieved anxieties about these matters would require helping to create a change in perspective, winning a new sense of conviction about what mattered. It is significant that 'this-worldly' wisdom could be used to this effect. Secondly, the sayings about judgemental attitudes towards one's brother and about good and bad speech may also testify to factions within the community. Such divisions might emerge in a community under stress. The general formulation of the instruction would successfully avoid any charge of undue partiality. It applies to all and ostensibly derives its authority as much from the nature of life itself as from particular individuals.[279] Thirdly, and not unrelatedly, another possible value of the aphoristic collections is that they are particularly well suited to encouraging *self*-evaluation. The function of parables to compel insight has been frequently argued in recent research, but the same can apply for aphoristic sayings.[280] For example, in Lk 6:45 par, aphorisms establish a differentiation between what is produced from the 'treasure' of the good and of the bad man, and it is observed that speech derives from 'the abundance of the heart'. This is presented by general aphorisms depicting correspondences. It is left to the hearer to ask which 'store' he is drawing upon. It is further left open for consideration what constitutes ἀγαθά or πονηρά. The issue is raised and persuasively related to one's speech, but it is open to the hearer to make the application to his own life. Obedience may thereby be won, but the demand upon him is one which develops through his own application of the general argument of the collection.

These observations may help to suggest reasons for the attractiveness of aphoristic collections of this kind. Any more precise explanation is necessarily more speculative. But such explanations seem preferable to a view which attributes the general nature of this teaching simply to 'catechetical' instruction of a pre- or post-baptismal kind. This hardly does justice to the powerful persuasive medium.[281] It also fails to account for the absence of many themes which one has come to associate with catechetical instruction, such as fornication, idolatry, fasting, submission to leadership, holiness.[282] Thus, it seems preferable to view the aphoristic collections as directed towards specific areas of concern where persuasiveness and sensitivity are required to deal with potentially divisive problems.

9. It may also briefly be noted that there is no explicit relationship established between the instruction of these aphoristic collections and the Torah. This is somewhat surprising in view of tendencies prevalent in Jewish wisdom literature going back at least to Sirach.[283] It is true that maxims dealing with retribution were found in Mt 7:1−2 par and Mt 10:32−3 par, and that the theme of retribution is easily related to legal concepts. Yet aphorisms of the retributive type are infrequent in these collections, and an equivalence between deed and consequence is in any case also well attested in experiential wisdom.[284]

The saying in Mt 10:32–3 par in particular has been interpreted in the light of a legal as well as prophetic background by Käsemann, although even here there is no express relation to Torah. This claim was analysed earlier, but it must also be noted that efforts have been made to demonstrate that the wisdom literature can account for this type of saying, in which a retributive relationship is established between what man does and what God does.[285] An interesting example is found even outside Jewish tradition amongst the wisdom instruction in Ahikar 2:33 (Syr A):[286]

My son, in the day of thy calamity revile not God;
lest when he hear thee, he should be angered against thee.

It is in any case indisputable that the material of these aphoristic collections is largely independent of any desire to relate it to legal precepts.

This observation may coalesce with another. Where God is invoked in the argument of the aphoristic collections, it is rarely in the sense of referring to his demands for moral obedience.[287] Only in Mt 10:26–33 par, where apostasy may be in view, does a hint of 'transgression' occur, but even in Mt 10:32–3 par divine punishment is expressed more as reflecting a general principle of reciprocation than as provoking an immediate divine outrage at immorality or sin. Elsewhere in the collections one encounters assurance of God's care for those addressed, but not often expressly linked to a fulfilment of God's demands or to righteousness. It is God's 'fatherhood' that is emphasized. He is frequently addressed as 'your Father' or 'the Father' (Mt 7:11 par; Mt 6:32 par; possibly the tradition behind Mt 10:29 diff Lk).[288] Von Rad traced the basis of the exhortation to trust in Yahweh which is found in the Jewish wisdom literature to the reality and evidence of the order which controls the whole of life. He noted that Yahweh is at work in this order in so far as he defends goodness and resists evil.[289] In the double-tradition collections, however, the trustworthiness of God is more clearly seen in his providential care for all the needs of his created world than in his sustenance of the 'righteous' in particular. The religious outlook of these collections, therefore, is not simply typical of Jewish piety.

10. Repeatedly during the analysis of the five collections of aphoristic sayings the question was asked as to how far eschatological motifs were evident. In no instance was an *imminent* eschatological awareness found necessary, despite contrary assertions by Schulz. The presence of eschatological motifs was most prominent in Mt 10:26–33 par, but even in this section the imagery must be examined with care. God's power to destroy not only the body but also the soul in hell (Mt 10:28 par) is immediately followed by an assurance of his protective care for his creatures, so that the force of the argument is deflected away from threat of eternal destruction to other 'caring' aspects of God's general control over the world. Man's eternal destiny does arise again in the concluding sayings (Mt 10:32–3 par), but in a slightly different way. Eschatological themes are used in the first instance in this collection to demonstrate the extent of God's control over men's fate, but in the final sayings to show how man's eternal destiny is the logical outcome of man's own prior confession. The common ground between experiential wisdom and the eschatological outlook is found primarily in an emphasis on the extent of God's effective care for those who trust in him, a care which encompasses both this world and the life to come, and in a recognition of the correspondence between present action (one's confession) and future consequence (judgement).

It is possible to indicate further eschatological allusions in other collections, but it is significant that the tendency is to have only possible 'allusions' rather than direct warnings or promises. In the one instance in which the βασιλεία (of ὁ πατὴρ ὑμῶν) is mentioned, it is something to be sought in the present, and implicit in its presence is not judgement, but God's care (Mt 6:33 par).

Especially interesting are the maxims which employ future and future passive verbs in the collections. Retributive maxims with future passive verbs occur in Mt 7:2 par and 10:32–3 par, and aphorisms indicating a future reversal of present conditions with use of future passive verbs are found in Mt 10:26–7. In addition to these sayings, the opening exhortations in Mt 7:7 par are also followed by future and future passive consequences, despite the fact that in the parallel maxims which immediately follow in Mt 7:8 par a future passive verb is found only once ('to him who knocks it will be opened') and that this appears to be interchangeable with the present tenses of the other clauses ('everyone who asks receives, and he who seeks finds'). Apart from Mt 10: 32−3 par, there are no clear indications, though, that any of these future tenses should be interpreted in an *exclusively* eschatological way. In Mt 7:2 par and 7:7−8 par, a remarkable ambiguity is maintained, in which it is possible to view these opening sayings as referring either to cause and effect in ordinary life or to End-time events.

There is, therefore, little basis for a claim that these aphoristic sayings collections have acquired a new and intensified meaning in the light of eschatological interests which in turn undermines the aphoristic and more universal nature of the sayings. The remarkable absence of direct eschatological sanction for the instruction of these collections, apart from Mt 10:26−33 par, cannot be wholly explained by the fact that 'insiders' rather than 'outsiders' are consistently addressed in these collections. The parables of watchfulness (Lk 12: 39−40, 42−6 par) and the opening beatitudes (Lk 6:20b−23 par) are examples of instructions seemingly for insiders which are supported by more direct eschatological promises or threats. A particular sensitivity among followers about the subjects raised in these collections may again go further to explain why careful and convincing argument is employed, avoiding announcements of judgement and reward, which could be more divisive than constructive. It is possible, however, that a further reason can lie behind the restriction of eschatological motifs in these collections. This may derive from an underlying tension between eschatological pronouncement and experiential wisdom, especially when the latter appears in a collected compilation. A further exploration of this tension will be carried out subsequently (cf. below, pp. 178−84).[290]

3. Other collections with similar structure

The discovery of a carefully elaborated pattern of argument in several aphoristic sayings collections of the double tradition leads to two further considerations. First, are there grounds for identifying any additional collections of this kind amongst the sayings of the double tradition? Secondly, are there any such collections outside the generally recognized bounds of the double tradition? These will be dealt with in turn. The first question is simply whether our findings for the double tradition can be extended to include another important group of sayings, the sayings on love of enemies (Mt 5:44−8; cf. Lk 6:27−36).

Mt 5:44−8/Lk 6:27−36

λέγω ὑμῖν,
(i) ἀγαπᾶτε τοὺς ἐχθροὺς ὑμῶν
καὶ προσεύχεσθε ὑπὲρ τῶν ἐπηρεαζόντων ὑμᾶς,
καὶ ἔσεσθε υἱοὶ τοῦ πατρὸς ὑμῶν [Lk: ὑψίστου]·

καθὼς θέλετε ἵνα ποιῶσιν οἱ ἄνθρωποι, οὕτως καὶ ὑμεῖς ποιεῖτε αὐτοῖς.

(ii) ὅτι τὸν ἥλιον αὐτοῦ ἀνατέλλει ἐπὶ πονηροὺς καὶ ἀγαθοὺς [καὶ βρέχει ἐπὶ δικαίους καὶ ἀδίκους].

(iii) εἰ γὰρ ἀγαπᾶτε τοὺς ἀγαπῶντας ὑμᾶς, τίνα μισθὸν ἔχετε;
οὐχὶ καὶ οἱ τελῶναι τὸ αὐτὸ ποιοῦσιν;

καὶ ἐὰν ἀσπάσησθε τοὺς ἀδελφοὺς ὑμῶν, τί περισσὸν ποιεῖτε;
οὐχὶ καὶ οἱ ἁμαρτωλοὶ [Mt: ἐθνικοὶ] τὸ αὐτὸ ποιοῦσιν;

(iv) γίνεσθε οἰκτίρμονες ὡς ὁ πατὴρ ὑμῶν οἰκτίρμων ἐστίν.

With the exception of Lk 6:43−5 par the sequence of sayings in all of the preceding collections has varied in only minor ways between Matthew and Luke. It has therefore been possible to have confidence that the pattern of argument which has been discussed has actually been that of the common underlying tradition. Unfortunately this agreement in sequence does not hold for the group of sayings on love of enemies; nor is there a consensus as to what the original sequence might have been.

Even if the antithetical constructions in Mt 5:38−43 and 44−8 are accepted as secondary,[291] this still leaves open the question of whether the teachings on non-retaliation and love of enemies were originally two separate blocks of teaching (as in Matthew) or one (as in Luke). The problems of reconstruction do not end here. The initial exhortations are presented differently in the two gospels (cf. Mt 5:44 [39b−42]/Lk 6:27−8, 29−30), and the supporting arguments betray further differences (cf. Mt 5:45, 46−7/Lk 6:32−3, 34, 35b). In Luke alone the command to love one's enemies is repeated at the close of the collected sayings (Lk 6:35a); and Luke alone also preserves the 'Golden Rule' (Lk 6:31; cf. Mt 7:12) in the context of these sayings. No one reconstruction of the original sequence can therefore expect to win complete agreement.

I

Nevertheless, the task is not hopeless. There is a striking discrepancy in the Lukan formulation of these sayings, which provides a starting-point for any analysis. It consists of the switch from the second person plural (6:27−8) to the second person singular (6:29−30) and back to the plural again (6:31ff.) in the opening series of exhortations. Because this apparent intrusion of the singular exhortations closely matches the material located in a separate block of teaching on non-retaliation by Matthew (Mt 5:39−42/Lk 6:29−30), it strongly suggests that the exhortations in Lk 6:29−30 have in fact been inserted into the series of exhortations about love of the enemies.[292] It is possible that at an earlier stage of tradition these exhortations preceded the love-of-enemies exhortations (although probably not in the antithetical form of Matthew). A possible proximity of the final Q-beatitude in Lk 6: 22−3/Mt 5:11−12 to the non-retaliation sayings is not significantly more difficult than proximity to the love-of-enemies sayings.[293]

There are other indications which support this suggested arrangement. Once it is recognized that the exhortations on non-retaliation have intruded into the teaching on love of enemies, it becomes clear why the love-of-enemies command had to be repeated later in the Lukan sequence in order to restore a connection with the motivation clauses found in Mt 5:45 (cf. Lk 6:35b).[294] It is also significant that the rhetorical questions in Lk 6:32ff. focus on the theme of love of enemies (6:32 καὶ εἰ ἀγαπᾶτε τοὺς ἀγαπῶντας ὑμᾶς ...), so that most of the collected sayings apart from Lk 6:29−30 deal most naturally with the theme of love of enemies rather than non-retaliation. That the two concepts are theoretically separable is clear from the stance taken by the Qumran covenanters.[295] Indeed, all the supporting argument centres on the love of enemies. The non-retaliation teaching simply consists of imperatives, not of supporting argument. It is only the secondary introduction of the exhortations of Lk 6:29−30 into this context that gives them the appearance of being commended by argument, but this is at the cost of disrupting the thematic coherence.

On formal and thematic grounds, the sayings in Lk 6:29–30 appear as a secondary insertion into the collection.

Luke, or his special tradition, may be responsible for further additions to the opening exhortations. While Matthew and Luke substantially agree on the two exhortations to love and to pray (Mt 5:44/Lk 6:27b, 28b), Luke includes also the commands to 'do good to those who hate you' (Lk 6:27c) and 'bless those who revile you' (Lk 6:28a). Not only is the former derivable from the beatitude in Lk 6:22 and the corresponding woe in Lk 6:26,[296] but also van Unnik[297] has argued that καλῶς ποιεῖτε belongs to the vocabulary of Hellenistic ethical teaching, not early Christian parenesis, and has been introduced here by Luke. This clause therefore would appear to be redactional in its present form, and several scholars also consider Lk 6:28a (cf. Rom 12:14; 1 Cor 4:12–13) to be so.[298] Although it is often argued that Luke tends to eliminate Semitic parallelism,[299] there is evidence that he shows some interest in 'catalogues of four', such as here and in the Lukan version of other material in this section including Lk 6:22, Lk 6:37–8 and the woes in Lk 6:24–6.[300]

The other saying which Luke includes among the opening exhortations, but which is not found here in Matthew, is the 'Golden Rule' (Lk 6:31). Matthew's location of the saying is likely to be the work of the evangelist rather than his source, with the significance of its location also highlighted by the appended statement: 'For this is the law and the prophets.'[301] Yet this in itself does not establish the originality of the location in Luke,[302] especially given the suitability of the saying as a floating unit of tradition. If the original sequence of the sayings collection has been disturbed in Luke by the incorporation of the teaching on non-retaliation at this point, then the gap caused by relocating the 'sons of the Most High' saying later (6:35) may have been filled by the Golden Rule.[303] Or, indeed, it may have been originally associated with the non-retaliation teaching. As it stands in Luke, the self-interest and reciprocity to which the saying appeals do superficially clash with the rhetorical questions which follow, encouraging one to go beyond mere reciprocity of love.[304] Since it encourages a benevolent attitude towards men generally, however, it is not completely lacking in suitability; and it does prepare for the emphasis on *active* love which follows.[305] There are, therefore, no conclusive grounds for omitting it here, although uncertainty remains. Strictly, it might be taken as an indicative rather than imperative,[306] so that it could conceivably mark the transition from exhortation to argument.

After the opening set of exhortations, the first supporting argument comes in Mt 5:45. This argument moves from the recognition of those addressed as 'sons of your Father (who is in heaven)'[307] to God's present action in the natural world in causing his sun to rise on both evil and good and sending rain on the just and unjust. In Lk 6:35b a more concise and less illustrative formulation of this argument is given.[308] Luke's formulation of the argument emphasizes more than in Matthew the *nature* of God himself (who is 'kind to the ungrateful and the evil'), thereby providing a smoother transition to Lk 6:36, where the nature of God as merciful is the focal point. His wording of 6:35, however, may well be secondary if his sequence of sayings is secondary.[309] The formulation in Matthew, coming earlier in the sequence of sayings, points less to the nature of God than to one's *experience* of God's world. Its experiential basis, attested in similar proverbs from other sources, is accordingly stronger.[310]

The reasons for considering the sequence in Matthew to be more original here have in part already been given. It is clear that the argument in Mt 5:45/Lk 6:35b must follow closely on the love command. The introduction of Lk 6:29−30 into the Lukan sequence, which has been discussed above, makes this impossible; and so the flow of argument can only be reinstated in Luke by a repetition of the love command in 6:35a. Although this seems to establish a kind of *inclusio*, which A. Jacobson has taken to be original,[311] it will be argued below that 6:35 is not in fact the end of the collection of sayings. Nor does this hypothesis do justice to Matthew's own interest in *inclusio*,[312] had one originally been present.

In Matthew's sequence, additional supporting arguments are presented by the multiple rhetorical questions in Mt 5:46−7 (cf. Lk 6:32−3). In Lk 6:32−4, there are three such questions, on the subject of loving, doing good (ἀγαθοποιεῖν) and lending; in Mt 5:46−7, the themes are loving and saluting. It is likely that Luke's third question on lending (6:34) is a secondary insertion, under the influence of the addition of Lk 6:30 (cf. Mt 5:42), and in line with Lukan interests.[313] The term ἀγαθοποιεῖν is also held by van Unnik[314] to be a formal Hellenization by Luke (cf. καλῶς ποιεῖν in Lk 6:27c). These observations suggest that Matthew has preserved the more original form of the rhetorical questions, and that a pair of questions came at this stage in the sequence of the collection.

This reconstruction of the sequence thus far corresponds to a large degree with that of D. Zeller[315] (apart from our tentative inclusion of Lk 6:31), as well as with R. Bultmann[316] and S. Schulz.[317] Zeller, however, proceeds to treat Mt 5:48/Lk 6:36 as separate and distinct from the present collection.[318] Although it can be seen as a saying transitional to the next section (Lk 6:37ff.), even in Luke it must be seen as the natural conclusion to the present collection.[319] Zeller himself notes the close connection of the call to imitate God with the idea of the hearers as 'sons of the Most High' (Lk 6:35/Mt 5:45) and with the rhetorical questions in Mt 5:46−7/Lk 6:32−4.[320] In the sequence in Matthew, which has been argued to reflect the original more closely, there is a clear need also for a concluding saying after the rhetorical questions.[321] Matthew and Luke agree in providing just such a saying, with no sign of any break in either case.

The concluding saying, therefore, is an imperative which draws for its support on the divine example. Earlier, in Mt 5:45, the relationship of the hearers to God was invoked along with observations about God's ordering of his world. But the concluding saying appeals more directly to the nature of God as a basis for human conduct. It is often held that the reference in Luke to God's mercy has greater claim to originality than the Matthean appeal to perfection.[322] The idea of perfection is particularly suitable for Matthew's purpose at this point in his discussion of the Torah,[323] and the theme of mercy is most apt for the context of loving one's enemies when it is divorced from the antitheses and the Matthean discussion of the law.

The result of this effort to reconstruct the underlying sequence of the sayings collected in Mt 5:44−8/Lk 6:27−36 may therefore be summarized as below:

(1) A double opening imperative, dominated by the command to love one's enemies (Mt 5:44; cf. Lk 6:27−28), but possibly also including Lk 6:31.

(2) An initial supporting statement appealing to the impartial provisions for both the just and the unjust in the natural world (Mt 5:45; cf. Lk 6:35b).

(3) A pair of supporting rhetorical questions (Mt 5:46−7/Lk 6:32−3)

(4) A short concluding exhortation based on the nature of God as merciful (Lk 6:36; cf. Mt 5:48).

In so far as this reconstruction is tenable, there is a basis here for showing that this collection of sayings shares the pattern of argument discernible in the previously analysed collections.

II

In addition to a similarity in structure, it can also be shown that the argument of this collection of sayings progresses in a way similar to that of the previously analysed collections. The opening admonition is typically universal in scope: you must love your enemies. While it may indirectly be a broadening of the command in Lev 19:18 (cf. Ex 23:4–5) to show love to one's neighbour, it need not be alluding specifically to the Mosaic law.[324] One's attitude towards one's enemy was a subject of wide discussion in the ancient world, and in the Jewish wisdom literature, although it was associated with a wide variety of motives.[325] It also must be allowed that a specific, concrete situation could give rise to such instruction,[326] but the exhortation is formulated in quite general terms.

The second of the opening imperatives introduces the idea of *prayer* for the enemy. This may introduce the idea that the enemy is in some sense a religious enemy, the enemy of Christians, and not merely a personal one.[327] Matthew would seem to imply this by his reference to the enemy as a 'persecutor'. But because διώκειν is considered characteristic of Matthean vocabulary, the description of the enemy as ὁ ἐπηρεάζων ('molester', 'insulter') in Lk 6:28b is likely to be more original.[328] The only other occurrence of this word in the NT is in 1 Pet 3:16, where also it is associated with the vocabulary of persecution.[329] In either case, therefore, hostility and abuse seem to be in mind, and the response is to be prayer.[330] The second imperative, therefore, begins subtly to introduce further clarification of the concept of love of enemies.

The presence of the 'Golden Rule' after these exhortations, if accepted here, would be to introduce also the idea of *active* love towards the enemy while maintaining the general idea of benevolence towards all. It is a universally phrased, self-contained saying with its own supporting logic within it,[331] yet not without some degree of self-interest in the motivation.

However, the first clear supporting statement (Mt 5:45 par) suggests that the dominant motive for active love towards one's enemies is not to be self-interest, but rather consistency with a status as 'sons of your Father/the Most High'.[332] This introduces into the argument an important new element which extends to all of the following sayings. It is because of this status that the hearers are expected to surpass the ordinary efforts of 'sinners' (Mt 5:46–7 par), and this also lays the foundation for the concluding saying (Mt 5:48/ Lk 6:36).

The difference between Matthew and Luke on whether 'being' or 'becoming' is the idea behind the appeal to sonship in Mt 5:45/Lk 6:35b is complicated by a corresponding reversal of terms in Mt 5:48/Lk 6:36.[333] How far is this really an appeal to the reader's present status, or how far is it a promise of future reward? The appeal to a future divine sonship could well draw on general futuristic eschatological ideas, but such seem to remain still in the background of the argument.[334] In the foreground is the *present* activity of God. The ὅτι-clause appeals not to a future judgement by God but to the *experiential evidence* of the present condition of God's world. This is the example that they are to reflect. It is a striking argument to use, because far from emphasizing the justice of God or his ultimate resolution of present injustices, it leaves disturbingly open the question of retribution.[335] In this sense the argument is highly realistic and experiential rather than theologically reflective. It realistically shows injustice in the present world. Divine sonship, therefore, reflects above all the present order of the natural world.

L. Schottroff,[336] however, insists that the attitude to be exemplified is not one of mere passive toleration of injustice. Already the idea of an active love was possibly raised by the 'Golden Rule'. This idea comes forth even more clearly as the argument progresses to the double rhetorical questions in Mt 5:46–7 par.[337] This second strand of argument for love of enemies builds on further observations of ordinary human conduct but presses the case for a 'special' conduct required of the hearers: 'If you love those who love you, what reward[338] have you? Do not even the tax-collectors/sinners do the same?' The required love must go beyond normal human conduct, beyond mere love of neighbour. Implicit in the argument is an assumption that extraordinary conduct should be expected of the hearers. Again, this may draw on the enticement of a future reward, but the present tense ἔχετε/ἐστίν ('what reward *have* you?') points interestingly to the present rather than to the future. The concept of reward is used here in a way which does not provide an ultimate resolution of the injustices of the world raised in Mt 5:45, or an anticipated word of assurance, but a present obligation.[339] The 'reward' merely expresses the obligation to exceed the conduct of sinners. It is not a word of comfort for the sons of God amidst persecution. The motive here for love of enemies is still the status of the hearers' relationship to God; it develops the argument begun in Mt 5:45.

However, the rhetorical questions raise more acutely not only the active quality of the love required, but also the question of those involved. In Matthew, those addressed are contrasted with τελῶναι and ἐθνικοί; in Luke, with ἁμαρτωλοί. Both Matthew and Luke use terms especially suited to their outlook, so an alteration might have been made by either or both.[340] Yet in another important double-tradition passage there is the pairing τελῶναι καὶ ἁμαρτωλοί (Lk 7: 34 = Mt 11:19), which provides a possible explanation of the versions of both evangelists here.

In the rhetorical questions, the terms seem to suggest a contrast between 'insiders' and 'outsiders'. In so far as these sayings had a *Sitz im Leben* within the Christian community, the 'insiders' would be Christians.[341] There is no denial or denigration of the status of the hearers (contrast Lk 3:7−9 with respect to the Jews), and their relationship to God is in fact the basis of the final appeal in Lk 6:36 par.

But who are the 'outsiders'? It is doubtful that the rhetorical questions themselves provide any clear answer to this question, since they are concerned less with specifying the enemy than with providing examples of 'ordinary' conduct.[342] Yet P. Hoffmann[343] attempts to align the teaching of love of enemies with his understanding of a general anti-Zealot stance on the part of the Q-missionaries. The enemy, therefore, would be the Romans, the enemy of the Jews. L. Schottroff,[344] however, has strongly criticized this position on the grounds that the enemy must surely be the enemy of the Christians, namely the Jews. In any case, the enemy is not just a personal enemy but in some sense can be associated with the 'unjust', and thus with *God's* enemies, the enemies of God's people.[345]

Only at the stage of the placing of the non-resistance teaching in close proximity to the collection on love of enemies is an apologetic argument regarding the non-violent and thus non-seditious behaviour of Christians also possible, but then one may also have to reckon with the proximity of other sayings, such as Lk 6:22−3 par. In the latter saying the enemy for Christians would again appear to be the Jews, and it is arguable that this is in any case a likely conjecture. A religious hostility is probable as a result of the church's early preaching activity amongst Jews.[346] The early church's difficulty in establishing for itself a satisfactory response to such hostility may have led to the careful formulation of a collection of teaching on the subject. The degree of such hostility in the experience of the early church (cf. Lk 6:22−3 par) could also explain the absence of any explicit hope of winning over the opponent. The response of the enemy to such love is left indeterminate; it is not sufficiently clear to be a motive.[347]

The concluding saying of the collection takes the argument to its natural conclusion: the imitation of God in his mercy. Although the idea develops from Mt 5:45 par and underpins the questions in Mt 5:46–7 par, it only becomes explicit at the end. The final imperative brings the collection to its conclusion in a way similar to Mt 7:5 par for the sayings on judging (Mt 7:1–5 par).[348]

The argument of the sayings collection therefore develops in a persuasive and careful way, reminiscent of the other sayings collections of the double tradition. It is not just a superficial similarity of structure, but a substantial similarity of argumentative style. The argument unfolds from the general instruction to progressive elaborations of what attitude is required and towards a final interpretative saying in which experience and reason lead to a statement of the distinctive basis for love of enemies. This is a call to imitate God in his mercy.

Like the collections in Mt 6:25ff. par and Mt 10:26ff. par, the cause of anxiety or threat is minimized in favour of an active, positive trust in God, who is revealed as the One who sustains the natural world.[349]

Like the sayings in Mt 7:1–5 par, the hearer is not made the judge of his opponent but is himself challenged.[350] This stands in striking contrast to other approaches to such hostility, including the beatitude in Lk 6:22–3 par, in which it is the promise of reward or of judgement that gives meaning to the suffering.[351] The assurance which is offered in the love-of-enemies sayings is primarily the identification of the hearers as 'sons of the Father/Most High' (Mt 5:45, 48 par), an affirmation of their relationship to the One who is in control. Both formally and thematically there is much to commend the harmony of this collection of sayings with the other aphoristic collections of the double tradition.

Having argued for the presence of an additional sayings collection among the material of the double tradition, the second question posed earlier must be asked. Are there any similar collections to be found outside the generally recognized bounds of the double tradition? There is one such collection which especially deserves consideration.

Lk 16:9–13

καὶ ἐγὼ ὑμῖν λέγω,

(i) ἑαυτοῖς ποιήσατε φίλους ἐκ τοῦ μαμωνᾶ τῆς ἀδικίας, ἵνα
ὅταν ἐκλίπῃ δέξωνται ὑμᾶς εἰς τὰς αἰωνίους σκηνάς.

(ii) ὁ πιστὸς ἐν ἐλαχίστῳ καὶ ἐν πολλῷ πιστός ἐστιν, καὶ ὁ ἐν ἐλαχίστῳ ἄδικος καὶ ἐν πολλῷ ἄδικός ἐστιν.

(iii) εἰ οὖν ἐν τῷ ἀδίκῳ μαμωνᾷ πιστοὶ οὐκ ἐγένεσθε, τὸ ἀληθινὸν τίς ὑμῖν πιστεύσει; καὶ εἰ ἐν τῷ ἀλλοτρίῳ πιστοὶ οὐκ ἐγένεσθε, τὸ ὑμέτερον τίς ὑμῖν δώσει;

(iv) οὐδεὶς οἰκέτης δύναται δυσὶ κυρίοις δουλεύειν · ἢ γὰρ τὸν ἕνα μισήσει καὶ τὸν ἕτερον ἀγαπήσει, ἢ ἑνὸς ἀνθέξεται καὶ τοῦ ἑτέρου καταφρονήσει. οὐ δύνασθε θεῷ δουλεύειν καὶ μαμωνᾷ.

A rather remarkable and unexpected parallel to the structure of the aphoristic sayings collections is found in the sayings which follow the notoriously difficult Parable of the 'Unjust' Steward in Luke's gospel. While opinions vary as to where precisely the parable ends, J. Fitzmyer has cogently argued that the 'parable proper' ends at Lk 16:8a, where the master (κύριος) of the parable commends the οἰκονόμος τῆς ἀδικίας.[352] Verse 8b ('for the sons of this world are wiser in their own generation than the sons of light') then appears to be an added explanation for the surprising commendation in verse 8a.[353] Considerable agreement exists, though, that the sayings in verses 9–13 are a later addition.[354] This is marked formally by the introductory phrase in verse 9, καὶ ἐγὼ ὑμῖν λέγω, and by the fact that this group of sayings seems at first sight to be a loose collection held together by the general theme of riches and the key term μαμωνᾶς (16:9, 11, 13).[355] The sayings in verses 9–13 have been thought to suggest a variety of individual comments on the parable,[356] although together they leave the reader rather perplexed as to both the original meaning of the parable and Luke's own intentions. Many of the sayings in 16:9–13 are not closely tied to the main points of the parable.

I

Leaving aside for the moment the thorny question of how to interpret these sayings in the light of the preceding parable, if verses 9–13 are taken on their own, a striking resemblance is found to the structure of the collections of aphoristic sayings which have been discussed earlier. With the possible exception of the opening saying in 16:9, to which we must return, all the sayings in Lk 16:9–13 could stand as self-contained aphoristic sayings. Even verse 9, consisting of a general exhortation followed by a supporting reason, could be classified as a wisdom admonition.[357] This admonition is the only imperative in the compilation of sayings. The use of an opening imperative formally resembles the opening of several of the previously analysed collections (cf. Lk 6:37 par; Mt 7:7 par, 6:25 par, 5:44 par).

The opening admonition is followed by the central sayings in verses 10–12, which include first an aphoristic statement in antithetical parallelism (10) and then the double rhetorical questions (11–12). These central sayings also introduce a change in imagery from the opening sayings. The double rhetorical questions and the change of imagery are characteristic of the central sections of the other aphoristic collections. The theme of making friends by use of 'mammon' in verse 9 has given way to a discussion of faithfulness in verses 10ff., but a progression of argument is maintained not just by the idea of the responsibilities of wealth but also by the thought of acting to secure one's future. Underlying verses 10ff. is also an *a minore ad maius* type of argument.[358]

The concluding sayings in verse 13 provide a final development in the imagery (servants and masters), in which the short proverb 'No servant can serve two masters' is elaborated and applied to the impossibility of serving both God and mammon. This is the first direct reference to God in the collection of sayings. The reference in the last clause to 'mammon' provides a final reflection back to the same subject introduced in the opening saying (verse 9), but only in the final clause in verse 13 is the critical challenge to choose God over mammon expressed. In this sense it is the climax of the collection. The climactic and interpretative role of the final saying has also been a consistent feature of the other aphoristic collections.

Hints of heavenly reward are found in the present form of verse 9 and perhaps even more obliquely in verse 11, where references to an eternal abode and 'true riches' are respectively mentioned.[359] However, these concepts are left encoded and without elaboration, and they can only be called 'eschatological' in the most general sense of the term. This is also a feature of most of the aphoristic sayings-collections. All of these structural and stylistic features point strikingly to a close relationship between this group of sayings and the collections of the double tradition.

II

Not only have these remarkable similarities of structure gone virtually unnoticed by scholars; they may also provide a new key to this *crux interpretationis* in Lk 16. It is with this in mind that we turn to a more detailed study of the progression of argument in these sayings.

First, we must return to the opening exhortation. There is a clear break from what precedes, indicated by the introductory formula in verse 9.[360] But even so it is not unlikely that in its present form verse 9 has in part been adapted to the preceding parable.[361] This saying more than any of the others reflects the themes of the parable itself. The exhortation to 'make friends' now so that 'they may receive you' later when your wealth fails[362] certainly matches important features of the parable; and the phrases τῆς ἀδικίας and δέξωνται ὑμᾶς εἰς may take over vocabulary from the parable itself (cf. 16:8a).[363]

Yet there are other features of this saying which make one hesitate to assign its construction wholly to the same source as the original parable or to the evangelist Luke later. It is immediately obvious, for example, that verse 9 has nothing to do with either a master or a steward in its content. To this extent it is distinct from the imagery of the parable. Regarding its formulation, the probable Semitic origin of μαμωνᾶς[364] (which also does not appear in the parable, but is found in verses 11 and 13) and the quite unexpected reference to 'eternal tents',[365] cast serious doubt upon whether Luke was in fact wholly responsible for the construction of the exhortation.[366] Many thematic features of verse 9 are found in other double-tradition sayings, and not always most clearly in the Lukan formulation of the sayings. The call to 'make friends' prior to a calamity is expressed in the saying in Lk 12:58–9/Mt 5:25–6. A similarity in the argument of Lk 16:9 to Lk 12:33/Mt 6:19–20, about laying up treasure in heaven which will not fail, is also evident.[367] In the latter case, Lk 16:9 is closer to Matthew's formulation than to Luke's. Unlike Lk 12:33, Lk 16:9 shows no specific application to the concerns of alms-giving or the disposal of one's possessions.[368] Does this not suggest only limited Lukan redaction in Lk 16:9? There is no clear indication that Lk 16:9 was actually composed from the sayings in Lk 12:33 or 12:58; on the contrary, the presence of these similar admonitions suggests that there is no good reason why the saying in Lk 16:9 could not have stood as an independent saying itself.[369] There is much, therefore, to suggest that J. Dupont[370] is correct when he suggests the possibility that Luke was content to retouch a pre-existing logion which at the very least spoke of 'mammon'.

The exhortation in Lk 16:9 can serve, therefore, as a general exhortation about one's attitude towards material wealth. It is unlikely that it applied only to ill-gotten gains, for H. Kosmala[371] has shown how the phrase τῆς ἀδικίας (modifying μαμωνᾶς) refers to 'this-worldly' rather than 'dishonestly acquired' possessions.[372] The negative connotations which it bears are primarily those made explicit in the final saying, 16:13, where material possessions show a tendency to distract man from devotion to God and thus are part of this evil world.[373] Even in verse 9 it is clear that there is no ultimate security in possessions ('when it fails'). This is the motive for the exhortation.

In the present admonition, one's worldly possessions are calculated to 'make friends'. Precisely how one is to use μαμωνᾶς to make friends is left unclear. The exhortation presents a broad goal or orientation rather than a call to particular actions, and is therefore all-inclusive. Whether this goal is to be accomplished by almsgiving, hospitality, cancellation of debts or more radical disposal of one's goods is unstated.[374]

The antithetically parallel maxim in Lk 16:10 introduces the new theme of faithfulness and unfaithfulness. Initially it is unclear how this imagery is related to what precedes in verse 9, apart from a catchword connection between ἀδικίας (9a) and ἄδικος (10b). The relationship becomes increasingly clarified, however, in two ways. First, verse 10 must be understood as setting the premise for the argumentative rhetorical questions in verses 11 and 12.[375] Therefore, one must ask how all of verses 10–12, focusing chiefly upon the double rhetorical questions, is related to the opening exhortation. The rhetorical question in verse 11 shows how the aphoristic statement on faithfulness in little and in much (10) applies to the matter of mammon.[376] Verse 11 refers again to ὁ ἄδικος μαμωνᾶς and contrasts it with τὸ ἀληθινόν. It becomes clear that verses 10ff. comprise an *a minore ad maius* type of argument to reinforce the earlier argument in verse 9. What in verse 9 is meant by making friends for oneself from one's μαμωνᾶς τῆς ἀδικίας is now presented as being faithful (πιστός) with one's ἄδικος μαμωνᾶς.[377] The better and more lasting security which is obtained by such behaviour is reflected in the one case by reception into 'eternal tents' (9) and in the other by access to 'true riches' (11).[378] What is exhorted in verse 9 is argued out from further human experience and reasoning in verses 10ff., but beginning with the maxim in verse 10. Thus, verses 10ff. provide additional arguments in support of verse 9, and further elaboration of the exhortation in terms of the vocabulary of 'faithfulness'. This connection in thought is important for understanding how these verses may form part of a collective argument.

Then, secondly, H. Kosmala[379] has argued that even in verse 10 itself the contrast between ἄδικος and πιστός is a contrast between, respectively, that which applies to the present and that which applies to the coming world. This is the result of his interpretation of ἄδικος as 'belonging to this evil world'. Therefore, the contrast between the 'this-worldly' and the eternal found in verse 9 may be subtly continued even in verse 10 itself through the ἄδικος–πιστός terminology.

The saying in verse 12, the second rhetorical question, formally takes the argument a step further by bringing to the fore the question of ownership and of stewardship. Stewardship may have been implicit in the earlier 'faithfulness' sayings but has not received explicit attention in verses 9–11, despite the preceding parable. Focus on the idea of stewardship or service is essential at this point in the structure of the argument, in order to provide a transition to the final sayings (13), which are completely concerned with service to a master. The saying in verse 12 provides this necessary transition in thought.

The precise interpretation of 'that which is another's' has proved troublesome, however. If it is taken as a wide reference to everything belonging to God, man acting simply as a steward in this world, then it leaves the ὑμέτερον (other MSS: ἡμέτερον)[380] difficult to explain. J.-P. Molina[381] attempts to see the contrast between that which is held by violent appropriation and that which one possesses without violence and without appropriation (i.e. by invitation; cf. verse 9). While importing the idea of 'violence' into the saying unnecessarily, the distinction between differing types of appropriation is probably to be preferred to the view of H. Kosmala, who sees verse 12 simply as a reiteration of verse 11. In his view, both sayings draw the contrast between worldly possessions (equivalent to 'that belonging to another') and what will be received in the age to come (equivalent to 'our [sic] own').[382] But such an explanation overrides the natural connotations of the vocabulary in verse 12, which speaks additionally of stewardship.

Verse 13, therefore, does not introduce a wholly new theme to the argument. It brings the question of use of worldly possessions to its focal point. Faithfulness in service now leads to a choice of whom one is to serve. But even at this critical point of decision, the choice is formulated on the premise of aphoristic wisdom: 'no one can serve two masters'.[383] This prepares for the final contrast, not between μαμωνᾶς and God, but between wholeheartedly *serving* μαμωνᾶς and wholeheartedly *serving* God.[384] While previously μαμωνᾶς τῆς ἀδικίας has been contrasted primarily with a more secure form of wealth (9b, 11), and most of the previous argument has put the case for 'faithful' use of mammon on the grounds of what provides one with greater security and benefit, here the all-important step is made in which that enticement of lasting riches, associated with the heavenly sphere all along, is linked to an inescapable either−or decision.[385] Will one seek to serve God or mammon? It brings one to a point similar to that found at the climax of the collection in Mt 6:25−33 par: 'Seek (first) the kingdom of God'. On a reduced scale, a similar development of thought underlies the admonition of Mt 6:19−21/ Lk 12:33−4 where seemingly bold appeal to one's interest in lasting treasure is capped by an insight into one's orientation of heart: 'where your treasure is, there is your heart also'.

Verse 13, therefore, provides both the climax and the interpretative clue for what precedes. Right use of μαμωνᾶς is not to be understood as merely competent management of possessions. Most of the discussion of possessions is in terms of other claims on them. This was tacit in the opening exhortation, in terms of 'making friends' with one's material possessions. It is also implicit in most of the discussion of 'faithfulness' and finally of 'service'. The insecurities of mammon can be overcome by the sharing of it before it fails (9) and by 'faithful use' in handling both large amounts and small (10−12). Accepting the obligations of service to God is the key by which one's use of mammon leads to true riches. Beyond this no details are given as to what constitutes right use of possessions, large or small.

Contrary to many treatments of Lk 16:9−13, we have endeavoured to show that there is an argument which proceeds through these assembled sayings. It has also been found that the argument progresses in ways similar to that found in the aphoristic collections of the double tradition. It moves from a general and supported admonition (9), to an initial supporting maxim introducing the new motif of 'faithfulness' (10), to the double rhetorical questions which pursue the case for faithfulness, looking forward to true riches (11−12), to the final set of maxims which presents the critical demand to choose between serving God and serving mammon (13). The similarity in style of argument to the other aphoristic sayings collections can hardly escape notice.[386]

III

How, then, is one to account for the presence and structure of the sayings collected together in Lk 16:9–13? The first task is to determine whether Luke himself was largely responsible for composing the sayings, whether his activity was limited mainly to their compilation, or whether he took up a previously existing collection of sayings.

Strong criticisms against A. Descamps's thesis that the parable and sayings (1–13) are closely united, and that Luke himself was largely responsible for composing the sayings in verses 9–13 in order to clarify points in the parable,[387] have been advanced by J. Dupont[388] and by J. Fitzmyer.[389] The latter scholars rightly observe the extrinsic nature of the connection of many of the sayings (especially verses 10–13) with the parable, the Aramaic background of the play on words between μαμωνᾶς and πιστός in verses 10–11,[390] and the fact that Lk 16:13 is clearly a saying added here from Q. It is only in verse 9 that one encounters the likelihood of Lukan composition. Nevertheless, it has been argued above that it is probable that verse 9 is a Lukan retouching of an existing saying, rather than entirely of his own composition. The mixture of elements in verse 9 which reflect Lukan interests and characteristics with other elements which cannot be easily related to Lukan style make one hesitate to assign its construction wholly to Luke.

It has also been previously noted how the themes in verses 9–13 go considerably beyond mere clarification of the parable. The insistence on 'faithful' use of wealth in verses 10ff. is hardly displayed by the steward in the parable, and it is likely in any case that verse 10a was an independently existing saying in the gospel tradition and not Luke's own composition (cf. Mt 25:21/Lk 19:17).[391] 'True riches' (11) and receiving 'that which is your own' (12) are also motifs not attributable easily to the parable. Even the key word μαμωνᾶς, repeated three times in verses 9–13, is foreign to the parable. Signs both of Lukan redactional activity and of connection with the parable in Lk 16:1ff. rapidly diminish as one proceeds through verses 10–12, 13. These considerations, therefore, cast serious doubt on the thesis that Lk 16:1–13 is an original unity or that Luke composed the sayings in verses 9–13 himself on the basis of the parable. They still allow the possibility, however, that Luke compiled the collection from several existing units (9, 10–12 and 13) or that he took up a previously existing collection. In either case, any traces of his own hand in verse 9, the opening of the 'collection', are readily explicable as an attempt to ease the transition between the parable and the other sayings which have been appended to the parable. Once the transition is made, the influence of his own hand is less frequently encountered.

Yet can the thesis that Luke even compiled this collection from originally independent units be maintained? First, in the light of our findings, this view would presume that Luke recognized the pattern of argument of the double-tradition aphoristic collections and here sought to reproduce this pattern himself. Against such a presumption is the fact that Luke has disrupted the pattern of these collections elsewhere: at Lk 6:39–40, 12:32, 12:4–7, and 6:27–36. This casts serious doubt upon whether he did recognize the pattern and especially upon whether he valued it enough to imitate it so carefully. Secondly, despite the placement of these sayings in a context which expresses criticism of love of money by the Pharisees (16:14–15), no polemical statements or direct warnings are included in verses 9–13, as one might have expected if Luke had taken a direct hand in the compilation of all the units in this context. He also has found no place for an explicit commendation of giving to the poor when discussing faithful use of mammon.[392] Thirdly, the preceding arguments from silence gain weight when combined with the observation that Luke fails here either to adapt the sayings to the reproof of the Pharisees which follows or to clarify significantly the parable which precedes.[393] It has been widely recognized that it is difficult to understand what Luke was trying to accomplish in this section.[394] This difficulty is less if one considers him to be taking up here a previously existing collection and presenting it *en bloc* than if one believes that he compiled it piece by piece himself with the parable or polemic in his mind. Fourthly, a common explanation of these sayings in verses 9–13 is that Luke records here three different ways in which the church moralized the difficult preceding parable.[395] However, this takes no account of the structure of the collection of sayings. Three independent sayings have not been merely appended here as three footnotes. They have been moulded into a definable structure and into a definite progression of argument. If Luke himself were responsible for such a careful construction, one might have expected that its purpose in this context would be plainer. Fifthly, the application of multiple aphoristic sayings to the end of a parable is not a device which Luke often employs. It is not unusual to find a single aphoristic saying concluding a parable (cf. Lk 18:14, 14:11, 12:48), but the few instances in which multiple sayings directly follow a parable in Luke's gospel are sufficiently rare to bear closer examination.

One instance of this occurs in Lk 8:4–18 (cf. Mk 4:1–25), in which the Parable of the Sower and its interpretation are followed without transition by the aphoristic sayings on lighting a lamp (8:16), nothing remaining hid (8:17), and its being given to him who has (8:18). In this instance, however, the interpretation of the parable has been made exceedingly clear previously (8:4–15). More importantly, the sayings are gathered at this point in Luke simply because they are so gathered already in Mark. There is also no correspondence between Lk 8:16–18 and the structure of the double-tradition aphoristic collections.

More significant is the other notable instance where multiple aphoristic sayings follow a parable in Luke. In this case it involves one of the previously discussed sayings collections![396] The parable, which is peculiar to Luke, appears in Lk 11:5–8 and is concluded with the interpretative saying in Lk 11:8. It then continues, however, in 11:9 with the formula κἀγὼ ὑμῖν λέγω and the series of aphoristic sayings in Lk 11:9–13 (cf. above, pp. 15–24). It has even been argued that Lk 11:9ff. can be understood as a second interpretation for the parable which precedes in Luke's gospel.[397] This provides a very close parallel to the situation in Lk 16:1–8, 9–13. Therefore, in both instances in which Luke does follow a parable directly with multiple aphoristic sayings, he does so by using a *previously existing collection of sayings*; and the closest parallel to his procedure in Lk 16:1–13 is found in Lk 11:5–13, in which a collection of double-tradition sayings follows a parable peculiar to his gospel, even using a very similar introductory formula.

IV

To go beyond this conclusion that Luke used a previously existing collection of sayings in Lk 16:9–13, and to argue more precisely for the original *source* of the collection of sayings, becomes necessarily more conjectural. Nevertheless, the close similarity of Lk 16:9–13 to the structure of the double-tradition aphoristic collections suggests the intriguing possibility that Lk 16:9–13 may have come to Luke along with the rest of his double-tradition material. This is not a wholly new suggestion. H. Schürmann, on very different grounds, indicates that it is possible that Matthew had a *Vorlage* including Lk 16:9–13. He tentatively makes this suggestion on the basis of some verbal reminiscences which he perceives in Matthew's Sermon.[398] Can one provide further arguments for this claim?

Apart from pointing once again to the significance of the structure of the collection, one would need to find reasons for Matthew's having broken up the collection and retained only Mt 6:24 in the Sermon. We observed earlier that Matthew did occasionally disrupt the structure of the sayings-collections (e.g., Mt 7:16−20, 12:33−5 par), so can one find reasons for his doing so here?

There are some indications that Matthew reflects knowledge of Lk 16:9−13 in his small collection of sayings in Mt 6:19−24. Certainly there are many general similarities between the two collections of sayings, both of which end with the double-tradition maxim about serving God or mammon (Mt 6:24/Lk 16:13).

As in Lk 16:9−13, the collection of sayings in Mt 6:19−24 centres upon the theme of riches, although in Matthew the danger of coveting riches is stressed, whereas the collection of Luke places emphasis more upon the attitude governing their use. In Mt 6:19−24, the collection of sayings is composed of three distinct units: Mt 6:19−21, 22−3 and 24. As in Lk 16, the collection in Mt 6:19ff. is introduced by an admonition with an integral supporting argument, has a change in theme in the central sayings, and changes theme again in the concluding sayings. More importantly, two of the sayings in Mt 6:19−24 (namely, 6:19−20 and 24) bear close relationship to two sayings in Lk 16 (9 and 13), and they appear at exactly the same points in the sequence of the Mt 6:19ff. collection as in Lk 16:9ff. This structural correspondence is sufficiently striking to go beyond mere coincidence. Even the central sayings, which appear the most different, share use of an *a minore ad maius* type of argument.

But what of the differences between the two collections? The opening sayings do, of course, differ, but the closeness in theme between Lk 16:9 and Mt 6:19−20 is clear and has been noted earlier.[399] Yet it is also clear why Matthew might have preferred Mt 6:19ff./Lk 12:33−4 to Lk 16:9 in the Sermon, if he had the choice. Not only is the latter a difficult saying as it stands in Luke, with awkward references to making friends from μαμωνᾶς τῆς ἀδικίας and being received in 'eternal tents', but the saying about earthly and heavenly treasures (Mt 6:19−20/Lk 12:33) puts these ideas in a more striking and less difficult way.[400] The implied contrast of earthly and heavenly in Lk 16:9 becomes explicit in Mt 6:19−20.[401]

If the central sayings (Mt 6:22−3; cf. Lk 11:34−5) are seen as the main variation of Matthew from the substance of Lk 16:9−13, it is because it is precisely here that the theme of covetousness comes to the fore. This may explain the absence of the sayings in Lk 16:10−12, which deal with 'faithfulness' rather than 'covetousness'. But there are still reminiscences of Lk 16:10−12 in Matthew's gospel.

H. Schürmann finds one in the Sermon itself, arguing that Mt 5:19 recalls Lk 16:10.[402] Lk 16:10a is also very similar to Mt 25:21/Lk 19:17, and the antithetical formulation of Mt 25:21 is in fact closer to Lk 16:10a than its counterpart in Lk 19:17. While such reminiscences suggest that Matthew may have at least known Lk 16:10, the main reason to be offered in support of the hypothesis that Matthew replaced the central sayings with Mt 6:22−3 must be Matthew's concern with the theme of covetousness. In Matthew's arrangement the teaching on covetousness is used to prepare for the sayings repudiating anxiety over material things which follow immediately in Mt 6:25−33. This teaching on covetousness is expressed in Mt 6:22−3 by the sayings about the evil and the good eye (contrast Lk 11:34−36; cf. below, pp. 127−30). The metaphor of the eye was commonly used in Jewish literature to signify either generous or grasping moral behaviour (cf. Dt 15:9; Prov 28:27; Sir 14:9).[403]

One passage of particular interest in this respect is Sir 31[LXX 34]. Sir 31[34]:8 is significant because it is here that one also finds the key term *māmôn* (LXX: χρυσίον). This is not a term of the canonical biblical literature, for *māmôn* never occurs in the Hebrew OT and μαμωνᾶς *only* appears in Lk 16:9, 11, 13 (cf. Mt 6:24) in the NT. Knowledge of the term is derived mainly from a few references at Qumran (cf. 1 QS 6:2; CD 14:20) and more frequently in the Mishnah (cf. M. *Aboth* 2:12), the Talmud and especially the targums.[404] Apart from these works, however, only two intertestamental references are known: the Hebrew of Sir 31[34]:8 and an assumed *Vorlage* to 1 En 63:10.[405] The significance of the Sirach text is heightened because it comes within an important section of teaching devoted to the theme of riches and covetousness.

The section in question is Sir 31[34]:1−13. The folly and ruin which come of an attachment to gold are stressed (Sir 31:5−8; cf. Mt 6:19−20), a link between the pursuit of riches and *idolatry* is indicated (Sir 31:7; cf. Mt 6:24), and the important word *māmôn* occurs (Sir 31:8; cf. Mt 6:24). The section also deals with the matter of anxieties about material wealth (Sir 31:1−2), a theme to which Matthew himself turns in Mt 6:25ff. Very significantly, however, a warning about the evils of a greedy eye immediately follows the discussion of *māmôn* in Sirach (31:12ff.):

> Are you seated at the table of a great man?
> Do not be greedy at it,
> and do not say, 'There is certainly much upon it!'

Remember that a greedy [Gk: πονηρός] eye is a bad thing. What has been created more greedy [πονηρότερον] than the eye? Therefore it sheds tears from every face ...

This immediate conjunction in Sirach of the exceedingly rare term *māmôn* with a warning about the 'evil' eye provides an important parallel to the themes found joined in Mt 6:22−4. The striking nature of the conjunction of terms and ideas is extended even further if one also takes account of a passage in Sir 29:11−12, which closely precedes Sir 31. The instruction about laying up 'treasure' (LXX: θησαυρός) 'according to the commandments of the Most High' (LXX) or 'of *righteousness* and love' (Syriac) occurs in Sir 29:11,[406] preceded by a warning 'to lose your silver *for the sake of a brother or a friend*, and do not let it rust under a stone and be lost' in Sir 29:10. Not only is there a parallel thought here to Lk 16:9, but the parallel with Mt 6:19−20 has long been recognized.[407] Thus one finds a sequence of correspondence as follows:

warning about laying up treasures, and the rust and ruin which threaten	Sir 29:10−12 Sir 31:5−8	Mt 6:19−20
anxieties about wealth	Sir 31:1−2	Mt 6:25ff.
the key word *māmôn*	Sir 31:8	Mt 6:24
the greedy (πονηρός) eye	Sir 31:12ff.	Mt 6:22−3

Neither Sir 31[34] nor Lk 16:9−13 alone is able to explain fully the construction of Mt 6:19−24, but *together* they show how the sequence of sayings and conjunction of themes may have originated. From Lk 16:9−13 one gets the pattern for the opening and closing sayings (Mt 6:19−20, 24), and the repeated key word μαμωνᾶς which directs one's attention immediately to Sir 31[34]. From Sir 31[34], one gets the conjunction of *māmôn* and the evil eye. Matthew, then, locates his saying about the eye precisely in the place where the central sayings of Lk 16:10−12 are omitted, the latter being directed to faithfulness, not to covetousness. The theme of anxiety over material needs also features prominently in Sir 31[34] and follows not unnaturally in Mt 6:25ff.

Such an understanding of Matthew's procedure is suggestive rather than conclusive and must be related also to the motives influencing the construction of the Sermon as a whole.[408] Yet the coincidences in thought and structure with Lk 16:9–13 cannot be ignored; nor can the parallels with Sir 31[34]. Here, then, is a further argument to add to those advanced earlier for believing the collection of sayings in Lk 16:9–13 to have been associated with the other collections of the double-tradition material formulated prior to either Matthew or Luke. It also explains how Mt 6:19–24 seems to approach the structure of one of these aphoristic sayings-collections while actually failing to conform to it at several points.[409]

Summary

The result of this analysis has been to add two further collections of sayings to those encountered in the preceding section. All of these can claim to share a similar basic pattern for the arrangement of the argument and a similar purpose of persuading Christians to adopt certain attitudes towards issues of special difficulty or sensitivity, such as the use of worldly possessions or confrontation with hardship and persecution. The approach is not mainly polemical or proclamatory or legislative, but persuasive.

The first of these additional collections (Mt 5:44–8/Lk 6:27–36) clearly consists of double-tradition material, the order of which has probably been better preserved by Matthew. The second collection, however, has not usually been assigned to the double tradition.

In the case of Lk 16:9–13, it has been argued that Mt 6:19–24 contains reminiscences of a similar collection to that in Luke. It is in any case reasonable to suppose that the collection did not originate with Luke. Indeed, this theory helps to explain what has occurred in this troublesome section of Lk 16, where the sayings of 16:9–13 are ill at ease with both the parable which precedes and the sayings which follow. Luke did not meticulously compile a multiple conclusion to the Parable of the Steward in 16:1–8. He probably attached a previously existing collection of sayings, as in Lk 11:5–8, 9–13. The structure of Lk 16:9–13, as well as its relationship to Mt 6:19–24, would then point to contact with the same circles as were responsible for the other aphoristic collections of the double tradition.

These results, therefore, merely extend the findings of the preceding sections (see, further, Appendix). It is again significant that in the one case Matthew seems to preserve better the original state of the collection (Mt 5:44–8), while in the other case this is true for Luke (Lk 16:9–13). There is little doubt, therefore, that this pattern stems from compositional activity prior to either of the evangelists.

3

THE USE OF APHORISTIC SAYINGS
OUTSIDE THE APHORISTIC COLLECTIONS

1. Introduction

The small collections of aphoristic sayings were an obvious place to begin our analysis of aphoristic traditions. They are of manageable number; they are reasonably well-defined in extent; they are sufficiently long to pursue profitably questions about compilational tendencies. Unfortunately, it is quite a different matter when one turns to consider those aphoristic sayings which occur apart from such collections. A major difficulty is the sheer number of individual aphoristic sayings in occasional usage in the gospel-tradition. Undoubtedly this explains in part the paucity of detailed scholarly analyses of these sayings and the difficulty of reaching generally valid conclusions about them. Attempts at analysis are also hampered by indeterminate contexts for the sayings, since individual aphorisms frequently 'drift' into differing contexts in the different gospels. One must also allow that at times the punctuation of teaching with an aphorism is simply a convenient rhetorical device, and accordingly that it might have no special significance as part of a pattern of usage. The task which one faces is, therefore, not an easy one; but if any patterns of usage do emerge, they will be all the more significant.

Indeed, the very frequency with which aphoristic sayings are encountered in the double tradition apart from the aphoristic sayings-collections[1] is itself a warning against any easy dismissal of such usages as 'merely' rhetorical. If there is a conscious interest in the collection of aphoristic sayings within the double tradition, as has been argued in the preceding chapter, then this fact too should alert one to such an interest extending to similar sayings occurring outside collections. It is thus on the double-tradition material that we shall again concentrate. But what kind of study is required?

One possible approach is to place the emphasis upon formal characteristics. While attempts have been made to classify formal categories of aphoristic sayings in OT literature,[2] this has seldom been applied in a comprehensive way to the synoptic tradition.

Aphoristic sayings do exhibit a wide variety of forms, and some formal categories which were prominent in the Jewish wisdom literature, such as 'better ... than' proverbs, are relatively scarce in the synoptic tradition. The early form-critical analysis of such logia by R. Bultmann[3] established some basic formal categories, but form critics made little headway with these logia until the stimulating short studies of W. Beardslee and N. Perrin, in which certain forms of proverbial statement are given special kerygmatic significance. The paradoxical formulation of the 'future reversal' form, for example, was taken to be a means of leading the hearer to a radical questioning of his existence.[4]

The most detailed recent study of any one type of aphoristic saying, however, is that of D. Zeller, who examines the 'wisdom admonitions'. Yet the conclusions reached from the form-critical aspects of his analysis are modest. Apart from identifying some stylistic tendencies to be associated with later tradition, and distinguishing the wisdom admonition from legal constructions, Zeller's main contention is that special significance is to be attributed to the direct second person plural admonitions.[5] Since the singular form of the admonition was most common in ancient wisdom literature, the prominence of the plural form in the synoptic tradition requires explanation. Zeller is prepared to argue that the use of the direct plural admonition is not usually an address to the Christian community, but is due to Jesus himself applying these warnings to *all* individuals. However, Zeller does have to admit exceptions to this theory.[6]

In 1983 J. D. Crossan produced another important study entitled *In Fragments: The Aphorisms of Jesus.* Crossan focuses not so much on individual forms as on a model for how the aphoristic tradition was applied and the processes by which it grew and became formulated in synoptic contexts. In a helpful way he elaborates the various possibilities which exist for an aphorism to come to expression in these contexts: single aphorisms being joined to form aphoristic compounds or clusters, isolated aphorisms being connected as conclusions to other linguistic forms, the use of aphorisms in dialogues and narrative so as to create aphoristic dialogues or aphoristic stories. This detailed study, however, has not yet led Crossan to a discussion of the originality of the traditions or to summary observations about the various influences of synoptic sources or stages of tradition.

Crossan is likely to be correct in putting his emphasis on the application of aphoristic traditions and on ways in which they come to expression rather than simply on a classification of individual forms of proverbial sayings. While distinctive individual forms may yield some results of interest, it is the actual application of the sayings in synoptic contexts that is most likely to reveal the role of practical wisdom and any conscious interest in its use amongst early Christians. Just as we have found that the way in which certain aphoristic 'clusters' were compiled has been very revealing and distinctive for a given stage of synoptic tradition, so also the key to the more diffuse use of aphoristic sayings may come in the application of the sayings and the purposes for which they are used. The association of smaller units, such as isolated aphorisms, with larger contexts can be an important indication of compilational activity.

The necessity of such an approach to the aphoristic sayings material is clear. Too seldom have questions about the actual use and significance of these particular sayings been investigated. While exegetical studies of many of the relevant passages are numerous, the questions treated have often given little place to understanding what contribution the aphoristic material itself makes. By asking these questions, new insights into the passages themselves are possible, as well as into the sapiential traditions which are represented.

2. Isolated wisdom admonitions

A considerable difference exists between the wisdom admonition and those aphoristic sayings in statement form. Formally, the wisdom admonition is a generally formulated imperative, usually followed by a supporting clause which is also formulated as a general statement.[7] With respect to function, the admonition is suited either for general encouragement or for exhortation in situations where some bolstering by brief argument may be advantageous. The majority of the aphoristic collections studied in the preceding chapter began with exhortations of this kind,[8] to be followed by more elaborate argument, and this raises the possibility of some kinship of function between the more isolated wisdom admonitions and these collections.

Apart from those admonitions appearing in the collections, there are three important instances of wisdom admonitions from the double tradition: Mt 6:19–21/Lk 12:33b, 34, on laying up incorruptible treasure in heaven; Mt 5:25–6/Lk 12:58–9, on making friends with one's accuser; and Mt 7:13–14/Lk 13:23–4, on entering by the narrow gate. Each will prove worthy of closer analysis.[9]

Mt 6:19–21/Lk 12:33b–34

μὴ θησαυρίζετε ὑμῖν θησαυροὺς ἐπὶ τῆς γῆς,
ὅπου σὴς καὶ βρῶσις ἀφανίζει,
καὶ ὅπου κλέπται διορύσσουσιν καὶ κλέπτουσιν.
θησαυρίζετε δὲ ὑμῖν θησαυροὺς ἐν τοῖς οὐρανοῖς,
ὅπου οὔτε σὴς οὔτε βρῶσις ἀφανίζει,
καὶ ὅπου κλέπται οὐ διορύσσουσιν οὐδὲ κλέπτουσιν·
ὅπου γάρ ἐστιν ὁ θησαυρός σου, ἐκεῖ ἔσται καὶ ἡ καρδία
σου.

The greater originality of Matthew's formulation of this saying has been widely recognized, even if Matthew's immediate context should prove secondary, as argued earlier.[10] In both Matthew and Luke, the passage is composed of two distinct units (Mt 6:19–20 par and Mt 6:21 par), which is evident by the switch from plural to singular in Matthew. The combination would appear to have occurred early in the tradition.[11] The result is a symmetrically balanced double warning, concluded by an observation about the relationship of one's treasure and one's heart. The imagery of θησαυρός ('treasure') is the connecting link.

In terms of argument, W. Pesch[12] suggests that the emphasis lies less on the negative warning against acquiring material riches than on 'das entscheidende Wort' of Mt 6:21. The accent lies on recognizing where one's heart is to be found, a saying which lacks contemporary parallels.[13] This motivation in Mt 6:21, therefore, alters the force of Mt 6:19–20. By itself, Mt 6:19–20 par contrasts the relative merits of earthly and heavenly treasure and contains its own implicit argument in favour of that which presents the more lasting investment. It is ironically a rather 'down-to-earth' appeal not to commit oneself to what is easily lost.[14] How far it draws upon early Christian prophetic-eschatological teaching is less certain. The rejection of material wealth is found in Jewish apocalyptic (see 1 En 38:2, 94:7–10; PssSol 9:5; 4 Ezra 6:5–6, 7:77, 8:33; 2 Bar 14:12; 2 En 50:5).[15] Yet in Mt 6: 19–20 par, while the imagery alludes to heavenly rewards, there is no direct judgement upon earthly treasure itself as 'unrighteous'. There is no direct, radical rejection of riches here. Earthly treasure is not 'unrighteous'; it is corruptible and temporary. So the appeal of the exhortations in Mt 6:19–20 par is more a practical reckoning of better alternatives than obedience to an authoritative or radical demand. Such an attitude towards material wealth is not unknown in Jewish wisdom literature (see Prov 23:4–5; Sir 29:10ff.).[16]

How far is this altered by Mt 6:21 par ('For where your treasure is, there will your heart be also')? Here any allusions to mere self-interest in Mt 6:19−20 are dispelled. As such it provides an important development in the argument, which directs attention away from self-interest to self-examination in the choice which confronts one. That on which the 'heart' is set is of ultimate concern. Yet such ultimate concerns are commended to the readers by citing a general principle which carries its own power of conviction. In this sense, it is still an appeal to reason. There is still no need for any explicit outside authority to be invoked, even though the new loyalty to which the hearer is called may be outside himself. The eschatological themes in their most general sense ('treasure in heaven') in Mt 6:19−20 par are the expression of that to which the hearer is called, but the absence of any explicit eschatological appeal in Mt 6:21 par makes clear that an imminent coming judgement is not the ultimate sanction or motive behind the exhortation.[17]

Both the exhortation and the development of argument bear noticeable similarities to two of the aphoristic sayings-collections. The similarity with Lk 16:9ff. has already been discussed with respect to those sayings.[18] Temporal wealth is contrasted with true (heavenly) riches, and one is finally led to an explicit choice as to where one's loyalties lie − with God or with worldly riches (cf. Mt 6:24/Lk 16:13). Both in Lk 16:9−13 and in Mt 6:19−21 par the theme concerns attitudes towards the use of wealth rather than its renunciation, although the final argument confronts the hearer with a stark choice of loyalties. Both encourage not so much any one specific action regarding wealth as, rather, a general orientation regarding the ultimate 'good' in which one should trust.

This orientation is also not far removed from that of the collection in Mt 6:25−33/Lk 12:22−31. Anxiety about material goods is shown to be useless. A greater priority claims one's loyalty (cf. Lk 12:31 par).[19] In both Matthew and Luke, the wisdom admonition in Mt 6: 19−21/Lk 12:33−4 is found in close proximity to this collection, which suggests that the similarity in theme and outlook was also recognized by the early compilers of the traditions.[20] It is, therefore, difficult to avoid the impression of a considerable overlap in the perspectives expressed by these three double-tradition passages.

Mt 5:25−6/Lk 12:58−9

ἴσθι εὐνοῶν τῷ ἀντιδίκῳ σου [ταχὺ] ἕως ὅτου εἶ μετ᾽ αὐτοῦ
 ἐν τῇ ὁδῷ,
μήποτέ σε παραδῷ ὁ ἀντίδικος τῷ κριτῇ,
καὶ ὁ κριτὴς τῷ ὑπηρέτῃ,
καὶ εἰς φυλακὴν βληθήσῃ·
λέγω σοι, οὐ μὴ ἐξέλθῃς ἐκεῖθεν ἕως ἂν ἀποδῷς τὸν
 ἔσχατον κοδράντην.

Considerable differences in the formulation, context and function of this logion in Matthew and in Luke hinder attempts to gain a clear understanding of its use in the underlying tradition.[21] Schulz argues that the wording in Matthew is largely to be preferred,[22] but he considers the context in both gospels to be secondary.[23] The differences in context reflect the very different applications made by the two evangelists.

In Luke the admonition is joined to the double-tradition saying in Lk 12:54ff. about interpreting τὸν καιρὸν τοῦτον on analogy with interpreting the skies. This unit is then followed in Lk 13:1ff. by special material about Pilate's persecution of Galileans. Luke thus indicates that the admonition is a warning to the ὑποκριταί ('hypocrites') to settle now with their accuser, who is presumbly either God himself or his representative, in the face of a coming judgement. In the light of Lk 13:1ff., this judgement is at least in part related to the political situation of the Jewish nation under Roman rule.[24]

In contrast to Luke's, Matthew's gospel applies this admonition not to the situation of Jews generally, but to followers of Jesus. It appears in the context of the Sermon on the Mount as an exhortation to be reconciled to one's *brother* (see Mt 5:21−6).[25]

In attempting to determine which context provides the more original sense for the saying, many scholars have tended to regard Luke as closer to the original.[26] This is in part based upon a supposed tendency of the tradition to apply ethical interpretations to earlier polemical material.[27] A contrasting view was expressed, however, by A. Jülicher,[28] who argued that the admonition had the original sense of Mt 5:39−40 (turning the other cheek), in which the offended or accused party is not to resist his accuser but to be reconciled to him.

This difference of interpretation demonstrates the influence of the context on the meaning of the saying; but where it is not possible to choose between the contexts provided by Matthew and by Luke with any measure of probability, one must then search for clues in the actual formulation of the saying. There are in fact some indications of this kind which incline one towards the early suggestion of Jülicher.

First, even in Luke's context the second person singular formulation of the admonition stands in uneasy contrast to the plural address of the polemic against the ὑποκριταί in Lk 12:54ff. (cf. Mt 16:2−3). This is therefore an indication that the admonition about reconciliation has no necessary connection with the polemical context in Luke.[29]

Secondly, the language of the admonition itself is not wholly polemical. Certainly the warning is strongly expressed by a threat of 'imprisonment' in Mt 5:25/Lk 12:58 which is reiterated in Mt 5:26/Lk 12:59. Yet this warning remains couched in the imagery set by the saying as a whole, dealing as it does with an accuser, a judge, an officer. It never emerges into a direct identification of the addressees or into a direct confrontation, such as would be more characteristic of prophetic speech. On formal grounds, Zeller shows little hesitation about describing Mt 5:25 par as a wisdom admonition.[30] So far as the concluding clause in Mt 5:26 par is concerned, he surmises: 'ein gängiger jüdischer Spruch auf seiner späteren Stufe durch Zusatz von v.26 eschatologischen Hintersinn bekam ... Überhaupt ist der eschatologische Bezug sehr verschlüsselt und eigentlich erst in einem entsprechend ausgerichteten literarischen Kontext wahrnehmbar.'[31] S. Schulz describes it simply as 'ein kommentierendes Abschlusswort'.[32] If this is so, the veiled eschatological features may themselves be a later addition to the wisdom admonition, and even so of limited significance. In support of the character of the saying as a wisdom admonition, Zeller also notes parallels in the Jewish wisdom literature, such as Sir 18:20; Prov 6:1−5, 25:7b−10.[33] Yet unlike Prov 25:7b−10 the encouragement to reconciliation in the synoptic admonition is not in order to escape shame, and unlike Sir 18:20 it does not stress the need to examine oneself before judgement. It is closest to Prov 6:1ff., where one must save oneself from one's neighbour's power. This is the motive which gives rise to the active efforts to appease one's accuser. Thus it serves as a prudential warning and not necessarily as a polemical attack on opponents.

Thirdly, reconciliation in the admonition does seem to be most easily interpreted as towards one's fellow-man rather than as directly towards God. There is no decoding of the imagery in the saying itself, but the distinctions made between ὁ ἀντίδικος, ὁ κριτής and the 'officer' are significant. They suggest that ὁ ἀντίδικος is not

God himself, for the latter would be more appropriately ὁ κριτής, if here at all. So the reconciliation seems to be with a human enemy. In this sense, the main thrust of the admonition may not be dissimilar to that of the 'love-of-enemies' admonition in the sayings collection, Mt 5:44–8 (cf. Lk 6:27–36). A parallel theme is again established between an individual wisdom admonition and one of the double-tradition aphoristic sayings-collections.

Mt 7:13–14/Lk 13:23–4

εἰσέλθατε διὰ τῆς στενῆς πύλης·
ὅτι πολλοὶ ζητήσουσιν εἰσελθεῖν,
καὶ ὀλίγοι εὑρήσουσιν αὐτήν.
(Following the reconstruction by A. Polag)[34]

Once again variations in both formulation and context have hindered attempts to reconstruct the tradition underlying the admonition. Both Matthew and Luke do place the saying in close conjunction to the saying about exclusion from the kingdom (Mt 7:22–3/Lk 13: 26–7), and this common association also lends support to the contention that the evangelists present two varying forms of a single underlying logion. But the original formulation of that admonition is still an open question.[35] Some agreement in wording does exist for the imperative itself (Mt 7:13a/Lk 13:24a: εἰσέλθατε διὰ τῆς στενῆς πύλης/θύρας), in which the main variations are the ἀγωνίζεσθε in Luke[36] and the difference between θύρα in Luke and πύλη in Matthew. Verbal agreement diminishes markedly, however, in the supporting statements introduced by ὅτι. The common reference to many (πολλοί) wishing to enter (εἰσελθεῖν) and the common idea that only a few (ὀλίγοι) will succeed are the main agreement in this clause.

The variations in wording are not unrelated to the different uses to which the admonition is put in the two gospels. In Matthew's gospel, the critical point is a choice between *two* ways. The nature of each way therefore requires and receives elaboration.[37] This choice between the two ways is ultimately a call to heed the high requirement of the teaching of Jesus which has preceded in the Sermon, although the question of entrance into the kingdom would also appear to rest on such a decision (cf. Mt 7:22–3).[38] Mt 7:13–14 itself provides the transition from the teaching of the Sermon, summarized finally in the Golden Rule (7:12), to the concluding warnings to heed Jesus' words (7:13–27).[39] This call to choose the difficult way of obedience is reinforced by a warning about the 'broad' way which leads to destruction for those who do not heed the teaching.[40]

In Luke's gospel the context is very different. Lk 13:22–30 is directed to the question of who will enter the kingdom of God. It is raised anonymously in Lk 13:22 as Jesus 'journeyed towards Jerusalem' with the question 'Lord, will those who are saved be few?' This prompts the answer to 'strive'[41] to enter by the narrow door, with the accompanying prediction that many will seek to enter and not be able. The latter point is illustrated by the slightly differing image of the *closed* door in Lk 13:25–7 (cf. Mt 7:22–3). The significance of many not entering is explained finally in Lk 13:28–9, 30 (cf. Mt 8:11–12), when reference is made to the rejection of the Jews in favour of men from the east, west, north and south. The many who do not enter the narrow door are therefore above all the Jews who have rejected Jesus, although there may also indirectly be a more general perspective in this passage.[42]

What, then, is the context in the underlying tradition? Has Luke correctly reproduced it in Lk 13:(22), 23–4, 25–7, 28–9 (30)? Strongly contrasting positions have been taken by P. Hoffmann and A. Denaux on this question. Hoffmann argues that Lk 13:22–30 was largely the compilation of the Lukan redactor from individual units of tradition.[43] Denaux, on the other hand, attributes to the 'Q-Redaktor' the addition of the small sayings-collection in Lk 13:24–30 par to the double Parables of the Mustard Seed and Leaven in 13:18–21 (cf. Mt 13:31–3). The collection of sayings in Lk 13:24–30 par balances the sense of certainty of the coming kingdom expressed in the parables with the necessary warning that it is not entered from the human side without repentance and moral effort. Admission to a meal is the motif which holds Lk 13:24–9 together.[44]

Hoffmann's view would appear to be difficult to support. First, it has already been noticed that Lk 13:23–4, 26–7 (cf. Mt 7:13–14, 22–3) preserves a sequence which is also found in Matthew. It therefore must be pre-Lukan. More doubtful is the early presence of Lk 13:25 (cf. Mt 25:10–12), however, which Hoffmann has rightly shown can only be attributed to Q with difficulty, and which in any case presents an awkward transition from Lk 13:24 par to 13:26–7 par.[45]

Secondly, Denaux demonstrates that there is a second common sequence shared by Matthew and Luke which extends to include

Lk 13:28–9/Mt 8:11–12, following Lk 13:26–7/Mt 7:22–3.[46] The transition from Lk 13:26–7 par to 13:28–9 par is made easier by Luke's form of verses 26–7, but S. Schulz[47] has independently argued in favour of Luke's formulation of this saying in any case. Matthew's application of the logion to false (Christian) prophets (cf. Mt 7:15, 22–3) appears to be a recurring concern of this evangelist and would explain why he separates the saying from Mt 8:11–12. In Luke, and perhaps in the earlier tradition, the saying is a warning to the Jews who have rejected Jesus. This leads easily to the comment on the expulsion of the Jews from the kingdom in Lk 13:28–9 par.

This context allows one to return to the question of the interpretation of the admonition in Lk 13:24 par itself. The question posed in Lk 13:23 about whether the number to be saved will be few is widely accepted as secondary.[48] Yet the formulations of the admonition in both Matthew and Luke have in common a contrast between the πολλοί and the ὀλίγοι, and in both the point is made that only few will enter the narrow entrance. Whether the more balanced 'two ways' formulation of Matthew is secondary or not,[49] there is a pessimism about the fate of the 'many'. This may be related to the later description of the rejection of the Jews. Yet in both gospels the imperative itself is a *positive* command.[50] So in the context of the admonition, even the pessimism about the salvation of the few serves as a positive prompting to choose the narrow way rather than simply being a cause of despair or a result of eschatological gloom. The imperative is a call actively to approach the difficult way of commitment.[51]

If the double-tradition context is preserved in Lk 13:(23), 24, 26–7, 28–9, the sequence of thought appears to unfold from a general imperative about facing the difficult way of commitment (Lk 13:(23), 24), to a warning against those who try to gain admission to the kingdom by the 'easy' way of mere 'association' with Jesus (also applying subsequently to Christian followers?), to a final clear warning about the expulsion of the Jews in favour of men from afar. The opening admonition prevents the entire sequence from being simply an announcement of judgement on the Jews. It contains a positive call to an admittedly difficult way. Judgement is the consequence for those who refuse to take it.[52] The instruction, therefore, is not simply aimed at opponents, but at those who still *might* respond to the positive call to commitment or perhaps have made a response which is still judged to be insufficient (cf. Lk 13:26–7). The rejection sayings are a warning of the hopelessness of any attempt at an easy compromise which fails to make a real break with this iniquitous generation of Jews who have largely rejected Jesus.

Ideas about the fate of men at the End of the age seem to have influenced the imagery in this section, and attention is often directed to 4 Ezra 7:6–8, 12–16.[53] The imagery, however, is somewhat differently used in 4 Ezra 7, where there is no real choice of an easy way in this life for men (4 Ezra 7:1, 7–8). The righteous man reconciles himself to the hardships of the present by keeping in mind the 'broad and safe' entrance to the greater world (7:13, 18). Nevertheless, 'many' will not have even this hope (7:20); and later, in 4 Ezra 8:13, one finds the statement: 'Many have been created but few will be saved.' In contrast with this pessimism, however, the gospel admonition more clearly presents a real choice in the present. The positive appeal which it makes distinguishes it from the thought of 4 Ezra; and, if J. D. M. Derrett is correct, then the image of the narrow gate may even evoke other images from everyday commercial life.[54] There are also striking parallels between the choice of two ways in Matthew and that in the *Tabula* of Cebes.[55]

The difficult way which the would-be follower must willingly confront is not elaborated in the admonition. The saying in Lk 13:26–7/ Mt 7:22–3 makes clear that it involves more than a casual confession. If followers faced material uncertainties and hostile opposition, as suggested by the aphoristic sayings-collections in Mt 6:25–33 par, 7:7–11 par and 10:26–33 par, then these might easily shed further light on the 'difficult way' indicated here. Thus, this wisdom admonition may be considered another which is complementary to the themes and argument of the larger aphoristic collections of the double tradition. Before this significant point is pursued further, however, we must consider other kinds of wisdom admonitions.

Other types of wisdom admonition

The classification of 'wisdom admonition' can be extended to include admonitions whose formulation departs from that considered above.[56] For example, there are two instances from the double tradition of admonitions where a general exhortation is constructed in conjunction with a *simile*, and both appear to come in the same aphoristic sayings-collection: the Golden Rule (Lk 6:31 par) and the exhortation to be merciful (Mt: 'perfect') as your heavenly Father is merciful (Lk 6:36 par). The presence at an early stage of the Golden Rule saying in the collection about love of enemies is not completely certain, but the compatibility of the saying with the theme of the collection has been discussed earlier and is of course recognized by Luke (cf. above, pp. 78–80).

Zeller argues that another type of wisdom admonition is that in which a general and widely applicable exhortation is presented *without any supporting clause*.[57] The presence of such instructions in the double tradition is of particular interest because it is contrary to the tendency which has previously been observed of using generally expressed admonitions in conjunction with careful and persuasive argument. Unsupported general admonitions are in fact rare in the material of the double tradition, but two instances should be discussed.

The first also occurs in close proximity to the collection of sayings on love of enemies. This is the set of admonitions about non-retaliation in Mt 5:39ff./Lk 6:29–30.[58] While the theme of non-retaliation bears no necessary relation to love of enemies,[59] it is complementary to the teaching on love of enemies, as both Matthew and Luke suggest.

Without any motivation clauses, the admonitions are clear, authoritative and challenging.[60] However, at some stage in the underlying tradition the sayings, still formulated in the singular, were brought together with the collection of sayings on love of enemies. In this context, they indirectly share the reasoned support which was absent previously.[61] This holds true even if the sayings of Mt 5: 39–40, 42 par were located outside the collection itself, as argued earlier.[62] The instruction on non-retaliation becomes a further demonstration of love of enemies, and the arguments advanced for the latter are effectively conferred by association on the former once the two sets of sayings have been brought together. There is no need to consider this joining of units only at the time of a compilation of the Q-material as a whole; it may have occurred at any time after the formulation of the sayings collection on love of enemies. The eventual conjunction in the tradition testifies to a merging of the interests expressed by these isolated general admonitions and one of the aphoristic collections.

Another significant point is to be noticed in the admonitions on non-retaliation. Amidst these exhortations is a general instruction on giving (Mt 5:42/Lk 6:30). The instruction about giving and lending in Mt 5:42 par may originally have been separate from the non-retaliation material.[63] The clause 'give to him who asks you'[64] is not directly concerned with retaliation or enemy at all. In its present context, its effect is to widen the concern beyond that of enemy to include anyone in need.[65] This clause, therefore, is significant because it sits so loosely to the theme of non-retaliation.[66] How is this to be explained?

It is doubtful that this call to 'give to him who asks' softens any of these demands by appeal to the more conventional piety of alms-giving. The other radical demands are still allowed to stand, and even this demand is challenging by its very breadth. It is more likely, therefore, that the bearers of the tradition saw some association of thought between 'giving' and a situation of hostility. If this is so, it cannot be assumed that it is hostile outsiders alone who are in mind. It may, indeed, be hostile outsiders who sue for one's goods, but the call to 'give to him who asks from you' is broad and suggests a relationship sufficiently close for the petitioner to have certain expectations of one. This impression is reinforced if one accepts S. Schulz's reconstruction of the following clause in Mt 5:42 par: καὶ τὸν θέλοντα ἀπὸ σοῦ δανείσθαι, μὴ ἀποστραφῇς.[67] The theme of lending reappears in Lk 6:34—5 and may therefore be reminiscent of the underlying source for Lk 6:30/Mt 5:42.[68] If lending is in view in this clause, then this also suggests that the saying applies to one's closer associates, perhaps including fellow-Christians.[69]

The instructions about giving and lending take one from actively seeking to meet the unreasonable demands of those hostile to one (Mt 5:39—40 par)[70] to being open to *any* claim on one's goods. Here again the question of one's attitude to material possessions arises, such as was also argued to underlie some of the aphoristic sayings collections. It is significant that a concern with material goods is at least, if not more, prominent in the admonitions in Mt 5:39—40, 42 par than the theme of physical abuse. Finding a setting which accounts for the association of these themes will be taken up below (pp. 184—92).

A second example of a double-tradition admonition without a sup-porting motivation, but which has been sometimes classified as a 'wisdom admonition', is Lk 17:3b, 4/Mt 18:15, 21—2. Whether stylistically this corresponds to a wisdom admonition is doubtful. Accepting the arguments in favour of the greater originality of Luke's formulation of the saying,[71] one finds that the unit comprises a threefold instruction about the rebuke of one's brother if he sins against one, the forgiveness of him if he repents, and repeated forgiveness in the case of repeated wrongs. Each imperative is set with a conditional clause, which gives the appearance of a casuistic form.[72] Nevertheless, Zeller has argued here for the presence of a sapiential style. He notes in particular the closer relationship of this saying to TGad 6:3−4, 6−7 than to either Lev 19:17b or the community rules of Qumran. In the Testament of Gad, he argues, the conditional sequence of instruction is 'im weisheitlichen Stil' and draws upon supporting reasons for the commands to forgive (TGad 6:3−4, 6−7).[73] The absence of any supporting argument in the synoptic passage, however, does cast doubt upon its 'wisdom style'. Even Zeller has to concede that this passage may testify to the union of wisdom and Torah familiar in the milieu of the time.[74] Certainly it is doubtful whether Lk 17:3b, 4 stylistically falls into the pattern of the other admonitions which we have considered. It contrasts markedly with the highly metaphorical admonition about reconciliation in Mt 5:25−6/Lk 12:58−9. This different style may be explicable above all in terms of its more closely prescribed purpose. It deals less with challenging the orientation of the hearer or winning his adherence than with setting forth a specific way of responding to an erring and repenting brother.[75]

Summary and comparison

What, then, emerges from this brief investigation? Certainly most of these double-tradition wisdom admonitions draw upon themes which recall those of the aphoristic sayings collections. At times the correspondence in theme is very close (cf. especially Mt 6:19−21/Lk 12:33−4; Mt 7:13−14/Lk 13:23−4; Mt 5:39ff./Lk 6:29−30). This rather surprising observation bolsters the hypothesis that these aphoristic traditions reflect concerns and a setting similar to those of the aphoristic collections. In the case of Mt 6:19−21 par[76] and Mt 5:39ff. par, it would appear that a direct joining of admonition and sayings collections may have taken place even in the tradition preceding the gospels.

The most important exception to these results is the saying in Lk 17:3−4 par. Yet, although it is considered a wisdom admonition (without a supporting argument) by Zeller, it is distinct in both form and metaphorical 'openness' from many of the other admonitions. It would appear that other influences and concerns are at work in this passage, resulting in an authoritative instruction in plain words.

Despite the challenge of most of these admonitions, there is again a general lack of direct or imminent eschatological appeal. The hearer is called to be reconciled with his enemy/accuser, to give without seeking repayment, not to lay up worldly treasures, and to embark on a difficult way. Alongside these challenges there may, indeed, appear to be allusions to judgement or to the heavenly sphere. One is warned of being hauled before the judge and imprisoned, or told to lay up treasure in heaven, or presented with the consequences of not entering by the narrow gate. Further, these general allusions to judgement, while basically non-polemical, do seem more pointed than such allusions were in most of the longer sayings collections, excepting Mt 10:26−33 par, where one's very discipleship was at stake. In most of the longer sayings collections, progress is made slowly from experiential observation towards an encouragement, for example, to 'seek the kingdom of God' (Mt 6:33 par). In the short isolated admonitions, however, the insight is necessarily telescoped and presented more pointedly. Yet, despite the more prominent eschatological allusions, these remain encoded in the metaphors of the familiar and everyday features of life. As a result, these admonitions are still capable of new and different applications (see especially Mt 5:25−6/Lk 12:58−9).

The function of these allusions can be described more closely for the admonitions in Mt 6:19−21/Lk 12:33−4 (laying up treasure in heaven) and Mt 7:13−14/Lk 13:23−4 (entering by the narrow gate). In these instances, the admonitions use the imagery of the heavenly sphere or judgement to contribute to contrasts which confront the hearer with a choice. The eschatological allusions help to point to the significance of that choice. But it is not presented as a simple choice between 'this world' or the 'world to come'. It is always on a this-worldly basis that one makes the decision. The form of the wisdom admonition is not undermined. One's past experience is not ignored or discounted. It is testimony to the strength of the tradition of practical wisdom behind these exhortations that *the effort to justify radical demands to accept this-worldly vulnerability is made in terms of this-worldly wisdom.*

How far, though, are these features peculiar to the material of the double tradition, as distinct from the rest of the synoptic tradition? A brief comparison with the wisdom admonitions in Mark certainly reveals some differences in style.

Admonitions in Mark's gospel, unlike those of the double tradition, are often expressed as promoting attitudes or conduct which relate specifically to the religious life of the follower, both individually and as a member of a Christian community.[77] For example, the two admonitions in Mk 11:24−5 both show a particular interest in 'prayer'. The first deals with 'asking' in prayer and the assurance that prayer *accompanied by belief* (cf. Mk 11:23) will be answered. While the theme of asking and receiving recalls that of Mt 7:7–11 par, 'asking' in the Markan context is not related to practical questions of material provision, but to the greater acts of faith typified by 'moving mountains' (11:23). In Mk 11:25, the admonition is about forgiving one another, but such forgiveness is again to be offered as one prays and with the explicit hope that the Father will in turn forgive oneself.[78] These explicit expressions of piety give a slightly different emphasis to the arguments from experience found in the double-tradition aphoristic sayings.

The admonitions in Mk 9:43, 45, 47–8 are concerned with another obligation of piety, the avoidance of 'sin',[79] which is not found in the double-tradition admonitions. This concern for Christian purity and for the abandonment of sinful hindrances in Mk 9 is explicit, as is the direct and intense eschatological warning. The latter is expressed in strong and vivid images, warning of being cast into the unquenchable fires of hell on the one hand (43b, 45b, 48) or promising entrance to the kingdom of God on the other (47b). General eschatological sanctions tended to remain encoded in the imagery of the admonitions of the double tradition (cf. Mt 5:25–6 par), but no such reserve is found in these sayings in Mk 9:43ff.[80]

The final instruction of the series of admonitions in Mk 9, however, is surprisingly different. The admonition in Mk 9:50b does remain general in imagery and application: 'Have salt in yourselves, and be at peace with one another.' But here the metaphor is so open-ended as to be virtually an enigma in this context.[81] Further, in terms of argument, it seems to lack any support or persuasive commendation, so that it cannot really be said to argue a case for any behaviour or attitude. It simply presents the general exhortation.[82] If the second clause is a legitimate guide, however, the theme is to encourage peace in the Christian community in quite general terms.[83]

Relationships in the Christian community may also be the concern of two further important sayings in Mark, which are very similar to each other:

εἴ τις θέλει πρῶτος εἶναι ἔσται πάντων ἔσχατος καὶ πάντων διάκονος.

(Mk 9:35b)

ἀλλ᾽ ὃς ἂν θέλῃ μέγας γενέσθαι ἐν ὑμῖν, ἔσται ὑμῶν
διάκονος,
καὶ ὃς ἂν θέλῃ ἐν ὑμῖν εἶναι πρῶτος, ἔσται πάντων δοῦλος.
(Mk 10:43–4)

In both logia the contrast between the first and the last (cf. also Mk 10:31) seems to have been mixed with the motif of service. In both contexts in Mark the logia are responses to disputes among disciples about which would be greatest. The problem, therefore, is associated with relationships among followers,[84] and this problem has emerged also in several logia of the double tradition which we have studied. Yet, again important differences exist, particularly in the form of argument. The sayings here in Mark are indeed only 'admonitions' if one takes the future indicative tense in the sense of an imperative.[85] More importantly, the encouragement to self-denial is without any motivation clause in Mk 9:35, and the supporting clause provided for 10:43–4 is the very interesting saying in 10:45, which makes direct appeal to the example of the Son of Man who came to serve rather than to be served and to give his life as a ransom for many. The saying, therefore, is given an overtly christological and soteriological point of reference, looking ahead to the Passion.[86] So, in neither of these sayings has Mark shown any obvious desire for experiential argument.[87] The rather intense demands of self-denial and religious faithfulness are for the most part not to be argued out from the pattern of ordinary human existence.[88]

Although the wisdom admonitions peculiar to Matthew and Luke can be only briefly considered, here too it is possible to observe distinctions. Matthew tends to preserve much of the orientation of the admonitions taken over from Mark. He adds several further general admonitions which are found only in his gospel, yet these are often specially concerned with matters of Jewish piety.[89] The instructions about oaths (5:34ff.), almsgiving (6:1–4), prayer (6:5–6, 7–8), and fasting (6:16–18) not only express concerns of Jewish piety, but in the latter instances are set in contrast with the hypocritical practice of such piety. Experiential argument occasionally enters the presentation of these instructions (cf. 5:36–7), but often the presentation reflects the style of works in which wisdom had become wed with Jewish piety and the Torah.[90] Even the general admonition to be reconciled to one's brother if he has something against one (5:23–4) is set in the context of presenting one's gift at the altar.[91] In Mt 23:8–10, instructing against the use of titles amongst followers, the application of specifically Jewish practice is again observed (see 23:8: 'rabbi').[92] Such a close relationship between wisdom and Jewish law and practice is not a prominent feature of the admonitions of the double tradition.

A more universal or experiential presentation, however, is found in two admonitions in Matthew. One is the double simile construction in Mt 10:16b: 'Be wise as serpents and innocent as doves.' This is used in the context of the hostility encountered in mission (cf. 10:16a). The saying is significant both for its explicit commendation of being 'wise' and for the *qualifying* commendation of purity. This is presented in an almost paradoxical combination, illustrated by the contrasting figures of the serpent and the dove. Even if the saying comes to the Jewish tradition from profane usage,[93] it is remarkable in how it serves partially to reconcile the contrasting attitudes towards the 'wise' found in the synoptic tradition (cf. Mt 11:25 par, 23:34 par). Matthew's use of it effectively suggests that wisdom can be commended if joined with purity. Such a qualification of wisdom is not found in the double-tradition material.

The second wisdom admonition peculiar to Matthew which shows a more universal and experiential style is in Mt 6:34: 'Therefore do not be anxious about tomorrow, for tomorrow will be anxious for itself. Let the day's own trouble be sufficient for the day.' The admonition immediately follows the sayings in Mt 6:25–33 (cf. Lk 12:22–31) about not being anxious for material provisions. The admonition in Mt 6:34 is supported by a fatalistic observation about human experience, not dissimilar to the outlook of the unique Matthean material supporting the warning against the making of oaths (Mt 5:36). While in the collected sayings in Mt 6:25–33 it is argued that the future lies in the general providential care of God, Mt 6:34 suggests man's inability to affect his future at all.[94] This abandonment to providence is tempered by the context in Matthew, which is set by the double-tradition collection.[95]

In Luke's gospel, one does discover a greater tendency to achieve a universality of statement and application for admonitions. Luke omits on occasion a Markan admonition which does not have such general reference (e.g. Mk 11:24–5, 9:43–8) or alters the Markan form so as to indicate a wider basis of support or application for the instruction (Lk 22:26–7; cf. Mk 10:43–5). Yet very few wisdom admonitions derive from Lukan special material. D. Zeller[96] identifies only two: Lk 14:8–10 (on places at table), and Lk 14:12–14 (on the invitation of outcasts to the feast). The themes of humility and sharing with the poor express common Lukan interests, although there is no evidence that these sayings are created by Luke himself. The sayings probably derive from his special tradition.[97] Luke unites the two admonitions in Lk 14:8–10, 12–14 by means of a 'future reversal' proverb. This proverb, which also appears in other contexts in the synoptic tradition,[98] declares that he who exalts himself will be humbled, and he who humbles himself will be exalted. The rabbinic tradition provides a further interesting parallel to Luke's procedure of linking advice on the ranking of places at table with a reversal saying on the exaltation of the humble.[99] In Luke, however, the entire section is given an explicit End-time reference by verse 14, in which reward is promised ἐν τῇ ἀναστάσει τῶν δικαίων.[100] Luke, therefore, does not hesitate to reinforce his instructions with direct and explicit appeal to eschatological reward.

This was also observed in Luke's treatment of some double-tradition material. It has been seen how Lk 12:58–9 was presented as a polemical pronouncement of judgement against the ὑποκριταί (12:56). Luke also appears to have accentuated the eschatological setting for the narrow door saying in 13:23–4 by its inclusion in a larger eschatological 'parable' in 13:25. This suggests that while Luke has preserved a form of these instructions which is quite open and general in terms of its potential applications, this has not precluded the evangelist's own efforts to apply these instructions to the particular issue of how one gains admission to the kingdom of God.[101]

There is in Luke, however, a general admonition followed by a supporting clause which is not analysed by Zeller.[102] It occurs in Lk 12:15: 'Take heed, and beware of all covetousness, for a man's life does not consist in the abundance of his possessions.' Here again Luke's concern about relying on possessions for one's security is expressed. This is an interesting example, because metaphorical or figurative qualities are largely lacking. It is a direct warning against covetousness, with a clear supporting clause. The setting seems to require a clear, authoritative declaration.[103]

The relative directness of this admonition, which may owe much to Luke himself, fits the picture of one who has been inspired to create so little of this kind of instruction. It would seem that Luke appreciated the literary power and the imaginative language of the instructions which he took from his sources, but he often used the openness of the imagery to apply the general exhortations to questions such as admissibility to the kingdom and the positive and negative responses of men to the kingdom. And when Luke was himself concerned to add an exhortation on a theme, it was in plain language for his readers to heed.[104] Although the use of wisdom admonitions in Luke probably kept closer to the nature of the double tradition than either Matthew or Mark, the characteristics of the double-tradition admonitions still stand out as distinct from the discernible efforts of any of the evangelists.

3. Isolated aphoristic sentences

Introduction

While wisdom admonitions speak the language of exhortation, aphoristic sentences often appear to be more detached observations. They often express insights rather than demands, although a challenge may be implied by the insight. Again it is essential to discover how the sayings are actually applied, for their metaphorical openness and applicability to a variety of contexts limit what can be learned from examining the sayings in complete isolation.

There are certainly some general indications that the use of aphoristic sayings in the synoptic tradition differs from that found in other literature of the ancient world. C. E. Carlston,[105] followed by J. Williams,[106] has drawn attention to a number of 'typical' themes of practical wisdom which are absent from the gospels. He bases his comparison on both Jewish wisdom literature and Graeco-Roman sources from outside Palestine. It is striking that in the synoptic tradition there is no explicit instruction to seek wisdom. Commendation of the virtues of character, warnings against follies,[107] exaltation of the golden mean of moderation, interest in sexual conduct and temptation, and concern with civil duties[108] are largely lacking. This restriction on the use of aphoristic insight would appear to be the result of the nature of the message of Jesus in the gospels and the interests of the early church, although the use of aphoristic sayings is by no means sparse.

These observations encourage one to try to discover more precisely what patterns exist for the use of such logia. As we turn to the scattered aphoristic statements outside the aphoristic sayings-collections, we shall endeavour to discover whether more evidence exists for the interests found in the double-tradition collections and whether it is also peculiar to the material of the double tradition. If so, these sayings may serve to confirm further our observations about the sapiential traditions at work in this double-tradition material.

The scope of this analysis, therefore, goes well beyond earlier and all too infrequent efforts to study aphorisms in the gospels. It is not concerned solely with the exegesis of the numerous passages containing aphoristic material, but also with the functions of the sayings and how far they conform to the patterns which we have begun to identify. Any such findings will be highly significant for the task of describing the sapiential traditions behind the gospel accounts.

Aphorisms used to defend or validate Jesus' ministry

The use of aphoristic sayings in 'controversy' stories is well attested in Mark's gospel. They are there used in response to questions about religious observance (2:17, 21–2, 27–8) as well as to personal attacks (3:23–7). While Mark can also show Jesus arguing from points of Law like the scribes (e.g., Mk 2:25–6), it is striking how the use of proverbs is even more prominent in these controversies in Mk 2–3 than legal argument. In general, the form of these proverbs in Mark depicts a contrast or something 'contrary to right order':[109]

'No one sews a piece of unshrunken cloth on an old garment' (2:21)

'No one puts new wine in old wineskins' (2:22)

'No one can enter a strong man's house and plunder his goods' (3:27)

'Those who are well have no need of a physician, but rather those who are sick' (2:17)

The absurdities or contradictions which are thereby exposed carry the argument. The opponent's challenge is shown to offend the normal order or practice. The defence is irrefutable, except conceivably by another proverb.

In Luke there is, indeed, an imagined controversy in which proverb and counter-proverb are quoted by both attacker and defender. Jesus quotes first a proverb which might be used against him ('Physician heal yourself') and then a proverb in response ('No prophet is acceptable in his own country'; Lk 4:23–4). Matthew also recognized the force of maxims in controversies, as shown in his adaptation of the double-tradition sayings about the blind leading the blind (15:14)[110] and about good and bad trees (12:33–5).[111] Few aphoristic statements peculiar to either Matthew or Luke are introduced into 'controversy' stories, although sometimes short parables or metaphors are applied in debates, often as a counter-question (e.g., Lk 7:41−2; Mt 17:25).[112]

The paucity of 'controversy' stories in the double tradition is itself of interest. If such controversy stories were, as Bultmann claimed,[113] one way by which the early Christians addressed issues of contention and concern within their church situations, then the relative scarcity of such stories in the double tradition requires some explanation. It is certainly true that the typical topics of such controversies in the gospels (viz. fasting, sabbath observance and ritual purity) play only a limited part in the opposition which Jesus faces from αὕτη ἡ γενεά throughout the double-tradition material.[114] However, it will become clear that issues of debate within the church are in fact often addressed by a different *means* in the double tradition. In place of stories about alleged controversies with opponents, one finds greater dependence on aphoristic teaching addressed to followers. Nevertheless, there is one important controversy story which must be considered, the 'Beelzebul' charge.

Mt 12:22−30/Lk 11:14−23
The 'Beelzebul' story provides a useful comparison between the approach to argument in Mark and that which appears to derive from a separate version, viz. the double tradition.[115]

Common features of Matthew and Luke which do not correspond to Mk 3:23−7 include the short exorcism account which introduces the controversy (Lk 11:14 par; but cf. also Mt 9:32−4), the reference to Jesus knowing his opponents' thoughts (Lk 11:17a par), the words πᾶσα βασιλεία, (δια)μερισθεῖσα and ἐρημοῦται in Lk 11:17 par, the phrase ἡ βασιλεία αὐτοῦ applying to Satan in Lk 11:18 par, and the inclusion in this context of Lk 11:19−20 par and 11:23 par. The number and strength of those agreements against Mark support the hypothesis of a distinct version of this story assignable to the double tradition.[116]

What is the significance of these differences from Mark? This only emerges on closer examination. For example, although both versions respond to the charges against Jesus with a maxim about the divided kingdom, there are differences in the formulation of that response. The initial rejoinder in Mark is 'How can Satan cast out Satan?' (3:23b), which serves from the outset as an interpretation for the maxims about divisions which follow in 3:24−5. The interpretation is finally restated, by reference again to Satan being against himself, in 3:26.[117] In contrast, Matthew and Luke have the *aphorisms themselves* as the initial rejoinder to the charge against Jesus. The general principle of the divided kingdom is stated at the outset (Lk 11:17 par) but only clarified later by specific application to Satan (Lk 11:18 par) and finally applied to the actual charge of casting out demons ἐν βεελζεβούλ only in Lk 11:19 par. This version, therefore, progresses in argument from a general principle to an increasingly specific application. This progression of argument is not unlike that of the aphoristic sayings-collections of the double tradition. In the Beelzebul pericope, however, the aphorisms simply provide the first stage in the progression.

The 'Beelzebul' pericope, however, does not end here. In Mark, the logion about binding the strong man is introduced next (Mk 3:27), providing a possible veiled allusion to Jesus as the Stronger One. W. G. Kümmel, for example, declares that the 'picture of the theft in the house of the strong man is doubtless intended as a metaphor; Satan is the strong man, Jesus is the stronger one who takes away from him those whom he dominates'.[118] Finally, Mark includes the blasphemy saying in 3:28–30 – an affirmation that Jesus is possessed by the Holy Spirit, not by the ruler of the demons (cf. 3:22), and a condemnation of the opponents who levelled the Beelzebul charge against Jesus, although it was perhaps meant to apply also to his family.[119]

The double-tradition version continues with noticeably different emphases. The evidence for a double-tradition version of the 'strong man' logion is uncertain.[120] The emphasis of the double-tradition version is not primarily claims *about* Jesus, but the question of *commitment to* what he represents (cf. Lk 11:23 par). Jesus did not exorcise by the power of Satan; rather he demonstrated the coming of God's kingdom. This establishes a contrast between Satan's kingdom (Lk 11:18 par)[121] and God's kingdom (Lk 11:20 par) and leads to the 'either–or' choice which is finally presented in Lk 11:23 par.[122] So, in Lk 11:20 par the positive claim is made that Jesus cast out demons by God's power, the power of God's kingdom.[123] Then follows the maxim 'He who is not with me is against me, and he who does not gather with me scatters' (Lk 11:23 par). This last saying may pick up the idea of 'divisions' found in the opening maxims, but it presents above all a challenge of commitment to Jesus. It faces the questioners with a decision; it does not rest with a condemnation of the questioners as in Mark. It puts them in a position in which even neutrality is excluded. This is an important extension of the earlier defensive argument.

The challenge in Lk 11:23 par is more radical than a similar saying in Mk 9:40. In Lk 11:23 par, it requires a positive decision 'for' Jesus, matching well the context in which it is assumed that those confronting him are not fully 'with' him.[124]

The basis on which this choice is presented is also very important to recognize. W. G. Kümmel[125] noted that Lk 11:19−20 par made little more claim for Jesus' authority than for that of *any* Jewish exorcist of his time. He argues therefore that the Q-context for the sayings cannot have been original. So what kind of argument has been created here? Clearly it gives only slight place to the *uniqueness* of Jesus' authority. Unlike Mark, which lacks these sayings, the distinctive feature of the double-tradition version of argument is that *unique* claims for Jesus are subordinate to more general persuasive reasons for accepting his *genuineness* as one who represents God's kingdom.[126] It is more important to show that Jesus' authority is valid than to show that it is unique. For this purpose, it is sufficient to show up the illogicality of the charges against Jesus. Even the challenge to accept his ministry is made on the basis that his ministry is *valid* rather than on the basis of a specific christological confession.[127] This basis of argument is therefore a distinctive feature of the double-tradition version of this controversy.

Another distinctive feature of the double-tradition account is how the Beelzebul pericope seems to have been joined eventually with pericopes on the return of the unclean spirit (Lk 11:24−6/Mt 12: 43−5) and the Sign of Jonah (Lk 11:29−32/Mt 12:39−42). These passages appear in close proximity in both Matthew and Luke; and, in view of Luke's tendency to preserve the order of his source-material, many favour his order here.[128] The union of these pericopes need not represent the same stage of compositional activity as the collection of logia in the 'Beelzebul' controversy. Nevertheless, it may shed light on subsequent early interpretations of the controversy story. What meaning had the 'Beelzebul' story for the early collectors of these traditions?

The relationship between the sayings about the return of the unclean spirit and the 'Beelzebul' story must be considered. R. Laufen[129] discusses a variety of explanations of Lk 11:24−6, including viewing it as an extension of the argument in 11:17−18 (E. Hirsch), a critique of Jewish exorcism (S. Schulz), a 'rule' of exorcism (P. Hoffmann), and an allegory of Jewish history (E. Käsemann). However, following Jülicher, Laufen himself observes that Lk 11:24−6 illustrates virtually as a 'parable' the challenge in 11:23:

'Das Tertium comparationis ... besteht in der Aussage, dass die Verneinung des Bösen (Bildhälfte: den unreinen Geist austreiben – Sachhälfte: kein Feind Jesu sein) noch nicht das Gute (Bildhälfte: Sicherheit vor der Rückkehr des unreinen Geistes – Sachhälfte: Jünger Jesu sein) ist.'[130]

Laufen thus rightly argues that in Q the focus has moved away from addressing the opponents of Jesus, to a new theme in Lk 11:23, 24–6 par, addressing the question of commitment to Jesus among those who wish to maintain some kind of neutrality or who are wavering. Indeed, the imagery of Lk 11:24–6 is that of a *relapse*. Thus, it is most naturally addressed to insiders, even those tempted to draw back from full commitment. That their eventual fate is described as becoming worse than their original state may provide the transition to Lk 11:29–32 par, linking them with 'this evil generation' which seeks a sign.[131]

This view helps to explain why Lk 11:24–6 par follows the maxim in Lk 11:23 par in the stage(s) of tradition where both passages were appended to the 'Beelzebul' pericope.[132] A unified perspective can be detected in the conjunction of these sayings. Any form of half-hearted response, any wavering or relapse or apostasy, is attacked through these sayings. It then presents a challenge not just to outsiders, but also to lukewarm insiders (cf. Mt 7:22–3/Lk 13:26–7; Mt 7:21/Lk 6:46; Mt 10:26–33/Lk 12:2–9).[133] As this theme has already been identified as a concern of the compilers of the double-tradition collections, a further link is possible between the argument of the 'Beelzebul' controversy and these collections. These sayings show how the double-tradition version uses the controversy not just as a defence of Jesus' ministry, but also as a challenge to vacillating followers.

Mt 11:7–19/Lk 7:24–35

The question of the 'validation' of Jesus' earthly ministry arises again in the longest continuous section of double-tradition material in Matthew and Luke, Mt 11:2–19 par. It is not itself a controversy story, but an extended section of teaching about the relationship of Jesus and John the Baptist and their rejection by 'this generation'.[134]

There are two sentences in this section which may reflect popular maxims:[135] Mt 11:8b par and 11:19b par. The first appears to be little more than an aside, in the midst of a series of rhetorical questions posed by Jesus to tease out the status of John. He asks the crowds, 'Whom did you go out to see? A man clothed in soft raiment?'

(Mt 11:8a par). These questions, like the preceding ones, require no answers. They clearly allude to the Baptist's austere appearance. But here alone the questions are followed by an apparently tangential observation that those who are richly dressed are to be found in kings' houses. It has the form of an aphorism, but seems superfluous. In this context, however, one would expect it to be relevant to the recognition of John as a prophet (Mt 11:9 par).

It has occasionally been argued that the imagery alludes specifically to the Essenes,[136] or to John's criticism of Herod,[137] or to Davidic–Messianic expectations.[138] On the other hand, other scholars have argued that the saying can be taken only in the most general sense of pointing to John's austere appearance (which is in fact already done by the rhetorical question in Mt 11:8a par)[139] or as a scornful contrast to the effeminacy ('soft clothing') of courtiers.[140] It is probably best neither to take the saying in so general a sense as simply to repeat the point of the question in Mt 11:8a par, nor to try to press too specific an allusion out of the imagery of what is essentially a general observation. Its plainest point, which goes beyond the rhetorical question, is to suggest that John was not amongst those to be found at court. How does this advance our recognition of him as a prophet? This is not difficult to understand if there is an underlying conviction that true prophets experienced rejection at the hands of the leaders of Israel. This theme of rejection has been identified by O. H. Steck[141] as the Deuteronomistic tradition of the fate of the prophets, which he traces to logia of the double tradition such as Lk 6:22–3/Mt 5:11–12; Lk 11:47–51/Mt 23:34–6; Lk 13:33–4/Mt 23:37–9. The theme of rejection also permeates the section of double tradition in which these John the Baptist sayings are located (cf. Mt 11:6, 12, (Lk 7:29–30), 16–19 par). Therefore, it may be fairly speculated that to point to John's contrast with the royal court is an allusion to his rejection and thus a subtle validation of his true prophetic status, which is the point towards which this series of rhetorical questions is moving.

A more direct validation of the activity of Jesus and John comes at the climax to the entire section, Lk 7:35 par: 'Yet Wisdom is justified by (all) her children.'[142] D. Lührmann[143] suggests: 'Der Satz klingt wie eine allgemeine Sentenz; er mag auch vielleicht auf ein jüdisches Sprichwort zurückgehen.' The reference to σοφία, however, suggests that this saying may be more than simply a popular proverb. It will, therefore, be examined in more detail below (pp. 162–70) as part of a consideration of other sayings that may allude to the figure of Sophia. Yet, two observations should be made at this point. First, the saying is a direct response to the rejection of John and Jesus (Mt 11:16–19a par). Secondly, it serves to validate the ministries of John and Jesus *together*. Although Jesus is differentiated from John in status in Mt 11:19a par, by use of the Son of Man designation, here they are defended on a common basis.[144] So again it is the *validity* of Jesus' authority rather than his uniqueness that is defended in the maxim-like saying in Mt 11:19b/Lk 7:35, especially given the priority of Luke's formulation of the saying which will be defended (with most scholars) below (pp. 168–9).

Summary

The use of aphorisms for defence in controversies is not unique to any one stage of the synoptic tradition, although controversy stories themselves are not at all prominent in the double-tradition material. But there are some distinguishing features in the use in the double tradition of aphoristic statements for the defence and validation of Jesus' ministry. These features are highlighted by comparison with the version of the 'Beelzebul' controversy in Mark.

One distinctive feature is the progression of argument from general principle to specific application which distinguishes the double-tradition version of Jesus' defence in the 'Beelzebul' controversy from that of Mark, and which conforms in this respect to the similar progression of argument in the aphoristic sayings collections of the double tradition.

Another distinguishing feature of the double-tradition version of the 'Beelzebul' controversy, which receives further confirmation in Mt 11:7–19 par, is that the validation of Jesus' authority against Jewish opponents rests less on any particular christological claims than on a general demonstration of his genuineness as a representative of God.[145] This is consistent with using general experiential maxims and demonstrating contradictions in opponents' arguments (Lk 11: 19–20, 7:33–5) in order to affirm the validity of Jesus' ministry. These provide general 'tests', sufficient to determine genuine from false. This may express the outlook of the wise man, drawing on his powers of reason and skill in argument in preference to special claims for Jesus which are more obviously confessional. Yet, it may go further than this. The treatment of Jesus' ministry as that of one in a line of prophetic messengers to Israel would seem to lie behind several other sayings of the double tradition (Lk 6:22–3 par; 13:34 par). These sayings confront the problem of Israel's rejection of the prophets in a way which places Jesus as a true representative of God in the line of other representatives who encountered Israel's opposition. There may, therefore, be a consistency of argumentative approach between all these sayings, whereby the validity of Jesus' ministry is demonstrated to opponents less by its uniqueness than by its conformity to the general tests of 'truth' and Israel's salvation-history. This will be pursued further in Chapter 4.

Aphorisms used as general teaching for disciples

It would be surprising if there were no isolated aphorisms used for general parenetic purposes within the double-tradition material. There are, indeed, a number of aphoristic sayings which seem to serve this purpose, although the scope of the general instruction offered in this way is not extensive.

Mt 5:15; 6:22–3/Lk 11:33, 34–6

οὐδὲ καίουσιν λύχνον καὶ τιθέασιν αὐτὸν ὑπὸ τὸν μόδιον
ἀλλ᾿ ἐπὶ τὴν λυχνίαν,
καὶ λάμπει [πᾶσιν] τοῖς ἐν τῇ οἰκίᾳ.

ὁ λύχνος τοῦ σώματός ἐστιν ὁ ὀφθαλμός.
ὅταν ὁ ὀφθαλμός σου ἁπλοῦς ᾖ, ὅλον τὸ σῶμά σου
    φωτεινόν ἐστιν·
ἐπὰν δὲ πονηρὸς ᾖ, [ὅλον] τὸ σῶμά σου σκοτεινόν.
εἰ [οὖν] τὸ φῶς τὸ ἐν σοὶ σκότος ἐστίν, τὸ σκότος πόσον.

εἰ οὖν τὸ σῶμά σου ὅλον φωτεινόν, [μὴ ἔχον μέρος τι
    σκοτεινόν],
ἔσται φωτεινὸν ὅλον ὡς ὅταν ὁ λύχνος τῇ ἀστραπῇ φωτίζῃ
    σε.

In Lk 11:33, 34–5, two sets of 'light' sayings which originally were probably independent are joined.[146] The first saying, about lighting a lamp and putting it on a stand, has a doublet in Luke (cf. Lk 8:16 and Mk 4:21).[147] Although the saying occurs only once in Matthew (5:15), this version shows some similarities with Lk 11:33 against Mark.[148] This indicates that Lk 11:33/Mt 5:15 preserves a double-tradition version of the saying distinct from that in Mark. The precise reconstruction of the wording of this version may be better represented in Matthew.[149]

The second unit of sayings (Lk 11:34–5, (36)/Mt 6:22–3) is about the eye, through which the whole body is full of light or darkness. There is little doubt that Matthew and Luke are ultimately dependent here on a common tradition, although Lk 11:36 is more open to question, having no direct parallel in Matthew.[150] Unlike in Luke, the sayings in Mt 6:22–3 are separated from the 'lamp on a stand' saying (5:15), although both passages do appear in Matthew's Sermon on the Mount, and we have previously argued that Matthew's immediate context for the sayings in 6:22–3 may be secondary.[151]

This difference in context is matched by a very different use of the sayings by the two evangelists. The terms ἁπλοῦς and πονηρός leave unclear how they are to be interpreted: whether in a physiological or ethical sense.[152] For Matthew, the eye which is ἁπλοῦς is effectively the 'generous' eye in contrast to the 'greedy' eye (cf. Mt 20:15; Sir 14:10, 31:13). The context in Matthew is concerned with the theme of covetousness and attitudes to riches (cf. Mt 6:19–21, 24).[153] For Luke, ἁπλοῦς may express 'integrity' or 'singleness' (cf. TIss 3:4, 4:6). It is concerned with the perception and reception of Jesus and his message, for it immediately follows the Sign of Jonah (Lk 11:29–32 par), in which 'this generation' seeks a sign. The references to light or darkness and to seeing in Lk 11:34–6 must be understood in terms of the lack of reception of the Sign of Jonah by 'this generation'.[154]

Did the sayings in Lk 11:33 par and 34–5 (36) par come together in the pre-gospel tradition and follow the Sign of Jonah in this tradition? The questions cannot be conclusively answered, but there is some indication that the 'lamp' saying and 'eye/light' saying were combined before Luke. Certainly Matthew's contexts for both sayings seem secondary.[155] The sayings are joined in Luke largely on the catchword λύχνος. While Luke might have been the first to join them, J. Dupont has observed that the language of verse 36b is not purely Lukan and that the image to which it refers does not correspond as well to the Lukan redaction at the end of Lk 11:33 ('so that those who enter may see the light') as to the ending preserved in Mt 5:15 ('and it gives light to all in the house').[156] H. Schürmann's[157] observation that most of Luke's doublets are not deliberately created by Luke, but derived from the scheme of his pre-existing sources, must also strengthen the argument in favour of the association of the two sayings in pre-Lukan tradition.

If the likelihood of this is accepted, then one is an important step closer to having a wider context, and therefore a more clearly defined meaning, for the sayings in the tradition underlying the gospels. As isolated sayings, the metaphorical openness has led to this being variously employed by the evangelists. However, once the 'lamp' saying is joined with the eye/light saying, as in Lk 11, the emphasis is firmly placed on the *reception* of the light. The motif of 'soundness' in perceiving and receiving the light so dominates Lk 11:34–5 (36) par that it also necessarily directs the interpretation of the 'lamp' saying in Lk 11:33 par towards the idea of the 'light' which is to be seen and received.

This emphasis on the reception of the light fits easily with the 'Sign of Jonah' sayings, in which receiving and understanding a sign is involved. This is not sufficient to establish the union of Lk 11:33, 34–5 (36) par with 11:29–32 par in the early tradition, but the thematic aptness of this sequence is evident.[158]

However, there are still ambiguities in the meaning of Lk 11:33, 34–5 (36) par, which lead to two quite distinct ways in which this combination of sayings can be understood. The soundness of one's reception of the 'light' can be interpreted either as a warning to disciples or as a warning to 'outsiders'. Whether the 'light' is taken to refer to Jesus' message or to Jesus himself,[159] the importance of 'soundness' in how it is received may be an encouragement to wholehearted commitment amongst disciples[160] or an allusion to the hypocrisy of the Jewish leaders (cf. Lk 11:39–52 par).[161] Most striking is the final warning against the light in one being darkness (Mt 6:23b/Lk 11:35).[162] Is this warning against a relapse in the commitment of followers, or again an allusion to the hypocrisy of the Jews? Even the 'lamp' saying in Lk 11:33 par could refer to Jewish efforts to obstruct the light.[163]

To choose between these possibilities it is helpful to recognize how similar these questions are to those posed by the sayings in Lk 11:23, 24–6 par, found in Luke between the Beelzebul controversy and the 'Sign of Jonah' pericope. The either – or choice of commitment to Jesus in Lk 11:23 is matched in the 'eye/light' sayings by the equally strong contrast between the body being *wholly* light or *wholly* dark, depending on the soundness of the eye. There is no middle ground.[164] Further, the image of the evil spirit having left its home only to return later (Lk 11:24–6 par) is matched by the warning against the light in one being darkness. Just as it was argued that the return of the evil spirits specified a relapse from a desirable state, so here too a relapse seems to be in view. This is an image not just for hypocrisy, but for reversion.[165]

Is such teaching about wholehearted commitment, however, out of place if these sayings did belong with the 'Sign of Jonah' pericope in the tradition? Opposition to Jesus on the one hand, and the wavering of disciples' commitment on the other, are by no means necessarily unrelated. Wavering may be the result of opposition. With respect to Lk 11:23, 24–6 par, Laufen argues persuasively that this in fact was parenetic material which was added to the defensive arguments of the 'Beelzebul' controversy. Here too one must allow that the general formulation of the sayings widens the application beyond opponents alone. The lack of invective in the sayings in Lk 11:33, 34–5 (36) par casts serious doubt upon whether their primary function is to warn *Israel* of judgment. They seem rather to encourage self-examination and commitment among those who have received light.[166] As H. D. Betz states,[167]

> It appears that having heard and understood the logion the thoughtful and conscientious person will be worried: What if my inner light is darkness? How can it be made bright again? The logion is so designed as to provoke this concern, but it does not answer it. It leaves the concerned hearer alone and restless, and this open-ended situation seems to be the parenetical goal of the passage.

The problem of less-than-wholehearted commitment among followers has been met earlier in our analyses. It is also expressed in a more direct way in the 'Lord, Lord' logion in Mt 7:21/Lk 6:46, in which the appellants are encouraged to put their deeds to the test.[168] In the 'lamp' and 'eye/light' sayings the test is of the soundness of one's 'eye' or reception of the light. The basic appeal is similar, although in this latter case we are perhaps a little closer to the concerns of the teacher[169] with the emphasis on understanding.

Mt 5:13/Lk 14:34–5

[καλὸν οὖν τὸ ἅλας·]
ἐὰν δὲ   τὸ ἅλας μωρανθῇ, ἐν τίνι ἁλισθήσεται;
οὐδὲ εἰς γῆν οὐδὲ εἰς κοπρίαν εὔθετόν ἐστιν·
ἔξω βάλλουσιν αὐτό.

Not unlike the 'light' sayings are the 'salt' sayings. Even though there is a group of 'salt' sayings in Mk 9:49–50[170] and no doublet in either Matthew or Luke, it is widely believed that Matthew and Luke may have drawn on a tradition other than Mark (cf. Mt 5:13; Lk

14:34−5).[171] Neither Matthew nor Luke reproduces the Markan context for the sayings. There are also some clear points at which Matthew and Luke agree in their wording against Mark. The most notable instances are their common avoidance of the 'salted with fire' saying in Mk 9:49 and of the exhortation to 'have salt in yourselves and be at peace with one another' (Mk 9:50c), the common use of the unusual μωρανθῇ against Mark's ἄναλον γένηται, and the common references in Matthew and Luke to its uselessness and being cast out (βάλλειν ἔξω).

The use of μωρανθῇ is especially significant because there is little clear attestation for its meaning 'become tasteless'. More usually it means 'become foolish',[172] as when Paul uses it in opposition to wisdom in 1 Cor 1:20. W. Nauck has shown that the word not only consistently means 'foolish' in the rest of the NT, but also does so in the LXX and in most of Greek literature. Moreover, 'salt' can be found as a symbol for wisdom or prudence (cf. Col 4:6).[173] The sapiential connotations of the double-tradition version are therefore intriguing.

The central image of salt-become-'saltless' has been a cause of considerable perplexity for commentators.[174] This saying, however, presents a similar paradoxical warning to that of the light in one being darkness.[175] Once again it would appear that the main point is a warning against reversion or relapse from what is a desirable condition − salt or light − to the contrasting opposite. This is all the more compelling if one adopts salt (as with light)[176] as a metaphor warning against those who have 'wisdom' becoming 'foolish' and therefore useless and 'cast out'. Although some commentators have considered this a warning originally to Israel,[177] both Matthew and Luke agree in this instance when they use it as an exhortation about discipleship. The formulation of the saying in the double tradition suggests the same. Fortitude is required of disciples; there is no place for wavering or compromise.

Mt 10:24−25a/Lk 6:40[178]

οὐκ ἔστιν μαθητὴς ὑπὲρ τὸν διδάσκαλον
οὐδὲ δοῦλος ὑπὲρ τὸν κύριον αὐτοῦ.
ἀρκετὸν τῷ μαθητῇ ἵνα γένηται ὡς ὁ διδάσκαλος αὐτοῦ,
καὶ ὁ δοῦλος ὡς ὁ κύριος αὐτοῦ.

The interests of the teacher of wisdom are expressed again by the aphorism in Mt 10:24−25a/Lk 6:40. Matthew and Luke agree in the first part of the saying ('a disciple is not above the teacher') and both include a following observation in somewhat different words about the disciple 'being as his teacher'. Luke's use of πᾶς in the clause is probably, as often, redactional;[179] and Schulz[180] argues that the verb καταρτίζειν was also due to Luke's effort to make the saying express the relation of the teacher and pupil with respect to their teaching rather than their condition or fate. It has already been argued (cf. above, pp. 39–42) that this saying probably did not belong to the double-tradition collection of sayings on judging one's brother, as in Luke.

Matthew's use of the saying also presents difficulties, however. First, Matthew's formulation of the saying is extended by the parallel 'δοῦλος – κύριος' motif. This motif alone is attested in Jn 13:16[181] and 15:20. Schulz argues again that Matthew may better preserve the tradition, because the 'δοῦλος – κύριος' image was inappropriate for Luke's context (cf. Lk 6:39) and because Luke in any case has a propensity to destroy such double parallelisms.[182] Matthew's rendering of the saying must therefore be seriously considered as reflecting that of the underlying tradition. Even so, the exact context in Matthew seems to owe more to Matthew himself than to his source. In Matthew it links the fate of the disciples with the foreshadowed Beelzebul charge against Jesus (10:25b). This is peculiar to Matthew and anticipates the controversy in Mt 12:24–30. A similar anticipation has already been made in Mt 9:34. This appears to be a particular concern for Matthew.[183]

Nevertheless, Matthew shares with the 'δοῦλος – κύριος' saying in Jn 15:20 the general use of the aphorism to indicate that followers must be prepared to accept a similar fate to their master's.[184] This may be a particular implication of the 'δοῦλος – κύριος' imagery,[185] and may accurately reflect the general conceptual context of the saying in the underlying tradition.[186]

But then what purpose does the 'teacher – pupil' metaphor serve? Although διδάσκαλος is a rare title for Jesus in the material of the double tradition,[187] H. Schürmann has suggested that it could have had an original christological sense. The 'μαθητής – διδάσκαλος' imagery generally corresponds to rabbinical teaching instructions. But Schürmann states: 'Mehr als im rabbinischen Lehrbetrieb gilt die Regel für die Jünger Jesu (vgl. Mt 23,8): der Offenbarung Jesu (Mt 13,52) gegenüber.'[188]

If one accepts that the double imagery of Matthew is original, it is nevertheless not impossible to combine these insights. By their very perpetuation and propagation of the message of Jesus, followers must be prepared to face a response similar to that faced by Jesus. These are the consequences that bearing this message brings.

In this disciple–teacher relationship is therefore a kind of counterpart to the tradition of the fate of the prophets, who were rejected and killed for the message they bore (cf. Lk 6:22–3 par, also 11:49–51 par, 13:34–5 par). The categories of prophet and teacher are also not mutually exclusive.[189] Ultimately, the absence of a firm context for the logion in Mt 10:24–25a par in the pre-gospel tradition renders any interpretation open to question. At best one can only argue for the suitability of such an interpretation in terms of the form of the saying itself.[190]

Mt 9:37–8/Lk 10:2

ὁ μὲν θερισμὸς πολύς, οἱ δὲ ἐργάται ὀλίγοι·
δεήθητε οὖν τοῦ κυρίου τοῦ θερισμοῦ ὅπως ἐκβάλῃ
ἐργάτας εἰς τὸν θερισμὸν αὐτοῦ.

The missionary instructions in Lk 10:2–12/Mt 9:37–8, 10:7–16 further set out the terms for the disciples' proclamation of Jesus' message and for the response which that message will draw. There are both some sayings here for the 'labourers' and also a good deal of emphasis on the rejection of that mission and on judgement.[191] Two maxims stand out in these sayings, with the first occurring in the introduction to the missionary charge. It is the metaphorical observation that 'the harvest is plentiful, but the labourers are few' (Lk 10:2a/Mt 9:37). This is immediately followed in both Matthew and Luke by an exhortation to ask the Lord of the harvest to send forth more ἐργάται.

The reconstruction of this saying presents no difficulties and the context for the logion differs only slightly between the two gospels.[192] The image of the 'harvest' is a common one for judgement (Joel 4:1ff.; Is 27:12, 9:2–3; Hos 6:11; Rev 14:15–20),[193] but this does not necessarily detract from considering the metaphor in Lk 10:2a par as 'proverbial'. C.E. Carlston[194] describes it as a 'generalization from nature', recognizing the inherently popular nature of the agricultural imagery and the concise formulation of the contrast, which suggests that the saying could have been coined as a sentential saying, however it was later used. The saying is sufficiently self-contained to have stood once as an independent maxim.[195]

The point of the saying about the plentiful harvest and few labourers is the contrast.[196] D. Lührmann[197] suggests that the 'plentiful harvest' is essentially an invitation to the Gentiles. P. Hoffmann[198] sees the readiness of the harvest as primarily an image pointing to the nearness of the End. A. Jacobson[199] rightly rejects interpretations which suggest a 'readiness to be converted', but himself takes the image of harvest to speak of judgement. One must do justice, however, to the fundamental pattern of the aphorism as a saying of *contrast*. Implicit in the contrast is a recognition of the daunting task which confronts the early Christian witnesses. This becomes explicit in the reference to the size (rather than readiness) of the harvest and the call to pray for more help in Lk 10:2b/Mt 9:38. Also, in view of the rejection theme which follows in Lk 10:2–12 par, it may be surmised that the daunting nature of the task lies at least partially in the difficulties which are to be faced (see especially Lk 10:3 par).[200]

Despite pessimism about the size of the task, the harvest does suggest an element of hope. This encouragement is essential for the missionary effort to continue. But the contrast between the plentiful harvest and the few labourers leaves no doubt that the task will not be easy. The theme of judgement lies in the background and is elaborated in the sayings which follow. The task requires the perseverance of the few in adverse conditions until their numbers are swelled. The need for perseverance has been a recurring theme of several of the preceding double-tradition aphorisms.

Mt 10:10b/Lk 10:7b

ἄξιος γὰρ ὁ ἐργάτης τοῦ μισθοῦ [Mt: τῆς τροφῆς] αὐτοῦ.

The situation of the ἐργάται[201] in their missionary activity is again the concern in the aphorism about the labourer being worthy of his hire/food.[202] The problem here is not perseverance, but the practical question of one's keep and physical provision. The aphorism is not even part of the actual instruction for the missionaries;[203] it is an almost parenthetical justification for their claims on hospitality. As Hoffmann remarks,[204] 'Lk 10,7b unterbricht den Zusammenhang und begründet die Essensanweisung Lk 10,7a; der Spruch ist dadurch leicht als sekundärer Einschub zu erkennen.' He goes on to observe:[205] 'Konkrete Fragen der Missionspraxis finden hier eine erste Antwort.'

The problem which emerges was one also known to Paul and which he met in a similar way (1 Cor 9:14).[206] In the context of Lk 10:2–12 par, it stands not far removed from the uncomfortable sayings in Lk 10:4 par about *not* making elaborate provisions for support.[207] Lk 10:7b par is the corrective to any possible misunderstanding: the labourer does deserve his support.

It is interesting that this obviously secondary comment, dealing with an issue of some sensitivity for the early church, is dealt with by a general aphorism. Surely here must be additional support for our general contention that *aphorisms were used to provide persuasive and seemingly impartial guidance on delicate matters of potential (or actual) conflict in the early Christian communities.* As A. E. Harvey observes on this point,[208] 'When friends have to discuss a delicate question involving payment of money, they are particularly apt to avoid calling a spade a spade.'

Summary and comparison

This brief examination of isolated aphorisms used for parenetical purposes within the sayings of the double tradition has continued to highlight interests which we encountered in our earlier analyses. Three of the five sayings are concerned with the question of perseverance in discipleship, warning against wavering (Lk 11:33–6 par, 14:34–5 par) or expressing encouragement despite the daunting task which lies ahead (Lk 10:2a par). The saying about a pupil's not being above his teacher (Lk 6:40 par) may also allude to the difficulties which disciples must expect to fact in their tasks. The main exception to this surprisingly unified picture is the aphorism in Lk 10:7b par. However, this maxim does deal explicitly with followers (ἐργάται) and the issue of material provision – which also accords with our earliest observations about the issues which gave rise to the argumentation of the aphoristic sayings collections. Further, it is a clear testimony to the use of aphorisms to deal with a situation of potential conflict amongst the early Christians.

The influence of teachers of wisdom seems to emerge particularly in the imagery of three of the sayings. The sayings on both light and salt present the essence of commitment to Jesus using metaphors closely associated with 'wisdom'. Also in Lk 6:40, the teacher – pupil relationship is prominent; the disciple is one who possesses the master's teaching or instruction.

These concerns can be found elsewhere in the synoptic tradition. They are not exclusive to the double tradition. But elsewhere such concerns appear much more diffusely mixed with other interests. The rather limited range of parenetical interest expressed in these double-tradition logia is quite remarkable.

Some differences can be briefly noted between the double tradition and Mark. On the theme of perseverance in discipleship, for example, Mark does use a sententious saying about perseverance in chapter 13: 'he who endures to the end will be saved' (13:13b). However, Mark treats the tribulations to which he refers as eschatological trials and accordingly uses the saying as virtually an eschatological promise of salvation (cf. 4 Ezra 6:25). This is not a denial of the parenetical application of the saying, but it does show the particular context within which Mark treats the instruction.[209] An aphorism which at first sight deals more with the general theme of temptation is Mk 14:38b: 'the spirit is indeed willing but the flesh is weak'. This brief remark must be seen alongside the call to 'watch and pray' (38a), which is a high point in this Passion material and recalls similar calls to watchfulness in the eschatological discourse (Mk 13:3, 9, 23, 33, 35−6, 37).[210] The suffering of the Passion and the suffering of the days of tribulation are perceived as together providing the pattern for what followers must face.[211] Therefore, Mark's development of the perseverance theme takes place in a theological context which is very much his own and closely related to his theology of the cross and his eschatological perspective.[212]

Mark's differences from the double tradition are most evident, however, in his version of the 'salt' and 'light' sayings (Mk 9:49−50, 4:21). Mark's version of the 'salt' saying lacks the significant μωρανθῇ of the non-Markan version[213] and mixes the saying about salt losing its taste with sayings about purification (being salted with fire, 9:49) and a call to be at peace with one another (9:50c). The meaning becomes accordingly diffuse, and appears to be more concerned with the theme of 'peace' than with perseverance or apostasy. The 'light' saying in Mk 4:21 only includes the 'lamp' aphorism and is part of Mark's 'parable theory' about the mystery of the kingdom.[214] These differences from the double tradition are all the more striking on account of the similarity of the logia themselves.[215]

Matthew and Luke show interest in an even wider range of parenetical purposes to which isolated aphorisms were applied. It has been noted how Matthew preferred to adapt the saying about the eye/light (6:22−3) to the theme of covetousness. Most characteristically, Matthew includes aphorisms which can be used to emphasize the high demands upon the disciple and the necessity of *doing* God's will. Examples of this follow:

'For many are called, but few are chosen' (Mt 22:14)[216]

'For there are eunuchs who have been so from birth,
and there are eunuchs who have been made eunuchs by men,
and there are eunuchs who have made themselves eunuchs
for the sake of the kingdom of heaven' (Mt 19:12)

'for they preach, but do not practise' (Mt 23:3b)[217]

Luke adds fewer new maxims for parenetical purposes but does adapt existing sayings to reflect his interests. His adaptation of the 'future reversal' sayings in Lk 14:11 and 18:14 as generalizing conclusions for parables on humility will be discussed below (pp. 151–2). Luke's concern with the use of wealth is also expressed in some of the few aphorisms peculiar to his gospel, such as 12:15 ('for a man's life does not consist in the abundance of his possessions')[218] and 12:48b ('Everyone to whom much is given, of him will much be required; and of him to whom men commit much they will demand the more').[219]

These special interests of the evangelists, and especially of Mark and Matthew, demonstrate some of the wider purposes to which isolated aphorisms are applied in the synoptic tradition, and also comprise a background against which the particular emphases of the double-tradition sayings can be recognized.

Aphorisms used in eschatological announcements

The use of aphoristic wisdom in prophetic – eschatological announcements is not just a matter of eschatological parenesis. This latter instruction is evident in works such as the closing chapters of 1 Enoch (92–105), the Testaments of the XII Patriarchs,[220] and even in Mk 13 and Revelation. However, the aphorism is seldom the chosen form for such instruction.[221] When aphorisms are used in such works, it is sometimes for quite different purposes from ethical instruction.

Aphoristic wisdom was on occasion integrated with prophetic eschatology as part of the prophetic announcement itself. The OT prophetic literature sometimes employed isolated aphorisms in this way. J. Lindblom[222] suggests that one common factor which led to wisdom being taken up by the prophets was the predilection of both for questions of retribution, underpinned further by the common idea of God's wisdom manifested in creation. But in several cases the aphorisms are of a type portraying not retribution, but rather impossibility or incompatibility.[223] These are often posed as rhetorical questions. For example, in Jer 23:28 ('What has straw in common with wheat?') the condemnation of false prophets is heightened. Or, in Is 49:24 ('Can the prey be taken from the mighty, or the captives of a tyrant be rescued?') the question is set forth only to be reproached in the following verses by the declaration that the mighty will in fact fall before God; and in Jer 13:23 ('Can the Ethiopian change his skin, or the leopard his spots?') the hopelessness of Israel's plight is illustrated.[224]

While the use of wisdom by the OT prophets is a subject much more extensive than can be pursued here,[225] these brief observations do illustrate two important points. First, it may well be that certain classes of aphorism are particularly suitable for adaptation to prophetic contexts, such as the 'questions of impossibility or incompatibility' set out above or those depicting 'future consequences'. But, secondly, only a close examination of how the sayings function in their contexts provides a firm basis for making generalizations about how prophetic and sapiential traditions have been brought together. It is with this latter point in mind that we shall turn first to three varied aphorisms used in End-time announcements in double-tradition material and then to some instances of an important class of aphorism, the 'future reversal' sayings.

Mt. 24:28/Lk 17:37b

ὅπου ἐὰν ᾖ τὸ πτῶμα, ἐκεῖ συναχθήσονται οἱ ἀετοί.

The form of this saying is a popular type of aphorism which expresses an invariable association or consequence ('where ... there'),[226] but of which there are surprisingly few examples in the synoptic tradition.[227] The precise meaning of this particular saying is notoriously elusive, despite only minor differences in the wording in Matthew and Luke.[228] This elusiveness is due in part to its metaphorical openness, which means that it is essential to determine the context for the saying in order to approach its meaning.

Both Matthew and Luke agree in placing the aphorism in the general context of double-tradition sayings which describe in vivid terms the events surrounding the coming of the Son of Man.[229]

Despite mixing with other source material, both gospels broadly agree in their sequence of double-tradition material in this section of Mt 24/Lk 17, but their location of this maxim about the corpse and the ἀετοί is one significant exception.[230]

Luke's location of the aphorism at the end of this section of eschatological sayings has been considered suspect by many scholars.[231] This suspicion arises particularly from the question which Luke alone has placed immediately before the aphorism, in which the disciples, after the description of the day(s) of the coming of the Son of Man, ask Ποῦ, κύριε; (17:37a). This question about locality does not follow easily on the preceding sayings in verses 26–35, in which spatial concerns are not present, and it would appear to be editorial.[232] Superficially the 'where ... there' aphorism in Lk 17:37b follows more easily on the 'Lo, here!' and 'Lo, there!' sayings in Lk 17:20–1, 23, which accords better with the placement in Matthew. J. M. Creed suggested that Luke might have moved the saying from such an earlier context to the end of the section so that 17:20–37 would end on a similar note to how it began.[233] In terms of the superficial structure, this is not unreasonable, but there may have been a further reason for Luke moving the saying. In Lk 17:20–1, despite the 'Lo, here!' and 'There!' sayings, the question which the Pharisees asked was *when* the kingdom of God was coming. Luke typically discourages such temporal speculation (cf. Lk 21:7–9; Acts 1:6–7),[234] and indications of the delay of the parousia are probably also to be seen in 17:22.[235] So, even in 17:23, Luke would appear to warn disciples against following after those who say 'There!' or 'Here!' on the grounds that temporally the appearance will be sudden, and therefore unexpected.[236] The 'where ... there' maxim, with its predominantly spatial imagery, would not therefore fit Luke's purpose in these earlier verses, so he has delayed it to the end of the section and given it a new, more appropriate question to answer: '*Where*, Lord?' The vagueness of the aphorism in reply at least suits well his general attempt to discourage apocalyptic speculation, whether temporal or spatial.[237]

But what of Matthew's setting for the saying? In Matthew, the aphorism immediately follows the saying 'For as the lightning comes from the east and shines as far as the west, so will be the parousia of the Son of Man' (Mt 24:27/Lk 17:24). Matthew may be secondary in his use of the word παρουσία in this chapter,[238] but of more significance is the stress on the spatial aspects of the parousia in Mt 24:26–8. The 'Lo, here!' and 'Lo, there!' sayings have received in

Matthew spatial points of reference: 'Lo, he is in the wilderness' or 'Lo, he is in the inner rooms.'[239] This fits Matthew's earlier discussion about attempts to 'lead astray' Christians (24:23–4). Perhaps some of these false Christs and false prophets[240] are to be associated with the 'wilderness'. Yet, however great their signs and wonders (24:24), they are isolated figures; and, in contrast to this, Matthew uses the 'lightning' saying to affirm the universally unmistakable nature of the recognition of the true parousia.[241] The 'where ... there' maxim fits easily into this context, which is already dominated by spatial motifs and affirms the point of unmistakable recognition:[242] 'Wherever the corpse/body is, there the eagles (vultures)[243] will be gathered together.'

The common tradition undoubtedly contains a close connection between a form of the 'Lo, here ... Lo, there' sayings (Mt 24:23, 26; cf. Lk 17:21, 23) and the 'lightning' saying (Mt 24:27; cf. Lk 17:24). The former sayings recall Mk 13:21, but S. Schulz follows Bultmann in assigning them to the double tradition.[244] The common sequence of Matthew and Luke with the 'lightning' saying supports this view, as does a doubling in both gospels of the 'Lo, here ... Lo, there' sayings. It is also very probable that the sayings about the coming of judgement in the day(s) of Noah and about the two men and two women, only one each of which is taken (Mt 24:37–41c; cf. Lk 17:26–30, 34–5), complete the section of double-tradition material.[245] In view of the reasons given for Luke's wishing to move the vulture saying, the natural affinity of the 'where ... there' imagery with the 'Lo, here ... Lo, there' sayings, and the difficulty of placing the aphorism alone at the end of the section without Luke's introductory question in Lk 17:37a, one is inclined to agree with many scholars who consider Luke's setting for the aphorism to be suspect and Matthew's to be the more original.

What, then, is the meaning of the saying in the double-tradition context? The sayings in Mt 24:26–8 par must be interpreted apart from Matthew's particular discussion of false Christs and false prophets. There is a common concern in these sayings about identifying the appearance of the Son of Man,[246] but whether the problem is particularly one of temporal or spatial questions is less clear.[247] Recognizing a somewhat spatial sense, S. Schulz[248] considers the force of the reply to be an assertion that the Son of Man's coming will not be missed when it takes place, yet part of a polemic against 'den spätjüdischen Topos vom verboren Auftreten des irdischen Messias'. The Son of Man's apocalyptic appearance will be of a heavenly kind, as the lightning saying implies.[249] Along more temporal lines, D. Lührmann,[250] who is less certain even of the inclusion of Mt 24:26 (cf. Lk 17:23) in Q, would define the problem as anxiety about the delay of the parousia. C. Tuckett[251] has recently argued persuasively for understanding the original source as emphasizing that the parousia is to come suddenly, without possibility of warning, like a lightning flash. This fits Lk 17:26–30 par, which is concerned with the suddenness of judgement intruding into ordinary life. These sayings encourage an active eschatological expectation. He would also wish to interpret the 'vultures' saying as representing a *sudden* event (cf. Job 9:26; Hab 1:8).

The 'lightning' saying and the 'vultures' maxim have in common the motifs of suddenness, unmistakable recognition and appearance from the skies. The 'Lo, here ... Lo, there' saying which immediately precedes in Mt 24:26/Lk 17:23 can, however, only indirectly be associated with the motif of suddenness. Tuckett argues that it implies 'that there will be no time for such advance notice when the event happens'.[252] But Matthew and Luke agree in considering this as a warning against being led astray *before* the event comes, which would seem the more natural interpretation. So, while the hearers seem to accept that the End will soon come, they seem uncertain about recognizing its coming, and this perhaps led to different opinions being expressed.[253] The reply in Mt 24:27–8/Lk 17:24, 37b is that its coming will be so decisive and universally recognized that there will be no possibility for error. Although the motif of suddenness is present and serves to keep the Christians living on the knife-edge of an imminent expectation, it is balanced by an assurance that the event will be physically recognizable when it comes despite the various uncertainties accompanying it.

This understanding of these sayings helps to make intelligible the use of the 'vultures' aphorism. But what does it add beyond the 'lightning' saying, where many of the same ideas are present in a much more direct and less enigmatic way? The answer lies with the function of the aphorism. Its logic is one of invariable association. Although the 'lightning' saying may *announce* (as an 'eschatological correlative'[254]) the unmistakable recognition of the Son of Man, the 'vultures' maxim carries with it a logic of *assurance*. Just as it is an invariable rule of experience that vultures will always find and gather around a corpse, there is no possibility that when the event of importance comes it will be missed. However uncertain, or even sudden, the timing may be, followers may be absolutely certain that it will be recognized and not missed or mistaken. This is the logic and certainty generated by invariable association ('where' ... 'there'), quite apart from any attempt to allegorize the imagery of the saying.[255] The aphorism carries with it the assurance of a 'rule', while the 'lightning' saying is strictly an announcement employing a simile.

This attempt to provide certainty about inherently uncertain End-time events also pervades the sayings which immediately follow in Lk 17:26−30/Mt 24:37−9. Here the appeal is to God's action in the past, in the days of Noah. D. Lührmann has described this as 'die weisheitliche Interpretation der im Alten Testament vorliegenden Geschichtsstoffe'.[256] While the theme of judgement is more conspicuous in these verses than in the preceding ones,[257] there is still the concern to demonstrate that it comes as a swift, overwhelming, inescapable intrusion into life. Like the coming of the flood in Noah's days, it is ultimately unmistakable and decisive.[258] There is no possibility of failing to recognize it or of mistaking it for the ordinary course of events (cf. also Lk 17:34−5 par). Given the likely absence of Lk 17:31−3 from the underlying source,[259] there is a quite noticeable absence of exhortation in this material. Apart from the initial warning not to be deceived (Lk 17:23 par), the section is descriptive and loaded with a cluster of comparisons of persuasive power.[260] Even direct exhortations to watchfulness are absent.[261] Dominant are a variety of arguments from experience and from the past acts of God, which provide assurances of the certainty and clarity of the coming of the Son of Man and his judgement, despite the uncertainties of when and where it will come. This is the way in which the problems of the eschatological hope are treated in these verses.

Mt 3:10b/Lk 3:9b

πᾶν οὖν δένδρον μὴ ποιοῦν καρπὸν καλὸν ἐκκόπτεται καὶ εἰς πῦρ βάλλεται.

A second example of a direct eschatological announcement which seems to incorporate an aphoristic saying as part of that announcement occurs in an early warning of John the Baptist about the imminent judgement. The warning (Lk 3:7−9 par) concludes with the logion: 'Therefore every tree which does not bear good fruit is cut down and cast into fire.'

In view of the strongly prophetic tone of Lk 3:7−9/Mt 3:7−10 as a whole,[262] in which those addressed are labelled 'a brood of vipers', it is somewhat striking that the parting shot is an allusion drawing upon everyday experience. It is all the more remarkable that an aphoristic formulation for this saying has been preserved so well, rather than having been substantially adapted to the specific threat of End-time judgement upon those addressed.[263] In particular, the generalized form of statement is preserved by the initial πᾶν; the present tense is consistently used rather than the future tense, preserving an aphoristic quality despite the context;[264] the passive verbs are left without more specific reference to divine agency;[265] and even the image of 'casting in fire' has its apocalyptic reference restrained and its everyday quality retained by the anarthrous use of πῦρ (contrast Jn 15:6).[266] The general formulation of the aphorism has therefore been kept intact despite the prophetic vigour of the context.[267]

The formulation of the saying indicates that the logion functions as more than simply an apocalyptic warning in metaphorical garb. Certainly in its immediate context its imagery does pick up that of the earlier command to 'bear fruit(s) worthy of repentance' (Lk 3:8/Mt 3:8) and of the warning that 'already the axe is laid at the root of the trees' (Lk 3:9a/Mt 3:10a). The popularity of such imagery can also be found in the parable at Lk 13:6−9, in the judgement saying at Jn 15:6 and in numerous texts in the OT and intertestamental literature.[268] But the fact that the saying stands as a self-contained aphorism is demonstrated by Matthew's precise repetition of it in another context (Mt 7:19): namely, in his version of one of the collections of aphoristic sayings (Lk 6:43−45 par). It is formulated as a 'rule' which can be applied in other contexts.

The question then becomes: what is the contribution of the saying to its context in Lk 3:7−9 par? If it was merely for rhetorical effect, might one not have expected at least some of the generalizing features to have given way to the directness which is characteristic of the rest of the passage, and which would provide a final direct thrust against the hearers? In its generalized form it retains an argumentative function. There are at least two ways, not mutually exclusive, in which this might be of use. First, because the logic of the aphorism is one of depicting expected consequences, it may serve to reinforce the general point that the expected consequence of fruitlessness is destruction. Secondly, it may suggest not only that such is the expected outcome of the condition of fruitlessness, but also that it is an *inescapable* consequence. There are no exceptions (see πᾶν in Lk 3:9b par). This is consistent with the earlier part of the Baptist's announcement, where not only are the hearers to 'bear fruit of repentance' (Lk 3:8a par), but also the question of Israel's privileged status is raised and quashed (Lk 3:8b/Mt 3:9).[269] There is no escape; there are no exceptions. And for this a general rule is a very suitable mode of expression. The logion, however, is of course more than simply the citation of a rule of life. In its present context, it is both a rule of life and also part of the Baptist's prophetic announcement. The general terms in which the saying is formulated suggest that the saying is a principle which applies to a wide field of human experience. Yet its specific use in the context of the Baptist's warnings of End-time judgement draws ultimately on a prophetic authority. The *application* of the proverb to this context lies with the *prophet*, but the saying remains a proverb nonetheless. As a proverb, it serves to relate the Baptist's announcement to mankind's wider experiences and expectations based on the past.[270] Thus, the Baptist's announcement is in some degree even supported by the wider field of validity which the proverb possesses. It is perhaps this wider validity that encouraged Matthew to apply the warning beyond the particular situation of the Baptist (cf. Mt 7:19).

Mt 25:29/Lk 19:26

τῷ ἔχοντι παντὶ δοθήσεται·
τοῦ δὲ μὴ ἔχοντος καὶ ὃ ἔχει ἀρθήσεται ἀπ' αὐτοῦ.

The aphorism 'To everyone who has it will be given; but from him who has not, even what he has will be taken away' (also cf. Mk 4:25 par; GThom 41) is more difficult to consider as part of an eschatological announcement, for it appears attached in the double tradition to a parable. Yet, the parable is concerned with the judgement of the End-time,[271] so that the aphorism makes its point within that context of judgement. It has been variously considered by some scholars as a generalizing addition,[272] and by E. Käsemann as a possible example of a 'sentence of holy law' proclaimed by early Christian prophets.[273]

One must begin, however, with the parable itself. The attribution of this parable to the double tradition is probable,[274] although the actual correspondence in wording in Matthew and in Luke is so slight at times as to demand either some different development of the common tradition prior to the evangelists,[275] or extensive reworking by the evangelists,[276] or both. It also would appear that the Lukan version witnesses to the incorporation of a second 'parable' about the throne claimant (Lk 19:12, 14−15a, 27).[277] Nevertheless, the similarity in the general story of the parable in Matthew and in Luke supports those who see the gospel versions developing from a single original story. L. McGaughy concisely traces the outline of this original story as follows, conforming most closely to Matthew's version:[278]

(1) Introduction

   (a) An anonymous man (Mt 25:14a; cf. Lk 19:12 'noble-man')

   (b) goes on a long journey (Mt 25:14a; Lk 19:12)

   (c) and entrusts certain capital to each of three servants (Mt 25:14b−15; cf. Lk 19:13 'ten', but only 'three' in 19:15−22)

(2) Development and crisis

   (a) Servants A and B increase their capital (Mt 25:16−17; cf. Lk 19:16, 18)

   (b) Servant C buries his in the ground (Mt 25:18; cf. Lk 19:20 'napkin')

(3) Dénouement

   (a) Upon the master's return, servants A and B report their gains and are commended and rewarded (Mt 25:19−23; Lk 19:16−19)

   (b) Servant C apologizes on the grounds that he was paralysed by fear of his master (Mt 25:24−5; Lk 19:20−1)

   (c) The master acknowledges servant C's fear (Mt 25:26; Lk 19:22)

      (i) but condemns him (Mt 25:27; Lk 19:23)

      (ii) and gives 'his' capital to servant A (Mt 25:28; Lk 19:24).

McGaughy does not include the maxim in Mt 25:29 par as part of the *original* conclusion to the parable, although it clearly was part of the tradition eventually used by the evangelists.

The closest verbal correspondences between the two versions of the parable come towards the end of the parable, and particularly with this aphorism about having and not having (Mt 25:29/Lk 19:26),[279] the claim of the third servant that the master reaps where he did not sow,[280] and the command of the master to take the mina/talent from the worthless servant and give it to the one who has ten (Mt 25:28 par). The plight of the third servant is the climax to the parable,[281] so it is significant that the correspondence should be greatest here. Further, McGaughy[282] observes that the apology of the servant also conceals an aphorism about 'reaping where one does not sow' and 'gathering where one does not scatter'.[283] This also resembles post-exilic criticisms of Yahweh's hardness (cf. Job 10:16, 23:13–17; Ps 119:120). At the climax of the parable, therefore, the worthless servant justifies his fear by using the aphoristic saying about reaping and sowing to point to his master's severity (Mt 25:24 par).

In the light of this, it is all the more significant that the master defends his action against the servant with use of his own aphorism in Mt 25:29 par. It appears that one proverb is countered by use of another; a play with aphorisms underpins the dialogue. This last aphorism is widely considered to have been a secondary conclusion to the parable,[284] but because of the play between aphoristic sayings it is likely that this must be seen not simply as an added conclusion for the parable, but *as a feature of the dialogue itself*. It may still be a secondary addition, but *within* the parable. This hypothesis is contrary to many treatments of this parable but gains support from three other observations.

First, W. Schenk[285] has indicated in the reply of the master to the first and second servants the presence of still another proverbial saying, which Schenk believes is also the product of 'Q-Redaktion'. It is the saying 'you have been faithful over a little, I will set you over much' (Mt 25:23; diff Lk 19:19). This closely resembles Lk 16:10–12, especially 'He who is faithful in a very little is faithful also in much' (16:10). Even if one must express more reserve than Schenk in the attribution of Mt 25:23 to double tradition at this point in the parable,[286] there is a distinct allusion to the principle of such an aphorism also in Luke's version of the master's reply to the first servant: ὅτι ἐν ἐλαχίστῳ πιστὸς ἐγένου, ἴσθι ἐξουσίαν ἔχων ἐπάνω δέκα πόλεων (19:17).[287] This presence of a further proverbial allusion in the dialogue between the master and the servants provides additional grounds for believing that a play on proverbs is supporting the main elements of the dialogue at each important point and therefore that this holds true also for the final maxim.

Secondly, few modern studies have given sufficient attention to the fact that both Mt 25:30 and Lk 19:27 depict a 'condemnation scene' as the actual conclusion to the parable. In neither Matthew nor Luke is the aphorism about 'he who has' and 'he who has not' the actual conclusion to the parable. S. Schulz,[288] for example, argues that, because the final condemnation in Lk 19:27 is adapted to the throne claimant parable and because Mt 25:30 shows evidence of favourite Matthean terminology (cf. 8:12, 22:13), neither form of the 'final condemnation' saying has a parallel in the other, and that neither saying preserves Q here. Accordingly, Schulz decides that the double-tradition formulation of the parable ended with the preceding aphorism. Yet, this does not do justice to the fact that some kind of 'final condemnation' saying is a common feature of the two versions of the parable. Indeed, Schulz's own analysis shows why each evangelist could have altered an earlier condemnation saying to obtain the saying each ultimately has. Given the divergences in wording earlier in the parable, it is hardly unexpected that there might be some divergence in the wording of a common saying here at the end. E. Schweizer[289] seems on firmer ground when he states that only Mt 25:30 ('outside in the darkness, where he will cry and gnash his teeth') is Matthew's own formulation, leaving open the possibility of an earlier ending of the parable which contained a final condemnation after the action of the master in verse 28. Even the version in the Gospel of the Nazaraeans 18 concludes with the third steward being cast into prison, although this may well be a later tradition. If a final condemnation or imprisonment scene was the actual conclusion to this parable in the underlying common tradition, then it becomes all the clearer that the aphorism in Mt 25:29 par is no longer simply a generalizing conclusion for the parable as a whole, because it *precedes* the actual conclusion. There are no other examples of such a penultimate use of an aphoristic 'conclusion' preserved in the synoptic tradition.[290]

Thirdly, the aphorism is a completely relevant comment on the precise action of the master in Mt 25:28 par. The reward of the industrious servant is actually increased, while the unprofitable servant bears further loss.[291] Luke's account appears to recognize this. The aphorism is there made the master's response to a direct objection from the onlookers to the master's action in Lk 19:25.[292] This captures the sense of debate and defence in the story which appears in any case to be implied.[293]

These various considerations suggest that the aphorism in Mt 25:29 par has been added to play a special role in the parable itself. This is evidence again of the propensity of the double tradition for employing aphorisms in an argumentative, and not simply a generalizing, way. The principle that 'to everyone who has it will be given' is indeed a commonplace of financial life.[294] The clause 'from him who has not, even what he has will be taken away' is the more difficult phrase, virtually presenting a paradox. Derrett[295] interprets it in the context of this parable as 'From him that has not (profits to show) is taken (withdrawn) even the capital which he still has.' If a manager shows no profit, no one is going to keep their capital with him. The entire saying is thus understandable as a rule of business and applicable within the terms of the parable itself to the master's defence of his action.[296]

In what sense, then, is the logion in Mt 25:29 par also an announcement about the End-time judgement? In so far as the master's action was seen by the early Christians as being of eschatological significance, so far the defence of that action within the parable would have had a similar bearing.[297] The implication would accordingly be that the principles which apply at the End-time judgement are not discontinuous with the principles which apply generally in everyday life. It is, indeed, the *principle* of judgement rather than the fact of judgement that is the concern of the aphorism.[298] Although the parable as a whole may also be applicable to the general issue of the expectation of the parousia,[299] the function of the aphorism about 'he who has' and 'he who has not' is applied particularly to the judgement against the third servant and to the principle of judgement which is involved.

This principle is itself interesting. It implies that this servant, who has done nothing dishonest,[300] is condemned for his half-hearted commitment and for his concern with his own personal security by 'playing it safe'.[301] Although he was originally entrusted with something, this lack of commitment is seen as irresponsibility, and he loses even what he had. This theme, even in its paradoxical formulation, is strikingly similar to what emerged from the equally paradoxical sayings about salt being 'saltless' (Lk 14:34−5 par) or the light in one being darkness (Lk 11:34ff. par). It is the assertion once again that only complete commitment, whatever the risk, must characterize the disciple.[302] Half-hearted commitment, trying to play it safe, is equivalent to having nothing.

The assertion of some scholars that the Parable of the Minas/Talents was originally directed against the leaders of the Jews[303] does not alter the fact that in the Christian tradition it was soon applied to Christians. The role of the 'servants', the absence of any actual dishonesty or obvious breaking of the servant−master relationship on the part of the last servant, and the likelihood that the church would see the master's 'journey' and 'return' as an allusion to the parousia of *Jesus*, who has entrusted his work to his followers, make it probable that Matthew and Luke correctly represent the underlying tradition in seeing this parable as at least in part for the church in the period preceding the parousia.[304] The aphorism leads naturally to a final condemnation of this third, half-hearted servant, who is recognized as a servant no longer.[305] This is not the same as simply general parenetical teaching about fruitfulness of discipleship; the stark contrast depicted in the saying calls into question the very status of the disciple.

Three 'future reversal' sayings

As early as Bultmann's *History of the Synoptic Tradition*, it was recognized that some sayings which are in concise, pithy, self-contained sententious sentences may go 'beyond popular wisdom and piety'. Notable amongst the sayings listed by Bultmann were sayings of a 'future reversal' formulation, 'sayings which are the product of an energetic summons to repentance, like Mk 8:35 (losing life and finding it)'; 'sayings about the first and the last (Mk 10:31)'; 'sayings which demand a new disposition of mind', like those about exaltation and humility (Lk 14:11 and 16:15).[306] In a later essay, Bultmann tried to explain further how general truths could share the genuine address character of the Christian proclamation. Above all, these generally valid truths can become a personal, authoritative address in so far as they *lose* their character as general truths and in concrete situations address the *present* situation of the individual.[307]

Interest both in this use of aphoristic sentences and in the 'future reversal' sayings in particular has been continued by a small group of subsequent scholars. A. N. Wilder, for example, in struggling with the problem of *Eschatology and Ethics in the Teaching of Jesus*, argues that observations from nature provide not only an appeal to commonsense which carry their own sense of truth, but in the message of Jesus could also 'serve as a ground from which to rise to a higher order of truth, not this time by "reason" but by a moral discernment'.[308] He quotes C. H. Kraeling that appeal to reason is 'brought into play especially where situations are met which are least apt to be acted upon on reasonable grounds'.[309] In later essays,[310] Wilder refers to the way in which the older distinct roles of sage and prophet are transcended, with Jesus' wisdom sayings having the character of prophetic revelations.

A more specific analysis of the use of the proverb, however, was made by W. A. Beardslee. Beardslee reaffirmed the use in the proclamation of Jesus of some sapiential forms which were not to be taken simply as general truths. Initially Beardslee wrote of these proverbs as showing how Jesus' radical eschatology was 'not simply world-denying', but was concerned also with inter-personal relationships.[311] In later works, though, he understood proverbs as 'compelling insight'.[312] Moreover, in its setting in Q a proverb can be found to be 'intensified'. A prudential rule can thus become (in its new eschatological framework) a saying which presents the total claim of God upon the hearer.[313] This was especially evident in beatitudes and in proverbs which express a paradox (such as the 'future reversal' sayings). In these the element of paradox is heightened and even results in 'a reversal of common sense wisdom'.[314] This serves to 'jolt' the hearer out of coming to a unified, comfortable and secure understanding of his life, so that he can make a new judgement about his existence and the claims upon him.[315] It is easier to see some aphorisms as acting in this way than others, but N. Perrin[316] followed Beardslee's lead and argued that those sayings which Bultmann identified as most characteristic of Jesus were those which most clearly demonstrated this intensification. Perrin set out three groups of sayings which could be seen in this way as a form of 'proclamation': the 'most radical' sayings (Lk 9:60a; Mt 5:39b−41),[317] the eschatological reversal sayings (Mk 8:35, 10:23b, 25, 31; Lk 14:11) and the conflict sayings (Mk 3:24−6, 27).[318] Jesus used these forms not in the manner of traditional Jewish wisdom, but to announce the eschatological inbreaking of the kingdom of God, which puts in question all 'established' insights. J. Roloff has also accepted the theological importance of this 'Zerschlagung vorgegebener Kategorien', which not only confronts the hearer with the kerygma but sends him out to think about why his usual way of thought must miss the manifestation of God in the kerygma.[319] A recent article by Beardslee[320] also draws on the findings of J. Crossan[321] and P. Ricoeur,[322] but attempts to balance the 'disorienting' thrust of these proverbs with some sort of recomposition of an understanding of reality which extends beyond just the self at a moment in time.[323] A distinct, but not entirely unrelated, effort to show how certain proverbial forms can become prophetic speech was made by E. Käsemann. Käsemann's efforts, however, are directed towards the category of 'sentences of holy law' which he attributes to early Christian prophets. He observes that a 'reversal' saying like 'Whoever exalts himself will be humbled, and whoever humbles himself will be exalted' could well be interpreted as a sentence of holy law showing the eschatological correspondence of deed and recompense.[324] Along similar lines, S. Schulz[325] does not hesitate to declare a change from gnomic to apocalyptic future in the 'kerygmatischen Horizont der Q-Gemeinde'.

It will be clear from this brief survey that the 'future reversal' sayings are especially important sayings for exploring how aphorisms can be used in eschatological announcements. Both Beardslee and Schulz have in different ways also identified the context of Q as particularly demonstrating this. Yet it is to the *general* context of Q that these scholars refer, because to a greater extent than many other sayings these 'future reversal' sayings appear to be 'floating' sayings. The three 'future reversal' sayings concerned are:

(i) Lk 17:33/Mt 10:39 (Mk 8:35/Mt 16:25/Lk 9:24; Jn 12:25), on losing one's life and saving it;

(ii) Lk 14:11/Lk 18:14/Mt 23:12 (18:4), on exaltation and humility;[326]

(iii) Lk 13:30/Mt 20:16 (Mk 10:31; [9:35b]/Mt 19:30), on the first and the last.[327]

In each case, there is no agreement on a precise context for the sayings in the double tradition. In the two cases where similar Markan sayings exist, it is even open to question whether it is proper to refer to 'double tradition' or Q at all. In none of these cases can one describe with confidence a context in common double-tradition material.

Recently, R. Laufen has claimed such certainty, however, for the saying on saving one's life and losing it in Mt 10:39.[328] Largely because the saying has a doublet in both Matthew and Luke, Laufen is confident that Mt 10:39 and Lk 17:33 represent a double-tradition formulation.[329] He also accepts Matthew's context as the more original because it is in connection with other double-tradition material (cf. Mt 10:37–8/Lk 14:26–7), because Luke seems to have introduced the logion himself into Lk 17:31–3,[330] and because Laufen sees in Lk 14:26 (ἔτι τε καὶ τὴν ψυχὴν ἑαυτοῦ) a reminiscence of the saying.[331] In the context of Mt 10:37–8, the logion in Mt 10:39 clarifies the sayings about the self-denial required in discipleship, but it also shows that the exhortations to self-denial are not just arbitrary commands, but based on a more fundamental principle.[332] In Laufen's interpretation, therefore, the saying is here not primarily an announcement about the End-time or judgement, but a supporting argument about the nature of discipleship.

Against the easy acceptance of this context for the logion, however, F. Neirynck has suggested that the supposed reminiscence of Mt 10:39 in Lk 14:26 (cf. Mt 10:37) may in fact depend on Mk 8:34–5 and not on a Q saying at all.[333] He also explores other influences of Mark on Lk 14:26 (cf. Mk 10:29), on the following verses in Lk 14:34–5 (cf.

Mk 9:50, 4:9) and, significantly on Lk 17:33 itself (cf. Mk 8:35).[334] Within the passage Lk 17:20ff., Neirynck detects signs of dependence on Mk 8 also for Lk 17:25 (cf. Mk 8:31).[335] The evidence for a Q-version of the saying about saving one's life and losing it therefore appears to be ambiguous; further consideration of this passage will be given in the Appendix.

No greater certainty attaches to the underlying tradition of the second 'future' reversal' aphorism. It is difficult to find any double-tradition context for this saying on exaltation and humility. In Mt 23:12, it is an instruction about discipleship, following special Matthean material in Mt 23:8–10 which encourages humility and the rejection of titles by disciples.[336] This logion portrays the teaching in a generalized way (cf. also Mt 18:4),[337] and even Beardslee admits that this is one of the less pointed of the reversal sayings.[338]

Luke uses the logion on exaltation and humility twice. There is no correspondence with Matthew's use, and in each case in Luke it is employed to conclude a parable peculiar to his gospel: 14:11, following 14:7–10 on places at table; 18:14b, following 18:9–14a on the Pharisee and the publican. The setting of each parable alludes to a criticism of Pharisaic pride. It is arguable that the logion in 14:11 was an early conclusion to the parable on places at table and therefore was not a Lukan insertion.[339] Whether or not Luke did place the saying here, there is no convincing evidence that it was derived from double-tradition material. It is interesting to observe, however, that for Luke the aphorism is not just a general ethical reformulation of the preceding teaching, but rather a warning of judgement against the pride demonstrated specifically by the Jewish leaders (cf. Lk 14:1, 3). Similarly, the clause which promises the exaltation of the lowly looks forward to the distinctly End-time reward which Luke describes in Lk 14:14.[340] Humility is not commended on general terms alone;[341] the promises and warnings are to be fulfilled at the day of resurrection and of judgement.

The same would appear to hold true for Luke's use of the previous 'reversal' saying in Lk 17. On the one hand, it occurs in the midst of a vivid description of End-time events and of the unmistakable intervention of God's judgement into the pattern of normal life (cf. 17:28–9). Yet, on the other hand, the saying in Lk 17:33 is frequently considered a general encouragement to disciples not to be unduly bound to worldly possessions (cf. Lot's wife in 17:32).[342] It would probably be wrong, however, to see the aphorism for Luke as simply the intrusion of some ethical teaching. It encapsulates a truth about the coming judgement which is also a truth about the gospel and of continuing relevance for the church. This is of little help, though, for establishing the context of the saying in his underlying tradition.

The saying about the first and the last is perhaps one of the most difficult to attribute to double tradition,[343] despite the agreement in the last–first ordering between Mt 20:16 and Lk 13:30 against Mk 10:31 parr. The contexts in Mt 20:16 and Lk 13:30 are vastly different. Matthew applied the saying as a general conclusion to his parable of the day-labourers (Mt 20:1–15), which results in an effective *inclusio* (in reverse formulation) with Mt 19:30 (par Mk 10:31).[344] Because there are no clear parallels to Luke here, this can hardly be considered a double-tradition context. In contrast, Luke does locate the aphorism amidst other double-tradition material, after the sayings about the exclusion of this present generation of Israel and the inclusion of men from afar in the kingdom (Lk 13:28–9/Mt 8:11–12). Here the 'last' which become 'first' probably refer to Gentile Christians.[345] Luke's form of the aphorism could serve as a further announcement of judgement on Israel, except that its force as an 'announcement' is weakened by the construction εἰσὶν ἔσχατοι, which prompts the translation *some* are last who will be first, and *some* are first who will be last' (cf. πολλοί in Mk 10:31/Mt 19:30).[346] The effect, therefore, is one of a reflection or summary, allowing for exceptions, rather than a direct radical challenge.[347] Of course, if at least Lk 13:29/Mt 8:11 was the common context for the logion in the earlier tradition, and if Lk 13:30 was originally in the bolder form found in Mt 20:16, then the saying could have had a different function in the tradition before Luke. This must, however, be assigned only to conjecture.

The results for the 'future reversal' sayings are therefore disappointing. While S. Schulz does not hesitate to postulate a meaning for two of these sayings in the general context of the late Q community and its *Martyriumsparänese*,[348] it is open to serious doubt whether any such interpretation is meaningful without a clearer idea of the precise context for the sayings in the tradition prior to the gospels. The grounds for taking these sayings as radical eschatological announcements or challenges are also slender. It may, indeed, be the very popularity of these paradoxically formulated sayings that hinders attempts to reconstruct a clear context in the underlying tradition.

Summary

Even within double-tradition contexts dominated by prophetic–eschatological announcements of coming judgement or by descriptions of the parousia, aphorisms occasionally, but not frequently, occur. The infrequency makes one hesitate to claim that any formal classification of aphorism is particularly suited to such announcements, but in most cases the aphorisms did depict 'future' consequences. This category serves only as a convenient umbrella under which to fit the present-tense formulation of Lk 3:9b par, the invariable consequence ('where … there') formulation of Lk 17:37b par, the antithetically formulated 'future consequence' maxim in Lk 19:26 par, and the 'future reversal' sayings. Yet, the idea of a future fate must be considered in most of these sayings.

It would be an oversimplification, however, to say that the main function of these sayings was to depict a future reward or judgement in a context dominated by an expectation of the End-time. The problem of function is more complex. Even in the early announcement of judgement by John the Baptist (Lk 3:7–9 par), the aphorism about the trees which do not bear good fruit takes on not only a declarative, but also an argumentative, role, providing familiar experiential support for the idea of the inescapable consequences awaiting those who do not bear good fruit against any claims of privilege or exemption. The universal nature of the expectation tells against any limitation of the consequences. This may help explain the preservation of the gnomic characteristics of the saying, despite the strong polemical tone of the context.

The aphorism incorporated into the Parable of the Talents/Minas (Lk 19:26 par) shows especially well the varied purposes to which an aphorism can be put. Not only is it caught up in a play of one proverb against another in the story of the parable, in which it serves in part to defend the master's action; it also, in declaring the principle of reward and judgement, presents a paradox ('from him who has not, even what he has will be taken away') which alludes to a recurring theme of the double-tradition sayings against half-hearted commitment.

Individual future reward or punishment is not the only theme of these sayings, however. Another problem was tackled by the 'vultures' aphorism in Mt 24:28 par. In this case the problem concerned the recognition of the parousia. The formula of invariable association in Lk 17:37b/Mt 24:28 served in the context of Mt 24:26–8 par to assure those addressed that, however uncertain the timing of the parousia may be, they may be certain that it will be unmistakable when it occurs. The aphorism fosters a sense of assurance amidst uncertainty.

The use of an aphorism to meet a particular problem of difficulty for the church, and the play on proverbs in the Parable of the Talents, denote a kind of sapiential activity which corresponds closely to that revealed in our earlier findings for aphoristic material in the double tradition. Unfortunately, it is not possible to extend these rather isolated findings by appeal to the use of the three 'future reversal' sayings in the double tradition, on account of the uncertainties of context and provenance.

The use of aphoristic sayings within eschatological announcements is also interesting for the theological questions which it raises about the continuity between the present (and past) experience of man and the nature of the eschaton which confronts him. Undoubtedly some continuity of expectations must exist. Could this be a reflection again of the teacher of wisdom who would strive to find an integrated understanding of these different kinds of knowledge? This issue must be raised again below (pp. 178–84).

4. General summary of Chapter 3

Before turning to look more widely at the sapiential traditions in double-tradition material, we must draw together our observations about the use of isolated aphoristic sayings. The variety of uses to which such sayings are put outside of the aphoristic sayings collections defeats any easy generalization. But it can hardly be claimed that this is unexpected. What is more surprising is the amount of coherence in some of the categories which have been examined, and the way in which this provides confirmation of some of the tendencies observed for the double-tradition aphoristic collections. By examining these isolated sayings within their immediate contexts in the pre-gospel tradition, and by noticing differences between double-tradition and Markan versions, corroborative evidence is obtained for some of the tendencies elucidated for the aphoristic collections.

First, it must be noted again how limited is the scope of ethical themes dealt with by the isolated double-tradition aphorisms. Several sayings (Lk 11:33–6 par, 14:34–5 par, 10:2a par) are used to express in particular the perseverance and wholehearted commitment needed by disciples. Even the logion about the disciple not being above his teacher (Lk 6:40 par) may contain hints that in the disciples' continuance of the message of their teacher they also must be prepared to face the response which he faced. These sayings on salt, light and the disciple–teacher relationship also contain in their imagery themes related to sapiential motifs, suggesting grounds for seeing here the proclivities of the teacher of wisdom.

The theme of a wholehearted commitment to discipleship emerged also in connection with two further aphorisms examined under different headings. Peculiar to the double-tradition version of the 'Beelzebul' controversy were the concluding sayings, which confronted the hearer with the stark choice between being 'for' Jesus or 'against' him (Mt 12:30/Lk 11:23); no middle ground was allowed. By the presence of the aphorism 'he who is not with me is against me' (Lk 11:23 par), the double-tradition version of the 'Beelzebul' story went beyond a controversy with Jesus' opponents, who were in any case clearly 'against' Jesus. The aphorism distinctly excluded any possibility of 'neutrality' or of half-hearted association with Jesus. The sayings which follow in Lk 11:24–6 par about the unclean spirit leaving and then returning also pointed to the hazards of an imperfect new allegiance. This theme is not integral to the 'Beelzebul' controversy, nor is it a feature of Mark's version of the controversy; it appears rather to indicate a deliberate effort to join sayings directed against those who are clearly hostile to Jesus with other sayings directed at those who may be more sympathetic but are trying not to 'burn their bridges' with their past completely. This situation is shown to be impossible and ultimately puts them in the same situation (or worse: see Lk 11:26 par!) as those against Jesus. A second saying, integrated into the Parable of the Talents/Minas, depicts the consequences for a servant who takes no risk (Lk 19:26 par). Here, too, the contrast is a stark one, with no middle ground for safety. To these two aphorisms may further be added the 'wisdom' admonition to enter by the narrow gate (Mt 7:13–14/Lk 13:24). These various sayings testify to an overriding concern with the quality of discipleship, measured in terms of risk and commitment rather than in terms of particular rules for moral guidance. The issue of discipleship itself is being forced, perhaps on account of a situation marked by the need for risk in view of external pressures and hostilities causing doubts among Christian adherents. This theme was not foreign to the double-tradition aphoristic sayings-collections (see especially Mt 10:26–33 par).

This convergence of interest in much aphoristic material of the double tradition contrasts noticeably with wider and differing interests that characterize the work of each evangelist. It is true that the double-tradition material also contains at least one wisdom admonition on the theme of reconciliation (Lk 12:58—9 par; cf. also Lk 17:3b—4 par) and on the theme of use of riches (Lk 12:33—4 par), both of which may merge with the other interests of the aphoristic sayings collections and continue the encouragement to this-worldly vulnerability. Yet, this does not approach the more developed concern with matters of Jewish piety found in Matthew or the extension of the concern with riches and humility found in Luke.

There is, however, a second dominant feature of the use of isolated aphoristic sayings in the double tradition. This too betrays a kinship with the aphoristic sayings-collections: the use of aphorisms to argue or defend a point at issue. Aphorisms are used not simply for generalized reflections; they are used much more pointedly and skilfully. The fondness for proverbial argument has been demonstrated, for example, in the play between proverbs in the Parable of the Talents/Minas (Mt 25:14—30/Lk 19:12—27). In controversy stories, the use of aphorisms is by no means confined to the double tradition, but the 'Beelzebul' controversy provides an informative example of the difference between the use of such sayings in Mark and in the double-tradition material. Mark basically answered the 'Beelzebul' charge by eliciting and illustrating the distinctiveness of Jesus' status. The version of the double tradition puts the emphasis on the illogicality of the charges. This is not to be attributed to an 'inadequate' christology, but rather to a greater confidence in the power of argument itself, which is sufficient to demonstrate Jesus' validity.

Confidence in the power of proverbial insight was also observed in the application within the double tradition of aphorisms to issues of practical concern for the early Christian communities, such as the problem of the recognition of the parousia (cf. also Acts 1:6—7; 1 Thess 5:1ff.). Mt 24:28/Lk 17:37 quash any doubts about mistaking the parousia by little more than the use of a proverb, an argument from nature. The delicate and divisive issue of the physical support of missionaries (cf. 1 Cor 9:4—14; 1 Tim 5:18) is met in a similar way in Lk 10:7b/Mt 10:10b. The latter case is an obviously secondary addition to the context of the sayings in Lk 10:2ff. par and is striking confirmation of our contention that the aphoristic sayings were deliberately used to meet practical problems requiring tact and sensitivity in the early Christian communities. This confirms again the findings for the aphoristic sayings collections.

This confidence in the persuasive effect of aphorism and reason goes beyond the use of aphorisms for argumentative purposes in either Matthew or Luke. In Matthew's gospel, aphoristic sayings add rhetorical colour to the strong invectives against false prophets (7:16–20) and Pharisees (12:33–7, 15:14, 23:24), but the point is carried ultimately not by persuasion but by warning and invective. This is illustrated particularly well in Mt 12:33 ('Either make the tree good and its fruit good; or make the tree bad and its fruit bad'), where an aphoristic sentence (cf. Mt 7:17–18/Lk 6:43) is actually turned into an admonition under the influence of the forcefulness of the invective. However, there are examples in Matthew of aphorisms used to support exhortations of a more instructional type, which thereby have an argumentative function: Mt 5:36 on swearing; Mt 6:34b on anxieties; cf. also Mt 26:52b. Yet, even in these cases the aphorisms seldom carry the argument alone. In the case of swearing, the maxim on the futility of swearing (5:36b), which supports the command not to swear by your head, is followed by another authoritative declaration that anything more than a 'Yes' or 'No' 'comes from evil' (5:37).[349] In Mt 26:52b, the aphorism about those who draw the sword carries rather less weight as an argument for restraint than the following assurance that Jesus could have called on the Father for angels in support if he really wanted them (26:53–4). Mt 6:34b ('for tomorrow will be anxious for itself') is a rare example of an aphorism which is part of a wisdom admonition but is allowed to stand as a sufficient argument in itself without a more prophetic or specifically authoritative declaration. It may owe this in part, however, to its position immediately after the aphoristic sayings collection of Mt 6:25–33 par on anxiety.[350]

Luke shows a slight interest independent of his tradition in the use of isolated aphorisms in debate or argument, but again the examples are limited. The most interesting is the short aphoristic 'debate' in Lk 4:23–4, but also peculiar to Luke is a concise saying of distinctly 'religious' terminology which occurs in argument against the Pharisees in Lk 16:15b ('For what is exalted among men is an abomination in the sight of God').[351] This latter saying was used in a way similar to Luke's use of the 'future reversal' sayings:[352] to show how humility was at the heart of the kingdom message of repentance, aimed often against Pharisees but with implications for the wider world (cf. also Lk 7:47). Sometimes isolated aphorisms were used by Luke to draw out general summary observations from parables (cf. Lk 12:48, 14:11, 18:14) rather than strictly to advance or support argument, but usually on the theme of renunciation of pride or riches. This is also the subject of more explicit teaching in Luke (see 12:15). Like Matthew, Luke also shows some evidence of the tendency to make aphorisms into exhortations for the church, as in Lk 22:26: 'let the greatest among you become as the youngest, and the leader as one who serves' (cf. Lk 9:48 par). On the whole, the use of aphorisms for advance or support of argument is not a marked redactional characteristic of Luke's gospel. While such a use is not wholly unique to double-tradition material, its prominence in this material relative to other sources or redaction must be recognized to be distinctive.

Finally, one must again return to questions about the perspective implicit in the use of practical wisdom of this kind. The aphorisms used in eschatological announcements such as Lk 3:9b/Mt 3:10b, raise the question of the continuity perceived between the present world and the imminent eschaton. It would seem that the principles of judgement are not new or unexpected, but grounded in the very fabric of ordinary life. Even the call to vulnerability in this life (cf. Mt 6:19–21 par) is supported in terms of this-worldly wisdom. This wisdom may be selectively applied, but it is difficult to escape the conclusion that the challenge with which men are confronted is viewed not as something running against their experience, but as that which draws conviction from that experience of life. Practical wisdom has not been undermined by the eschatological perspective.

A similar emphasis seems to influence the presentation of Jesus and his ministry in some of the sayings analysed. In the 'Beelzebul' controversy the defence of Jesus shows a predilection for demonstrating his validity as an exorcist by applying tests of reason against the charges made by his opponents. This approach sharply contrasts with attempts to defend Jesus by asserting his distinctive status from an explicit confessional stance. This need not imply a 'deficient' recognition of the status of Jesus, but for the purpose of the controversy his validity is demonstrated apart from claims for uniqueness. The lack of differentiation between Jesus and John the Baptist in the saying in Lk 7:35 par is also evidence of this tendency. H. J. Cadbury observed in general terms that originality and novelty were not necessarily coveted characteristics in the ancient world. He concluded:[353]

> Certainly claims of continuity and antiquity are much more
> likely to have been made for Jesus by his friends than the

reverse. Since our gospels come from friendly sources they are unlikely to stress novelty and originality ... Even when novelty in Christianity was regarded as an asset it had to compete with or combine with the still valid and valuable claim of antiquity.

These lines of continuity with experience and the past did have to be reconciled, however, with a recognition of the special status of Jesus and with the announcement he proclaimed. Of particular interest, therefore, will be the way in which the tradition of practical wisdom was united with other branches of sapiential thought which treat wisdom as a special revealed knowledge and Jesus as representing divine Sophia. This will be our next subject of enquiry.

4

THE PLACE OF APHORISTIC WISDOM IN THE SAPIENTIAL TRADITIONS OF THE DOUBLE TRADITION

Introduction

The distinctiveness of structure and argument which has been found to characterize several aphoristic sayings-collections of the double tradition leads one to infer the existence of a unique circle of people who formulated these collections.[1] It is unlikely that such a pattern of collection and argument is due to accident or coincidence during the transmission of the traditions. Because many isolated aphoristic sayings of the double tradition can also be shown to share some of these argumentative functions, and because of some overlap with the themes of the aphoristic collections, it seems also that the activity of this circle of early Christians extended beyond the compilation of collections alone. Indeed, if such a circle existed it would be surprising if its activity were limited to a set of seven collections of Jesus' logia alone.

How much more widely, however, was this sapiential activity exerting its influence in the formulation of the Jesus-tradition? It is doubtful that this question can be answered directly, yet there are some clear indications as to where one might investigate further. On the one hand, M. Boring[2] argues that early Christian teachers in general were often not far removed from prophets: that is, they often seemed to have a charismatic function as well as employing the natural gifts of learning. While few would doubt that the 'teacher' must have played an important role in early Christianity, the figure itself is remarkably poorly defined.[3] This makes distinctions between different types of teachers difficult to verify. Boring's observations suggest, though, that a sapiential circle might have had an interest also in 'the revelation of Spirit-given "mysteries"'.[4]

This possibility arises also in another way. In Chapter 1 it was noted how 'wisdom' is not an undifferentiated tradition. While this book has concentrated on the relatively neglected area of aphoristic wisdom, other sapiential traditions existed by NT times which considered wisdom as an interpretative construct for Torah, or which alluded to a divine Sophia figure, or which referred to a secret wisdom to which access was only by revelation. These categories allow again for some kind of 'revelatory' wisdom, alongside the aphoristic tradition.

It will not necessarily be the case that these other branches of sapiential thought have stemmed from the same circle as that which was responsible for collecting the aphoristic sayings of the double tradition. These other sapiential traditions may be functionally and even epistemologically distinct. Yet there may be overlap as well. It is striking, for example, that one of the most fruitful sources for sayings about *divine* Sophia in the synoptic tradition has been double-tradition material. A brief description of this material will therefore be our starting-point, and then the question will be posed as to how the various streams of sapiential tradition are related.

Divine Sophia in the double tradition

The origin and development of thought concerning the figure of divine Sophia has been widely discussed, and it is not necessary for our present purposes to reproduce that discussion. It is sufficient to note that it is unlikely that there was any simple fixed myth about the Sophia-figure, if, indeed, there was a 'myth' at all.[5] The portrayal of divine Sophia was, therefore, open to varying emphases and new characteristics according to the tradition in which it was used. For example, Küchler[6] has traced how changes occurred in the nature of Wisdom's call to instruction. Increasingly, he notes, Sophia's instruction and guidance were seen to be a divine gift and the particular possession of Israel. This is detectable in Sir 24, where Sophia becomes directly associated with the Torah.[7] A similar step was taken in 1 Bar 3:9–4:4[8] and can be traced later in rabbinic literature.[9] Yet, in the Wisdom of Solomon the call to heed Wisdom is expressed less directly in terms of Torah than in terms of a more heterogeneous blend of concepts, including an intimate religious or intellectual experience which guides man to perfection and union with God.[10] Wisdom is also presented as an active principle in Israel's history (WisSol 10–19). The reasons for these changing emphases are open to debate, especially regarding the relative importance of theological and apologetic influences.[11] But there can be little doubt that the presentation of divine Sophia did vary and was subject to changing influences.

Traditions about Sophia also became incorporated into some apocalyptic literature. Here Sophia becomes hidden from all but the elect, and her withdrawal in 1 En 42 and 4 Ezra 5:8−10 takes on the character of a warning and prelude to judgement.[12] M. Hengel has also sought to trace the merging of ideas about Sophia with Spirit, Son of Man and Messiah.[13] He cites a tradition extending from Is 11:1−4 through PsSol 17 and 18 to WisSol 7:22−7. The conjunction of Sophia and Son of Man is also presented in 1 En 37−71.[14] This merging of ideas is not systematically worked out, and even in the Similitudes of Enoch no explicit identification of Sophia with Son of Man or Messiah is made. The Sophia figure itself remains rather obscure, but there is a flowing association of ideas in which Wisdom has a part. The 'spirit of wisdom' is a special gift or revelation, associated with salvation and judgement. It is far removed from being a simple guide for everyday life.

Another constraint on the emergence of a well-developed Sophia myth in Jewish thought may have been the monotheistic presupposition of Yahwism. Despite the allusions to a Sophia figure in Sirach, 1 Baruch, 1 Enoch, Wisdom of Solomon and Philo, Dunn argues that Wisdom remains largely the personification of a '*function* of Yahweh, a way of speaking about God himself, of expressing God's active involvement with this world and his people without compromising his transcendence'.[15] G. Macrae also observes that the tendency to hypostatization was greater in the gnostic literature than in the earlier Jewish literature.[16] For whatever reasons, Sophia's personification in Jewish circles did not apparently result in a clearly defined myth by the first century AD.[17]

In view of this openness to various emphases, it is imperative to discover how the concept of Sophia fared in the synoptic tradition. This particular aspect of sapiential thought has received considerable attention in recent decades, and much of the interest has in fact focused on the double tradition. Not only has it become clear that most of the synoptic sayings which seem to allude to Sophia are double-tradition material, but also distinctive emphases have been suggested for these sayings. One important exception is Mt 11:28−30, which cannot easily be identified as double-tradition material. But G. N. Stanton has recently cast doubt on how far this 'yoke' saying in Matthew does in fact allude to the figure of Sophia in Sir 6 and 51, and on whether these themes are indeed the key to the passage *as it now stands*.[18] Even if this be allowed as an exception, however, the importance of the double-tradition 'Sophia' logia cannot be denied.

A fresh analysis of each of these logia would take us beyond the scope of our present endeavour and would in any case simply duplicate many of the findings which are easily accessible in a variety of recent studies.[19] It will be sufficient to indicate some of the more important conclusions reached by these studies.

An important contribution of M. J. Suggs' influential study of *Wisdom, Christology and Law in Matthew's Gospel* is the argument that the Sophia sayings of the double tradition have identifiable and distinctive characteristics which can be differentiated from the later tradition, and from Matthew in particular. He argues that in the Q-form of the sayings Jesus is considered the final envoy of divine Sophia, while in the later formulation of Matthew Jesus is identified with Sophia.[20] Suggs' observation that Luke preserved the more original form of the saying about Wisdom's children in Lk 7:35 (cf. Mt 11:19b) and of Wisdom's oracle in Lk 11:49−51 (cf. Mt 23:34−6), which Matthew then turned into sayings about and by Jesus himself, has been confirmed by C. Tuckett.[21] These are the two synoptic sayings which refer to σοφία explicitly and in terms compatible with a divine figure.

Suggs finds a similar change in speaker in the lament of Lk 13: 34−5/Mt 23:37−9,[22] although in this case it is more difficult to establish that Sophia was intended, even in Luke, as the speaker of the lament. Tuckett, however, argues that Luke's difficult ἥξει phrase ('you will not see *me* until *he* [or the time] comes when you will say, Blessed is he who comes ...') suggests that originally there was a distinction between the speaker (Wisdom) and the 'coming one', which Matthew then removed[23] and which Luke glossed over. The speaker of the lament in its pre-Lukan form was Sophia.

In favour of an attribution to Sophia in the pre-gospel formulation of this saying are the following observations: (i) The possible conjunction of the saying with Lk 11:49−51/Mt 23:34−6 in the underlying tradition may provide the context of a 'Sophia' saying.[24] (ii) The image of the hen gathering its brood is a maternal image for divine being in 4(5) Ezra 1:30 and 2 Bar 41:3−4. It is further applied to Sophia in Sir 1:15 (Gk: 'She made as a nest among men an eternal foundation') and to the Shekinah.[25] (iii) The lament ('How *often* would I have gathered your children together') presupposes a supra-historical figure.[26] (iv) The sending of the prophets and their rejection recalls Lk 11:49−51/Mt 23:34−6. (v) The withdrawal of the speaker recalls 1 En 42 or at least a reworking of Sir 24, both of which deal with Sophia's seeking a place to dwell (cf. also Prov 1:28; Sir 15:7).[27] (vi) The Jerusalem reference may also recall Sir 24.

While these arguments are highly suggestive, one still faces the difficulty of the absence of any direct attribution to Sophia in either Matthew or Luke.[28] Thus J.D.G. Dunn, without denying the allusions to Sophia, argues that the saying is presented in the Lukan and pre-Lukan tradition as coming from Jesus himself, who speaks the lament as the *messenger* of Sophia.[29] This also somewhat eases the problem of identifying the 'I' who directly addresses the Jews with a supra-historical figure.[30] Yet, this does little to resolve the distinction between the speaker and 'he who comes in the name of the Lord' in the saying. For this reason one must still allow the possibility that in the pre-Lukan tradition the saying was a lament of Sophia, whether or not already joined with Lk 11:49−51 par.

In addition to these three important logia, another small set of double-tradition sayings has sometimes been identified as containing allusions to a Sophia-figure. One passage, Mt 11:25−7/Lk 10:21−2, will receive separate consideration below. However, one must also cite sayings such as the 'homelessness' logion in Lk 9:58/Mt 8:20 and the declaration that 'something greater than Solomon is here' in Lk 11:31/Mt 12:42.[31]

In the case of the latter saying, the σοφία of Solomon is expressly superseded, but without any direct reference to a Sophia-figure. The 'something greater' is almost deliberately vague. The references to σοφία and to the example of Solomon[32] are very unexpected in their general context of Lk 11:29−32 par, where the focus is consistently on Jonah (Lk 11:29, 30, 32 par) except for Lk 11:31 par. Even the use of the term κήρυγμα in parallel with σοφία is quite exceptional, apart from 1 Cor 1:21−3, 2:4.[33] While R.A. Edwards has sought to draw attention to the redactional significance for Q of the 'eschatological correlative' Son of Man saying in Lk 11:30 par,[34] one might with equal forcefulness cite the unexpectedness of the motif of σοφία in this context as a redactional creation of a 'double saying' in the underlying tradition.[35] In this respect, it is not unlike the surprising occurrence of the σοφία reference in Lk 7:35 par at the end of a long double-tradition section on John the Baptist.[36] Yet, if one is to see any allusion in Lk 11:31 to divine Sophia, it is only in a veiled way by an extrapolation from the σοφία of Solomon to 'something greater'.

Perhaps even more elusive is any Sophia motif in the 'homelessness' logion (Lk 9:58/Mt 8:20). In both its Lukan and its Matthean formulation it is indisputably a saying about the Son of Man, but an allusion to Sophia has been urged by some scholars, largely on the basis of a comparison with 1 En 42:1−2 (contrast Sir 24:8ff.).[37] In the 1 Enoch passage, Sophia finds nowhere among men to dwell. Yet, in 1 En 42, this leads to Sophia's withdrawal, while there is no such suggestion in the double-tradition 'Son of Man' logion.[38] Also, it must be admitted that the general motif of homelessness can be derived from sources other than 1 En 42 − sources which do not directly refer to Sophia. The phenomenon of wandering teachers was well known in the ancient world,[39] and Bultmann even suggested that the logion could have been adapted from a proverb.[40] It would appear that 1 En 42 is only one possible source for the imagery in this saying.[41]

Another argument which has been offered in support of a 'Sophia' allusion in Lk 9:58 par, however, is based upon the order of logia in a fixed Q-source. In the reconstruction of the sequence of Q made by A. Polag, Lk 9:58 par immediately follows the 'Sophia' logion in Lk 7:35 par.[42] Further, A. Jacobson has recently argued that in the later redaction of Q Lk 9:58 par introduced the second major section of Q and that the 'sections' of Q generally were denoted by Sophia sayings.[43] However, Jacobson's case would be stronger if the Sophia allusion itself were stronger for this logion, and unfortunately the later 'sections of Q' do not apparently exhibit the same demarcations by 'Sophia' logia.[44] Again, it seems that one must conclude that an allusion to Sophia's search for a place to dwell is only one possibility for this logion, and that any observations about the 'Sophia' logia must not rest too heavily on it alone.[45]

One can thus detect in the double-tradition material a set of 'Sophia' pericopes which at least includes Lk 7:35 par and Lk 11:49−51 par as the clearest examples, and Lk 11:31 par, 13:34−5 par and possibly 9:58 par as further allusions. The next step is to consider whether these sayings have any other common features. Here, too, significant strides have been made in recent studies. Two important observations have emerged.

First, these 'Sophia' sayings are used to express the rejection of God's messengers by Israel. O. H. Steck[46] draws attention to how Lk 11:49ff. par and 13:34−5 par continued the Deuteronomistic tradition of the fate of the prophets, a tradition which has its roots even in Neh 9:26 and Ezra 9:11. It came into contact with the 'Sophia'-tradition in 1 Bar 3:9−4:4. Yet Steck clearly shows that the tradition of the fate of the prophets is not restricted to 'Sophia' texts of the double tradition (cf., e.g., the beatitude in Lk 6:22−3 par).[47] Mk 12:1−9 is a further example of the motif, but attributed to a different context, namely 'im hellenistischen Urchristentum';[48] and possibly other synoptic texts (cf. Mk 6:4) also reflect this rejection theme.

Steck's thesis has drawn wide interest,[49] but his observations have been pressed yet further by A. Jacobson and C. Tuckett. Tuckett argues that the *combination* of the Deuteronomistic tradition of the fate of the prophets with Sophia is a *distinctive* theme of the double tradition (Lk 7:35 par, 11:49−51 par and 13:34−5 par).[50] Jacobson considers additional 'Sophia' and other logia of the double tradition, suggesting that the motif of the rejection of Jesus also applies to Sophia's search for a place to dwell in Lk 9:58 par, as well as to Lk 13:34−5 par and Lk 11:24−6 (the return of the unclean spirit). Further, he notes that the sending of messengers to Israel can be found in Lk 11:29−32 par and Lk 10:16 par (lacking reference to Sophia).[51] Jacobson considers all of these passages distinctive of 'the compositional stage of Q'.[52] For our purposes, however, it is sufficient to note how the theme of the rejection of God's messengers by Israel has been combined with 'Sophia' terminology in the double-tradition material, so that the rejection motif has become integral to (even if not limited to) the employment of the 'Sophia' motif.

This point hardly needs further elaboration for Lk 11:49−51 par or for Lk 13:34−5 par, if one accepts an allusion to Sophia in the latter. The same would apply to Lk 9:58 par. Jacobson rightly argues that this 'homelessness' logion is not just about discipleship, but is a statement about Jesus himself and his own rejection.[53] The homelessness does not appear to be chosen; the contrast with 'homes' of foxes and birds suggests that the 'homelessness' is something unnatural[54] and thus a sign of rejection. For Lk 7:35 par, the rejection motif is quite clear in the preceding verses, Lk 7:31−4 par. The reference to Sophia in verse 35, however, is unexpected[55] and may provide evidence of a deliberate, if somewhat strained, effort in the underlying tradition to bring the rejection motif together with the concept of Sophia.[56] This applies also, as noted above, to the σοφία reference in Lk 11:31 par within the context of the 'Sign of Jonah' pericope (Lk 11:29−32 par). As in Lk 7:31−5 par, the men of 'this generation' are specifically criticized in the 'Sign of Jonah' pericope for their rejection of the message brought to them by Jesus (Lk 11: 29, 30, 31−2 par). They therefore stand condemned by the men of Nineveh and the Queen of the South, who, as non-Jews,[57] responded positively to the message of God delivered to them. The rejection motif is a consistent feature of each of the Sophia passages of the double tradition.

Secondly, the 'Sophia' pericopes of the double tradition were considered by M. J. Suggs to portray Jesus as the final eschatological envoy of divine Sophia, but not yet as Sophia herself.[58] In terms of the Deuteronomistic tradition of the fate of the prophets, Jesus is the culmination of the messengers sent by God/Sophia. Earlier studies of these double-tradition pericopes largely tended to identify Jesus with Sophia,[59] but more recent studies have followed the lead of Suggs.[60] It is Matthew who is credited with the actual identification of Jesus and Sophia (cf. Mt 11:19b, 23:34–6).[61]

The evidence for Jesus as the final envoy of Sophia is mainly derived from Lk 7:35 par. Most recent studies accept the greater originality of Luke's τέκνων to Matthew's ἔργων for the reason that Matthew's 'works' echoes Mt 11:2 and thereby forms an *inclusio* around an important Matthean theme.[62] Matthew effectively identified the 'works of Sophia' (11:19b) with the 'works of Christ' (11:2). For Luke the point is different. The contrast is set up in Lk 7:29–30 between 'all the people and the toll-collectors' who acknowledged God to be right (ἐδικαίωσαν), and the Pharisees and lawyers who rejected the βουλὴ τοῦ θεοῦ. This is continued in Lk 7:33–5. Unlike the children in the market-place (7:32) and those who criticize both John the Baptist and Jesus the Son of Man (7:33–4), all the τέκνα τῆς σοφίας are those who 'acknowledge' Sophia to be right (7:35). Luke's use of πάντων makes clear that τέκνα are not simply Jesus and John the Baptist, but all those who have responded to her revealed announcement (cf. Lk 7:29).[63]

M. J. Suggs differentiated between Luke's interpretation and that of Q, however. Suggs argues that because the πάντων may be a Lukan addition to 7:35, and because 7:29–30 cannot be assigned to Q, in Luke's underlying source there were only *two* sets of principals: the men of this generation on the one hand, and Jesus and John the Baptist on the other. So for Q, he argues, only Jesus and John are Sophia's children, her End-time representatives.[64]

But Suggs' conclusion has been subject to recent questioning. This has arisen on three main grounds: the meaning of δικαιόω in Lk 7:35 par, since it is difficult to see how Jesus and John 'acknowledge' Sophia;[65] the possible pre-Lukan origin of πάντων in Lk 7:35 par;[66] and the parallel of Lk 7:29 with Mt 21:32, which suggests that Lk 7:29 can be attributed to double tradition and had a place in the underlying source for the 'Sophia' pericope.[67] The effect of these arguments is to deny to Jesus and John alone the category of τέκνα τῆς σοφίας in the pre-Lukan tradition, and to apply it instead to those who *respond* to Sophia (cf. 'sons of Wisdom' in Sir 4:11; Prov 8:32). The pre-Lukan tradition was represented essentially in Luke. To differentiate between Jesus and the τέκνα τῆς σοφίας in Lk 7:35, however, is not to deny that Jesus was viewed as 'representing' Sophia. This remains a legitimate inference from the conjunction of Lk 7:35 par with 7:(29–30), 31–4 par. But Jesus is not a unique representative of Sophia. Although as Son of Man he is differentiated from John the Baptist in Lk 7:33–4 par, Jesus is clearly placed alongside John in the rejection of his ministry by 'this generation' in the final collection of sayings. Also, no assumption is necessarily implied that this understanding of Jesus and John drew upon a recognized role from Jewish ideas about Sophia's 'representatives'. It may well have been in the double tradition itself that the role of the representative of Sophia was first defined.[68]

These inferences about Jesus and Sophia drawn from Lk 7:35 par are supported by the other 'Sophia' logia of the double tradition. It is true that the Sophia oracle in Lk 11:49–51 par[69] makes no direct reference to Jesus himself. But, because the guilt for all those prophets and messengers[70] sent to Israel and killed by her is placed upon 'this generation', the implication is that the rejection and killing of Jesus (and John the Baptist?) is the culmination of this history of rejection. Whether the followers of Jesus also form part of this experience of rejection by 'this generation' is less clear, but in view of Lk 6:22–3/ Mt 5:11–12 it cannot be wholly ruled out.[71]

If Lk 13:34–5 par is a saying of Sophia, it does little to alter the conclusions already drawn. The main interest centres on 'he who comes in the name of the Lord' (Lk 13:35 par), who seems distinct from the speaker (Sophia), but in some way to be representing the speaker: 'you will not see *me* until *he* comes ...'. Other previous representatives of Sophia may be implied in the lament 'How often I would have gathered your children together', but this is hardly explicit.[72]

In Lk 11:31 par, it is the presence before this generation of πλεῖον Σολομῶνος that implies that Jesus' message at least is a message of 'wisdom'. Lk 11:31 par is not in itself an obvious christological statement at all. Emphasis is put on the message that is borne rather than on the precise status of the bearer himself.[73] Therefore, in these five logia there is a consistent attempt to *relate* Jesus and his message to Sophia, but the *precise* relationship is not made explicit. It seems doubtful that Jesus was actually identified with Sophia, so the inference that he 'represents' her is probable. This is also consistent with the use of the Deuteronomistic tradition of the prophets' fate in Lk 11:49−51 par and Lk 13:34−5 par, with the placing of Jesus alongside John the Baptist in Lk 7:33−5 par, and with the parallelism with the prophet Jonah in Lk 11:29−32 par.

G. N. Stanton observes about the christology of the double-tradition material that, in general, 'christological titles are of less interest to Q than the grounds of the authority of Jesus'.[74] Certainly the 'Sophia' logia would support such a view, both in their ambiguity about providing a precise role for Jesus and in their implicit authentication of Jesus and his message by associating him with other messengers to Israel who also suffered rejection. Yet, there are still some indications of the uniqueness of Jesus' ministry too. One important one is the way in which the culmination of this history of rejection of Sophia's messengers is identified with 'this generation'. D. Lührmann has argued that the polemic against 'this generation' is also a compositional motif of 'Q-Redaktion'. It appears in conjunction with the 'Sophia' sayings in Lk 7:35 par, 11:49−51 par, 11: 29−32 par and 13:34−5 par.[75] Indeed, the Sophia logia themselves have strong claim to being a compositional motif within the double-tradition material, as has been variously argued by A. Jacobson with respect to the composition of Q as a whole[76] and by J. Wanke with respect to the secondary nature of Lk 7:33−4, 35 par, 9:57−8 par, and 11:31−2 par in their immediate contexts.[77] The association with the polemic against '*this* generation', though, inevitably gives special significance to Jesus even as a 'representative' of Sophia. He is not just another in a long line of envoys; he marks the culmination of that history (cf. Lk 11:50−1 par).[78]

Mt 11:25−7/Lk 10:21−2 and access to revelation

One double-tradition pericope in which sapiential influences are to be found, but which has been felt by some scholars to differ from the other 'Sophia' logia, is the notoriously difficult passage in Mt 11: 25−7/Lk 10:21−2.[79] Precisely how, though, do these sayings conflict with the previously examined Sophia sayings?

A. Jacobson has pointed to three important indications that Lk 10:21−2 par must be a later addition to Q than the other Sophia passages. First, in the 'thanksgiving' saying (Lk 10:21 par) the Deuteronomistic tradition appears to be contradicted, because Israel no longer seems to be culpable for her unbelief. It is God's will that the revelation has been hidden from her. Secondly, in the 'revelation' saying (Lk 10:22 par) Jesus as Son becomes the *sole* mediator of the knowledge of God. He no longer stands in a line of prophets and envoys of Sophia. Thirdly, in both sayings Wisdom is now inaccessible, in contrast to Wisdom's call to men in the 'Sophia' pericopes.[80] Jacobson has not been alone in finding Lk 10:21–2 par somewhat alien to the synoptic tradition,[81] and his conclusion that it is a later reflection on sapiential themes need not seriously affect one's assessment of the other 'Sophia' logia of the double tradition.

Yet, Lk 10:21–2 par may in fact be closer to the outlook of the other 'Sophia' logia than is often recognized. Each of Jacobson's arguments is open to further consideration.

Regarding the culpability of Israel in the 'thanksgiving' saying, it is surely doubtful that Israel is viewed as no longer responsible for her blindness. In the first place, Jacobson himself notes that the criticism of the σοφοὶ καὶ συνετοί must be understood as a 'sarcastic inversion of a current Jewish claim'.[82] This kind of attack against the leadership of a religious establishment is not without parallel (cf. Jer 8:8–9; Is 29:14, cited also in 1 Cor 1:18–19; 1 QpHab 12:2–10;[83] 11QPs^a 18:3–6).[84] It therefore contains an implicit rebuke, which in turn must imply a degree of culpability. These men above all *should* have understood the significance of Jesus' ministry. Secondly, this observation is reinforced by the immediate context of Lk 10:21–2/ Mt 11:25–7 in double-tradition material. It is immediately preceded by the woes pronounced upon the Galilean cities (Lk 10:12–15/ Mt 11:20–4), in which the culpability of those who have failed to respond is clear: 'if the mighty works done in you had been done in Tyre and Sidon, they would have repented long ago'. Thirdly, the language of the hiddenness of revelation is found also in apocalyptic traditions where the withdrawal of Wisdom before unrighteous men is a sign of the eschatological age (cf. 4 Ezra 5:9–10; 1 En 42). It is doubtful that this withdrawal was seen as removing the culpability of the people; rather, it is the prelude to eschatological judgement on unrighteousness.[85] Finally, one must beware of reading the 'thanksgiving' logion primarily as a detailed statement about the opponents of God's revelation. While opponents have been addressed in the preceding woes, the thanksgiving itself is primarily for the *recipients* of God's saving revelation.[86] These may be seen as similar to the τέκνα τῆς σοφίας of Lk 7:35 par, in opposition to 'this generation'. The case for the irreconcilability of the 'thanksgiving' saying with the other double-tradition 'Sophia' logia is therefore open to doubt.

Regarding the emphasis on the sole mediation of 'the Son' in the 'revelation' saying (Lk 10:22 par), Jacobson's argument is again open to re-evaluation. The reference to 'the Son' needs to be elucidated, but it must be examined in its own right, not simply as a variant for 'Sophia'[87] or even for 'the Son of Man'.[88] The use of the term 'Son' expresses a filial relationship, although it is unlikely that Lk 10:22 par simply refers to *any* son and *any* father.[89] The phrase 'no one knows the Son ...'[90] would itself seem to require a more specific interpretation of ὁ υἱός. J. Dunn, following Suggs, has been impressed by the parallels with the righteous and wise Israelite, who is described as God's 'son' in WisSol 2:13, 16−18 and 4:10−15.[91] The righteous disciple of Wisdom is also described in WisSol 7:27−9, 6:21−2. It is open to question whether this 'son' is the 'organ of revelation' in the Wisdom of Solomon,[92] but the rather more special use of 'Son' in Lk 10:22 par is explained by Dunn in terms of the 'eschatological immediacy of his knowledge of God's will'.[93] Such a special eschatological status for Jesus exists even in the Deuteronomistic tradition of the 'Sophia' logia (see Lk 13:34−5 par, 11:49−51 par). A.E. Harvey[94] has pointed to still further nuances in the 'Son' terminology, such as obedience (cf. Prov 4:4), the transmission of knowledge from teacher to pupil (cf. Prov. 4:1)[95] and the authorization to act as fully empowered agent (Tob 5:2 א). The last is particularly striking, for Harvey concludes that 'the designation of him as Son of God clearly implied that he was God's authorized agent and representative'.[96] This is precisely the 'role' ascribed to Jesus in the previously studied 'Sophia' logia! Thus, sapiential traditions may illumine aspects of Lk 10:22 par without implying an identification of Jesus with Sophia,[97] and in ways consistent with the other 'Sophia' logia.

But what of the limitation of access to revelation through the Son alone? As Jacobson observes, the question of access to revelation is more the focal point of this saying than christology.[98] The restriction of revelation, though, is almost certainly a *foil* against which to show where wisdom in fact *has* been received. The 'Son' is God's agent, and the limitation of revelation is essential to highlight the division already made in Lk 10:21 par between those who have received the revelation and those who have not. It serves to validate those to whom the revelation *is* given (cf. Lk 7:35 par) and for whom thanksgiving is made. The fact that the Deuteronomistic history of the fate of the prophets is not directly invoked may well be due to the fact that this saying is addressed to those who have received God's message rather than to its opponents. For similar reasons, this Deuteronomistic history was also not directly invoked in Lk 7:35 par.

If these considerations for the 'thanksgiving' and 'revelation' sayings in Lk 10:21−2 par are given full weight, it can be shown how one is not compelled to postulate for Lk 10:21−2 par a markedly contrasting viewpoint from that of the other 'Sophia' logia. It need not represent a distinctly 'later' perspective.[99]

The interaction of sapiential traditions in double-tradition material

It is clear that within the double tradition there are sayings which reflect a variety of sapiential emphases. We have seen that, in addition to the aphoristic wisdom which is formulated as wide-ranging observations from human experience and as general instructions, there is the tradition in which Jesus appears as the rejected representative of divine Sophia. There may also be hints of the apocalyptic notion that the coming of the End-time will be marked by wisdom being hidden from unrighteous men (cf. Lk 10:21d par). A variety of such concepts was present also in the Jewish wisdom literature, as M. Küchler has shown,[100] so that it is hardly surprising that these various strands of sapiential traditions should mingle with one another wherever a conscious interest in 'wisdom' is present.

Perhaps more surprising, however, is the relative lack of speculation about the Torah in connection with these other sapiential themes. Such speculation was clearly present in Sir 24:23−9; 1 Bar 4:1 and the rabbinic literature, as well as less directly in many other Jewish works.[101] This absence does not seem to be due to a sustained attempt to challenge the validity of the Torah itself in double-tradition sayings (cf. Mt 5:18/Lk 16:17; Mt 23:23/Lk 11:42).[102] Yet, the failure to develop a clear sapiential understanding of the Torah in double-tradition material may be less surprising if one gives full weight to the way in which the 'divine Sophia' logia have been used to express Israel's rejection of God's messengers. Sophia is set in opposition to the authorities who represent Israel. They are the learned custodians of the Torah. In contrast to their rejection of Jesus, the message of Sophia is received by her children (Lk 7:35 par) or the 'babes' (Lk 10:21 par). The message comes to them as κήρυγμα and σοφία (Lk 11:31−2 par) rather than the Torah. It would not have been impossible to challenge 'this generation' through a sapiential interpretation of the Torah,[103] but the fact that this has not been done would suggest that this line of attack proved less attractive or less successful than putting the emphasis on linking wisdom and prophecy,[104] as in Lk 11:31–2 par and in the association of Sophia with the Deuteronomistic tradition of the fate of the prophets.[105] One can only speculate as to why a sapiential interpretation of the Torah did not itself prove more attractive.

Even if the Torah has not been integrated into the sapiential streams of tradition running through the sayings of the double tradition, it must be recognized that tensions may exist even between the sapiential traditions which *are* represented. The instance of Lk 10: 21–2 par has already been discussed, but found less problematic than often argued. However, one must also allow for an epistemological difference between the emphasis on experiential knowledge in the aphoristic material and the implication of a 'revelation' to be presented by those who represent divine Sophia (and especially in Lk 10:21–2 par).[106] Although both are alternatives to finding the locus of knowledge of God supremely in the Torah and scribal learning, it is doubtful that this alone is sufficient to reconcile the two. Further, our own findings have indicated that these two sapiential streams are functionally well defined and distinct within the double tradition. On the one hand, the aphoristic collections were aimed at persuading followers to adopt certain attitudes in response to particular issues of sensitivity within the fellowship. Their appeal was thus phrased in a non-partisan and universal way, which allowed the hearers to be distanced somewhat from emotionally sensitive issues and open to persuasion. Hyperbole and even humour are employed (cf. Mt 7:1–5 par) to this effect. On the other hand, the concern of the Sophia logia was primarily the problem of the rejection of Jesus by Israel and his accreditation. The concerns are thus differently directed. Is it possible, then, to speak of any interaction between these two streams of wisdom in the double tradition?

J.M. Robinson has raised the possibility that such a conjunction of traditions can be understood in terms of a 'trajectory', whereby 'it is partly because the *Gattung* was itself associated with the "wise" that it could be easily swept into the christological development moving from personified Wisdom to the gnostic redeemer'.[107] Apart from recent questioning of whether such a gnosticizing tendency was in fact implicit in the Q-material,[108] the suggestion of an implicit connection between the sapiential nature of the sayings collection and the christological development of sapiential categories is worthy of closer consideration. It would be a reasonable *a priori* hypothesis that the *Gattung* of λόγοι σοφῶν would encourage viewing Jesus in relation to Sophia. Yet, there is surprisingly little direct evidence in the double tradition to show that Jesus was understood christologically as Sophia's representative *because he spoke in proverbs*. The 'Sophia' logia in the double tradition are concerned with the rejection by Israel of Jesus' message, not with the aphoristic formulation of that message. It is true that the comparison with Solomon in Lk 11:31 par may come closest to the latter idea, but σοφία is so closely parallel to κήρυγμα in the context that it is unlikely that the σοφία of Solomon is viewed primarily as the proverbial sayings of a wise man. Similarly, despite some claims that the sayings in Lk 7:35 par or 9:58 par were originally aphorisms,[109] it is doubtful whether this observation in itself demonstrates any effective integration of the sapiential traditions. Lk 7:35 par is not universally accepted as aphoristic in form,[110] and the understanding of 'the Son of Man' in Lk 9:58 par may also affect any allegedly universal qualities of the saying.[111] Robinson may well be correct about implicit associations between sapiential traditions, but explicit attempts to integrate these traditions are difficult to pinpoint in the double tradition.

The question of the interaction of sapiential traditions can be avoided by simply assigning the various streams of sapiential expression to different stages in the development of the pre-synoptic tradition. This is most noticeable in the works of those scholars who have emphasized distinct stages in the development of Q. Even D. Lührmann assigns the 'Sophia' logia and Lk 10:21–2 par to a late stage of the redaction of Q, while most of the aphoristic sayings collections are assigned to an earlier period of compilation.[112] S. Schulz divides the material in a similar way, although Lk 6:43–5 par, Lk 12:2–3 par, and many individual aphoristic sayings are assigned to the later 'Syrian' Q-community.[113] A. Polag distinguishes more stages, assigning most of the aphoristic collections to an early stage of Q-tradition prior even to the main Q-collection, the 'Sophia' logia to the redaction of the main collection, and Lk 10:21–2 par to a still later redaction.[114]

The most substantial attempt to show how the 'Sophia' logia were added at the compositional stage of Q has been made by A. Jacobson. Jacobson's task is not to study the entire composition of Q, but he does argue persuasively for a theological coherence between the primary 'Sophia' logia and many other double-tradition sayings, especially in terms of the Deuteronomistic tradition.[115] Lk 10:21–2 par is attributed, as discussed above, to a still later stage of Q-redaction. But how does Jacobson treat the aphoristic sayings material? Lk 6:27–35 par seems to have been a small group of sayings prior to the redactional stage of Q-composition.[116] Lk 6: 37–42 par is not seen in this way, however, for Jacobson sees 6:39 par as arising at the compositional stage out of a redactional activity which has also affected Lk 6:41–2 par.[117] Lk 6:43–5 par is also viewed as affected by this activity, but it was perhaps already largely formulated at a pre-redactional stage.[118] In contrast to these collections, Lk 11:9–13 par is assigned to the late ('final') redaction of Q (alongside Lk 10: 21–2 par), and Jacobson hints that Lk 12:22–31 par and even Lk 12:2–9 par should also be assigned to this late stage, deriving from a 'highly enthusiastic' form of Christianity.[119] Thus, Jacobson recognizes no coherence amongst the aphoristic collections, and only finds the sayings in Lk 6:37–42, (43–5) as reflecting concerns similar to those of the main 'Sophia' texts (the stage of 'Q-composition').

Our own analysis of the structure and argument of the aphoristic collections requires recognition of much stronger affinities amongst them than Jacobson suggests, although the questions which he raises about the larger source Q have not been the subject of the present study. Once a coherence between the aphoristic collections is recognized, however, the problem of their relationship to the 'Sophia' logia still remains. Are the 'Sophia' logia in themselves necessarily *later* products of sapiential thought than the collections? M. Hengel has argued that there are no *a priori* reasons why many of the Sophia sayings themselves could not have gone back even to Jesus, particularly in view of the lack of a developed christological statement in Lk 7:35 par and 11:49–51 par.[120] Also, how discontinuous need different stages of development be? Even if the various sapiential traditions are relegated to different 'stages', does the question of interaction never arise? Do different sapiential interests appear and then disappear in a community in a relatively quick succession?

Our starting-point towards answering these questions is clearly the coherence of much of the aphoristic material of the double tradition, and particularly amongst the aphoristic collections. A coherence amongst the main 'Sophia' logia of the double tradition must also be accepted. Functionally, the two sapiential traditions seem distinct. Yet, this need not presume different bearers of the traditions or even widely differing situations. Complementarity must always be considered. Even the general concept of a 'trajectory' illustrates how a period of development need not imply discontinuity.

So the recognition of functionally distinct sapiential traditions, and even of development within these traditions, does not allow one to avoid the question of an interaction of traditions, especially as the sapiential outlooks described above are both distinctive of double-tradition material. Is it possible, then, to describe any such interaction for this material?

The most direct approach to this question is to look for any specific interests which overlap. The results here are limited, but most significant is how some of the aphoristic collections present the theme of anxiety about one's life in view of external threats. This fundamental concern is not unrelated to the declared fate of Sophia's representatives, although the aphoristic collections make no *direct* reference to the 'Sophia' motif or to the Deuteronomistic tradition of the fate of the prophets. The cluster of sayings in Lk 12:4−7 par, which may have been re-worked into Lk 12:2−9 par,[121] implied threats against the followers of Jesus. Lk 12:2−3, 8−9 par linked these fears of death with the problem of those followers wavering in their confession of Jesus. Hints of physical threats may be found secondarily inserted into the collections of sayings on love of enemies (especially Mt 5:44; cf. Lk 6:27−8) and on anxiety about material needs (Mt 6:27 par).[122] Some isolated aphorisms also dealt with the theme of the hardships of commitment and the loss of commitment (cf. Lk 11:23 par, 11:33, 34−6 par, 13:23−4 par, 19:26 par).[123] It is not impossible that the suffering of Jesus' *followers*, as well as of Jesus and his precursors, was itself envisaged in some of the 'Sophia' logia (see Lk 11:49 par). Those who responded to Jesus were referred to by the terms τέκνα (Lk 7:35 par) and νήπιοι (Lk 10:21−2). In Lk 6:22−3 the fate of these rather vulnerable followers of Jesus is related to the Deuteronomistic tradition of the fate of the prophets.[124] Yet, in the aphoristic collections past history is not invoked to explain the critical situation. Sometimes persuasion of an almost fatalistic kind to trust in God (cf. Lk 12:7 par, 12:25 par; Mt 5:45 par) is used to encourage the addressees to face what lies ahead. This can be understood as a difference in function. Past history is used to provide an *explanation*. The argument of the aphoristic collections seeks less to explain than to exhort and encourage. Thus, the 'Sophia' logia are used mainly with respect to *understanding Jesus'* fate; the aphoristic collections for *encouraging* anxious *followers* in their present crises. But allusions to Jesus' followers in the 'Sophia' logia and the existence of sayings such as Lk 6:22−3 par, and even Mt 10:24 par, show how not only an overlap but even an interaction between these concerns was possible.

Another important example of such interaction can be cited. In the 'Beelzebul' pericope, an attack on Jesus and the source of his authority is countered with the aphoristic statement about the divided kingdom (Lk 11:17 par). The aphorism is appropriate in that it effectively meets the specific charge levelled against Jesus. It was noted, however, in the discussion of the double-tradition pericope how the use of the generally formulated aphoristic reply naturally placed emphasis on the validation of Jesus rather than his uniqueness. Little more is claimed for his authority than for that of any legitimate Jewish exorcist. This is strikingly similar to observations about how there appears to be little developed christological reflection in the main 'Sophia' logia. Jesus is God's/Sophia's authorized representative, but apparently falls into a sequence of other such envoys. So again one finds an interesting overlap between the different sapiential traditions, in that it was clearly more important to establish the validity of Jesus' ministry than to show either its uniqueness or its specifically christological basis. Here is testimony to a general sapiential outlook which seems to bridge the distinct sapiential traditions.

The question of the interaction of the sapiential traditions can be approached in two further ways, however. First, one can seek to clarify how far the more fundamental presuppositions of the various sapiential traditions are reconcilable. Secondly, one can seek an actual setting in early Christianity which might testify to the interaction of these traditions. These will be approached in turn.

Wisdom, revelation and eschatology

The epistemological tension between divine Sophia as a source of 'revealed' knowledge on the one hand and general, 'experiential' aphoristic insights on the other is one which can easily be overstated. Within double-tradition material, there are signs of a convergence in such perspectives from both sides. It is a striking fact that the 'Sophia' logia of the double tradition are not really used to convey any divine revelations. As has been shown, they are more concerned with the acceptance and validation of the 'messengers' than with any particular 'message' which they bear. This is the main function of these sayings. It is true that Lk 10:21−2 par refers to a 'revelation' of limited access, but it has been argued that the dominant theme is the acceptance or rejection of that unspecified revelation.

The openness of 'babes' typifies the attitude of acceptance. Similarly, the σοφία of Solomon appears alongside the κήρυγμα of

Jonah in Lk 11:31–2 par, but it is the attitude of 'this generation' that is the dominant concern. No specification of the σοφία or κήρυγμα is offered in this context. So while it remains important for the validation of Jesus' ministry to maintain that his message is divinely authorized, the 'Sophia' logia are not themselves made the vehicle for presenting his message. This suggests that the main motive behind this stream of sapiential tradition is to *commend* the message rather than to declare it.

This emphasis on *commending* a message is shared by the aphoristic tradition, particularly through the design of the aphoristic collections. It has been argued that persuasion is of the utmost importance in the structure of these collections. Here, then, is a very important area of common ground in the sapiential traditions of the double tradition.

In a sense it is the aphoristic tradition, however, that is more related to a 'message'. This is because the aphoristic collections are often concerned with exhortation. In Mt 6:25–33 par this even leads to a call to seek the kingdom of God. But how far, then, does the content of these collections, and of other isolated aphorisms, allow for a 'divine' authorization of its message?

The question about the relationship of general truths to the kingdom-preaching of Jesus is not a new one, particularly with respect to the teaching of Jesus himself.[125] It has frequently led to the question of whether proverbial sayings can preserve anything 'characteristic' of Jesus;[126] the theories of N. Perrin, W. Beardslee and J. Crossan on the 'intensification' of some kinds of proverbs in the context of Jesus' preaching were introduced above (pp. 149–50). The role which experience, general truths and aphoristic wisdom play in the proclamation of Jesus in the double-tradition sayings themselves, however, has recently been explored in an important essay by W. Grundmann.[127]

Grundmann argues that the 'experiential' wisdom found in the double tradition has been transformed into a new 'eschatological' wisdom, which he describes as 'Weisheit im Horizont des Reiches Gottes'. It is this transformation that ultimately allows him to view the aphoristic material as complementary to the Sophia logia and Lk 10:21–2 par. The influence of the kingdom-awareness on wisdom is expressed in the new eschatological trust in the 'Father' (cf. Mt 7: 7–11 par; and Mt 6:25–33 par, which itself concludes with a call to seek the kingdom of God)[128] and in the perception of God as the merciful Creator and Governor of the world (cf. Mt 6:25–33 par, 5:45 par, and 10:29–31 par).[129] Further, hypocrisy is attacked in aphoristic sayings such as Mt 6:22–3 par, 7:3–5 par; and Lk 6:43–5 par. Integrity and wholeness of commitment are essential to the message of the kingdom.[130] The power of faith is also exemplified in the instructions against anxiety about one's life (cf. Mt 6:25ff. par, 10:29–31 par).[131] Finally, the message of judgement which forms part of the warning to Israel in the double tradition can be related to aphoristic instructions which encourage one to be responsible in one's actions.[132] In these various ways, he argues, the old wisdom has been newly grounded in alignment with the announcement of the kingdom.

But is it necessarily the 'old wisdom' that is altered and brought into alignment with the new awareness of the kingdom? While Grundmann refers to 'Weisheit im Horizont des Reiches Gottes' and suggests a new basis for the old wisdom and its deed–consequence nexus, D. Lührmann puts the emphasis somewhat differently and refers to Jesus calling God and his kingdom back from apocalyptic into the horizon of experience, which opens up new and concrete possibilities of speaking about God.[133] The result of each of these studies, however, has been to suggest that something has happened to the aphoristic insight so that it no longer simply refers to practical consequences or functions in a fundamentally *persuasive* way.[134]

It is this last point that must be questioned with respect to the use of double-tradition aphorisms. How far is persuasion still a function of aphoristic material? And how can aphorisms 'persuade' one to 'seek the kingdom of God'? Inadequate attention has been given in modern studies to the role of persuasion in the use of these sayings.

Two reasons may account for an aversion towards recognizing the persuasive power of aphoristic sayings in Jesus' proclamation, especially when formulated into collections with an argumentative structure, as in the double-tradition collections. These will be considered in turn. The first is that if an emphasis is put on the *persuasive* role of aphoristic sayings in these contexts, then it may seem to make experiential observation a prerequisite to and a kind of stepping-stone towards the kingdom proclamation itself. It is as though it might imply that the 'old wisdom' could lead one to an awareness of the kingdom. This would be open to the objections facing a 'natural' or 'general' revelation. But great care must be taken here. By the stage at which the double-tradition material was formulated into aphoristic collections, Jesus' 'kingdom' proclamation was itself a nuclear part of the 'Jesus-tradition'. There is no question of experiential wisdom being the 'origin' of the perceptions about the kingdom of God; it is rather that experiential insights have been selectively brought to bear in arguments designed to encourage the followers of Jesus towards particular attitudes or priorities,[135] such as Grundmann has shown are consonant with the 'kingdom' message. This selectivity in the use of aphoristic insights is important. Aphorisms never serve as comprehensive or complete statements about reality. By their concrete nature, they focus only on *aspects* of reality, and thus it is quite possible to find apparently contradictory 'truths' about life because of the very ambivalence of the phenomena themselves.[136] If aphorisms are themselves *selective* insights from experience, then it is equally true that they are selectively applied in the course of argument or even proclamation. Bold sapiential sentences, such as 'everyone who asks receives' have amazing force in winning assent, even though they present an exaggerated view of reality as a whole.[137] The persuasive power of sapiential insight must not be underrated, even though experience of the world alone may not be sufficient to originate the line of argument, and even though the argument may be logically dependent on the authority of a more fundamental interpretation of reality.

It is significant, though, that in the circles responsible for these collections, even a selective use of experiential wisdom was still seen as an *appropriate* means of leading to exhortations such as 'seek the kingdom of God' (Mt 6:33 par). Even the kind of argument which was employed stressed this. In Mt 7:7–11 par, an *a minore ad maius* argument helped one to leap from observations about human fathers to an observation about the heavenly 'Father'. In Mt 10:28ff. par, this type of argument may also be operative ('Do not fear those who kill the body but cannot kill the soul; rather fear him who can destroy both body and soul in hell'),[138] as well as the *a minore ad maius* progression between God's care of nature and God's care of 'you' (Mt 10:29–31 par; also cf. Mt 6:25ff. par). Inherent in this extrapolation from nature and human conduct, though, is not simply an attempt to say something convincing from human experience about God's present rule; the distance between man and God is also established. The finitude of man is made apparent (cf. especially Mt 6:27 par, 10:29–30 par). This creature-consciousness is itself an important element in a 'religious' consciousness whereby the controller of the world is recognized to be God, the Father (Mt 6:26ff. par) and eschatological Judge (Mt 10:26ff. par).[139] There are, therefore, grounds in this kind of argument for some convergence between the general perspective implicit in the use of aphoristic wisdom in the double tradition and the more distinctly revelatory implications of Jesus' role as a representative of Sophia and prophetic announcer of God's kingdom. This surely helps to cast light on the way in which many of the actual teachings expressed in the aphoristic collections sought to persuade the hearer to think beyond this-worldly securities (which are necessarily finite and limited like man himself), through the this-worldly form of argument which was applied.

A second criticism of a view of aphoristic wisdom as a persuasive medium has been expressed by W. Beardslee. He criticizes the older attempts to see proverbs as stressing the ordering processes of the world and merely allowing for a vision of God within these. In contrast, he points to how the paradoxical aphorisms open up *discontinuities* in one's existence, which in turn open up a new vision of God altogether. Paradox and surprise are fundamental to this kind of saying and are seen by him as important elements in Jesus' own employment of parable and proverb.[140]

Beardslee's observations are largely based on how individual proverbs of this particular kind might have been used in Jesus' own proclamation and challenge to people.[141] But by the time of the formulation of aphoristic collections, the reversal-type and paradoxical-type of maxim are much less prominent, and it is difficult to deny that an emphasis on continuity of experience exists even for those aphoristic sayings which do appear in eschatologically dominated, double-tradition contexts. This is to claim not that the future is simply an extension of the present conditions, but rather that an overlap of expectations does exist between the present age and the age to come. The connection between deed and consequence in the present is not totally disrupted in the eschatological future,[142] and thus decisions which affect one's standing in the future age are informed by past and present experience.[143] This is expressed clearly in sayings such as Lk 3:9b par ('Every tree therefore which does not bear good fruit is cut down and cast into fire') or Lk 19:26 par ('To everyone who has will more be given; but from him who has not, even what he has will be taken from him') or even Lk 17:37 par ('Where the body/corpse is, there will the eagles/vultures be gathered together'). In these sayings a continuity rather than discontinuity exists between expectations derived from past experience and the future age, and this does contribute to the *persuasive* impact of the sayings in exhortation or proclamation.

D. Lührmann has suggested another way in which this appears to hold true for double-tradition sayings. He draws attention to a 'weisheitliche Interpretation der im Alten Testament vorliegenden Geschichtsstoffe', which he associates with the redaction of Q.[144] While it has already been seen how the Deuteronomistic tradition of the fate of the prophets was united with 'Sophia' concepts in the double tradition, Lührmann's observations apply particularly to texts about the coming day of the Son of Man in Lk 17:26–30, where Noah, the flood, Lot and Sodom are employed almost as 'proverbial' images drawn from OT history. They are applied as old stories which everyone knows, mediated experiences, which lead the hearer to new connections in a compelling way.[145] The use of familiar concepts from past knowledge or experience does not preclude new and even startling applications, but in Lk 17:26–30 par they do lend *conviction* to the announcement of future judgement by reference to judgement in Israel's past, to continuities with her experience.

Thus, aphoristic wisdom is used in the double tradition at times to demonstrate a continuity between future expectations and expectations based on past experience. But often the confrontation of the hearer with the kingdom also concerns the establishment of priorities. In these cases aphoristic wisdom plays a somewhat different role. Here it is often a matter of demonstrating the 'prudent' course of action in view of the situation which confronts one. 'Prudence' in the light of coming judgement may, however, involve extraordinary commitments (see Mt 5:25–6 par, 6:19–20 par, 7:13–14 par; Lk 16:9ff.). In Mt 10:26ff. par, for example, two functions are combined. First, aphorisms are used to set forth an expectation/warning of present conditions coming to fulfilment ('nothing is hidden that will not be known': Mt 10:26 par). Then it is shown how a prudent decision in the light of this expectation involves commitment to God above the fear of man ('Do not be afraid of those who kill the body but not the soul; rather fear him who can destroy both the soul and the body ...': Mt 10:28ff. par). This commitment is persuasively set forth as the wisest choice. The perspective of judgement does not lead to a denial of normal reasoning or experience; it provides a new frame of reference within which the choice of priorities must take place. The extraordinary and critical nature of that new frame of reference is what results in this-worldly reasoning calling one to go beyond this-worldly securities. There is no suggestion, though, that the process of this-worldly reasoning is itself undermined. Indeed, the design of argument in the aphoristic collections would suggest the very opposite.

In these ways aphoristic insights go beyond general ethical teaching. By the selective application of the insights within arguments which also draw on an awareness of the kingdom of God, this-worldly concerns, priorities and experience have been applied to decisions which draw the hearers to the claims upon them of the kingdom and the needs of their fellow-Christians. There are, therefore, unifying factors in the way in which aphoristic insights in the double tradition and the more prophetic aspects of Jesus' message are used. These unifying factors are not based so much upon superficial themes held in common, or upon a radical suspension of the persuasive qualities of aphoristic wisdom, as upon more fundamental convictions about continuities between God as Creator as well as Judge, between present and future expectations and between man's decision-making as based on this-worldly experience and his consideration of other-worldly prospects. This is the basis for the selective application of persuasive argument. An important implication of this is that, despite functional distinctions in the use of aphoristic sayings and of 'Sophia' sayings in the double tradition, the epistemological gulf between the two may not be so wide as to require that these sapiential traditions derive from widely separated circles or times.

The bearers of the sapiential traditions

Can an actual setting in early Christianity now be identified for these traditions of wisdom? On the one hand, the information available about the earliest Christian communities is hardly extensive enough for one to expect to be able to identify clearly an actual setting of the kind required. Too little is known. Yet, on the other hand, many of our results have indicated that a distinctive intellectual activity was involved, so that the search for a setting is not in itself inappropriate.

The concerns which dominate the aphoristic material are relatively closely delimited when compared to the wider range of interests which have been held to typify early Christian catechesis and ethical instruction. There is no express concern, for example, about idolatry or fornication, and the nature of argument is in any case unlike that of a 'holiness code'.[146] The concerns of this material also do not conform particularly closely to what one might expect of early Christian missionary instructions. Regarding the formulation of the aphoristic collections, while D. Zeller fails to show how distinctive the structure of the collections is, he nonetheless is probably correct in his view that, generally, larger compilations of sayings seem to presuppose communities rather than individual missionary preachers.[147] Also, while the sayings encouraging one not to be anxious about material needs (Mt 6:25ff. par) and not to waver in the face of external opposition (Mt 10:26ff. par) might have been applicable to missionary activity, it is doubtful whether either of the collections was intended primarily or solely for such a setting. The arguments about not judging one's brother (Mt 7:1ff. par) or about purity in heart and speech (Lk 6:43−5 par) would easily apply to inner-community relationships. Even the calls to wholehearted commitment might be as easily seen as aimed at wavering Christians on the 'fringes' as at those in the forefront of the Christian proclamation.

Before speculating about a setting for the sapiential activity, it would be useful first to list briefly the main features of the aphoristic sayings and 'Sophia' sayings which might bear upon the question of a setting. In doing so, we shall initially deal with the aphoristic double-tradition material and the 'Sophia' logia separately.

The following characteristics are present in the aphoristic collections and in other aphoristic material of the double tradition:

1. Some sayings-collections are concerned with anxieties about basic material needs, especially with respect to food (Mt 6: 25−33 par, 7:7−11 par). Other aphoristic sayings (such as Lk 16:9−13 par; Mt 6:19−21 par; and possibly Mt 5:39ff. par) place less stress on actual need than on the false securities offered by material goods. In both cases the question of one's attitude towards material security is uppermost, although this question is approached from differing points of view. Some unevenness in the distribution of material goods might be presupposed if these perspectives are to be held together.

2. Physical security as well as material security is a concern of followers in Mt 10:26−33 par and may also emerge in sayings such as Mt 6:27 par and Mt 5:44 par, which intrude into other sayings-collections. Fear for one's life is specifically mentioned in Mt 10:28ff. par. This latter example shows how such fears may have led also to questions about the commitment of some followers (cf. also Lk 11:33, 34−6 par, 14:34−5 par, [19:26 par], 13:23−4 par).

3. Tolerance among followers features prominently in Mt 7:1−5 par, where the hearers are exhorted to examine themselves before judging their ἀδελφοί. Self-examination is also encouraged in Lk 6:43−5 par, with the themes of one's speech and of 'treasure' in close proximity. If one is correct in inferring an unevenness in the distribution of wealth amongst

the hearers, it is not impossible that this itself was one cause of factions and disharmony amongst followers. Certainly the encouragement simply to put God above all else in material questions corresponds to the equally simple, and perhaps even simplistic, implication here that purity of heart will dispel causes of tension.[148]

4. The aphoristic collections and the 'Beelzebul' pericope (Lk 11:14ff. par) have consistently shown how generally formulated arguments take precedence over direct assertions of the unique authority of Jesus and his message. Only in Lk 12:8−9 par, where the issue of apostasy is pressing, is the unique status of Jesus invoked, and even here the identity of Jesus with the heavenly Son of Man is not explicit in its earliest form.

5. From the design of the aphoristic collections and the importance attached to persuasive argument, one might be led to expect teachers or 'wise men' to play an important part in the leadership of the community (cf. also Lk 6:40 par).

Further themes relevant to a setting are found in the 'Sophia' logia. These include the following:

1. Most prominent is the theme of religious opposition and possible persecution at the hands of the Jews (cf. Lk 11: 49−51 par, 13:34−5 par). Certainly Jesus' own fate is viewed in these terms, but it is less clear whether Christians are also directly in view.[149] This theme may converge with the anxieties about physical security found in the aphoristic collections, but the 'Sophia' logia differ in function in that they do not appear to be directed to wavering Christians so much as against opponents, viz. 'this generation'. In Lk 13:34 par, the persecution specifically refers to 'stoning' and 'killing'.

2. Jesus' own role, though, is again portrayed in an ambiguous way. More emphasis again falls on the validity of Jesus' ministry and message, in succession to the prophets, than on a unique status. This is found particularly in Lk 7:33−5 par, where he and John the Baptist are considered in parallel. This is only partly compensated for by the use of 'Son of Man' in Lk 7:34 par, but even here we found little evidence of christological speculation on the relationship between the 'Son of Man' and the representative of Sophia. The main exception to the lack of christological speculation is Lk 10:21−2

par, but the significance of the 'Son' terminology may point primarily to a representative function in which most stress is on the reception of the message which he mediates.[150]

3. It is clear, however, that the role of prophet emerges more clearly than that of teacher in the 'Sophia' logia. The Deuteronomistic tradition of the fate of the prophets is the model employed in conjunction with the sapiential themes. Further, the wise man Solomon and the prophet/preacher Jonah are virtually complementary concepts in Lk 11:29–32 par, as are σοφία and κήρυγμα. In Lk 10:21–2 par a rather harsher attitude is adopted to the σοφοί altogether, in that it is from these that the revelation is hidden. Yet it is doubtful that σοφοί there can be taken as a general term for all teachers.[151] Prophecy is nonetheless more prominent in the 'Sophia' logia.

When these features are considered together, one is led to envisage a situation in which a group of Christians was facing significant difficulties. These appear to have been partly concerned with economic hardship (at least for some) and partly with the threat of Jewish opposition. Such difficulties are well attested in the early church (see Acts 6–7, 11:27–30, 24:6; Gal 2:10; Rom 15:25–7; 1 Cor 16:1–4). One may infer that those pressures contributed to problems of wavering commitment amongst some followers and even to factions critical of one another. These issues were addressed by the aphoristic sayings-collections.

The attempt to pinpoint an identifiable situation in early Christianity which corresponds to these characteristics is of course fraught with difficulties. Not only do our extant sources give a very incomplete picture of early Christianity, but the validity of what *is* described in sources such as Acts is often open to question. Yet, a superficial similarity does exist between what has been inferred above and what Luke records about Stephen and the Hellenists in Acts 6–7. One hesitates to put too much historical weight on these chapters of Acts,[152] but it is certainly true that the similarities to Acts 6–7 are much closer than to any other part of Acts. It is for this reason that it is illuminating to list briefly these characteristics.

The following features of Acts 6–7 are of special interest for our study:

1. The initial issue with which Luke associated Stephen and the Seven was the practical problem of a quarrel between

two parties over the distribution of food. Both groups were apparently subject to 'the Twelve' (Acts 6:2). The needy group was described as widows belonging to the 'Hellenists' (Acts 6:1), for Luke does not appear to describe here a general situation of need (but cf., later in Acts, 11:27–30, 24:6). At face value it therefore appears to present a problem of an uneven distribution of poor relief, particularly of food. Even though the 'Seven' are not actually described by Luke as having looked after the poor,[153] this is not in itself an indication that the problem did not exist. Indeed, many scholars have conjectured that the problem of distribution of food to widows did not represent the complete nature of the rift in the community,[154] and this may be true. But this precise cause of the 'murmuring' in Acts 6:1 is so little developed in what follows in Acts 6–7 (or even in Acts 6: 8–15), and is so subordinate to Luke's overall purposes in the Stephen material, that it is difficult to dismiss these details as simply due to Lukan creativity, even if much more may have been behind it.[155] Thus, some correspondence can be found with the first and third inferences about a setting derived from our study of the aphoristic collections.

2. A second important feature of the situation depicted in Acts 6–7 is the active opposition of the Jewish authorities to Stephen (6:9, 12). This persecution does not seem to be directed against the entire Palestinian Christian community, but primarily against Stephen and perhaps, by implication, against the Hellenist group (see Acts 8:1, 11:19).[156] In the case of Stephen, this persecution led to his being stoned, so that the threat to life was real, even if it cannot be demonstrated that other deaths followed. This threat again provides a point of similarity with both the aphoristic and the 'Sophia' sayings of the double tradition.

3. Of exceptional significance, however, is the appearance of the Deuteronomistic tradition of the fate of the prophets in Stephen's speech. This was a prominent characteristic of the 'Sophia' logia of the double tradition (see Lk 11:49–51 par, 13:34–5 par). Further, in O.H. Steck's analysis of the Deuteronomistic tradition the only places outside the synoptic tradition in which he finds evidence of it are in Acts 7:52 and 1 Thes 2:15–16.[157] The presence of the motif in Stephen's speech is, therefore, an exceptional occurrence,[158] although

it must be admitted that no direct reference to divine Sophia appears in Acts 7:52.

4. Yet sapiential terminology is exceptionally prominent in Acts 6–7 as a whole. The term σοφία occurs four times in Acts 6–7 (6:3, 10, 7:10, 22) and nowhere else in all of Acts! It is never used in Acts to describe any other early Christians; nor is the cognate, σοφός. Even in Luke's gospel the terms are used with reserve outside of double-tradition material. They occur twice in the infancy narrative with respect to Jesus' own growth in wisdom (Lk 2:40, πληρούμενον σοφίᾳ, and Lk 2:52) and once in Lk 21:15 referring to the gift given to Jesus' followers enabling them to answer charges levelled against them by adversaries. As this last use is strongly reminiscent of Acts 6:10, it may even serve as a Lukan 'prophecy' which has its specific fulfilment in Acts 6.[159] This limited use of the term σοφία by Luke makes the fourfold concentration of the terminology in Acts 6–7 all the more remarkable.

What exactly σοφία means here is, however, less clear. When Luke describes Stephen and the Seven, he uses the following pairs of terms: πλήρεις πνεύματος καὶ σοφίας (6:3);[160] πλήρης πίστεως καὶ πνεύματος ἁγίου (6:5); πλήρης χάριτος καὶ δυνάμεως (6:8); and τῇ σοφίᾳ καὶ τῷ πνεύματι (6:10). The terms πίστις, χάρις, πνεῦμα and δύναμις all occur frequently in Luke–Acts, unlike σοφία.[161] These conjunctions suggest that 'wisdom' is perceived here as a kind of spiritual gift,[162] but it is still unclear how this 'gift' is specifically manifested or exercised. Lk 21:15 would suggest that it may not be unrelated to the persuasive nature of Stephen's reply to the charges against him, but in Acts 6:1–10 it seems equally to apply to the overall ministry of Stephen or the Seven.[163]

The speech of Stephen is hardly secure ground for gleaning information about Stephen, the Hellenists or their theology.[164] Yet, in Luke's presentation of Stephen's speech two of the main figures, Joseph and Moses, are specifically associated with σοφία.[165] It is precisely these two who are also shown to have been rejected by their own people: Joseph by his brothers (Acts 7:9), Moses as a rejected prophet/wise man (Acts 7:25ff., 35, 39ff.).[166] Thus, σοφία and the rejection motif are united here – a kind of union which is also distinctive of the double-tradition material. 'Wisdom' itself appears as a divine endowment given to Joseph (7:10), but also takes on the character of 'instruction' when applied to Moses, who was 'instructed in all the wisdom of the Egyptians, and he was mighty in his words and deeds' (Acts 7:22). One cannot, therefore, exclude from the sense of σοφία a pragmatic core of learning in Acts 6−7.[167]

It is interesting to find near the climax of Stephen's speech a further OT figure whom Luke does not describe as 'wise' but who was nonetheless the popular archetype of the wise man, Solomon (Acts 7:47ff.).[168] Reference to Solomon is just as exceptional as Luke's use of σοφία. Outside the genealogy in Matthew, the only other occurrences in the NT of the historical figure Solomon are the two instances of double-tradition sayings, one in an aphoristic collection (Mt 6:29 par 'even Solomon in all his glory was not arrayed like one of these') and one in a possible Sophia logion (Lk 11:31 par: 'something greater than Solomon is here').[169] In Acts 7:47ff., Solomon is associated with the building of the Temple. Luke is not entirely clear about his attitude towards Solomon or the Temple at this point, for while 7:48ff. criticizes the idea that God dwells in man-made buildings, 7:46 links the original concept of the Temple to the favour which David had before God.[170] The real attack comes in 7:51ff. against 'you stiff-necked people' and 'your fathers'. Yet Solomon's somewhat ambiguous role here is not unlike that found in both double-tradition sayings. Solomon's glory is *surpassed* by God's adornment of nature (Mt 6:29 par), and 'something *greater* than Solomon is here' (Lk 11:31 par). Perhaps it should not be surprising that the very Christian traditions which give emphasis to σοφία should consider the popularly recognized supreme wise man, Solomon, as surpassed by this subsequent σοφία.

The prominence of sapiential traditions is certainly striking in Acts 6−7. While Luke might have been attracted to the Deuteronomistic tradition as an explanation of Stephen's martyrdom, there was no need for him to apply sapiential terminology here to the extent and in the way in which he does. Why did he do so? Can any redactional explanations be found for this? Is not an appeal to traditions (bearing marked correspondence to distinctive double-tradition motifs) equally, if not more, likely?

5. One may now briefly note how the description of the leadership of the Hellenist group has emphasized both σοφία and πνεῦμα (Acts 6:3, 10). This is not far removed from the joining of 'wisdom' and 'prophecy' in the 'Sophia' logia of the double tradition.

6. Finally, one should not fail to ask how Jesus himself is presented in Acts 6−7. Again, one is dependent on Luke's own presentation of Stephen's speech, but with this warning in mind one finds that Jesus is only introduced explicitly in the last two verses of the speech (7:52−3).[171] The bulk of the speech is not devoted to proclaiming Jesus' unique authority; it is an extended argument which seeks to show persuasively how Jews are resisting God's purposes. Once this is established, Luke briefly alludes to the misunderstanding of Jesus (ὁ δίκαιος) and his rejection and death. The implication is clearly that Jesus' fate at the hands of the Jews is not dissimilar to that of Israel's prophets (7:52). This is the totality of 'Stephen's' statement about Jesus, until his extraordinary vision of the 'Son of Man' in 7:56.[172] Therefore, despite the term ὁ δίκαιος (cf. WisSol 2:12−20),[173] the significance of Jesus in this speech appears to lie less with any unique title or status than with a selective historical survey in which Jesus comes at the climax of the Jews' failure to respond rightly to God. The affinities with the presentation of Jesus in the sapiential streams of the double tradition are again clear.

Taken together, the number of important features which are distinctive of Acts 6−7, and which also correspond to characteristic features of the sapiential material of the synoptic double tradition, is surprising. The correspondence holds for both the aphoristic material and the 'Sophia' logia, so that Acts 6−7 provides a description of circumstances and emphases which unite this material. It is also significant that the correspondences are found in both the descriptive narrative section of Acts 6 and the speech material in Acts 7. An example of this is the use of σοφία terminology.

Many of these features are sufficiently distinctive even within Acts not to be easily dismissed as Lukan redaction. The Deuteronomistic tradition of the fate of the prophets, the σοφία terminology, the Solomon reference, the dissension in the Christian community, are examples of unusual features in these chapters.[174] This does not, of course, imply the complete historicity of Acts 6 or of the speech in

Acts 7; nor does it require the use of a particular source upon which Luke drew for his formulation of the chapters.[175] However, these are not simply favourite Lukan themes. Can it be that Luke drew on information known to him in one way or another about Stephen and the Hellenists? Do some of these distinctive features of Acts 6–7 not show Luke's attempt to reflect some of the spirit of these events in his composition?[176] This need not be inconsistent with some appreciation of Lukan redaction.

One may not be able to claim direct evidence of a historical link of these sapiential characteristics with the Hellenists, but the correspondences are intriguing and suggestive. At the very least they lend credibility to the general picture which has been inferred about the situation of the bearers of the double-tradition sapiential material. It is possible to envisage a Christian community with these characteristics.[177] Whether the Hellenists indeed represented that community must remain a possibility for further investigation extending beyond the sapiential themes to other aspects of Hellenistic theology, such as Law, Temple and attitude to non-Jews, in so far as these can themselves be reconstructed.[178]

CONCLUSION

This study began with the aim of investigating the ways in which aphoristic sayings were used in the synoptic tradition prior to the written gospels. The goal was to define and describe an early sapiential activity interested in aphoristic wisdom, particularly evident in the material of the double tradition. It was hoped that this might make some progress in a much-neglected field and complement the interest shown in other kinds of sapiential motifs in the double tradition, particularly in the figure of divine Sophia.

The starting-point for such an investigation was the aphoristic collections of the double tradition. Five such collections (Lk 11:9–13 par, 12:22–31 par, 6:37–42 par, 6:43–5 par, 12:2–9 par) were found to exhibit a perceptible, recurring formal structure and pattern of argument. Far from their being loose or haphazard collections of aphorisms built simply around catchwords and common themes, a clear design of argument was evident. This design moved in a steady progression from general propositions or admonitions to specific application. A wide variety of persuasive techniques was employed, including the use of the *a minore ad maius* kind of argument, rhetorical questions and illustrations from one's experience of the world. The argument proceeded, however, through four distinct steps:[1] (1) the general opening maxim or admonition, (2) a supporting argument following closely on from the opening sayings, usually being a maxim, (3) further new illustrations and arguments in a rhetorical question formulation, typically being double rhetorical questions, (4) a concluding saying drawing together the argument of the collection and providing the final interpretative key for the collection as a whole. This design of collection is remarkable not only for its argumentative and persuasive power, but also because it testifies to a deliberate effort to formulate the teaching of Jesus in such a way. Here is the basis for the inference of an early sapiential activity with respect to aphoristic traditions.

In support of this contention, it was observed that this pattern of argument is distinctly associated with double-tradition material. Of two further aphoristic collections, Lk 6:27–36 par and 16:9–13, the latter is not usually associated with the double tradition, but it was argued that the contact with double-tradition material is in fact closer than is often recognized and that the collection not only preceded Luke but may also have been known to Matthew. This relatively restricted source-critical range within which the collections are found strengthens the theory of a unique sapiential circle behind the collections.

The themes of the collections are also clearly circumscribed. They focus on attitudes towards basic material needs and possessions, critical attitudes towards 'brothers', probably including critical speech, and wavering faith in the face of external threats. It is argued that the object of the collections was therefore to address some of the more sensitive issues faced by early Christian communities, and the parallel with the situation depicted in Acts 6–7 is particularly suggestive.

Confirmation of these observations was sought from the isolated aphoristic sayings of the double tradition. A surprising degree of coherence in theme and argumentative style was in fact found, particularly for the wisdom admonitions (except Lk 17:3b–4 par). But further elucidation of this sapiential activity was also possible. First, although the use of aphorisms for defence in controversies is not a feature unique to the double tradition, the 'Beelzebul' controversy and Lk 7:31–5 par showed how there is a tendency in the double-tradition material to emphasize Jesus' genuineness as a messenger of God rather than to insist always on his uniqueness. A more general formulation of argument than in Mark is therefore presented and seemingly emphasized. Secondly, general maxims are widely employed in the synoptic tradition for teaching in discipleship, but double-tradition sayings are restricted in the issues which they address and show a more discernible interest in sapiential motifs than is consistently true of any single evangelist or other source. Thirdly, even in the context of eschatological announcements, maxims not only appear, but are used in an argumentative rather than just rhetorical or even proclamatory way in double-tradition material. The sayings never entirely lose their aphoristic quality and their usefulness in persuasion (cf. Lk 11:33, 34–5, [36] par; Mt 24:28 par, 25:29 par, 3:10b par). These observations again lead one to infer a distinct sapiential activity with an interest in universally valid forms of argument, and they extend the range of contexts within which this is observed in double-tradition material.

While little difficulty is thus encountered in supposing that the aphoristic sayings in double-tradition material as a whole testify to a distinctive sapiential activity, it is more difficult to relate this to other sapiential motifs in double-tradition material, especially that of divine Sophia. Yet some areas of shared interests can be identified. In addition to the general mixing of such motifs in intertestamental times and some overlaps of theme (viz. persecution) between the two groups of double-tradition sayings, other indications of common attitudes can be found. One of these may again be the way in which Jesus' genuineness (as one in the line of the prophets) is stressed over his uniqueness.

The limitations of this study have not allowed further important questions to be pursued, however. Only slight attention has been given to the next important step in such an investigation: namely, how and when this sapiential activity was integrated with the rest of the double-tradition material, and probably incorporated into a source, Q. Ultimately this entails a full-scale study of Q itself and of the larger units within Q in the light of these results. The theory of a Q-source itself received some indirect support from our findings. When examining the aphoristic collections, it became clear that neither Matthew nor Luke was responsible for creating the distinctive design of argument which is employed in the double-tradition collections, for neither evangelist seemed concerned to imitate it or even to preserve it consistently. The most likely hypothesis is that the formulation of the collections preceded both Matthew and Luke and was known to both. This is not strictly sufficient to prove the existence of Q as a whole, but it does lend credibility to that hypothesis.

Not only is it important to follow up the subsequent development of this sapiential activity in the synoptic tradition; it may be necessary to investigate the earlier history of the traditions. This ultimately leads back to the teaching activity of Jesus himself. The careful compositional style of the double-tradition aphoristic collections does not suggest the spontaneous creation of a preacher, and its reappearance in seven instances also most naturally implies a studied approach and method. In itself this need not totally preclude the activity of Jesus, particularly in view of some revival of interest in Jesus as a 'teacher'.[2] The use of individual isolated aphorisms poses even fewer obstacles in this regard. But, if the aphoristic collections were the result of a careful compilational activity by Jesus himself, this would require some re-evaluation of Jesus' role. Was he a trained 'wise man'? How would such collections fit into the pattern and style of his 'kingdom' proclamation? These questions would need to be answered.

However, the likelihood that the aphoristic collections in fact were compiled at a stage later than the ministry of Jesus himself is also supported by the fact that they are not evenly distributed in the Jesus-tradition. They are distinctive of double-tradition material. This concentration at one source-critical stage of the synoptic tradition, coupled with a similar concentration of the 'divine Sophia' logia in the double tradition, must most naturally imply a unique sapiential activity deriving from one stream of the synoptic tradition and thus probably from one circle in the early church.

If this is so, as seems likely, then the question which remains is how far the units which comprise the aphoristic collections, and some of the isolated maxims, go back to Jesus, and in what contexts, and how far is Hengel correct that Jesus may also have viewed himself as a 'messianischer Lehrer der Weisheit', even an envoy of Sophia, providing the foundation for the 'Sophia' logia?[3] It is doubtful that a general answer will prove a suitable substitute for the analysis of individual texts, but the sapiential characteristics of Jesus' own teaching should not be overlooked. However distinctive the kind of sapiential activity found in double-tradition sayings may be, aphoristic sayings generally are in evidence in considerable numbers throughout the synoptic tradition. They are at least as prominent in the Jesus-tradition as the parables. This itself lends credibility not just to the limited attempts of Perrin and Beardslee to find aphoristic sayings which might be distinctive and 'authentic',[4] but also to the more general observation of Carlston that excessive concentration on the unique elements in Jesus' message may unduly lead to an outlook which prejudices one at the outset against aphoristic elements in Jesus' teaching. He concludes that 'Christian exegetes will have to become somewhat more open to the creative possibilities of the universally human elements in Jesus' life and teaching'.[5] The agenda is therefore set for recognizing in Jesus that not only 'something greater than Jonah', but also 'something greater than Solomon is here'.

APPENDIX
Mk 8:34b—38 and Lk 14:26—35

Some small collections of aphoristic sayings can be found in Mark's gospel — as, for example, in the defence of Jesus against the charge of the Pharisees concerning fasting (Mk 2:19—22), in the sayings following the interpretation of the Parable of the Sower (Mk 4:21—5), and, mixed with other types of sayings, in the warnings against temptations (Mk 9:42—50).[1] It has often been noted that the sayings in Markan collections are arranged quite artificially[2] and that in Mk 9:42—50 the scheme of compilation seems largely dependent on catchword connections.[3] Even if greater scope is given to the evangelist's role in forming the collections, none of those groupings portrays a structure which resembles that of the aphoristic collections of the double tradition.

There is, however, one collection of sayings in Mark which comes closer to this structure. This is found in Mk 8:34b—38, which is part of a slightly larger section on discipleship (Mk 8:34—9:1). The differences between this collection of sayings and those of the double tradition are as telling as the similarities, so that neither must be neglected in the consideration of this collection.

εἴ τις θέλει ὀπίσω μου ἀκολουθεῖν, ἀπαρνησάσθω ἑαυτὸν καὶ ἀράτω τὸν σταυρὸν αὐτοῦ καὶ ἀκολουθείτω μοι.

ὃς γὰρ ἐὰν θέλῃ τὴν ψυχὴν αὐτοῦ σῶσαι ἀπολέσει αὐτήν·
ὃς δ' ἂν ἀπολέσει τὴν ψυχὴν αὐτοῦ ἕνεκεν ἐμοῦ καὶ τοῦ εὐαγγελίου σώσει αὐτήν.

τί γὰρ ὠφελεῖ ἄνθρωπον κερδῆσαι τὸν κόσμον ὅλον καὶ ζημιωθῆναι τὴν ψυχὴν αὐτοῦ;
τί γὰρ δοῖ ἄνθρωπος ἀντάλλαγμα τῆς ψυχῆς αὐτοῦ;

ὃς γὰρ ἐὰν ἐπαισχυνθῇ με καὶ τοὺς ἐμοὺς λόγους ἐν τῇ γενεᾷ ταύτῃ τῇ μοιχαλίδι καὶ ἁμαρτωλῷ, καὶ ὁ υἱὸς τοῦ ἀνθρώπου ἐπαισχυνθήσεται αὐτὸν ὅταν ἔλθῃ ἐν τῇ δόξῃ τοῦ πατρὸς αὐτοῦ μετὰ τῶν ἀγγέλων τῶν ἁγίων.   (Mk 8:34b—38)

The similarities in structure and argument are to be found at the following points. The collection begins with a threefold exhortation (8:34b: 'Let him deny himself, take up his cross and follow me'),[4] followed immediately by an expanded aphoristic saying which supports the opening commands ('For whoever would save his life will lose it …': 8:35).[5] No imperatives appear in the collection except here at the beginning. Next follow two rhetorical questions (8:36—7) which set out further reasons in support of the initial commands. In this context they clearly further the argument about abandonment of the world.[6] Finally comes a saying similar to that in Lk 12:9/Mt 10:33, threatening that those who are ashamed of Jesus and his words will likewise suffer shame at the judgement by the coming Son of Man. The theme of the collection deals not just with an ascetic ideal of self-denial, but with fidelity in a situation which calls for courage and sacrifice, possibly in view of persecution.[7] This is not unlike the sayings collection in Mt 10:26—33/Lk 12:2—9, with which it has a close parallel in the concluding saying.

The differences between Mk 8:34b—38 and the aphoristic sayings collections of the double tradition must also be recognized, however. First, the use of the first person in a specific sense to designate obedience to Jesus in Mk 8:34b, 35 is unlike the more general sapiential admonitions which appear in the previously analysed collections. This sharply limits the universal force of the initial exhortation and its support.[8] Zeller rightly does not classify this as a 'wisdom admonition' at all.[9] The only example of the use of the first person, referring to Jesus, in the double-tradition collections was in the final interpretative sayings of Lk 12:8—9 par (cf. also Mk 8:38). The initial and recurring use of the first person in Mk 8:34b—38, however, contrasts notably with the restraint in its use in Lk 12:2—9 par and emphasizes from the outset the importance in Mark of the specific recognition of Jesus.

There are also other limitations to the general applicability of the sayings in Mk 8:34b, 35. The use of the conditional εἴ τις in 8:34b limits the situations to which the exhortations can apply. Such conditional clauses have not been present in the admonitions of any of the double-tradition collections.[10] Also the use of the words καὶ τοῦ εὐαγγελίου (8:35), which are notably Mark's own addition[11] from missionary terminology, contributes further to the dissipation of the generalized character of the saying.[12] Since this move away from a generalized formulation seems to be advanced in part by Mark's own editorial activity, it can fairly be claimed that Mark himself attaches no particular value to citing arguments here which specifically draw their force from universal human experience.[13]

A second area of difference between this collection and most of the previously examined collections is that the double rhetorical questions in verses 36—7 logically develop the theme of the loss of ψυχή expressed in verse 35.[14] This is in contrast to the tendency noticed in the other collections to provide a new set of images in the central section of the collection. Double questions are not in themselves unusual in Mark;[15] yet, instead of drawing fresh imagery from the natural plant or animal world, Mk 8:36—7 is closely integrated in theme with the preceding sayings, especially through the catchword ψυχή.[16] This effectively keeps the emphasis on the decision confronting the individual: 'For what does it profit a man to gain the whole world and forfeit his ψυχή? For what can a man give in return for his ψυχή?' Just as the opening sayings betrayed an intense concern with the need for self-denial in discipleship to Jesus from the very outset, rather than a broad, experientially based opening, so in Mk 8:36—7 the intensity of the individual's decision is maintained, rather than more diffuse aphoristic perceptions.

This intensity is expressed in yet another way in the concluding saying,

Mk 8:38. Despite the similarity of this saying to Lk 12:9/Mt 10:33 at the conclusion of the collection in Lk 12:2–9 par, the Markan saying exhibits a much stronger apocalyptic colouring than its counterpart in the double tradition (for which see pp. 58–61 above). This is evident particularly in the phrase ἐν τῇ γενεᾷ ταύτῃ τῇ μοιχαλίδι καὶ ἁμαρτωλῷ[17] and in the less ambiguous agency of the Son of Man as judge and not simply as witness.[18] The influence of Dan 7:13ff. is also discernible in the allusions to 'coming', 'glory' and 'angels'.[19] In contrast to Lk 12:8–9 par, Mk 8:38 presents only the negative warning of judgement for those who are 'ashamed'[20] of 'me and my words'.[21] The positive promise for followers occurs in Mark only through the addition of 9:1,[22] although its distinctive formulation and the separate introduction (καὶ ἔλεγεν αὐτοῖς) make it likely that it was at an earlier stage distinct from 8:34–8.[23] It was later introduced to conclude the section in Mark consisting of 8:34–9:1.[24]

Although it is still subject to debate, many scholars consider the formulation of Mk 8:38 to be less original than Lk 12:9.[25] It is in any case significant that the increased intensity of the Markan version over against the double-tradition version is matched generally in Mk 8:34b–38 by a lessened interest in purely aphoristic formulation when compared with the sayings collections of the double tradition. Although the appeal to universal experience is not far from the surface, especially in 8:35–7, it is dominated by an underlying concern to warn the hearers in strong terms of the consequences of disloyalty to Jesus in situations of hardship.

How, then, is one to explain both the similarities and the differences between Mk 8:34b–38 and the double-tradition collections? Here one must pose the question of whether Mk 8:34b–38 was a pre-Markan collection. E. Best[26] has presented five arguments in favour of this hypothesis: (i) the apparently independent example in Mt 10:38, 39 of the union of the sayings in Mk 8:34b and 35, which is of extra significance because of the close proximity in both cases of a third saying (cf. Mk 8:38; Mt 10:33); (ii) the repeated use of the connective γάρ by Mark to add emphasis to the existing links between sayings; (iii) the tendency of Mark to draw long sequences of logia from tradition, often based on the initial saying only (as in Mk 4:21–5, 9:42–9), rather than compile them himself; (iv) the presence of the catchword connections in Mk 8:35–7 as a sign of *oral* tradition; and (v) the sudden change of introductory formula in Mk 9:1, indicating a joining of originally distinct units. Not all of these arguments may be of equal weight, as Lambrecht seeks to show,[27] but the stylistic arguments are particularly significant. The fresh introductory formula in Mk 9:1 does seem to indicate a joining of two sets of tradition rather than a continual compilation by Mark, such as Lambrecht seeks to establish. The similar conjunction of Mk 8:34b, 35, 38 in the material of Mt 10 is also difficult to attribute entirely to direct Markan influence on Matthew, since the obvious parallel to Mk 8:34ff. comes in Mt 16:24ff., and since the similar conjunction of sayings in Mt 10:37–8 and Lk 14:26–7 suggests a source other than Mk 8 at this point.[28] One might still question whether this 'source' was pre-Markan and used by Mark; but when the arguments about style and source are viewed together, it is not surprising that successive studies by M. D. Hooker,[29] M. Horstmann,[30] E. Trocmé,[31] R. Pesch,[32]

W. Grundmann,[33] among others,[34] have argued for a pre-Markan collection behind Mk 8:34b—38.

If one considers both the fact that three of these sayings have 'doublet' parallels preserved in close proximity in Matthew[35] and the evidence given above concerning the similarities in structure between this sayings-collection and those of the double-tradition collections, then one is led to ask whether Mk 8:34b—38 is a group of sayings which had its roots in a tradition corresponding to that of the other aphoristic collections. Is it likely that the correspondence is simply coincidental? Certainly there is little ground for suggesting that Mark himself was aware of this structure of argument. The structure appears nowhere else in Mark. Indeed, it is more typical of the structure of sayings collections in Mark to follow a pattern of beginning with a single rhetorical question and continuing with a series of maxim-like sayings in statement form (cf. Mk 2:19—22, 4:21—5, also 3:23—7). Thus, the hypothesis of either a coincidental correspondence or a Markan imitation has many weaknesses. More likely is the view that Mark has here taken up a previously existing collection of sayings which shows many affinities with the double-tradition collections.

Yet, how does one account for the differences? Mk 8:34b—38 is not as it stands simply another cast from the same mould. It is at least a stage removed from the emphases at work in the construction of the other aphoristic sayings-collections, and not simply by Mark's own probable additions (cf. Mk 8:35, 9:1). While reasonable persuasion is not abandoned in the argument of 8:34b—38, there is evidence of a more pressing concern to confront the hearer continually with the loss necessarily involved in following Jesus and a warning against retreating from this. In this way, Mk 8:34b—38 is different even from its closest sister-collection, Lk 12:2—9/Mt 10:26—33. So, while the similarities between the collections may suggest a common origin, the differences suggest at least a differing development in the tradition. It would seem, therefore, that before the collection reached the hands of Mark any contact with the circles responsible for the double-tradition collections was probably lost and a more intense apocalyptic influence was exerted on the collection.[36] There is no question here of arguing for Markan access to a complete Q-source. This merely suggests what is in any case probable: that there was a continuing growth in the sayings-tradition in the early period of the church, and that in isolated cases Mark had access to a tradition shared with the double-tradition material,[37] but not necessarily *directly* from the Q-source.[38]

The 'overlap' of Mk 8:34b—38 with sayings of the double tradition, and its likely existence as a pre-Markan collection, have both been long recognized. This presents, therefore, no serious challenge to the hypothesis that all these collections derive from an early stage of gospel-tradition in which they have been compiled not just according to the anonymous tendencies of amalgamation, but influenced by a particular outlook steeped in the interests of persuasion and aphoristic wisdom and emerging above all in the material of the double tradition. It is hardly accidental, however, that just as this pattern of argument was most under pressure for the collection in Mt 10:26—33/Lk 12:2—9, where the question of continuing loyalty to one's confession of Christ amidst external threats was raised, so also in Mk 8:34b—38 one is furthest removed from simple persuasion by appeal to universally observed phenomena. Where the threat to the very confession of Christ is at stake, exhortation becomes more concentrated and specific, with explicit and dramatic eschatological promises and warnings emerging finally in the concluding sayings (Mk 8:38; cf. Lk 12:8−9/Mt 10:32−3). Where Mk 8:34b−38 differs from Lk 12:2−9 par is in that the former appears more intense and threatening, a step further removed from the outlook of the other collection.

An examination of the parallels to Mk 8:34b−38 in Mt 16:24−8 and Lk 9:23−7 does little to alter this hypothesis. However, it is significant that, while each evangelist makes alterations to the formulation of the Markan collection, neither does so in such a way as to accentuate the similarity to and reduce the differences from the other aphoristic collections which it has received. Both evangelists remove the introductory formula in Mk 9:1a and connect the saying in 9:1 more closely with the preceding sayings, rather than stressing the saying in 8:38 as the natural conclusion to the collection. Luke even eliminates one of the two rhetorical questions in the centre of the collection. Neither evangelist attempts to heighten the universal aphoristic character of the sayings significantly, for while each removes the reference to the adulterous and sinful generation in Mk 8:38, both retain much of the apocalyptic imagery of the Son of Man's coming in glory.[39] This all provides further evidence for the claim that neither Matthew nor Luke demonstrated a particular interest in the proliferation or imitation of the structure of the double-tradition collections, and thus the compositional style responsible for the similarities in structure of these collections lay prior to both.

A further variation of this call to discipleship, however, occurs in *Lk 14:26−33, 34−5*. This collection of sayings begins with a double-tradition form of the 'cross' saying, preceded by the saying about a break with family ties which also seems to belong to the double tradition (Lk 14:26−7). As we have seen, these logia are found similarly linked in Mt 10:37−8.[40] Although the passage which follows in Luke contains no other sayings of the double tradition[41] or of Mk 8:34b−38, it does at first glance bear similarity to the design of the aphoristic sayings-collections of the double tradition. The central unit consists of double rhetorical questions, and a seeming *inclusio* occurs in Lk 14:33 to mark the conclusion.

Yet here is an example of a collection of sayings where the similarities with the design of the other aphoristic collections do seem to be superficial rather than substantial. They in fact consist of little more than a pair of illustrative sayings formulated as questions and located near the middle of the section. Even the existence of this pairing is less significant once it is recognized that these two 'parables', like several others in the synoptic tradition, may have circulated together.[42] They could have simply been drawn together from additional source-material used by Luke.[43] Many of the other apparent similarities to the aphoristic collections fail on closer analysis:

    (1) In Luke, the conclusion to the section of sayings on discipleship actually comes with the 'salt' sayings in 14:34−5 (Mt 5:13; cf. Mk 9:49−50),[44] to which is attached the warning 'He who has ears to hear, let him hear.' The seeming *inclusio* in 14:33 is, therefore, not

the actual end of the section for Luke.[45] It is also widely believed that the evangelist himself constructed verse 33 on the model of the sayings in verses 26–7[46] in order to press home again his concern for the renunciation of wealth. Thus Lk 14:33 is unlikely to have come from the tradition or to have formed part of any earlier tradition, and for the evangelist the natural conclusion to the section on discipleship is Lk 14:34–5.

(2) It has already been noted how the opening sayings in Mk 8:34b–35, consisting of imperatives and supporting argument, differ from the formal style of the 'wisdom' admonition by their conditional formulation and by the specific references to following Jesus. The same could be said of the opening sayings in Lk 14:26–7, except that, unlike even Mk 8:34b–35, there is no immediate supporting argument for the admonitions (contrast Mk 8:35). The sayings in Lk 14 are, therefore, even further removed from the style of general 'wisdom' admonition as found in most of the aphoristic sayings-collections.[47]

(3) Finally, a study of the progression of argument in Lk 14:26–33, 34–5 discloses a very uneven development of thought, which contrasts significantly with the style of the double-tradition aphoristic sayings collections and which lends credibility to the view that Lk 14:26ff. is not a carefully designed argument but, rather, a loose conjunction of diverse source-material.

The flow of argument in Lk 14:26–33, 34–5 has been a cause of continuing perplexity, centring especially on the role of the 'parables' in their present context.[48] It appears that some of the sayings in this section are concerned with absolute self-renunciation as the requirement for discipleship (cf. Lk 14:26–7, 33?), while others call the disciple to make a calculated evaluation of his position and to test himself (cf. Lk 14:28–32, 34–5).[49]

Even if these diverse elements can be made to appear less disjointed,[50] it is nonetheless clear that Lk 14:26–35 is not the carefully unfolding kind of argument found in the previously studied collections. In contrast, it is a poorly integrated conjunction in which Luke himself (as in 14:33) tries to provide some cohesion for the diverse sayings which he has brought together.[51] There is no compelling case for finding here either another pre-existing collection of aphoristic sayings comparable to the others studied, or for finding Luke himself in direct imitation of these other collections. It serves above all only to demonstrate the difference between occasional, superficial, stylistic similarities and the substantial similarities of design which link the other collections.

NOTES

Introduction

1 *Formgeschichte*, 151 (= *Tradition*, 153).
2 *Tradition*, 151–2.
3 *Geschichte*, 73ff.
4 'Study', 52.
5 *Geschichte*, 77–84. 'Grundsätze' were then further subdivided.
6 'Parables', 297.
7 'Wisdom Tradition', 231–40; 'Uses', 61–73; *Criticism*; 'Thomas', 92–103; 'Koan', 151–77; 'Saving', 57–72.
8 *Language*, 48–54; 'Wisdom', 543–72.
9 *Mahnsprüche.*
10 *Fragments*, ix.
11 *Fragments*, ix, 330–41.
12 'Proverbs', 91.
13 *Weisheitstraditionen*, 587–92.
14 *Tradition*, 105. The four exceptions are sayings which (i) arise from the exaltation of an eschatological mood, (ii) are an energetic summons to repentance, (iii) demand a new dispensation of mind, and (iv) are of the type 'the first will be last', or 'many are called but few are chosen'.
15 *Proverb*, 3.
16 W. McKane, *Proverbs*, 23–4, 124–5; J. Crossan, *Fragments*, 18–25; J. Williams, *Ponder*, 78–80.
17 Against the distinction, see A. Taylor, *Proverb*, 4–5; R.A. Edwards, *Theology*, 59 (following R. Murphy). But favouring a distinction, see H. Fischel, *Literature*, 40, 50.
18 Cf. A.R. Johnson, ' מָשָׁל ', 162–9; W. McKane, *Proverbs*, 22–33; J. Crenshaw, 'Wisdom', 229–39; F. Hauck, 'παραβολή', 744–61, and 'παροιμία', 854–6; J.W. Sider, 'Meaning', 453–70.
19 Cf. below, pp. 162–70.

1. Aphoristic wisdom and the New Testament era

1 *Form*, 21.
2 W. McKane, *Proverbs*, 23.
3 E.g., is the 'Foxes have holes' saying (Mt 8:19–20/Lk 9:57–8) an

adaptation of or fragment of an earlier aphorism? Cf. R. Bultmann, *Tradition*, 28.

4 W. McKane (*Proverbs*, 23–4) uses this as a basis for distinguishing 'proverbs' from 'aphorisms or apophthegms'.

5 *Form*, 20; cf. G. von Rad, *Wisdom*, 31–2. J. Crossan (*Fragments*, 20–5) and J. Williams (*Ponder*, 79–80) attempt to distinguish 'proverb' from 'aphorism' on the basis of being able to distinguish a 'collective' voice from an 'individual' voice or authority, respectively. This will not be accepted because, as they admit, this relates to usage rather than form or content. The terms 'proverb' and 'aphorism' will be used interchangeably in the present study. Other synonyms are gnomes and maxims.

6 G. von Rad, *Wisdom*, 32. For rare exceptions, see A. Taylor, *Proverb*, 82–6.

7 Cf. above, Introduction, n. 4. On the use of *sententiae* in ancient rhetoric at the hands of teachers and students, see also H. Fischel, *Literature*, 50, 132 n. 48, 138 n. 111.

8 *Studien*, 36, 92–3.

9 It should be clear from these criteria how aphoristic sayings also differ from 'parables', which are described by Crossan as 'separable narrative metaphors or short stories' (*Fragments*, vii). The 'authority' of the parable also differs from that of the aphorism. The parable makes no pretence of being a generalization about life.

10 R. N. Whybray, *Tradition*, 1–54, 69–70, 71–6, 155–6. Whybray considered the intellectual tradition to have been characterized by certain terminology, but hesitated to identify this with any particular group. J. McKenzie ('Reflections', 1–9) adopted another fairly general definition of wisdom. It is a way of thought and speech which is not limited to the schools. It is an 'approach to reality' characterized by a firm belief in the validity of experience. For other such views, see discussions by J. Crenshaw, 'Prolegomenon', 3–6; D. Morgan, *Wisdom*, 17–29; G. Sheppard, *Wisdom*, 1–12.

11 Cf., e.g., G. E. Bryce, 'Book Review', 596–8.

12 'Prolegomenon', 1–45, and 'Method', 129–42.

13 *Wesen*, 119–20; Schmid notes that the Sumerian lists were taken over by the Accadians for their philological value.

14 'Method', 130, 132.

15 Cf. M. Hengel, *Judaism*, I, 202–10, who describes it variously as 'apocalyptic wisdom' or 'apocalyptic encyclopaedic wisdom'; also J. Blenkinsopp, *Wisdom*, 150–5.

16 J. Crenshaw ('Prolegomenon', 9–13) rejects a prophetic *Sitz im Leben* for wisdom; cf. also R. E. Murphy, 'Assumptions', 411. Murphy ('Consideration', 159–61) does, however, allow the cult as a setting for wisdom psalms.

17 *Studien*, 188, 192. Also, for the association of this wisdom with the royal court, see W. McKane, *Prophets*, 48ff., who identifies the old wisdom as a wisdom of statecraft in view of court associations, prophetic opposition, and lack of ethical or religious content. G. von Rad (*Wisdom*, 11–23) refers to the rise of 'school wisdom' in

the early monarchy period, but rejects the view that Proverbs was 'merely a product of court knowledge and serving for the training of high officials' (*ibid.*, 17).

18 *Studien*, 33–4, 36, 50–1; contrast the view of O. Eissfeldt, *Introduction*, 81–7.

19 Aphoristic forms are still important in Qoheleth, but no longer as straightforward expressions of the wise man's learning. Often they appear as 'quotations' for elaboration in the preacher's own discursive manner, and sometimes he uses contrasting proverbs (cf. Qoh 4:5–6) in which the second view is apparently favoured. Cf. R. Gordis, 'Quotations', 123–47. In addition to these three works, one might also include Tobit (especially the speeches of advice in chapters 4 and 12, which may be of the testament genre). WisSol is largely in the form of extensive poems or discourses rather than collections of individual sayings, but some individual maxims are isolatable (cf. 6:24b, 4:1, 3:13–14; see further O. Eissfeldt, *Introduction*, 601; J. M. Reese, *Influence*, 90–121; C. Larcher, *Études*, 85–180, 348).

20 *Weisheitstraditionen*, 174. Also cf. J. Robinson, 'Logoi Sophōn', 71–113.

21 J. T. Sanders, *Ben Sira*, 3–26; M. Hengel, *Judaism*, I, 131–2; W. Roth, 'Wisdom', 59–79.

22 Cf. J. Blenkinsopp, *Wisdom*, 130ff.; E. Schnabel, *Law*, 8–92; G. von Rad, *Wisdom*, 244–6. O. Rickenbacher attributes the thematic integration of the 'Wisdom' pericopes into the work as a whole as evidence of Ben Sira's redactoral hand (*Weisheitsperikopen*, esp. 214). Also note 1 Bar 3:9–4:4, and the study by G. Sheppard, *Wisdom*, 19ff.

23 Cf. discussion in J. T. Sanders, *Ben Sira*, 57–9, 105–6; E. Schnabel, *Law*, 10–15, 84–7. In particular, note the debate between Th. Middendorp (*Stellung*) and M. Hengel ('Book Review', 83–7) over Sirach's stance towards Hellenism. On Sirach's attitude towards the priesthood and scribal learning, see also H. Stadelmann, *Ben Sira*. Theologically, J. Marböck (*Wandel*, esp. 129–32) argues that the figure of divine Wisdom signified the immanence of God and was part of Sirach's attempt to establish the unity of reality, of God and the world.

24 Cf. above, n. 15.

25 M. Hengel, *Judaism*, I, 153; G. von Rad, *Wisdom*, 262 (citing also the work of V. Hamp). Nonetheless, there may be similarities between Sirach and apocalyptic, especially when the latter is not concerned solely with eschatology: cf. J. D. Martin, 'Child', and (regarding hints of Messianism in Sirach but without any developed 'doctrine') 'Hymn'.

26 *Kingdom*, 382ff.; and, similarly, U. Wilckens, 'σοφία', 503. For the dating of these chapters of 1 Enoch, cf. M. Hengel, *Judaism*, II, 134 n. 600.

27 'Message', 309–28.

28 But Nickelsburg ('Message', 327) does note that both the 'woe' form

and the 'say not' refutation form occur in Sirach and that the righteous are called 'wise'. He attributes this to a re-emergence of prophetic consciousness in 'wisdom circles' (yet different from classical prophecy). See also M. Hengel, *Judaism*, I, 206.

29 Cf. B. Reicke ('Apocalypticism', 148–50), who suggests that sectarian pietists were behind 1 En 91–102, urging endurance but criticizing the materialism and lack of zeal for the Law of the later Hasmoneans.

30 More general teaching is found in 2 Enoch, but it is difficult to determine the date and origin of this material: see O. Eissfeldt, *Introduction*, 623; J. Milik, *Enoch*, 107–16. There is of course interest in sapiential traditions other than of an aphoristic kind in 1 Enoch: in particular the speculation about divine Wisdom in 1 En 42 (and possibly 84:3; 91:10; 93:8; 94:5). 2 Enoch shows no interest in this figure.

31 Cf. 1QS 11:5f; 1QH 9:23–4, 10:2–4; 13:13–14; 1QpHab 7:14. That this wisdom was fundamentally esoteric, however, has been challenged by M. Hengel, *Judaism*, I, 176, appealing particularly to 11QPs[a] col 18. J. A. Sanders (*Psalms Scroll*, 69) reaches the opposite conclusion from this hymn! Much of this debate, though, centres on the role of the 'educated' at Qumran. More generally, see J. Worrell, 'Concepts'; E. Schnabel, *Law*, 190–226.

32 Cf. 1QS 10:24–5, and further in U. Wilckens, 'σοφία', 504–5; M. Hengel, *Judaism*, I, 222.

33 Cf. E. Schnabel, *Law*, 199: 'No proverbial texts have been found in Qumran.' But there are fragments of Sir 1:19–20 (?); 6:14–15 (?), 6:20–31 (2QSir), 51:13–20b, 30 (11QPs[a]); Qoh 5:13–17, 6:3–8, 7:7–9 (4QQoh[a]). A possible allusion to Prov 15:8 is found in CD 11:20–1. The interest in Sirach may be due to interest in Zadokite priesthood, Aaron and Torah: cf. J. Marböck, *Wandel*, 110–12.

34 Is the harlot the negative counterpart to divine Wisdom? M. Hengel (*Judaism*, I, 218–19) sees no concept of hypostatized Wisdom as mediator at creation anywhere in Essene writings, for she is replaced with perfect knowledge by God himself. But also cf. J. A. Sanders (*Psalms Scroll*, 66–7, 68–9) on 11QPs[a] col. 18; J. Lebram, 'Chokmah', 202–11; and D. Lührmann, 'Weisheitspsalm', 87–98.

35 A list is given in R. Charles, *Pseudepigrapha*, II, 293; cf. also H. Hollander, *Joseph*, 94–5. A list of general exhortations is also given by A. Hultgård, *L'Eschatologie*, II, 148–9, 154–5.

36 *Joseph*, 11.

37 References to the will and law of God are common in the admonitions in the Testaments: cf. TIss (4:1, 6; 5:1–3; 6:1) and TAsher (1:3, 2:6, 10; 4:5; 5:4; 6:1, 3; 7:5).

38 This applies even in Sirach; but cf. M. Hengel, *Judaism*, I, 78ff., 134–6. For Palestinian sages during the Pharisaic period, see E. E. Urbach, *Sages*, although his evaluation of the early period is inevitably conjectural. Also see E. Schürer, *History*, II, 415–22; S. Safrai, 'Education', 945–70.

39 D. Georgi, 'Records', 530−42. On Josephus' identification of scribes and 'the wise', cf. U. Wilckens, 'σοφία', 502.
40 'Records', 538−9; J. Neusner, *Rabbinic Traditions*, 224−6.
41 J. Neusner, *Rabbinic Judaism*, 106.
42 Cf. U. Wilckens, 'σοφία', 517−23; *Weisheit*; and his later assessment in '1Kor 2, 1−16', 501−37; H. Conzelmann, 'Paulus', 231−44, and *1 Corinthians*, 40−8, 55−69; B. Pearson, 'Speculation', 43−66; R. Horsley, 'Wisdom', 224−39; J. Dunn, *Christology*, 176−96; J. Davis, *Wisdom*, esp. 65ff.; A. van Roon, 'Relation', 207−39; A. J. M. Wedderburn, '1Kor 1.21', 132−4; P. Richardson, 'Thunderbolt', 91−112; E. Schnabel, *Law*, 236−64.
43 For aphoristic and moral wisdom in Paul, see E. Schnabel, *Law*, 323−42; V. Furnish, *Theology*, 29−33, 35−37, 42−3, 69−70, 90−2; also, in a limited way, D. Georgi, *Geschichte*, 68−9.
44 Cf. E. A. Judge, 'Society', 30 n. 60.
45 'Transformation', 67−101, and *Literature*.
46 'Transformation', 73.
47 For a survey of wisdom instruction amongst nations of the ancient world, see M. West, *Hesiod*, 3−25.
48 G. Highet, 'Anthology', 67.
49 W. Watt, 'Sententia', 977−8; M. Clarke, *Education*, 28−45; D. Clarke, *Rhetoric*, 177−212.
50 The question of Q cannot be reviewed here in detail. Even the list of studies of Q from 1972 to 1980 compiled by F. Neirynck ('Studies', 409−13) came to over 90 entries. For the early history of the Q hypothesis, cf. R. Worden, 'Analysis', 23−61, and 'Redaction', 532−46; S. Schulz, *Q*, 11−44. Many opponents of Q argue for Luke's use of Matthew, either from a neo-Griesbach stance (W. Farmer, B. Orchard) or from a Markan priority stance (A. Farrer, M. Goulder).

Some scholars (cf. J. Jeremias, 'Hypothese', 147−9; R. M. Grant, *Introduction*, 113−14; H.-T. Wrege, *Bergpredigt*, 2−3) have preferred to think of Q as consisting of various strata of oral tradition rather than as a largely fixed, single source. It has become increasingly clear, however, that if Matthew and Luke drew on a common tradition, it was in a largely fixed form (cf. V. Taylor, 'The Order of Q', 27−31; 'Original Order', 246−69; A. Polag, 'Mitte', 104; *Fragmenta*). Against the supporters of Luke using Matthew, however, most Q reconstructions prefer to think of Luke as better preserving the original order than Matthew. Ultimately support for Luke's use of Matthew depends on a plausible case being made for a Lukan reordering of Matthew's sequence of double-tradition material. C. Tuckett (*Revival*, 145) points out: 'Griesbach himself never dealt with the problem of the relationship between Matthew and Luke in any detail.' Even in the modern debate, Luke's alleged rearrangement of Matthew's order of double-tradition material has seldom been discussed in more than broad terms (cf. C. Tuckett, 'Arguments', 207; and even M. Goulder, 'Order', 111−30; H. B. Green, 'Credibility', 149).

Another difficulty for the theory that Luke used Matthew is the requirement for the Lukan form of double-tradition sayings to be secondary to the form in Matthew. M. Goulder accepts that it must always be so (*Midrash*, 452; 'Farrer', 193–4), although W. Farmer is willing to accept other hypothetical sources available to Luke where it is necessary to explain instances in which Luke's formulation seems more original ('Approach', 42, 46–7). On the basis of the 'Sophia' logia, however, Tuckett argues even against Farmer, by noting that the appeal to parallel traditions is less plausible when the wording of Matthew and Luke is very close for a given passage, as it is in the cases he considers (*Revival*, 146–66).

Regarding whether the 'minor agreements' show Luke's knowledge of Matthew, see the debate between M. Goulder ('Test', 218–34, and 'Mark XVI.1–8', 235–40) and C. Tuckett ('Relationship', 130–42). F. Neirynck ('Transfiguration', 810) also argues that a subsidiary indebtedness of Luke to Matthew need not entail the demise of the Q hypothesis, following R. Morgenthaler, *Synopse*, 301–5, and E. Simons, *Evangelist*, 107–8.

51 'Logoi Sophōn', 71–113; see also M. Küchler, *Weisheitstraditionen*, 157–318, 562–7. Robinson noted, though, a lack of investigation of the Greek literature for the *Gattung* (*ibid.*, 73). For a different assessment of *Gattung*, cf. E. Bammel ('Ende', 39–50), who considers Q a 'testament'. A recent discussion of Q's *genre* is found in J. Kloppenborg, 'Tradition', 57–62.

52 See also P. Pokorný, 'Worte', 172–80.

53 *Redaktion*, 98–9; and 'Verweis', 188.

54 *Q*, 50–1 *et passim*.

55 Lührmann (*Redaktion*, 98) specifically draws the contrast with Matthew and Mark.

56 D. Lührmann (*Redaktion*, 76–7) specifically compares Lk 17:26–30 with Sir 16:7–8.

57 *Jesus*. The double-tradition passages include Lk 7:31–5 par, Lk 10:21–2 par, Lk 11:49–51 par and Lk 13:34–5 par.

58 *Theology*. He apparently recognizes different kinds of wisdom (*ibid.*, 146), but makes no attempt in the end to elaborate on this. He concludes that wisdom in Q differs from 'conventional' wisdom, however, and describes it as an eschatological form of wisdom (*ibid.*, 148).

59 *Q*, 50 contains a brief paragraph on the subject.

60 *Q*, 153: 'Jesus der "Lehrer" und Jesus als eschatologischer Charismatiker, Weisheit und Prophetie bzw Weisheit and Apokalyptik sind keine Gegensätze, eine Beobachtung, die wir immer wieder in den ältesten Q-Stoffen gemacht haben.'

61 Relatively little discussion of wisdom is found in P. Hoffmann, *Studien*, apart from the relationship of the Son of Man to the prophetic-wisdom tradition found particularly in the divine Sophia passages (*ibid.*, 158ff.). He inclines towards seeing the Son of Man references as a later layer of development over the prophetic-wisdom traditions (*ibid.*, 232). D. Lührmann (*Redaktion*, 97–8) holds the more common view that the divine Sophia sayings belong to a late

!ayer of tradition, as Q moved into a wider Hellenistic Jewish environment. Cf. also A. Polag, *Christologie*, 137–8. Unfortunately, the recently published work of J. Kloppenborg, *The Formation of Q: Trajectories in Ancient Wisdom Collections* (Philadelphia, Pa, 1987) appeared too late to be evaluated in the present study.

62 A. Jacobson is sensitive to the problem of distinguishing tradition from redaction in Q and to Devisch's argument that the theological content of the tradition is not itself adequate for defining the theological character of the composition Q ('Christology', 11; cf. also M. Devisch, 'Q', 90–1). Jacobson therefore seeks to study the stages in the literary growth of the document Q as a whole, with special reference to Wisdom christology. Even so, the latter part of Q receives scant attention. The conclusions of our study of the structure of aphoristic collections themselves will conflict in part with Jacobson's wider and more theological approach regarding this material (see below, pp. 175–6).

63 E.g., the recognition of the formal and structural similarities between the aphoristic sayings collections will provide an important 'control' over the assignment of these to widely different stages of Q on thematic grounds such as is found in A. Jacobson's work. An early unity of these traditions must be recognized, and then the later use traced in correlation with other material and still larger units.

2. Collections of Aphoristic Sayings in the Double Tradition.

1 'Transformation', 72ff.

2 In addition there are a number of smaller clusters or pairs of aphoristic sayings, but these will be considered in Chapter 3 under the heading of 'isolated aphoristic sayings'. Some of these may have been elaborated forms of a single saying or closely integrated conjunctions of similar sayings: see R. Bultmann, *Tradition*, 85–93; J. Crossan, *Fragments*, 120ff.

3 Lk 6:43–5 par shows the greatest divergence.

4 *Fragmenta*, 48–51. On this passage, also see my earlier essay, 'Evidence', 411–18.

5 *Tradition*, 87; see further D. Catchpole, 'Friend', 416–17.

6 P. Minear (*Commands*, 115) argues that Mt 7:8 par is 'an innocuous and unnecessary restatement' in proverbial form of Mt 7:7 par. This evaluation is rightly challenged by Zeller, *Mahnsprüche*, 128–9, although Zeller still considers Mt 7:8 to have been modelled on 7:7.

7 R. Bultmann, *Tradition*, 86; P. Minear, *Commands*, 117; also apparently W. Ott, *Gebet*, 99–112, and J. Jeremias, *Parables*, 144–5. In contrast, cf. S. Schulz, *Q*, 163; I. H. Marshall, *Luke*, 465–6; and D. Zeller, *Mahnsprüche*, 128. Zeller's observations that 'enthüllt erst V. 11 das theologische Passiv von V. 7' and that a catchword connection on αἰτεῖν and διδόναι exists between the two units are hardly unambiguous arguments for original unity. Parallels to Mt 7:7–8 par alone are preserved in GThom 2, 92, 94.

8 See D. Zeller, *Mahnsprüche*, 128–30.

9 For the qualifications added to similar sayings elsewhere, see P. Minear, *Commands*, 114–15, 126–30; J. Gnilka, *Matthäusevangelium*, I, 261–2.

10 J. Jeremias, *Theology*, 11.

11 A. H. McNeile, *St Matthew*, 91–2; I. H. Marshall, *Luke*, 466–7.

12 'Seeking' can be with reference to God (Deut 4:29; Isa 55:6; Jer 29:13; cf. H. Greeven, 'ζητέω', 892–3), to wisdom (Prov 8:17b), to the Law (Sir 32:15), or to entry into the kingdom (Mt 6:33 par). Similarly, 'knocking' may serve as an image not only for prayer (bMeg. 12b) but also for study of the law (bPesikta 176a) and possibly for entry to the kingdom (cf. J. Jeremias, 'θύρα', 178).

13 The Lukan ordering, in which these sayings follow soon after the Lord's Prayer in Lk 11:2–4 (par Mt 6:9–13), might also provide a clue to the interpretation of the sayings once they were joined to the larger section. But on this conjunction of passages, see further below.

14 Whether or not this was originally 'beggar's wisdom' (cf. J. Jeremias, *Parables*, 159), it has been formulated in a more universal way.

15 Cf. note 12 above, and D. Zeller, *Mahnsprüche*, 128–9. One may also conjecture that the well-attested application of 'seeking' to wisdom (Prov 2:4–5; 8:17b; 14:6; Qoh 7:25; Sir 4:12; 24:34; 51:13; WisSol 8:2,17) further commended this saying to the interest of those clearly skilled in the use of practical wisdom. There is nothing to suggest, however, that this would have been more than a secondary interest. On 'seeking' and 'finding', see further N. Brox, 'Suchen', 17–36.

16 Cf. J. Gnilka, *Matthäusevangelium*, I, 262.

17 Cf. S. Schulz, *Q*, 161–2; W. Ott, *Gebet*, 102–12.

18 S. Schulz, *Q*, 162; A. Harnack, *Sayings*, 10.

19 Cf. the discussion of D. Catchpole, 'Friend', 413–14, supporting many features of Matthew's version as more original.

20 *Gebet*, 109–12.

21 'Friend', 414; also note parallels cited by U. Luz, *Matthäus*, I, 384.

22 Arguing for an original series of three questions, see K. Bailey, *Poet*, 135–7.

23 S. Schulz, *Q*, 162–3, 63; cf. H. Greeven, 'Wer', 86–101.

24 But cf. K. Berger, 'Materialien', 31–3, citing examples from sapiential literature as background.

25 Cf. D. Zeller, *Mahnsprüche*, 83 n. 217; U. Luz, *Matthäus*, I, 384.

26 J. Jeremias (*Parables*, 144–5) also argues that this speech form is usually addressed to opponents. But the use of the formula varies considerably with context: see D. Catchpole, 'Friend', 415 n. 28. The context set by Mt 7:7–8 par makes it likely that it is here addressed to followers, since Mt 7:7–8 par would hardly be addressed to opponents.

27 Regarding ὑμεῖς πονηροὶ ὄντες, see below.

28 Cf. U. Luz, *Matthäus*, I, 384.

29 The phrase in Luke, ὁ πατὴρ [ὁ] ἐξ οὐρανοῦ, is likely to reflect earlier tradition than Matthew's ὁ πατὴρ ὑμῶν ὁ ἐν τοῖς οὐρανοῖς, since the former phrase is unusual for Luke, whereas the latter conforms to Matthew's characteristic terminology. Cf. S. Schulz, *Q*, 162, who notes that Matthew's phrase occurs 11 times in Matthew (never where it can be attributed with certainty to tradition), only once in Mark, and never in Luke.

30 P. Minear, *Commands*, 117.

31 *Gebet*, 107–8; also S. Schulz, *Q*, 162.

32 *Bergpredigt*, 108; also I. H. Marshall, *Luke*, 470.

33 See also D. Catchpole, 'Friend', 414; A. Harnack, *Sayings*, 10; S. Schulz, *Q*, 162.

34 See J. Fitzmyer, *Luke*, I, 227–31; II, 913.

35 *Gleichnisreden*, II, 41–4; also W. Ott, *Gebet*, 107–9.

36 So also P. Minear, *Commands*, 118; W. Ott, *Gebet*, 108; E. Schweizer, *Matthew*, 174; D. Zeller, *Mahnsprüche*, 130–1.

37 See also D. Catchpole, 'Friend', 415–16, against J. Jeremias and W. Grundmann.

38 Cf. U. Luz, *Matthäus*, I, 385.

39 So also A. Polag, *Christologie*, 76; J. Dunn, *Jesus*, 24.

40 See M. Hengel, *Property*, 34; G. Theissen, *Followers*, 57; J. Jeremias, *Jerusalem*, 121–3.

41 *Q*, 163–4. Schulz particularly finds evidence of prophetic declaration in the two formulas τίς ἐξ ὑμῖν (discussed above) and κἀγὼ ὑμῖν λέγω. Curiously, Schulz accepts the secondary provenance of κἀγὼ ὑμῖν λέγω in Luke, but still believes that such a formula *would* have introduced this unit of sayings (*ibid.*, 161). Certainly the use of κἀγώ is exceptional in double-tradition material (cf. Lk 19:23 par?), whereas Schulz identifies it twice in Luke (redaction) and 5 times in Acts. On ὑμῖν λέγω, see further F. Neirynck, 'Developments', 56–69.

42 Cf. G. von Rad, *Wisdom*, 71, 87, 113, 311; J. Collins, 'Proverbial Wisdom', 5–6; J. Crossan, *Fragments*, 27–8.

43 J. Crossan, *Fragments*, 27.

44 A. Jacobson tentatively suggests that Mt 7:6 might have belonged to Q, referring to secret traditions not to be shared with outsiders ('Christology', 217).

45 Against a purely 'eschatological' understanding of Lk 11:3 par, cf. M. Goulder, 'Composition', 32–45; E. Yamauchi, 'Daily Bread', 145–56; S. van Tilborg, 'Form Criticism', 94–105 (who also cites other important works). Van Tilborg considers Lk 11:3 par as an addition of Q-redaction to a more basic form of the prayer found in Mk 14:36, 38. He also draws attention to the similar concerns in Mt 6:25, 31 par.

46 *Fragmenta*, 48–51.

47 'Original Order', 251.

48 *Synopse*, 61–5.

49 A. Jacobson ('Christology', 215–21) sees Lk 11:9–13 as 'an exposition of the Lord's Prayer, with the striking feature that it

denies that God would lead anyone into temptation'; see also J. Crossan, *Fragments*, 98. Jacobson sees Lk 11:9–13 itself subsequently corrected by the Temptation account. He takes no specific account, however, of the theme of asking for food (which is in the Lord's Prayer itself), or of the non-polemical character of Lk 11: 9–13.

50 On the relationship of these sayings to Mt 7:7–8 par, see recently C. Tuckett, *Nag Hammadi*, 86 n.311 and 153–4.

51 *Fragments*, 99–104.

52 H. Koester, 'Witnesses', 243–4.

53 A. Jacobson ('Christology', 215–21) attempts to draw further parallels between Lk 10:21–2 par and Lk 11:9–13 par.

54 Catchpole notes: (i) both have τίς ἐξ ὑμῖν formulations, (ii) both concern petitioning, (iii) both concern a lack of food, (iv) both emphasize the willing gift of food, (v) both make a comparable assertion about God, but with it only being explicit in v. 13. He also argues (against Schulz, *Q*, 161) for the originality of Matthew's ή, which 'reads most naturally as a reminiscence of such an earlier scheme' ('Friend', 414, 416). Also cf. H. Schürmann, 'Reminiszenzen', 202. But arguing specifically for the original independence of Lk 11:9–13 par from 11:5–8 is K. Bailey, *Poet*, 134–5.

55 'Friend', 421–3, where he also suggests Mt 6:7–8 was an editorial introduction into this material in Q.

56 A possible parallel to Catchpole's hypothesis will be found in our later discussion of Lk 16:9–13. Its connection with the Parable of the 'Unjust' Steward in Lk 16:1–8 could conceivably have also been pre-Lukan and thus another example of an aphoristic collection composed in response to a parable. The parable in this case is sufficiently awkward to pose no problems for explaining Matthew's omission of it if it were known to him. Cf. below, pp. 86–99.

57 For various form-critical theories on the units comprising this passage, see D. Catchpole, 'Ravens', 77–8. But against such theories generally, see J. Gnilka, *Matthäusevangelium*, I, 246.

58 J. Fitzmyer (*Luke*, II, 977) compares this verse with the 'idyllic summaries of Acts 2:42–47; 4:32–35; and the divisive episode of Ananias and Sapphira (Acts 5:1–10)'.

59 So also S. Schulz, *Q*, 149ff.; A. Harnack, *Sayings*, 140; T.W. Manson, *Sayings*, 111ff. (who discusses Lk 12:32 separately as a Q-saying); E. Schweizer, *Luke*, 209; G. Strecker, *Bergpredigt*, 145; W. Schenk, *Synopse*, 89–92. But A. Polag (*Fragmenta*, 62) tentatively includes Lk 12:32, and U. Luz (*Matthäus*, I, 364) assigns Lk 12:32 and Mt 6:34 to QLk and QMt respectively, while H. Wrege (*Bergpredigt*, 119) follows Justin *Apol.* I.15.16 in accepting Mt 6:33/ Lk 12:31 as the conclusion to the section.

60 For the introductory phrases, see below p. 35. For the exhortation, see GThom 36 and OxyP 655. The GThom logion only contains a brief exhortation on anxiety about clothing. J. Jeremias (*Sayings*, 98) seems undecided whether OxyP 655 is 'no more than a précis of Matt. 6.30' or 'a primitive tradition'.

61 S. Schulz (*Q*, 149) suggests that Luke omitted ὑμῶν to make the saying more universal.

62 J. Gnilka, *Matthäusevangelium*, I, 247. This is characteristic of the form of wisdom admonitions: see S. Schulz, *Q*, 152.

63 Cf. R. Bultmann, *Tradition*, 93; A. Harnack, *Sayings*, 6; H. Cadbury, *Style*, 81–3, 138–9; H.-T. Wrege, *Bergpredigt*, 117; G. Strecker, *Bergpredigt*, 142.

64 Arguing that Mt 6:25a, b might already have stood together before the formulation of the collection, see R. Bultmann, *Tradition*, 88.

65 'Ravens', 79.

66 For the greater originality of Luke's 'ravens' to Matthew's 'birds of the sky', cf. J. Fitzmyer, *Luke*, II, 978; D. Catchpole, 'Ravens', 85–6; U. Luz, *Matthäus*, I, 364–5; J. Gnilka, *Matthäusevangelium*, I, 246. But, on the basis of Mt 8:20; 13:32 par, S. Schulz (*Q*, 150) inclines towards Matthew's wording.

67 For differences in wording between Mt 6:26 and Lk 12:24, see S. Schulz, *Q*, 149–50; H.-T. Wrege, *Bergpredigt*, 117–18; J. Fitzmyer, *Luke*, II, 976–8. Fitzmyer attributes the substitution of κατανοεῖν in vv. 24, 27 to Luke.

68 *Q*, 150.

69 *Bergpredigt*, 118; see W. Schenk, *Synopse*, 91.

70 A. Polag (*Fragmenta*, 60) opts for Luke's wording, πόσῳ μᾶλλον, but treats it as a question.

71 Cf. below, p. 190.

72 Cf. S. Schulz (*Q*, 150), who notes that ὁ οὐράνιος is certainly a Matthean predication of the Father ('sonst im NT nur Lk 2, 13 und Apg 26, 19; bei Mt red 5,48; 6,14; 15,13'); also U. Luz, *Matthäus*, I, 364–5; J. Gnilka, *Matthäusevangelium*, I, 246.

73 Cf. also D. Catchpole, 'Ravens', 85–6.

74 D. Catchpole, ('Ravens', 80) also notes: 'its man-centred appeal to the ineffectiveness of anxiety is to be contrasted with the God-centred appeal to the inappropriateness of anxiety in the surrounding material'. U. Luz (*Matthäus*, I, 369–70) argues that ἡλικία must mean either 'age' or 'size of body', but not 'span of life'.

75 Cf. J. Fitzmyer, *Luke*, II, 976, who also dismisses G. Schwarz's attempt to recover an Aramaic form of the saying as 'farfetched' (*ibid.*, 979); D. Catchpole, 'Ravens', 88; G. Strecker, *Bergpredigt*, 143; J. Gnilka, *Matthäusevangelium*, I, 246; S. Schulz, *Q*, 152. Schulz accepts that the saying is a later insertion into the context but believes that it was present prior to the redactional stages of Q. No support is provided for this contention, and cf. W. Schenk, *Synopse*, 91–2.

76 Cf. R. Bultmann, *Tradition*, 81; J. Creed, *Luke*, 174. J. Fitzmyer (*Luke*, II, 976) suggests that Luke modifies his form of v. 26 considerably; cf. also D. Catchpole, 'Ravens', 84.

77 *Luke*, II, 977.

78 Cf. Mt 10:28ff. (and L. Schottroff/W. Stegemann, *Jesus*, 61); Mt 5:44 par. Also, what kind of oral mnemonic technique would account for the preservation of this disruption in both Matthew and

Luke, as H. Wrege must argue (*Bergpredigt*, 119–20, 123–4)? D. Catchpole ('Ravens', 83) also rules out Goulder's theory of a unified Matthean midrash.

79 G. Strecker (*Bergpredigt*, 143) draws attention to Matthew's οὖν (6:31) as marking the conclusion.

80 S. Schulz, *Q*, 151; A. Polag, *Fragmenta*, 62; but, in contrast, cf. W. Schenk, *Synopse*, 91.

81 S. Schulz, *Q*, 151; A. Polag, *Fragmenta*, 62; again contrary to W. Schenk, *Synopse*, 91.

82 *Gebet*, 108–9.

83 *Gebet*, 109. But τοῦ κόσμου in Lk 12:30 is probably secondary: see S. Schulz, *Q*, 151; H.-T. Wrege, *Bergpredigt*, 122 (who agrees that it was not known to Matthew, but considers it pre-Lukan); D. Seccombe, *Possessions*, 150 ('It may be meant as an intentional contrast to the kingdom').

84 Cf. U. Luz, *Matthäus*, I, 364; J. Gnilka, *Matthäusevangelium*, I, 246. S. Schulz (*Q*, 152) argues against many for the originality of πρῶτον (cf. also Mt 23:26), but not of πάντα. The καὶ τὴν δικαιοσύνην is almost certainly Matthean: G. Strecker, *Weg*, 152, and *Bergpredigt*, 144–5; H.-T. Wrege, *Bergpredigt*, 122–3; D. Catchpole, 'Ravens', 86.

85 W. Ott, *Gebet*, 33–4.

86 For other differences in wording, see further S. Schulz, *Q*, 151–2.

87 On the three items in GPh 57:7–8, cf. C. Tuckett, *Nag Hammadi*, 74–5.

88 Cf. D. Catchpole, 'Friend', 418, who also notes the common 'seeking' imagery, but sees verse 33 as less 'quietist and passive' than a call simply to prayer.

89 *Tradition*, 104.

90 D.P. Seccombe, *Possessions*, 148; cf. E.G. Selwyn, 'St Luke xii. 27,28', 163–4.

91 *Q*, 152–7.

92 *Q*, 156.

93 *Q*, 154–5.

94 Cf. D. Zeller, *Mahnsprüche*, 155–7, regarding λέγω ὑμῖν. On τίς ἐξ ὑμῶν, see *ibid.*, 83–4.

95 *Q*, 154–5, 111–12.

96 *Q*, 155–6.

97 Rightly L. Schottroff/W. Stegemann (*Jesus*, 70): 'für sie die Königsherrschaft Gottes primär heisst: Gott ist kyrios/Herr und Gott ist patēr/Vater'.

98 See D. Catchpole, 'Ravens', 82.

99 So D.P. Seccombe, *Possessions*, 150. See further D. Zeller, *Mahnsprüche*, 83–92; citations of Stoic and rabbinic texts in G. Strecker, *Bergpredigt*, 142; L. Schottroff/W. Stegemann, *Jesus*, 57.

100 *Theology*, 236–7, and *Parables*, 214–15. See also P. Hoffmann, *Studien*, 265; and even D. Zeller, *Mahnsprüche*, 93 (who does, however, note that 'Unser Text ist nicht ausdrücklich auf solche Adressaten eingeschränkt').

101 Even the double-tradition sayings in Lk 12:10, 11–12 par strictly refer more to the challenge to be faced from Jewish opposition than to the life of the wandering missionary *per se*.

102 Cf. L. Schottroff/W. Stegemann, *Jesus*, 62, 64–9, who allow that the exhortations could also address Christians settled in communities, although the message was seemingly borne by 'Q-Propheten'.

103 'Christology', 135.

104 'Christology', 136.

105 D. Zeller, *Mahnsprüche*, 85, considers such directness as closer to a prophetic than sapiential style, but see also his discussion on p. 90. J. Jeremias (*Theology*, 161–2) notes the possibility of an Aramaic nucleus for the term.

106 Cf. D. Catchpole, 'Ravens', 81.

107 D. Zeller, *Mahnsprüche*, 90. See also ἐθνικοί in Mt 5:47 (see below, p. 85).

108 *Aramaic*, 176–8. Cf. G. Strecker (*Bergpredigt*, 144): 'die Masse der unbekehrten, gottlosen, Menschen'. Much double-tradition material is favourable towards Gentiles who do respond to the Christian proclamation: cf. D. Lührmann, *Redaktion*, 86–8.

109 'Friend', 421.

110 'Friend', 421. Cf. also the doubts about this conjunction expressed by D. P. Seccombe, *Possessions*, 147, who, however, accepts the unity of Lk 12:13–34, where vv. 13–21 provided the transition to vv. 22–34. For a further discussion, see D. Zeller, *Mahnsprüche*, 83, n. 213.

111 'Friend', 421–4.

112 The καί in Lk 6:37a, linking the saying with Lk 6:36/Mt 5:48, should not be allowed to obscure the integrity of theme in Lk 6:37–42 par: *contra* A. Jacobson, 'Christology', 56.

113 Preferring Mt's ἵνα μή, see S. Schulz, *Q*, 146.

114 *Luke*, I, 641.

115 On the more positive attitude towards 'judging' (discernment) at Qumran and in rabbinic circles, see H. Braun, *Radikalismus*, II, 92–3 n. 2.

116 Stating that a divine passive is implied, see J. Fitzmyer, *Luke*, I, 641.

117 Against S. Schulz, *Q*, 148, who views the passives as referring to the apocalyptic judgement of God.

118 *Fragments*, 179–82. W.-P. Funk (*Apokalypse*, 155–6) cites other similar sayings (SentSext 183–4; GMary 15:17–8; Thunder 20: 11–12; TeachSilv 102:11–13; 2ApJas 57:20–2), but C. Tuckett considers the saying 'proverbial', so not all these texts need be related to the synoptic logion (*Nag Hammadi*, 39, 105).

119 *Fragments*, 180.

120 R. Bultmann, *Tradition*, 79–80, 86–7; S. Schulz, *Q*, 146; D. Zeller, *Mahnsprüche*, 113; J. Fitzmyer, *Luke*, I, 641: *contra* H. Schürmann, *Lukas*, I, 362.

121 Cf. J. Dupont, *Béatitudes*, I, 52–3 (a change from his 1954 edition).

122 See M. Goulder, *Midrash*, 91.

123 The parallel order and common vocabulary between Mt 7:1—2 and Lk 6:37—8 make it difficult to accept H.-T. Wrege's (*Bergpredigt*, 125—6) view of no common literary contact.

124 It may be argued, however, that at some stage in the compilation of the underlying tradition a 'critical attitudes' section was arranged (cf. the 'cares' section of Q supported by D. Catchpole, 'Friend', 419—24), consisting of Lk 6:27—36 par, 6:37—42 par, 6:43—5 par. In this case the appeal to 'forgive', 'not to condemn' and possibly to 'give' (cf. Lk 6:29—30 par) may have been added at this compilational stage to strengthen the transition between sub-units.

125 This was also true however for Mt 7:7—8 par with respect to the parallel clauses on 'seeking' and 'knocking'.

126 Neither Matthew nor Luke here adds the phrase in Mk 4:24: καὶ προστεθήσεται ὑμῖν. The wider use of the saying is noted in Strack-Billerbeck, I, 444—6; K. Deissner, 'μέτρον', 633—4; E. Neuhäusler, 'Masstab', 110.

127 *Q*, 146; see also A. Harnack, *Sayings*, 8—10, 130.

128 *Matthäus*, 65.

129 *Mahnsprüche*, 113.

130 For the difference in viewpoint between Mt 7:2b and Mt 25:14—30 par (where God's gifts follow no measure), see E. Neuhäusler, 'Masstab', 104—13.

131 E. Urbach, *Sages*, I, 371—2; see also below, n. 133, and M. *Sotah* I.7—10.

132 B. Couroyer, 'Mesure', 366—70.

133 H. Rüger, 'Mass', 174—82, confines his study to Jewish literature; he finds one instance in the Palestinian Targum in which the equivalent of the Greek passive occurs, and claims that it draws on End-time judgement. He assumes that Mt 7:2 is also eschatologically employed. See also the references of J. Crossan (*Fragments*, 179—82) to 'apocalyptic sanctions'.

134 On GThom 34 being dependent upon Matthew, see W. Schrage, *Verhältnis*, 85—6. But elsewhere Schrage notes how sayings about blind guides have many parallels ('τυφλός', 292 n. 159); see also TeachSilv 88:20—2; ApPet 72:12—13.

135 See J. Crossan, *Fragments*, 85—8.

136 S. Schulz, *Q*, 472—3; A. Polag, *Fragments*, 36; W. Schenk, *Synopse*, 30—1.

137 *Tradition*, 93; see also J. Dupont, *Béatitudes*, I, 57 n. 2; S. Schulz, *Q*, 473; A. Polag, *Fragmenta*, 36; W. Schenk, *Synopse*, 31; W. Schrage, 'τυφλός', 292.

138 S. Schulz, *Q*, 473. But H.-T. Wrege (*Bergpredigt*, 127) judges otherwise for μήτι.

139 Cf. G. Strecker, *Weg*, 139; J. Dupont, *Béatitudes*, I, 54; T. W. Manson, *Sayings*, 57.

140 For hints of a connection between Lk 6:39 and 6:41—2, see H. Schürmann, *Lukas*, I, 370 (but cf. further below); A. Polag, *Christologie*, 82.

141 S. Schulz, *Q*, 472–3, detaches Lk 6:39 from the unit 6:37–8, 41–2. However, if it was a polemic against the Pharisees in the early sayings tradition, it is perhaps surprising that Lk does not preserve this (cf. the woes in Lk 11).

142 J. Dupont, *Béatitudes*, I, 55–6; J. Fitzmyer, *Luke*, I, 641.

143 This assumes ὁδηγοὶ τυφλῶν is not considered a rabbinic title of honour in the saying: against E. Haenchen, 'Matthäus 23', 47; A. Jacobson, 'Christology', 57.

144 For discussion of this and other variations, see below, pp. 131–3.

145 'Christology', 63–4; but contrast J. Crossan, *Fragments*, 86. Jacobson argues that Lk 6:39 was added redactionally in Q to Lk 6:39–45 to give a unit of inner-community exhortation a new polemical slant. But he admits that 'Lk 6:40 fits only poorly into this polemical scheme'.

146 J. Fitzmyer, *Luke*, I, 641–2.

147 H. Schürmann, 'Reminiszenzen', 206–7, and *Lukas*, I, 370–1.

148 *Christologie*, 81–2.

149 R. Bultmann, *Tradition*, 93, 99; S. Schulz, *Q*, 449–50; and see further below, pp. 131–3. DialSav 139:11 refers only to the disciple resembling his teacher.

150 S. Schulz, *Q*, 450–1; A. Polag, *Christologie*, 82.

151 *Q*, 450–1.

152 On the two different *Sitze im Leben*, see H.-T. Wrege, *Bergpredigt*, 128.

153 *Lukas*, 153.

154 H. Cadbury, *Making*, 304, 236.

155 The differences in wording between Matthew and Luke are slight: see J. Fitzmyer, *Luke*, I, 642; S. Schulz, *Q*, 147.

156 'Christology', 56; also R. Bultmann, *Tradition*, 86; S. Schulz, *Q*, 147. On the parallel with GThom 26, which lacks Lk 6:42a and has the first 'question' in statement form, see further A. Jacobson, 'Christology', 57–8; Jacobson considers the GThom version more original than the Q-saying.

157 Rightly, J. Fitzmyer, *Luke*, I, 642.

158 *Ibid.*

159 Against A. Jacobson, 'Christology', 58. For other aphoristic parallels, see D. Zeller, *Mahnsprüche*, 116–17; J. Gnilka, *Matthäusevangelium*, I, 257.

160 'R. Tarphon said, I wonder whether there is anyone in this generation who accepts reproof, for if one says to him: Remove the mote from between your eyes, he would answer: Remove the beam from between your eyes!' (b. *Arakin* 16b).

161 G. Strecker, *Bergpredigt*, 150; and see above, n. 159.

162 Against A. Jacobson, 'Christology', 63. In support of an inner-community setting for Mt 7:3–5 par, see also D. Zeller, *Mahnsprüche*, 117.

163 Cf. D. Zeller, *Mahnsprüche*, 116.

164 *Q*, 147–8. But Lk 6:39 is assigned to the later, rather less enthusiastic Syrian community (*ibid.*, 472ff.).

165 Schulz explains this most succinctly in his discussion of the Golden Rule (*Q*, 140—1).
166 *Q*, 172.
167 *Q*, 148, 154, 141.
168 Schulz develops the view of E. Käsemann that parenesis in the early post-Easter community was founded primarily in apocalyptic. This can be found in Käsemann's discussion of 'sentences of holy law' (see *Questions*, 66ff., and esp. 92—3, 98—9).
169 Cf. the criticisms made by U. Luz, 'Logienquelle', 527—33; R. A. Edwards, 'Book Review', 609—12; P. Hoffmann, 'Rezensionen', 104—15; A. Jacobson, 'Christology', 13—14; J. Kloppenborg, 'Tradition', 39—45.
170 *Q*, 147.
171 J. Crossan, *Fragments*, 159—60; W. Schrage, *Verhältnis*, 101—2. But the Matthean order of 'grapes' and 'figs' in Mt 7:16 (cf. Lk 6:44) is found in GThom 45a. The aphorism 'The tree is known by its fruits' is attested also in IgnEph 14:2; GTr 33:30, 38—9; TriTrac 118:23—4; ApPet 75:7—9; TestTr 31:21—2; ValExp 36:32ff. Cf. C. Tuckett, *Nag Hammadi*, 60—1, 71, 122, 152—3.
172 *Fragments*, 159.
173 R. Bultmann, *Tradition*, 124, 127; T. W. Manson, *Sayings*, 59; A. McNeile, *St Matthew*, 94; G. Strecker, *Bergpredigt*, 165—8; U. Luz, *Matthäus*, I, 401; J. Gnilka, *Matthäusevangelium*, I, 272—3; A. Polag, *Fragmenta*, 36—7; S. Schulz, *Q*, 316; E. Schweizer, *Gemeinde*, 126—7; D. Hill, 'False Prophets', 331—2, 335. But cf. J. Dupont, *Béatitudes*, I, 126—7. For the sheep—wolf imagery, see also Mt 10:16 par, where, however, it is differently used.
174 S. Schulz, *Q*, 318; H. Schürmann, *Lukas*, I, 375; R. Bultmann, *Tradition*, 74, 95: against M. Krämer, 'Hütet', 358—9, 372. J. Drury (*Tradition*, 136—7) has argued that in Lk 6:37—45 Luke briefly tries to give a practical judgement upon bad living to balance the blessing of the good life described earlier, just as at the outset of the Sermon blessing and woe balance each other. According to Drury, Luke is looking for judgement material here in Matthew. When he finds it in Mt 7:15, Drury explains his not taking it up because it refers to a local Matthean problem of false prophets. Drury, however, fails to explain why then Luke does not take up Mt 7:19, which is not specifically related to false prophets and which provides exactly the judgement motif for which Luke is allegedly looking. Furthermore, why does Luke forsake the polemical forms of Mt 12:33—35 for the neutral gnomic forms which he employs? According to Drury, Luke is keen to sharpen the judgement emphasis in Mt 7:21. This is but one example of the failure of Drury to prove the Q-hypothesis unnecessary by his view of Luke's purpose and design. Another example is Lk 6:39—40, which Luke allegedly adds to the Sermon despite his tendency to abbreviate Matthew and his alleged 'fatigue' at just this point (*Tradition*, 134, 137).
175 So J. Crossan, *Fragments*, 159; A. Polag, *Fragmenta*, 36; U. Luz, *Matthäus*, I, 401; J. Gnilka, *Matthäusevangelium*, I, 272—3, 456—7.

176 J. Fenton, 'Inclusio', 174–5; M. Goulder, *Midrash*, 27. This is even admitted by M. Krämer, 'Hütet', 371–2.

177 S. Schulz, *Q*, 316–17; A. Harnack, *Sayings*, 69.

178 On other slight differences, see S. Schulz, *Q*, 316–17. He notes that the plural καρπῶν in Mt 7:16a, 20 may well be secondary.

179 *Q*, 316.

180 R. Bultmann, *Tradition*, 93; A. Harnack, *Sayings*, 69; M. Krämer, 'Hütet', 355; H. Schürmann, *Lukas*, I, 375; S. Schulz, *Q*, 317. Schulz also argues that Luke has secondarily inserted τρυγᾶν.

181 H. Schürmann, *Lukas*, I, 375–6; A. Polag, *Fragmenta*, 36: against S. Schulz, *Q*, 316–18; and W. Schenk, *Synopse*, 32.

182 See also GThom 45; and, arguing for the originality of this tradition, H. Montefiore, 'Comparison', 238–9.

183 *Q*, 318.

184 S. Schulz, *Q*, 318, but without recognizing the parallel structure between Lk 6:45 and Lk 6:43, 44a. Schulz also discusses differences in the wording between Matthew and Luke for the sayings in Lk 6:45 par.

185 *Q*, 319–20; also A. Jülicher, *Gleichnisreden*, II, 116ff., 122–3. J. Jeremias (*Parables*, 90, 92, 94) refers to a 'double parable' here: the two trees and the two treasures.

186 Schulz appears to ignore the other sayings, Lk 6:44a, b par, which are found here.

187 *Q*, 319–20.

188 *Tradition*, 83–4; also J. Crossan, *Fragments*, 159.

189 Mt 7:17 is a positive construction parallel to the negative formulation of Mt 7:18 (par Lk 6:43) and may be a secondary doubling due to Matthew, since in both Mt 12 and Lk 6 only one saying occurs: S. Schulz, *Q*, 316 n. 417, 318; R. Bultmann, *Tradition*, 74; H. Schürmann, *Lukas*, I, 375; M. Krämer, 'Hütet', 353. It is possible however that Luke shortened the parallelism and that a shortening in Mt 12 was due to the reformulation as an imperative: see A. Harnack, *Sayings*, 69. Cf. also G. Strecker's remarks on the awkwardness of the positive formulation of Mt 7:17 (*Bergpredigt*, 169).

190 The imperatival formulation is probably due to the polemical nature of the context in Mt 12; but cf. M. Krämer, 'Hütet', 353–4.

191 The πονηρός–ἀγαθός terminology in Mt 7:17–18 is probably secondary because Mt 12:33 helps to confirm the καλός–σαπρός terms in Lk 6:43.

192 Cf. A. Jacobson ('Christology', 59): 'There is in Lk 6:43–45 par (excepting Matthew's redacted version in 12:33–35) no call to "bear fruit"; rather the imagery is turned toward distinguishing between the "good tree" and the "bad tree".'

193 See R. B. Y. Scott, *Way*, 60–1.

194 See S. Schulz, *Q*, 317: 'Eine Entscheidung, welches der jeweiligen Gegensatzpaare ursprünglicher ist, ist kaum noch möglich (Lk ἄκανθα–σῦκον; βάτος–σταφυλή/Mt ἄκανθα–σταφυλή; τρίβολος–σῦκον).' J. Fitzmyer, *Luke*, I, 643, notes that the pair

ἄκανθαι–τρίβολοι is found in the OT (Gen 3:18; Hos 10:8; cf. Heb 6:8), and this is preferred by M. Krämer, 'Hütet', 355–6; but the allusion could equally be attributed to Matthew.

195 The final unit of this aphoristic sayings collection would appear therefore to consist of two discrete sayings.

196 GThom 45 adds 'and speaks evil things' to the phrase 'an evil man brings forth evil things out of his evil treasure, which is in his heart'. H. Montefiore, 'Comparison', 235, observes a similar addition in the Diatessaron. But the counterpart to Lk 6:45c in GThom 45 makes no direct reference to speech: 'for out of the abundance of the heart he brings forth evil things'. Cf. also TNaph 2:6.

197 Against S. Schulz, *Q*, 319; also T. W. Manson, *Sayings*, 60. J. Fitzmyer, *Luke*, I, 643, notes how in the OT 'fruit' often was a figure for 'deeds' (Hos 10:13; Isa 3:10; Jer 17:10; 21:14). But, regarding 'speech', cf. Prov 12:14; 13:2; 18:20.

198 *Christologie*, 14, 81–2; also probably cf. A. Jacobson, 'Christology', 63–5 (who also at times refers to a polemic against false leaders of the community).

199 *Lukas*, I, 378, and *Untersuchungen*, 300–2.

200 H. Schürmann, *Lukas*, I, 378, and *Untersuchungen*, 293–4; A. Polag, *Christologie*, 2, 12, 81–2; also A. Jacobson, 'Christology', 57, 62.

201 *Lukas*, I, 375–6. A. Jacobson, 'Christology', 59, admits 'what is striking is that Lk 6:43–45 lacks any connection to judgement and, in contrast to John's use of this imagery, is part of a general reflection on the human condition'. Cf. n. 145 above.

202 Note the repeated linkage with γάρ throughout Lk 6:43–5 (44a, 44b, 45c). In v. 43a it may be added by Luke to create a transition from Lk 6:37–42, or possibly was an earlier compilational link when the two aphoristic traditions were joined in the underlying tradition (cf. above, n. 124).

203 False teaching, though, may be the issue in Luke: see J. Fitzmyer, *Luke*, I, 633; H. Schürmann, *Lukas*, I, 373–9.

204 However, the theme of judgement is alluded to in Lk 6:46, 47–9 par when the issue is more clearly related to a response to *Jesus'* authority.

205 D. Zeller, *Mahnsprüche*, 94–101; W. Schenk, *Synopse*, 84–5; S. Schulz, *Q*, 157–61; D. Lührmann, *Redaktion*, 50. The similar exhortation in Mt 10:26a is probably an attempt by Matthew to relate Mt 10:26–7 to the context: see R. Bultmann, *Tradition*, 91, 333; S. Schulz, *Q*, 461; J. Fitzmyer, *Luke*, II, 956; J. Gnilka, *Matthäusevangelium*, I, 384.

206 Cf. L. Schottroff/W. Stegemann, *Jesus*, 59–62.

207 *Q*, 157–8. In support, Schulz notes Matthew's fondness for λέγω ὑμῖν (7 times introduced by Matthew into Markan material and only once deleted). Φίλος is a favourite term of Luke, but is not usually applied to disciples.

208 *Q*, 157–8; also J. Fitzmyer, *Luke*, II, 956; W. Schenk, *Synopse*, 84; D. Zeller, *Mahnsprüche*, 94.

209 S. Schulz, *Q*, 158: μὴ φοβηθῆτε (Lk) is more refined than μὴ φοβεῖσθε (Mt); μετὰ ταῦτα is a favourite of Luke (see also R. Bultmann, *Tradition*, 359); the rare use of ἔχειν in this sense is more common in Luke; the absence of ψυχή in Luke is possibly because the Greeks considered the death of the ψυχή as unthinkable. Ψυχή elsewhere in double-tradition material is almost equivalent to σῶμα (cf. Mt 6:25 par). For Lk 12:5 par, Schulz notes how ὑποδείκνυμι may be Lukan; μᾶλλον (Mt) is corrected by Luke, as is ἀπολέσαι ἐν γεέννῃ ('ungriechisch'). He also accepts ναὶ λέγω ὑμῖν as Lukan, although it only occurs elsewhere in Mt 11:9 par and in Lk 11:51; 10:21.

210 R. Bultmann, *Tradition*, 93; H. Cadbury, *Making*, 152–3 (but also noting Luke's restraint). D. Lührmann, *Redaktion*, 50 n. 5, thinks Matthew may have created the strict parallelism, but gives little support for his supposition.

211 H. Cadbury, *Making*, 217–18, 236–8. But some reservations are expressed by I. H. Marshall, 'Fear', 277.

212 Cf. J. Crossan, *Fragments*, 271–2 on the parallel tradition in 2 Clem 5:2–4.

213 D. Zeller, *Mahnsprüche*, 96; S. Schulz, *Q*, 160–1; J. Gnilka, *Matthäusevangelium*, I, 387; J. Fitzmyer, *Luke*, II, 959; against D. Lührmann, *Redaktion*, 50 (referring it to Satan), and W. Schenk, *Synopse*, 85.

214 J. Fitzmyer, *Luke*, II, 957; and D. Zeller, *Mahnsprüche*, 96–101, who relates it to the 'Topik frühjüdischer Martyriumsparänese' as in 2 Macc 6:26, 30; 7:29; as well as 4 Macc 15:8; 13:13–15; 1 En 100:5; 102:5; 103:4.

215 Cf. L. Schottroff/W. Stegemann, *Jesus*, 60–1. J. Fitzmyer (*Luke*, II, 960) notes that sparrows were 'sought after as food by the poor'.

216 J. Fitzmyer, *Luke*, II, 956.

217 *Sayings*, 84.

218 Against S. Schulz, *Q*, 159.

219 S. Schulz (*Q*, 159) misses the significance of this point. Note, however, also the rabbinic saying of R. Schim'on b. Jochai, cited in Strack–Billerbeck, I, 582–3.

220 *Q*, 159; followed by D. Zeller, *Mahnsprüche*, 94–5.

221 E.g., A. Harnack, *Sayings*, 84; J. Jeremias, *Prayers*, 39.

222 D. Zeller, *Mahnsprüche*, 95–6.

223 Supporting the priority of Luke's version is J. Fitzmyer, *Luke*, II, 956; but Schulz (*Q*, 159) sees the more correct formulation in Luke as a sign that it is secondary. The difference in sense is slight. For a late rabbinic parallel, see D. Zeller, *Mahnsprüche*, 100, who also notes corresponding sapiential themes.

224 Cf. the argument of Mt 6:26, 28b–30 par.

225 Cf. also Prov 1:7. J. Fitzmyer, *Luke*, II, 959, states: 'It is Luke's way of repeating an OT teaching: "Fear of the Lord is the beginning of knowledge".'

226 Concern about priorities is typical of Jewish wisdom, but is often expressed by 'better ... than' proverbs, which seldom occur in the gospels. Cf. G. Bryce, 'Better', 343–54.

227 *Q*, 160–1. J. Gnilka also notes on Mt 10:29–31: 'Die Argumentation ist weisheitlich' (*Matthäusevangelium*, I, 384).

228 Mt 10:32–3 par is assigned by Schulz to the earlier Q-community along with Mt 10:28–31 par, but Mt 10:26–7 par is assigned to the later Q-community (*Q*, 66ff., 461ff.). D. Zeller (*Mahnsprüche*, 94–101) also considers Mt 10:28–31 par in isolation from the other sayings because of his interest only in the admonition form, but he recognizes Lk 12:2–10 as a 'Q-Block'.

229 A. Polag (*Christologie*, 4) indicates that the Q-unit should include Lk 12: (1b), 2, 3, 4–5, 6–7, 8–9, 10, 11–12 (and Mt 10:23). Lk 12:1b and Mt 10:23, however, have little claim to being Q-sayings at all, and the Matthean parallel to Lk 12:10 is in Mt 12:31–2, which casts doubt on its location in this collection. The Matthean parallel to Lk 12:11–12 does appear earlier in Mt 10 and seems related in theme ('do not be anxious'), but the different placement in Matthew and in Luke makes the exact location uncertain. The close parallel of these verses with Mk 13:11 may even call into question their assignment to Q: cf. R. A. Edwards, *Theology*, 123. It is possible that Lk 12:10, 11f. par were added subsequently in pre-Lukan tradition to Lk 12:2–9 par, but it will be argued that Lk 12:2–9 par itself is a well balanced and well defined unit, which need not be concerned simply with legal proceedings.

230 Viewing Mt 10:26–33 par as a complete collection are D. Lührmann, *Redaktion*, 49ff.; J. Fitzmyer, *Luke*, II, 956. Fitzmyer dismisses T. W. Manson's view (*Sayings*, 105) that Lk 12:2–3 was the conclusion to the speech against Pharisaism, following on Lk 11:52 par.

231 D. Lührmann, *Redaktion*, 49–52.

232 Cf. discussion below favouring the priority of Luke's version of Lk 12:3 par.

233 Cf. also Lk 8:17; Mk 4:22; GThom 5, 6; OxyP 654 5, 6; OrigWorld 125:17–18; and further in R. Laufen, *Doppelüberlieferungen*, 156–73. Seeing a 'theological passive' here is J. Fitzmyer, *Luke*, II, 958; but a similar ambiguous usage was found in Mt 7:7–8 par.

234 On the opening exhortation in Mt 10:26a, see above, n. 205. The compound verb συγκαλύπτειν may be Lukan: S. Schulz, *Q*, 461–2.

235 R. Bultmann, *Tradition*, 95; D. Lührmann, *Redaktion*, 50.

236 *Tradition*, 95. Contrast the imperatival formulation in GThom 33. There it introduces the 'lamp' saying, which may reflect a secondary joining of Mk 4:21–2 with Mt 10:26–7, but dropping the common denominator.

237 *Luke*, II, 957.

238 Cf. J. Creed, *St Luke*, 170; G. Caird, *St Luke*, 160–1; J. Drury, *Tradition*, 152–3; J. Fitzmyer, *Luke*, II, 957. Creed, though, notes the uneasy conjunction with the persecution theme in Lk 12:4–7 (*loc. cit.*).

239 R. Bultmann, *Tradition*, 95; B. Lindars, *Jesus*, 55, 202 n. 60; D. Lührmann, *Redaktion*, 50; E. Percy, *Botschaft*, 212–13; J. Fitzmyer, *Luke*, II, 956; but contrast J. Wanke, *Kommentarworte*,

67; J. Gnilka, *Matthäusevangelium*, I, 384–5. S. Schulz (*Q*, 462) includes ἐν τοῖς ταμείοις as a possible Lukan addition.

240 Against J. Wanke, *Kommentarworte*, 67; R. Laufen, *Doppelüberlieferungen*, 160–3.

241 J. Wanke (*Kommentarworte*, 70): 'Das zweite Logion hat deutlich eine erläuternde Funktion.' But Wanke sees Matthew's version of the second saying as more original and therefore all the more specific in its application of Mt 10:26 par to mission.

242 Cf. D. Catchpole, 'Son of Man', 255–65; A. J. B. Higgins, 'Menschensohn', 117–23, and *Son of Man*, 80–4; B. Lindars, 'Advocate', 484–9, and *Jesus*, 48–55; M. Casey, *Son of Man*, 193–4, 231–2.

243 Cf. list of adherents in Schulz, *Q*, 68 n. 66; and A. J. B. Higgins, 'Menschensohn', 117–23. Note also the use of the passive verb in Lk 12:9 with no specified agent (diff Mt).

244 Against M. Goulder, *Midrash*, 350–1, who attempts to establish a tendency in later tradition to insert 'Son of Man' into Markan material because of the greater frequency of the title in Matthew and Luke. But this can only be held if one gives little place to sources of tradition in the early church other than Mark. Also, Matthew's modifications of Mk 8:38 in Mt 16 lend credibility to theories of Matthean redaction in Mt 10, and there is no evidence that Luke elsewhere introduces the term into contexts where possible confusions are created. Cf. also Lk 6:22 par.

245 'Son of Man', 255–6.

246 D. Catchpole, 'Son of Man', 255; S. Schulz, *Q*, 68–9.

247 H.-E. Tödt, *Son of Man*, 57; A. Polag, *Christologie*, 99; D. Catchpole, 'Son of Man', 261.

248 This is indicated by its self-contained quality and its presence in other synoptic contexts: so D. Catchpole, 'Son of Man', 256.

249 *Questions*, 66–81, esp. 77.

250 *Q*, 67.

251 Cf. D. Catchpole, 'Son of Man', 255; and on Lk 12:4, even Schulz himself (*Q*, 157–8).

252 Disputing that such sayings should necessarily originate with Christian prophets are D. Hill, 'Evidence', 262–74; J. Dunn, 'Utterances', 175–98. Suggesting possible sapiential or other backgrounds for the sentences are K. Berger, 'Sätzen', 10ff.; E. Schweizer, 'Observance', 226 n. 3 (citing the work of G.-C. Kähler); D. Hill, 'Evidence', 271–4. But, in general support of Käsemann, see J. Crossan, *Fragments*, 175–8; A. J. B. Higgins, *Son of Man*, 107–11; M. Boring, 'Mark 3:28–29', 501–21, esp. 514.

253 'Verhalten', 221–2.

254 This is more true of Lk 12:8–9 par than the parallel in Mk 8:38, which is widely considered less primitive in its formulation: see discussion in S. Schulz, *Q*, 66–7.

255 *Son of Man*, 111.

256 *Q*, 463–5. But against J. Jeremias (*Parables*, 221 n. 66), Schulz does not accept an 'apokalyptische' interpretation of the saying, referring

to an eschatological reversal on the Last Day (*Q*, 464). A. Polag tentatively suggests that it 'ursprünglich gegen die Gesetzeslehrer gerichtet war' (*Christologie*, 14).

257 *Q*, 66ff., 157ff.

258 Rightly, B. Lindars, *Jesus*, 55. L. Gaston (*Stone*, 323) suggests that Lk 12:2–3 was bound at a very early stage with the light sayings (Lk 11:33–6; cf. Mk 4:21, GThom 33), which presented a call to mission in the early Palestinian church. Yet Matthew and Luke make clear that they had the saying in the context of Lk 12:2–9 par.

259 Showing how this beatitude may belong to Q-redaction, see A. Jacobson, 'Christology', 52–5.

260 On many reconstructions of Q, these sayings immediately preceded Lk 12:2ff. par: cf. V. Taylor, 'Order', 30; A. Polag, *Fragmenta*, 56–8; T. W. Manson, *Sayings*, 105–6.

261 Cf. further below, p. 169.

262 In the small collection Mt 10:28–31 par, the opening command not to fear men (Mt 10:28a) seems to derive initial support from the following command to fear him who can destroy both body and soul in Gehenna (Mt 10:28b).

263 Cf. S. Schulz, *Q*, 163 n. 193.

264 The proclivity for using double rhetorical questions is also observable in these concluding sayings. But, unlike the earlier ones, these final questions are not allowed to stand on their own, but are followed by a direct rejoinder proclaiming the correct attitude to adopt.

265 The use of the *a minore ad maius* argument appears in connection with the rhetorical questions and not simply at the conclusion of the collection.

266 *Mahnsprüche*, 142.

267 *Ibid.*, 142.

268 It is possible also that Lk 12:10, 11–12 par were added at some subsequent stage, but the specific concern with legal proceedings and 'blasphemy' seem outside the scope of Lk 12:2–9 par.

269 On such 'impossible questions', see J. Crenshaw, 'Questions', 19–34. Double rhetorical questions are not uncommon in the Jewish wisdom literature, perhaps because of the influence of Semitic parallelism: cf., e.g., Prov 6:9, 27–8; Qoh 6:8; Sir 34:4; WisSol 5:8. Yet often a rhetorical question appears at the beginning or end of a section rather than in the centre.

270 Cf. W. McKane, *Proverbs*, 321, 326–31. Also J. Crenshaw, 'Questions', 23, identifies the larger didactic unit as Prov 6:20–35.

271 Cf. also Prov 27:23–7, though it lacks the central rhetorical questions and is not evidently composed of independent sayings using varied imagery, and Prov 6:6–11. On the peculiar nature of the section Prov 6:6–11 and on the classification of Prov 27:23–7 as an instruction with 'extended motivation', see W. McKane, *Proverbs*, 320, 607, 618–19.

272 Other more distant examples include Sir 34:1–8; Sir 27:4–7; and possibly Sir 27:16–21.

273 It is conceivable that the *a minore ad maius* type of argument can be interpreted as a kind of 'heightened' simile. This type of argument is observable occasionally in Jewish wisdom literature: see Prov 21:27; Sir 10:31; and a reversal of this argument in Job 25:5–6. In the gospels, the *a minore ad maius* argument occurs mainly in double-tradition material: Mt 6:30/Lk 12:28 (24); Mt 10:31/Lk 12:7; Mt 7:11/Lk 11:13. It does, however, also occur elsewhere: e.g., Mt 12:12; 10:25; and possibly Lk 16:10ff. The argument is found in Paul's writings (see Rom 11:12, 24) and Hebrews (9:13–14), but not in James, and once in inverted form in the Didache (4:8).

274 On Mk 3:23b–27, see below, pp. 121–4.

275 Cf. above, n. 174.

276 *Tradition*, 152.

277 Further questions will arise concerning Luke's procedure in Lk 6:27–36 par: see below, pp. 78–86.

278 The beatitude for you who mourn/weep (Lk 6:21b) is more difficult to relate. Could it refer to bereavement under persecution? Or to oppression generally?

279 J. Crossan (*Fragments*, 24–5) distinguishes between 'proverb' (which is 'the summation of the wisdom of the past') and 'aphorism' (which is 'a personal counter-vision and counter-order'). We make no such distinction because the aphorism/proverb is always a selective observation about life, not a comprehensive one. It always carries the 'authority' of a universal statement about life, and formally it is virtually impossible to determine the origin of the generalization. But it will also always carry the 'personal' authority of its use in a given context for a given purpose.

280 On proverbs, see W. Beardslee, 'Uses', 66, and 'Koan', 151–77; N. Perrin, *Language*, 48–54.

281 Contrast the explicit instructions of Did 1 and 3:1ff. Only some have supporting reasons like wisdom admonitions, and most of these demonstrate only the implications of the command: e.g., Did 1:5:

> To everyone that asketh of thee give and ask not back, for the Father desireth that gifts be given to all from his own bounties.
> Blessed is he that giveth according to the commandment, for he is guiltless.

282 The sources for 'catechetical instruction' are unfortunately very limited; but see P. Carrington, *Catechism*, 12–21, 58ff.; E. Selwyn, *St Peter*, 363ff.

283 See M. Küchler, *Weisheitstraditionen*, 33–61.

284 Concerning the act – consequence relationship in sapiential thought, see G. von Rad, *Wisdom*, 124–37; R. B. Y. Scott, *Way*, 62–3.

285 Cf. above, n. 252.

286 See R. Charles, *Pseudepigrapha*, II, 733.

287 Contrast with Proverbs: W. McKane, *Proverbs*, 10–22; R. B. Y. Scott, *Proverbs*, 22–3.

288 A. Polag (*Christologie*, 59–62) investigates the use of the title
       'Father' in Q and notes that 'your Father' sets forth the relation-
       ship of God to the disciples and his care for them.
289 *Wisdom*, 190–5, esp. 192.
290 Mt reveals no attempt to intensify the eschatological significance
       of the collections in Mt 6:25–33, 7:1–5, 7:7–11, 10:26–33. But
       the evangelist applies Mt 7:16–20; 12:33–5 against opponents and
       in so doing introduces pronouncements of judgement.
            Although in Luke the collections of sayings in Lk 6:37–42,
       6:43–5 follow closely on the beatitudes and woes in Lk 6:20b–26,
       there is no noticeable attempt to emphasize an eschatological interest
       in these collections. Similarly, Lk 11:9–13 and 12:2–9 do not seem
       to be subject to eschatological intensification in Luke. The collection
       in Lk 12:22–31 is located after warnings against covetousness
       (12:13–15) and the parable of the rich fool (12:16–21), but the only
       apparent intensification of eschatological motifs in this collection
       is the addition of Lk 12:32, which assures those addressed of the
       Father's desire to give them the βασιλεία. This is then elaborated
       by the sayings on treasure in heaven which does not fail, which refer
       to the heavenly sphere but not strictly to End-time events.
291 Cf. R. Bultmann, *Tradition*, 135; E. Lohse, 'Ich', 189–90; J.
       Gnilka, *Matthäusevangelium*, I, 188; I. Broer, 'Antithesen', 50–63;
       M. J. Suggs, *Wisdom*, 109–15, and 'Antitheses', 433–44; R. A.
       Guelich, 'Antitheses', 444–57; G. Strecker, 'Antithesen', 38–47;
       D. Lührmann, 'Liebet', 412–13; V. P. Furnish, *Love Command*,
       45 n. 60; S. Schulz, *Q*, 127. Unconvinced are J. Jeremias, *Theology*,
       251–3, who cites the ἀλλά in Lk 6:27 as an echo of an original an-
       tithesis; and also W. D. Davies, *Setting*, 388. The introductory ἀλλὰ
       ὑμῖν λέγω in Luke has been variously described: as a Lukan in-
       troduction (R. Bultmann, *Tradition*, 96), as a Lukan transition from
       the preceding woes (D. Zeller, *Mahnsprüche*, 102; V. P. Furnish,
       Love Command, 55), or as a preface to the entire collection of
       sayings which follows (R. Banks, *Law*, 183). H. Schürmann
       (*Lukas*, 345) is inclined to see an introductory formula in the
       underlying tradition; S. Schulz (*Q*, 127) argues that just the words
       common to Matthew and Luke (λέγω ὑμῖν) were an introductory
       formula in Q, which was altered by Matthew to form an antithesis
       and by Luke to signal the transition after the woes in Lk 6:24–6.
       Schulz's view has much to commend it, but his insistence that
       λέγω ὑμῖν is a *prophetic* formula prejudges the material which
       follows; cf. also F. Neirynck, 'Developments', esp. 65.
292 So A. Harnack, *Sayings*, 59–63, 129; R. Bultmann, *Tradition*, 79,
       96; J. M. Creed, *St Luke*, 93; J. Dupont, *Béatitudes*, I, 149–50;
       S. Schulz, *Q*, 120–1; D. Zeller, *Mahnsprüche*, 101–2. But favouring
       Luke's sequence, cf. H. Schürmann, *Lukas*, I, 345–6, 357–8; A.
       Polag, *Fragmenta*, 34; D. Lührmann, 'Liebet', 416–22; R. Guelich,
       'Antitheses', 449–50; H. Hübner, *Gesetz*, 82–3, 92–3; U. Luz,
       Matthäus, I, 291; D. Catchpole, 'Jesus', 305 (Lk 6:29–31 secondary
       but in Q).

293 *Contra* D. Lührmann, 'Liebet', 416–17. R. Gundry (*Matthew*, 96) argues that the 'singular derives from the individuality of having your cheek struck and your things asked for and taken'; but many of the commands in the Lukan sequence could be seen as 'individual' (esp. Lk 6:27c, 31), despite the plural formulation.

294 Cf. D. Zeller, *Mahnsprüche*, 101, who also notes differences on the question of whether the introductory πλήν in Lk 6:35 is a sign of Lukan redactional effort. E. Percy, *Botschaft*, 149, considers Lk 6:35 to be reminiscent of an original antithesis.

295 1QS 1:9–11, 10:17–20. Cf. K. Stendahl, 'Hate', 343–55.

296 D. Lührmann, 'Liebet', 416–17; J. Fitzmyer, *Luke*, I, 637–8.

297 'Feindesliebe', 289–95, 297–8; followed by V.P. Furnish, *Love Command*, 55, and L. Schottroff, 'Gewaltverzicht', 214. Cf. also Acts 10:33.

298 S. Schulz, *Q*, 130 (but see his n. 296 for contrary views); J. Fitzmyer, *Luke*, I, 638; D. Lührmann, 'Liebet', 416–17; D. Zeller, *Mahnsprüche*, 102. For a list of variations in the later Christian tradition, see H.-T. Wrege, *Bergpredigt*, 84–5.

299 With respect to this passage, cf. R. Bultmann, *Tradition*, 79 (but doubt expressed on 96!); O.J.F. Seitz, 'Love', 44, 52; J. Dupont, *Béatitudes*, I, 155 n. 1.

300 M.D. Goulder, *Midrash*, 91.

301 G. Barth, 'Matthew's Understanding', 73; E. Schweizer, *Matthew*, 172; V.P. Furnish, *Love Command*, 56–7; G. Strecker, 'Antithesen', 42; U. Luz, *Matthäus*, I, 387–94.

302 Cf. R. Bultmann, *Tradition*, 96; A. Polag, *Fragments*, 34–6; J. Fitzmyer, *Luke*, I, 639. In favour of the position in Luke, cf. D. Lührmann, 'Liebet', 419; U. Luz, *Matthäus*, I, 387–8.

303 Cf. J. Piper, *Love*, 54. H. Schürmann (*Lukas*, I, 350–2) defends a pre-Lukan connection of Lk 6:31 with Lk 6:30, although the change to the plural in Lk 6:31 would remain a difficulty.

304 V.P. Furnish, *Love Command*, 57; J. Fitzmyer, *Luke*, I, 639. D. Zeller, *Mahnsprüche*, 118, also rightly rejects the view of Dihle that Lk 6:31 is a reference to the behaviour of men in general, which is also elucidated in Lk 6:32–4 as that which must be surpassed.

305 See W. Grundmann, 'Weisheit', 190.

306 A. Dihle, *Regel*, 113–14; but cf. above, n. 304, and U. Luz, *Matthäus*, I, 388.

307 While τοῦ ἐν οὐρανοῖς is likely to be Matthean, the title ὁ πατὴρ ὑμῶν may be more original than ὑψίστος in Lk 6:35 because (1) πατήρ is suited to the context which concerns υἱοί, and (2) ὑψίστος is characteristic of Lk as a divine designation. See S. Schulz, *Q*, 128; J. Piper, *Love*, 193 n. 162; W.C. van Unnik, 'Feindesliebe', 288; H. Schürmann, *Lukas*, I, 355 n. 94 (who considers a wide range of possibilities). The connection of υἱοί and ὑψίστος can be found, however, in Sir 4:10 (LXX). D. Zeller (*Mahnsprüche*, 102f) and H. Schürmann (*Lukas*, I, 355) conjecture that the source read θεοῦ.

308 Lk 6:34, 35a have no counterpart in Mt and are unlikely to have been in the tradition common to Matthew and Luke: see J. Fitzmyer,

Luke, I, 640. On the command ἀγαθοποιεῖτε, see W. C. van Unnik, 'Feindesliebe', 288−98, and below. The command to lend recalls Mt 5:42 (cf. Lk 6:30, 34), which it has been argued above does not belong to this context: see R. Bultmann, *Tradition*, 96; J. Piper, *Love*, 59; D. Zeller, *Mahnsprüche*, 102; S. Schulz, *Q*, 130−1; D. Lührmann, 'Liebet', 420. The phrase ὁ μισθὸς ὑμῶν πολύς in Lk 6:35 matches exactly Lk 6:23b and may have been inserted here by Luke, possibly indicating also that the phrase τίνα μισθὸν ἔχετε was in the *Vorlage* of Lk 6:32 (as in Mt 5:46−7): see H. Schürmann, *Lukas*, I, 355.

309 D. Lührmann, 'Liebet', 421; S. Schulz, *Q*, 128; J. Piper, *Love*, 62; I. H. Marshall, *Luke*, 265; D. Catchpole, 'Jesus', 305.

310 H. D. Betz, *Plutarch*, 59ff., cites parallel ideas from Plutarch. J. Piper, *Love*, 62, cites the proverb attributed to the Stoics: 'If you are imitating the gods then bestow benefits also upon the ungrateful; for the sun rises also upon the wicked and the sea lies open also to pirates' (Seneca, *De Beneficiis*, 4.26.1). Yet, although he sees here 'nothing specifically Christian in the command to imitate God', he argues that 'Mt 5:45 does not introduce an observation of nature which intends to prove in this instance the kindness of God; it introduces an absolute statement about the kindness of God which is realized ... in rain and sunshine' (62). He seems to suggest that it presents an 'illustration' of God's kindness rather than a 'proof' of it, and thus a different epistemological starting-point. But it is unlikely that the question of the *source* of our knowledge of God is involved here at all; it is a matter of *commending* this perception by reference to experience, and in this sense is an argument from nature. Because kindness to enemies is superficially at odds with the strong retributive outlook of Jewish eschatology, such a point would need commendation.

311 'Christology', 56.

312 M. D. Goulder, *Midrash*, 27; J. Fenton, 'Inclusio', 174−9.

313 See above, n. 308.

314 'Feindesliebe', 288−98. Cf. also 1 Pet 2:20.

315 *Mahnsprüche*, 102−3.

316 *Tradition*, 79.

317 *Q*, 127−31.

318 *Mahnsprüche*, 110−13. So also H. Schürmann, *Lukas*, I, 357−9; D. Catchpole, 'Jesus', 309−10; U. Luz, *Matthäus*, I, 306.

319 The καί in Lk 6:37 does suggest a close connection, yet it also (*contra* Schürmann: see above, n. 318) can suggest a conscious joining of distinct units. There is no break at all between 6:35c and 6:36.

320 *Mahnsprüche*, 110. The implication that the command to mercy is not in line with the preceding love-of-enemies sayings (cf. H. Schürmann, *Lukas*, I, 357, 359) fails to allow for the development of the argument from the initial broad command of love for enemies to the proper motivation from which this should be approached.

321 So, rightly, S. Schulz, *Q*, 132; J. Piper, *Love*, 63, 194 n. 169; D. Lührmann, 'Liebet', 421−2; R. Bultmann, *Tradition*, 79.

322 G. Strecker, *Weg*, 141; D. Catchpole, 'Jesus', 310; S. Schulz, *Q*, 130; U. Luz, *Matthäus*, I, 313; D. Lührmann, 'Liebet', 421–2; V. P. Furnish, *Love Command*, 59; J. Piper, *Love*, 63 (but see 194 n. 170, citing M. Black, *Aramaic*, 181, and the contrasting opinion of J. Jeremias, *Theology*, 212). Less certain is R. Bultmann, *Tradition*, 79. On the mercy of God in Judaism, see D. Zeller, *Mahnsprüche*, 111–12 and citations such as TZeb 7–8.

323 G. Barth, 'Matthew's Understanding', 97; B. Przybylski, *Righteousness*, 85–7; G. Strecker, *Weg*, 141–2. U. Luz (*Matthäus*, I, 312) suggests that περισσός (Mt 5:47) also refers back to 5:20.

324 But cf. S. Schulz, *Q*, 134; J. Piper, *Love*, 89–99.

325 See the background discussions in J. Piper, *Love*, 19ff.; J. Fitzmyer *Luke*, I, 637–8; L. Schottroff, 'Gewaltverzicht', 204–8; D. Zeller, *Mahnsprüche*, 104–9; K. Stendahl, 'Hate', 343–55; M. Bouttier, 'Hésiode', 129–30. Within the Jewish wisdom literature, esp. cf. Prov 24: 17–18, 25:21–2; Sir 10:6–7, 27:30–28:7, but also Sir 12:1–7 and 6:13!

326 L. Schottroff, 'Gewaltverzicht', 197–221.

327 *Ibid.*, 213–15.

328 S. Schulz, *Q*, 128; H. Schürmann, *Lukas*, I, 344 n. 11; J. Piper, *Love*, 56.

329 I. H. Marshall, *Luke*, 260. L. Schottroff, 'Gewaltverzicht', 213 n. 77, writes: 'die Differenz zwischen διωκόντων und ἐπηρεαζόντων (Mt 5,44 par) ist unerheblich'.

330 Cf. TJos 18:1–2; Ps 109:4–5. In later tradition, cf. also Did 1:3b ('pray for your enemies'); OxyP 1224; Justin *Apol.* I.15.9; Polycarp *Phil.* 12:3.

331 For the history of this traditional saying, see H.-W. Bartsch, 'Regel', 128–32.

332 See V. P. Furnish, *Love Command*, 51.

333 Contrast ὅπως γένησθε (Mt 5:45)/ἔσεσθε (Lk 6:35b) with ἔσεσθε (Mt 5:48)/γίνεσθε (Lk 6:36). Against A. Harnack (*Sayings*, 61, 129), S. Schulz (*Q*, 128) and W. C. van Unnik ('Feindesliebe', 288), the view is expressed in D. Zeller (*Mahnsprüche*, 102 n. 356) that ἔσεσθε is more original in Lk 6:35/Mt 5:45 on the grounds of a redactional use of ὅπως by Matthew and the Semitic style, illustrated in Sir 4:10.

334 The strength of the eschatological future prospect is modified somewhat by the recognition of the place which divine sonship can play in the Jewish wisdom tradition (Sir 4:10–11; WisSol 2:18, 5:5): see D. Lührmann, 'Liebet', 426; G. Theissen, *Soziologie*, 161–2. S. Schulz, *Q*, 134–5, recognizes this, but believes the wider eschatological context of Q overrides it: 'Zwar fehlt die explizite apokalyptische Begründung der Sohnschaft Gottes, aber sie kann fehlen, weil sie im Hintergrund steht und durch die gesamte prophetische Verkündigung des ältesten Judenchristentums in Q gegeben ist' (135). D. Zeller, *Mahnsprüche*, 103, 107–8, attempts to do greater justice to the immediate collection of sayings by noting that the future tense is not a strong one and that Mt 5:45b connects

the eschatological future with the present command through reference to the present divine ordering of the world.

335 It is true that the ultimate righteousness of God is not at stake (cf. D. Zeller, *Mahnsprüche*, 110, against Lührmann), but one nonetheless might have expected some assurance of resolution such as in TJos 18:2 ('and the Lord will rescue you from all evil'), 2 En 51:3, or even Did 1:3c, 5bc.

336 'Gewaltverzicht', 215–16.

337 *Contra* S. Schulz (*Q*, 131), who seems to see Mt 5:46–7 interrupting the connection of Mt 5:45 and 5:48. Better is V. P. Furnish, *Love Command*, 52, or even H. Hübner, *Gesetz*, 91–2. On 'greeting' possibly referring back to 'prayer' in Mt 5:44 par, see D. Zeller, *Mahnsprüche*, 102.

338 On μισθός as more original, see W. C. van Unnik, 'Feindesliebe', 295–7; D. Lührmann, 'Liebet', 420; S. Schulz, *Q*, 129; V. P. Furnish, *Love Command*, 58. Less convinced is J. Piper, *Love*, 59.

339 Unlike μισθός in Lk 6:23/Mt 5:12!

340 For τελῶναι and ἐθνικοί as secondary, see Mt 18:17, and D. Lührmann, 'Liebet', 419. On the secondary nature of ἁμαρτωλοί, see S. Schulz, *Q*, 129–30, and possibly J. Piper, *Love*, 59, 192 n. 148; H. Schürmann, *Lukas*, I, 353 n. 79; and W. Walker, 'Tax Collectors', 224–9. The term ἔθνη (cf. ἐθνικοί) does appear, however, in Mt 6:32 par: cf. above, p. 34.

341 L. Schottroff, 'Gewaltverzicht', 216–18.

342 D. Zeller, *Mahnsprüche*, 104.

343 *Studien*, 309–10, 332; also D. Lührmann, 'Liebet', 437. For the situation of Jesus himself, see O. J. F. Seitz, 'Love', 39–54; M. Hengel, *Revolutionär*, esp. 20–2. Could this also be what B. Reicke ('Apocalypticism', 150) has in mind when he cryptically refers to the presence in the NT of a peaceful anti-zealot pietism called 'wisdom', such as in 1 En 91–108 and the Testaments of XII Patriarchs?

344 'Gewaltverzicht', 203–4.

345 *Ibid.*, 216–220; L. Schottroff/W. Stegemann, *Jesus*, 77–84. Also see V. P. Furnish, *Love Command*, 48.

346 With respect to Q, Schottroff seems to recognize that Jews would be particularly in mind ('Gewaltverzicht', 214 n. 79; and L. Schottroff/ W. Stegemann, *Jesus*, 77–84); also see S. Schulz, *Q*, 132–3, 135–8, 172.

347 *Contra* L. Schottroff, 'Gewaltverzicht', 215–16. Although the winning-over of enemies has a clear place in later Christian tradition (1 Pet 2:12; Rom 12:20–1; Justin, *Apology*, I. 14.3) and Jewish tradition (TBenj 4–5; TGad 6–7), this hope is not raised in the present sayings collection. See also the varying interpretations of Prov 25:21–2 in W. Klassen, 'Coals', 337–50; and K. Stendahl, 'Hate', 346–8. A different motive is present in Prov 24:17–18.

348 Recognized but not accepted by D. Zeller, *Mahnsprüche*, 110 n. 424.

349 J. Piper, *Love*, 60–1. For trust in the 'Father', see also Mt 7:7–11 par. While direct reference to the 'Father' is left to the final stages

of the arguments about food in Mt 7:11 par and Mt 6:32 par, this relationship seems to be invoked earlier in the sayings collections about opponents, here and in Mt 10:28ff. par. May this be due to the intensification of the threat?

350 Cf. N. Perrin, *Language*, 53–4.

351 So also Rom 12:17–21.

352 J. Fitzmyer, *Essays*, 165ff., and *Luke*, II, 1094–111, who also provides a valuable discussion of other interpretations of Lk 16:1–13. Other useful surveys are found in L. J. Topel, 'Injustice', 216–27; M. Krämer, *Rätsel*, ch. 6: R. Lunt, 'Steward', 132–6; and H. Preisker, 'Lukas 16, 1–7', 85–8. Preisker, *ibid.*, 89, prefers to see the parable itself end with verse 7, a view shared by J. Jeremias, *Parables*, 45–6; E. Kamlah, 'Verwalter', 276–7; E. Klostermann, *Lukas*, 163. However this makes a very abrupt ending for the parable. Supporting Fitzmyer, see also I. H. Marshall, 'Luke xvi. 8', 617–19 (and *Luke*, 619–20); F. Horn, *Glaube*, 72–3.

353 It need not have been first added by Luke, though. For attempts to solve the problem of the master's commendation, see esp. J. D. M. Derrett, 'Steward', 198–219, and 'Bond', 438–40; J. Fitzmyer, *Essays*, 165–84; K. Bailey, *Poet*, 86–110; G. Schwarz, 'Verwalter', 94–5 (appealing to an Aramaic mistranslation); P. Gächter, 'Steward', 121–31.

354 Yet, for attempts to include verse 9 with the original parable, see D. Fletcher, 'Riddle', 19–20; R. Hiers, 'Friends', 30–6. But even A. Descamps ('Composition', 47–53), who tries to show a close connection of verses 9–13 with the parable, admits a clear break between verses 8 and 9. For other attempts to see verses 1–13 as a unity, cf. discussion in M. Krämer, *Rätsel*, 192–211.

355 See, among others, J. Jeremias, *Parables*, 45–7; H. Kosmala, 'Steward', 118; R. Lunt, 'Steward', 133, 136; J. Dupont, *Béatitudes*, I, 109ff.

356 See esp. C. H. Dodd, *Parables*, 30.

357 But D. Zeller, *Mahnsprüche*, 51, sees verse 9 as an allegorizing imperative based on the parable and therefore not 'independent'.

358 This type of argument has appeared in the central section of the aphoristic sayings collections on anxiety about riches (Mt 6:26, 28–30 par) and on whom to fear (Mt 10:31 par). It is also found at the conclusion of Mt 7:7–11 par.

359 H. Kosmala, 'Steward', 118–20.

360 V. Hasler (*Amen*, 101, 108) attributes this break to Luke himself, disagreeing with Jeremias' view (*Parables*, 105) that κἀγὼ ὑμῖν λέγω with ὑμῖν preceding, is characteristic of 'Lucan source'. But H. Schürmann, *Untersuchungen*, 226, considers the possibility that Lk 16:9 came from Q with this formula. There are only three clear cases of ὑμῖν λέγω in Luke (none in Matthew), and both other cases (6:27, 11:9; cf. also 12:22) not only introduce double-tradition material, but introduce aphoristic sayings collections! Cf. F. Neirynck ('Developments', 60–1) for various understandings of the phenomenon.

361 Attempts, however, to relate verse 9 to the parable as an ironic or sarcastic demand (D. Fletcher, 'Riddle', 22; G. Paul, 'Steward', 192) or to punctuate it as an unthinkable rhetorical question (R. Merkelbach, 'Haushalter', 180–1) are strained and unnecessary.

362 On the variant ἐκλίπητε, cf. H. Kosmala, 'Steward', 118–19; I.H. Marshall, *Luke*, 621. Also Lk 12:33 (diff Mt 6:19–20).

363 R. Hiers, 'Friends', 31–2. Some of Hiers' parallels, however, are dubious: e.g., ὑπάρχοντα (1) with μαμωνᾶς (9).

364 H.P. Rüger, 'Μαμωνᾶς', 127–31; E. Nestle, 'Mammon', 2912–15.

365 Considered a technical term by E. Klostermann (*Lukas*, 164) for the 'grave' or 'die Wohnung im Jenseits'; cf. the example of 5 Ezra 2:11 (and 1 En 39:4–5). Against this, cf. F. Horn, *Glaube*, 77–9 (who attempts to argue away the significance of these Jewish features in favour of seeing verse 9 as a Lukan composition based on 16:4); D. Fletcher, 'Riddle', 24; M.D. Goulder, *Midrash*, 301. Yet as D. Seccombe (*Possessions*, 168) notes, 'the idea of the righteous inhabiting σκηναί in the new age is not unattested'.

366 M. Black (*Aramaic*, 126–7) also takes the impersonal plural δέξωνται as a sign of Aramaic construction. Doubting that verse 9 was a Lukan creation are D. Seccombe, *Possessions*, 161; J. Fitzmyer, *Luke*, II, 1105.

367 Cf. R. Hiers ('Friends', 33), who raises the possibility that Lk 12:33 is a variant recension of Lk 16:9, although he later notes that 12:33 must be regarded as part of the Q-tradition (*ibid.*, 35). W. Schmithals, *Lukas*, 167, notes similarities also with Lk 6:27ff., 12:20–1, 14:14 and 18:22.

368 It is probable that Luke has altered 12:33 (cf. Mt 6:19–20) to express more clearly his own interests: S. Schulz, *Q*, 142; H.-J. Degenhardt, *Lukas*, 86–91; W. Pesch, 'Exegese', 356 –61. Luke's positive concern for almsgiving is also expressed in Acts 9:36 and 10:2–4, 31, and for more general sharing in Acts 2:45, 4:35; 20:33–5.

369 *Contra* D. Zeller (see above, n. 357). One might also compare Lk 16:9 with the parable of the φρόνιμος and πιστός steward in Lk 12:42–6/Mt 24:45–51, who cares for the household, but the thought of this parable is probably nearer the sayings in Lk 16:10–12.

370 *Béatitudes*, I, 111. Cf. also R. Bultmann, *Tradition*, 176 (who considers Lk 16:9 as a saying drawn from (Jewish?) tradition); and K. Bailey, *Poet*, 111.

371 'Steward', 115–21; also followed by D. Seccombe, *Possessions*, 165–7.

372 Against the interpretation of J. Jeremias, *Parables*, 46 (but cf. his *Theology*, 222); F. Hauck, 'Μαμωνᾶς', 390.

373 See J. Fitzmyer, *Essays*, 169 n. 15, and *Luke*, II, 1109; E. Schweizer, *Matthew*, 164; L.J. Topel, 'Injustice', 220 n. 23. H. Rüger ('Μαμωνᾶς', 129) argues against F. Hauck ('Μαμωνᾶς', 390) that *māmôn* was a fully neutral term which was qualified by genitive attributes into positive or negative connotations. For τῆς ἀδικίας, see also Lk 18:6.

374 *Contra* F. E. Williams ('Almsgiving', 295), who argues that 'friends' here is a personification of almsgiving. One must give due weight to the actual formulation of the saying and the ambiguities presented in it.

375 So, rightly, D. Seccombe, *Possessions*, 170.

376 So, rightly, D. Fletcher, 'Riddle', 21.

377 Some scholars also see a pun in the Aramaic between μαμωνᾶς and πιστός; cf. L. J. Topel, 'Injustice', 220 n. 23, citing other scholars.

378 D. Seccombe, *Possessions*, 170.

379 'Steward', 119.

380 See B. M. Metzger, *Commentary*, 165.

381 'Mamon', 374.

382 'Steward', 120. A. Feuillet, 'Riches', 41-2, prefers to interpret it as 'qui est étranger, qui est d'un autre pays'. 'Your own', then, is that which is properly spiritual (cf. Mt 25:34); see also D. Seccombe, *Possessions*, 171.

383 R. Bultmann, *Tradition*, 87, 105, 168, conjectures as to the original independence of this proverb. S. Safrai/D. Flusser ('Slave', 30-3) draw the parallel with a saying of R. Shimeon: 'Man, while he lives, is the slave of two masters: the slave of his Creator and the slave of his inclination.' These authors believe the fusion of this saying with wealth is the grafting by Jesus of an Essene idea into the rabbinic saying. Cf. also GThom 47 (which sets the saying amidst other proverbs of impossibility); 2 Clem 6 (which sets it in a section contrasting this world and the world to come); 2 LogSeth 60:2 (which claims serving two masters typifies persecutors of the community); and TestTr 29:24-5 (which applies it to those under the Law).

384 Cf. K. Rengstorf, 'δοῦλος', 270-1.

385 Cf. F. Williams, 'Almsgiving', 293-4. M. Barth's distinction ('Steward', 65-6) between Lk 16:1-9 (illustrating 'Be wise as serpents') and 16:10-13 ('Be innocent as doves') misleadingly ignores the prudential character of verses 10-12.

386 K. Bailey, *Poet*, 110-18, provides interesting independent support for the contention that verses 9-13 have a unified structure and theme which did not originally belong to the parable, and which consist of a threefold progression. He considers that it reflects the work of a 'skilled poet', but not the work of Luke. See also A. Feuillet, 'Riches', 43, who sees unity in at least verses 9-12.

387 A. Descamps, 'Composition', 47-53 (who does accept that Luke used sayings also found in 12:42 par and 19:17 par in his composition).

388 *Béatitudes*, I, 109 n. 1.

389 *Essays*, 166, 169-70; so also E. Fuchs, 'Argent', 5.

390 J. Dupont (*Béatitudes*, I, 109-10 n. 1) would also include ἀληθινός in the word play. See also above, n. 377.

391 So also F. Williams, 'Almsgiving', 296-7.

392 Contrast Lk 11:41, 12:33, 6:38, 14:13-14, 10:34-5, 19:8, and, more polemically, 6:24-5, 12:15ff., 16:19-31. Also see above, n. 368.

Renunciation of wealth does not seem to be the ideal here at all: see D. Seccombe, *Possessions*, 172.

393 J. Fitzmyer, *Essays*, 179–80. L. J. Topel ('Injustice', 221–7) has to see two distinct stages of 'Lucan redaction' at work to explain how the units of the section fit together. This problem is also not adequately dealt with by M. Krämer (*Rätsel*, 239), who argues that Luke received verses 1–12 already united and added verses 13 and 14–18 himself.

394 Cf. even I. H. Marshall, *Luke*, 614, 624–5.

395 Cf. n. 356, and, more recently, J. Fitzmyer, *Essays*, 179–80.

396 A third example involves another aphoristic double-tradition collection: Lk 12:22–31, following the parable of the rich fool in 12:16–21. In this case, however, the break between the parable and the sayings collection appears stronger because the parable has its own concluding simile in verse 21, and verse 22a has a more pronounced narrative introduction: εἶπεν δὲ πρὸς τοὺς μαθητὰς (αὐτοῦ). Of course Lk 12:22–31 is clearly not Luke's own compilation.

397 Cf. W. Ott, *Gebet*, 100–1; and, more recently, D. Catchpole, 'Friend', 407–24. On the parallel construction, see also V. Hasler, *Amen*, 100–1.

398 H. Schürmann, *Untersuchungen*, 132–4, 213, 236–7.

399 See above, n. 367.

400 Matthew has also preserved one saying about 'making friends' (5:25–6) already in his Sermon.

401 If the antithetical formulation of the saying is due to Matthew (see H.-J. Degenhardt, *Lukas*, 88–9), then the contrast between earthly and heavenly riches may reflect also the contrast in Lk 16:11 (and not just Lk 12:21: H. Schürmann, *Untersuchungen*, 120). The originality of the Matthean formulation is widely held, however: see S. Schulz, *Q*, 142; D. Zeller, *Mahnsprüche*, 77–8.

402 *Untersuchungen*, 213, 236–7.

403 See esp. H. J. Cadbury, 'Eye', 69–74. He observes: 'If we may judge by context Matthew did not miss the meaning of the good and single eye when he placed the message between one which recommended treasures in heaven (i.e. generous alms), and one which condemned the service of mammon' (p. 72). For more detailed analysis, see C. Edlund, *Auge*, esp. 104–13; on Matthew, see U. Luz, *Matthäus*, I, 360–2; and, more widely, A. Dundas, *Eye*.

404 F. Hauck, 'Μαμωνᾶς', 388–90; H. Rüger, 'Μαμωνᾶς', 127–31 (and in *TRE* III, 607); M. Black, 'Aramaic', 139–40. J. Fitzmyer, *Luke*, II, 1109. The term does make its way later into TestTr 68:4, which may recall Lk 16:9: see C. Tuckett, *Nag Hammadi*, 143.

405 'Our souls are sated with possessions gained through iniquity, but they do not prevent our going down into the flames of the torment of Sheol' (trans. M. Knibb); cf. H. Preisker, 'Apokalypsen', 202–3; H. P. Rüger, 'Μαμωνᾶς', 128. The statement by D. Hill (*Matthew*, 143) that 'the term is found frequently in 1 Enoch' is without foundation.

406 Early theories suggested that *māmôn* was etymologically derived from the root *maṭmôn* ('hidden treasure'). This has been brought into doubt by A. M. Honeyman ('Etymology', 60–5). He argued that, while the theory was based on the double μμ found in some Greek spellings of 'mammon', these spellings were all late. Our oldest attested Hebrew spelling is from Sirach. Nevertheless, Honeyman suggested that in meaning *māmôn* included the ideas of 'safe deposit, of hoarding or concealing' (*ibid.*, 63).

407 Cf. W. Pesch, 'Exegese', 363; D. Zeller, *Mahnsprüche*, 79; R. H. Charles, *Apocrypha*, I, 411.

408 G. Bornkamm ('Aufbau', 426–7), for example, argues that Mt 6:19ff. is taken up here in Matthew's Sermon as a comment on the petitions of the preceding Lord's Prayer. The sayings in Mt 6:19ff. reinforce the first three petitions of the Lord's Prayer, while 6:25ff. reinforces the fourth petition about the daily existence of the petitioner. While Bornkamm's general thesis does seem to explain some of Matthew's arrangement of his material, a weakness of his discussion here is that the parallels with the initial three petitions of the Lord's Prayer appear to be found mainly in the earth–heaven contrast in Mt 6:19–20 rather than in the theme of covetousness which runs throughout Mt 6:19–24. Bornkamm also makes no attempt to show a one-to-one correspondence between the three sayings in Mt 6:19–24 and the three petitions of the Prayer. One feels that his thesis would be little changed if Mt 6:22–3, 24 were not here at all. While he observes the unity of 6:19–24, his theory does little to explain it.

409 The differences include (a) the absence of rhetorical questions in the central section (6:22–3), and (b) the absence of a progression of argument from general exhortation to specific application.

3. The use of aphoristic sayings outside the aphoristic collections

1 Lk 3:9 par, 6:29–30 par, 6:40 par, 7:25b par, 10:2a par, 10:7b par, 11:17 par, 11:23 par, 11:33, 34–5 par, 12:33b, 34 par, 12:58–9 par, 13:23–4 par, (13:30 par), (14:11 par), 14:34–5 par, (17:33 par), 17:37 par, 19:26 par. In addition, see above, pp. 79–80, on Lk 6:31 par, and below, p. 175, on Lk 7:35 par and 9:58 par. See also C. E. Carlston, 'Wisdom', 108–11; J. D. Crossan, *Fragments*, 330–45.

2 R. B. Y. Scott, *Way*, 59–63; J. Crenshaw, *OT Wisdom*, 67–72; H.-J. Hermisson, *Studien, passim*; J. M. Thompson, *Form*, 59–68; R. Murphy, 'Form Criticism', 475–83.

3 *Tradition*, 69ff.; see above, pp. 1–2.

4 W. Beardslee, 'Uses', 66–70; N. Perrin, *Language*, 52.

5 *Mahnsprüche*, 142–3, 147–85.

6 E.g., Mt 23:8; Mk 11:25, and possibly Mk 9:50c and 10:43–4.

7 W. McKane, *Proverbs*, 1–10, 139–40; R. Murphy 'Form Criticism', 479–80; D. Zeller, *Mahnsprüche*, 21–2; P. J. Nel, *Structure*, 7–18, 70–82.

8 Lk 6:27 par, 6:37 par, 11:9–10 par, 12:22–3 par, 16:9 par.

9 D. Zeller (*Mahnsprüche, passim*) assigns the three sayings to different form-critical classifications. Mt 6:19–21 par is interestingly considered a direct admonition, as distinct from those employing imagery! Mt 5:25–6 is differentiated from the other two because it is singular. These formal differences, though, may actually obscure similarities in use.

10 See above, pp. 96–9. W. Pesch ('Exegese', 356–9) argues for Matthean originality on three grounds: (1) Matthew has better Semitic style; (2) Luke resolves difficulties found in Matthew's version; (3) Lk 12:33a is a Lukan construction. See also S. Schulz, *Q*, 142–3; D. Zeller, *Mahnsprüche*, 78; J. Fitzmyer, *Luke*, II, 981–2; U. Luz, *Matthäus*, I, 356; M. Steinhauser, *Doppelbildworte*, 236–7. Some doubts, though, are expressed by H.-T. Wrege, *Bergpredigt*, 110–13 (on Lk 12:33a), and by H. Schürmann, *Untersuchungen*, 120, 123.

11 R. Bultmann, *Tradition*, 84; J. Crossan, *Fragments*, 128–31. Yet W. Pesch ('Exegese', 369) speculates that the connection may go back to Jesus. It is preserved loosely in Justin, *Apol.*, I.15.11–16; but GThom 76 has no parallel to Mt 6:21 par and has somewhat awkwardly set its version of the 'unfailing treasure' saying at the conclusion of the parable of the merchant who finds a pearl. More widely, cf. C. Tuckett, *Nag Hammadi*, 153 *et passim*.

12 'Exegese', 369; see also H.-T. Degenhardt, *Lukas*, 88.

13 H.-J. Degenhardt, *Lukas*, 88, 92; E. Percy, *Botschaft*, 90–1. But cf. D. Zeller (*Mahnsprüche*, 80), who believes that the thought is not so unusual, even if exact parallels cannot be found; also J. Fitzmyer, *Luke*, II, 983; J. Gnilka, *Matthäusevangelium*, I, 239.

14 Cf. S. Schulz, *Q*, 144.

15 W. Pesch ('Exegese', 365) also cites 1Qp Hab 6:1, 8:10f, 9:2–6, 12:10. Yet, exact contrasts between earthly and heavenly treasure are not found even here. J. Fitzmyer, *Luke*, II, 982, observes for Lk 12:33–4 par 'that background is not the eschatological crisis, but the fate of the individual after death'.

16 See also Tob 4:8–11, and the remarks of D. Zeller, *Mahnsprüche*, 80–1.

17 This seems to be overlooked by H. Windisch (*Meaning*, 33) when discussing how Mt 6:19–20 has been 'enforced with eschatological sanction'.

18 See above, pp. 96–9.

19 E. Schweizer (*Matthew*, 162–3) claims that 'the riches in heaven can be only the Kingdom of heaven itself', but this simple identification is doubted by D. Zeller, *Mahnsprüche*, 81.

20 Cf. L. Schottroff/W. Stegemann, *Jesus*, 54, 70–1; M. Steinhauser, *Doppelbildworte*, 242–4, who also notes a link with Lk 12:15–21; and H. Riesenfeld, 'Schätzesammeln', 47–8.

21 On Lk 12:57 as Lukan redaction, see S. Schulz, *Q*, 421; R. Bultmann, *Tradition*, 91; A. Polag, *Fragmenta*, 66–7. Less certain

are I. H. Marshall, *Luke*, 550–1; H. Schürmann, *Untersuchungen*, 116 (see below n. 23).

22   *Q*, 421–2; also , with reservations, D. Zeller, *Mahnsprüche*, 64–5; U. Luz, *Matthäus*, I, 252; J. Fitzmyer, *Luke*, II, 1001; A. Polag, *Fragmenta*, 66–7. J. Drury (*Tradition*, 145) suggests that Luke imposed here a pattern of three on his material; Matthew has only two officials. For a contrary view, see G. Strecker, 'Antithesen', 50 n. 37.

23   *Contra* H. Schürmann (*Untersuchungen*, 116) who finds a pre-Lukan connection between Lk 12:54ff. and 12:57ff. on the basis of a somewhat tenuous assumption that κρίνειν was worked into 12:57 by Luke because of διακρίνειν in the *Vorlage* of 12:56 (= Mt 16:3); so also J. Crossan, *Fragments*, 248.

24   G. B. Caird, *St. Luke*, 169–70 and 'Defendant', 36–9; J. Drury, *Tradition*, 155.

25   J. M. Creed, *St. Luke*, 179: 'instead of a parable, the saying becomes in Mt a direct precept'.

26   J. Jeremias, *Parables*, 43–4; W. G. Kümmel, *Promise*, 56; D. Zeller, *Mahnsprüche*, 66.

27   J. Jeremias, *Parables*, 44.

28   *Gleichnisreden*, II, 245.

29   This is not given weight by H. Schürmann: see above, n. 23.

30   *Mahnsprüche*, 64–6. See also J. Fitzmyer, *Luke*, II, 1002; U. Luz, *Matthäus*, I, 252.

31   *Mahnsprüche*, 66–7.

32   *Q*, 423.

33   *Mahnsprüche*, 65–6.

34   *Fragmenta*, 68.

35   For the greater originality of Matthew's version, see R. Bultmann, *Tradition*, 77, 93; J. Creed, *St Luke*, 185; D. Zeller, *Mahnsprüche*, 139; S. Schulz, *Q*, 309ff.; M. Steinhauser, *Doppelbildworte*, 148–52. Favouring Luke's version, see J. Jeremias, 'πύλη', 922–3; J. Dupont, *Béatitudes*, I, 97–101; R. Gundry, *Matthew*, 126–7; P. Hoffmann, 'Lc 13.22–30', 195–6. Supporting separate developments of tradition, see W. Knox, *Sources*, II, 31; H.-T. Wrege, *Bergpredigt*, 135; I. H. Marshall, *Luke*, 563–5; W. Michaelis, 'ὁδός', 70–1. C. Tuckett (*Nag Hammadi*, 45, 69–70) notes possible dependence on Matthew's version by TeachSilv 103:19–26, and TreatRes 44:8–10.

36   See below, n. 41.

37   For brief discussions of the 'two ways' motif, see P. Winter, 'Ben Sira', 315–18; D. Zeller, *Mahnsprüche*, 140–1; A. Denaux, 'Wegen', 309 n. 8; and, more fully, W. Rordorf, 'Voies', 109–28; F. Nötscher, *Gotteswege*; M. McKenna, *Two Ways*. Against taking Mt 7:13–14 as a direct reference to the 'two ways' tradition, though, see M. J. Suggs, 'Two Ways', 63.

38   The words ζωή and εἰσέρχομαι may also be taken in this sense. Cf. A. Mattill, 'Way', 531–4; G. Schwarz, 'Matthäus vii 13a', 229–32; E. Schweizer, *Matthew*, 176; R. Schnackenburg, 'Bergpredigt', 29;

A. Denaux, 'Wegen', 309. Mattill also interprets τεθλιμμένη in Mt 7:14b as a reference to End-time tribulations.

39 D. Hill, *Matthew*, 149–50, and 'False Prophets', 335; E. Schweizer, *Matthew*, 176, 184–5; G. Bornkamm, 'Aufbau', 421, 423; A. Denaux, 'Wegen', 305–15.

40 A. Denaux ('Wegen', 313) sees a chiastic structure in which Mt 7:13–14 and 7:24–7 address *all* disciples (and even all men), while 7:15–20 and 7:21–3 refer to specific prophetic leaders in the community. D. Hill ('False Prophets', 333–48) would distinguish the false prophets (Pharisees!) in 7:15–20 from charismatic Christians in 7:22–3; but on 7:15–20, see above, pp. 44–51.

41 P. Hoffmann ('Lc 13, 22–30', 196–7) sees the influence of the parenetic tradition on Luke. Also attributing this to Lukan redaction are S. Schulz, *Q*, 310; A. Polag, *Fragmenta*, 68–9. In contrast, cf. A. Denaux, 'Wegen', 323–4.

42 H. Flender (*Heil*, 100–2) suggests that Luke's introductory question in 13:23 is provoked by the parables in 13:18–21. He also sees Luke's concern in chapter 13 with the Jews 'als Typos der Wege Gottes mit der Welt'. Cf. also A. Denaux, 'Wegen', 327; P. Hoffmann, 'Lc 13, 22–30', 203–5, 213–14; M. Steinhauser, *Doppelbildworte*, 152–4.

43 'Lc 13, 22–30', 206.

44 A. Denaux, 'Wegen', 328.

45 P. Hoffmann, 'Lc 13, 22–30', 198–200; so also S. Schulz, *Q*, 424; R. Bultmann, *Tradition*, 130. In contrast, A. Denaux ('Wegen', 328 n. 85) recognizes the awkwardness of 13:25 but attributes it to the 'Q-Redaktor'.

46 'Wegen', 315.

47 *Q*, 424–5 (citing other scholars in his n. 158); cf. P. Hoffmann, 'Lc 13, 22–30', 200.

48 D. Zeller, *Mahnsprüche*, 139; J. Fitzmyer, *Luke*, II, 1021; S. Schulz, *Q*, 310; P. Hoffmann, 'Lc 13, 22–30', 193 (citing in his n. 16 other scholars in support).

49 A. Denaux ('Wegen', 317–18) notes that the majority of scholars opt for the greater originality of Matthew's form, although Denaux finds redactional re-working by both evangelists (*ibid.*, 318–29).

50 The ethical significance of this call is equally clear from Luke's ἀγωνίζεσθε (P. Hoffmann, 'Lc 13, 22–30', 197) and from Matthew's 'two ways' formulation (D. Zeller, *Mahnsprüche*, 140; A. Denaux, 'Wegen', 309 n. 8). Even if the original imperative was simply 'Enter by the narrow gate', the requirement for effort or commitment is implied in the command.

51 R. A. Edwards, *Theology*, 130–1; J. Jeremias, 'πύλη', 923.

52 E. Bammel ('Ende', 45–6) suggests that a positive promise for the ὀλίγοι is broken off and preserved in Lk 22:28, 30a, which (with 29, 30b) is the 'end of Q'.

53 E.g., D. Zeller, *Mahnsprüche*, 141; S. Schulz, *Q*, 311; J. Jeremias, 'πύλη', 923. The difference between Matthew and 4 Ezra, however, is rightly described by M. McKenna, *Two Ways*, 407.

54 'Gate', 20–9. Non-apocalyptic parallels to the 'two ways' image can also be found, e.g., in Sir 21:10, or the saying of Bion of Borgsthenes (cited in Diogenes Laertius, *Lives*, IV, 19; cf. C. Carlston, 'Proverbs', 102 n. 119): 'The road which leads to Hades is easy to follow.'

55 The difficult, seldom-used path leading to a small gate is that which leads to true education (*Tabula*, 15:1–4) in contrast to the false paths described in *Tabula* 4:3–14:4.

56 D. Zeller, *Mahnsprüche*, 21–2.

57 *Ibid.*, 21–2, 55ff.

58 Cf. above, pp. 78–80. For a discussion of the reconstruction of the logia, see S. Schulz, *Q*, 121–3. Against Schulz's view that these are 'legal sayings', however, see D. Zeller, *Mahnsprüche*, 56.

59 K. Stendahl, 'Hate', 343–5.

60 For background parallels to these commands, see again D. Zeller, *Mahnsprüche*, 57–9. G. Strecker, 'Antithesen', 64, attributes Mt 5:41 to either Q^{Mt} or Matthean redaction.

61 This is clearest in Luke: see V. P. Furnish, *Love Command*, 56. D. Zeller (*Mahnsprüche*, 59) prefers to draw a motivation from general background ideas, such as perseverance in light of the End, rather than from the immediate context.

62 See above, pp. 79–80.

63 H. Schürmann, *Lukas*, I, 348–9; D. Zeller, *Mahnsprüche*, 59–60; F. W. Beare, *Matthew*, 159.

64 Common to Matthew and Luke, though the παντί is usually attributed to Luke himself.

65 J. Fitzmyer, *Luke*, I, 639.

66 F. W. Beare, *Matthew*, 159. This is more obvious in Matthew's formulation, although the subject of loans is also worked into Lk 6:34–5. Note also the observation of G. Strecker ('Antithesen', 65 n. 85): 'Die matthäische Reihenfolge [in Mt 5:39b–42] ist die einer Antiklimax'; and cf. L. Schottroff, 'Non-Violence', 38 n. 96.

67 Produced by D. Zeller (*Mahnsprüche*, 55) from S. Schulz, *Q*, 123. So also G. Strecker, 'Antithesen', 65: 'Übernimmt Matthäus in v. 42b offenbar den Wortlaut der Q-Vorlage.'

68 S. Schulz, *Q*, 123; H. Schürmann, *Lukas*, 348–9; *contra* I. H. Marshall, *Luke*, 261, who prefers to see a separate development in the sources. The use of αἴρειν in Lk 6:30 both generalizes the saying and recalls the theme of hostility from Lk 6:29.

69 D. Mealand (*Poverty*, 29) comments that this was 'no doubt especially relevant in the straitened circumstances of the early Christians'.

70 H. Sahlin ('Bemerkungen', 69–77), however, considers references to supererogation as secondary, or as misunderstandings of an underlying Aramaic.

71 R. Bultmann, *Tradition*, 141; S. Schulz, *Q*, 320–2; D. Zeller, *Mahnsprüche*, 60–1; J. Crossan, *Fragments*, 272–4; I. H. Marshall, *Luke*, 643; G. Barth, 'Kirchenzucht', 168–9. For a contrary view, see D. Catchpole, 'Reproof', 79–90. In addition to the considerable

differences in wording between Matthew and Luke, there is also the textual problem of the εἰς σέ in both Lk 17:3b/Mt 18:15: see J. Galot, 'Publicain', 1012–13, 1029.

72 S. Schulz, *Q*, 322.

73 'Love one another from the heart, therefore, and if anyone sins against you, speak to him in peace. Expel the venom of hatred, and do not harbour deceit in your heart. If anyone confesses and repents, forgive him. But if anyone denies his guilt, do not be contentious with him, otherwise he may start cursing, and you would be sinning doubly ... Even if he denies it and acts disgracefully out of a sense of guilt, be quiet and do not become upset. For he who denies will repent, and avoid offending you again; indeed he will honour you, will respect you and be at peace. But even if he is devoid of shame and persists in his wickedness, forgive him from the heart and leave vengeance to God' (cited from J. H. Charlesworth, *OT Pseudepigrapha*, I, 816).

74 *Mahnsprüche*, 61–2.

75 However unlimited forgiveness is to be in terms of its repetition, it still presupposes a pattern of rebuke and repentance. This also contrasts with other 'reconciliation' sayings which are less qualified and which advocate not judging one's brother (Mt 7:1–5 par) or love of one's enemies (Mt 5:44–8 par).

76 H. Riesenfeld, 'Schätzesammeln', 47–8.

77 K.-G. Reploh, *Markus*, esp. 87ff.

78 For the view that these sayings became attached to the 'withered fig-tree' pericope by later catechetical interests, see V. Taylor, *St Mark*, 465–7; H. Anderson, *Mark*, 268 (suggesting catchword connections); E. Schweizer, *Mark*, 235–6. W. Telford (*Temple*, 54–6, 108–10) suggests that the 'prayer' logia may be an early scribal insertion (later than Mark himself) to soften the thaumaturgic interpretation of Mk 11:23. Alternatively, G. Biguzzi, 'Pater', 57–68, argues that Mk 11:23–5 recalls the Lord's Prayer.

79 H. Koester ('Mark 9:43–7', 151–3) takes this as a rule for the community, not the individual. The explicit references to sin apply most naturally, however, to an individual, although 'scandal' is present in Mk 9:42.

80 The logia may still be classified as 'wisdom admonitions', because the reckoning (losing a little is better than losing everything) is clearly practical, and because the 'better than' form is widely attested in Jewish wisdom literature: see G. Bryce, 'Better', 343–54; C. E. Carlston, 'Wisdom', 100. These sayings, however, highlight the differences possible even within the category 'wisdom admonition': see D. Zeller, *Mahnsprüche*, 74–7. For the view that the references to 'fire' in 9:43, 48 are Markan redactional additions, see H. Fleddermann, 'Discipleship', 69.

81 In the context, it does not seem to be a logical conclusion to 9:33–50, or even to 9:50a: see M. Krämer, 'Ihr seid', 136–7. For various interpretations, see J. Latham, *Salt*, 226–7; J. Gnilka, *Markus*, II, 67; E. Schweizer, *Mark*, 199–20; W. Nauck, 'Salt', 166–70 (who

equates salt with being 'wise' or 'bright'); H. Fleddermann, 'Discipleship', 73 (who links it to covenant fellowship); J. D. M. Derrett, 'Salted', 364–8 (who relates it to amputation and cauterization); M. Lattke, 'Salz', 44–59 (who considers it 'ein Appell zur Tischgemeinschaft und damit zur Gemeinschaft' (p. 58).

82 D. Zeller, *Mahnsprüche*, 137, rejects the possibility that εἰρηνεύετε ἐν ἀλλήλοις is indicative rather than imperative on the grounds of his *Motivkritik*.

83 O. Cullmann, 'Salz', 198–9. K.-G. Reploh (*Markus*, 154–6) suggests that this may refer to community strife.

84 D. Zeller, *Mahnsprüche*, 137, also notes a correspondence between ἐν ἀλλήλοις in Mk 9:50b and ἐν ὑμῖν in Mk 10:43–4. J. H. Elliott ('Ministry', esp. 388–90) argues that the *Sitz im Leben* of this tradition is baptismal catechesis, primarily reflecting the concerns with rank in Qumran admission traditions. K.-G. Reploh, *Markus*, 140–8, 163–72, suggests a problem of a developing hierarchy of church leaders. It is doubtful whether the problem is primarily christological and only secondarily about discipleship, *contra* T. Weeden, *Mark*, 34–5, 52–3.

85 So D. Zeller, *Mahnsprüche*, 122.

86 That Mk 10:45 may have been added secondarily here (R. Bultmann, *Tradition*, 155) does not alter the fact that it is used here by Mark to support 10:43–4. On Mk 10:45 in the context of these chapters, see N. Perrin, 'Christology of Mark', 115–21; B. Lindars, 'Mark 10:45', 295. J. Roloff ('Todes', 51), however, views verses 42–5 as a pre-Markan combination of sayings.

87 Q. Quesnell, *Mind*, 134ff., notes that most of the 'universal moral directives' occur in Mk 8:27–10:52 and thus are closely related to the Passion. See also V. Robbins, *Jesus*, 158–63.

88 On Mk 8:34ff., however, see Appendix.

89 So esp. D. Zeller, *Mahnsprüche*, 195–6.

90 For attempts to see in Matthew a more direct and christological union of Torah and wisdom, see M. J. Suggs, *Wisdom*, 99–127 (also discussing other sayings material in this light); R. Hamerton-Kelly, *Pre-Existence*, 67–83; E. Schweizer, *Matthew*, 446–7.

91 On the problem of Temple worship in the time of Matthew, see K. Clark, 'Worship', 269–80; or, alternatively, M. D. Goulder, *Midrash*, 287: 'Matthew may well be living in the rabbis' dreamworld where the Temple-service will soon be restored.' But cf. G. Strecker ('Antithesen', 49–50), who sees this close union of ethical and cultic as pre-Matthean, with Matthew himself putting the ethical above the cultic (9:13, 12:7).

92 G. Bornkamm, 'End-Expectation', 38–40. W. D. Davies, *Setting*, 297–8, sees Jamnian usage underlying Mt 23:8. Regarding opposition to a kind of 'Christian rabbinism' by charismatics, see E. Käsemann, *Questions*, 84–5; E. Schweizer, *Matthew*, 178–84, and 'Observance', 213–30. Finally, for the hypothesis that it was a midrash directed particularly against Jewish elders, see J. D. M. Derrett, 'Mt 23, 8–10', 372–86.

93 R. Bultmann, *Tradition*, 107, cites the midrash in Cant. 2:14 (101a): 'God says of the Israelites: To me they are upright as doves, but to the nations they are wise as serpents.' Bultmann considers it a secular proverb (*ibid.*, 103); cf. also Rom 16:19.

94 T. W. Manson, *Sayings*, 173.

95 Cf. parallels in Prov 27:1; b. Sanh 100b; b. Ber 9; and others cited by D. Zeller, *Mahnsprüche*, 94 n. 298. The final clause, 'Each day has enough trouble of its own', is considered a Matthean composition by R. Gundry, *Matthew*, 119; E. Schweizer, *Matthew*, 166.

96 *Mahnsprüche*, 67ff., 69ff.

97 E.g., W. Grundmann, *Lukas*, 292–5; E. Klostermann, *Lukas*, 150–1. 'Table rules' comparable to Lk 14:8–10 are found in Prov 25:6 and rabbinic literature (see Strack-Billerbeck, II, 204). R. Bultmann (*Tradition*, 103) finds Lk 14:12–14 akin to the 'grudging spirit' of 1 En 108; but see also M. Ab 1:5.

98 Cf. Lk 18:14; Mt 23:12, 18:4; and see below, pp. 151–2.

99 Cf. J. Jeremias, *Parables*, 192; also Prov 25:6–7. M. Black (*Aramaic*, 171–5) finds a more original version of the saying in the D text of Mt 20:28–9, which, he claims, 'may have come from the Greek Q'.

100 J. Jeremias, *Parables*, 192–3.

101 See also Lk 12:35, an admonition with no motivation clause, which introduces the parables on watchfulness. L. Johnson (*Possessions*, 148) notes how Luke uses language about possessions to symbolize negative and positive responses to the crisis of God's visitation.

102 D. Zeller, *Mahnsprüche*, 51, considers it a redactional, 'transitional' saying in its context. Cf. also E. Klostermann, *Lukas*, 135; W. Schmithals, *Lukas*, 144; R. Karris, 'Poor', 120; J. Jeremias, *Sprache*, 215, who identifies the εἶπεν δὲ πρὸς (+ acc.), ἐν τῷ (+ inf.), and the substantive participle of ὑπάρχω (with the dative of person) as Lukan. I. H. Marshall (*Luke*, 523) argues, however, that the clumsiness in the style suggests that 'Luke is not composing freely'. Perhaps it is best to see Luke composing the admonition but with some other saying or phrases in mind; *contra* H. Schürmann (*Untersuchungen*, 232), who would see all of Lk 12:13–14, 15–21, 22ff. as a pre-Lukan collection. A version of the parable in Lk 12:16–21 appears, without the admonition in Lk 12:15, in GThom 63.

103 L. Johnson, *Possessions*, 153, observes that this saying 'acts as a thematic statement for the whole subsequent development', which includes the story of the Rich Fool. D. Seccombe (*Possessions*, 139) adds that it begins with 'the strongest warning formula in Luke–Acts'.

104 Cf. the observations of W. McKane, *Proverbs*, 139–40, on the absence of metaphor in the Egyptian instructions.

105 'Proverbs', 91–9.

106 *Ponder*, 31, 54, 56.

107 But cf. Mt 7:24–7 par.

108 But cf. Mt 22:21.

109 Cf. R. B. Y. Scott, 'Folk Proverbs', 420−3, for a description of this classification of proverb.
110 On Matthew's adaptation of the saying, see R. Bultmann, *Tradition*, 52, 99; S. Schulz, *Q*, 472−3; and above, pp. 39−42.
111 On Matthew's adaptations here and in 7:16−20, see R. Bultmann, *Tradition*, 52, 95, 104; and above, pp. 45−7.
112 Cf. R. Bultmann, *Tradition*, 41.
113 *Tradition*, 49−54.
114 The main exception is the woes in Lk 11:39−52 par, but it may be fairly argued that these lead up to the σοφία saying in Lk 11:49−51, which is concerned primarily with Israel's rejection of the messengers of God sent to her: see D. Lührmann, *Redaktion*, 43−8. In any case, the sayings are not controversy stories: see S. Schulz, *Q*, 95: 'im Unterschied zu den Streitgesprächen der Markus-Stoffe − wo dasselbe Thema polemisch verhandelt wird allerdings in der Gattung der Anekdote − wird hier nicht erzählt bzw gestritten, sondern definitiv der Fluch verkündet!'.
115 See esp. R. Laufen (*Doppelüberlieferungen*, 126ff.), who observes: 'In der Forschung wird die Existenz dieser Perikope in Q von fast niemandem geleugnet, der auf dem Boden der Zweiquellen-Theorie steht.'
116 See also R. Laufen, *Doppelüberlieferungen*, 427 n. 3; A. Jacobson, 'Christology', 162−3; J. Fitzmyer, *Luke*, II, 917−18.
117 Other features assigned to Markan redaction by R. Laufen (*Doppelüberlieferungen*, 149−55) include the 'sandwich arrangement' of 3:22−30 amidst the friends/relatives sayings in 3:20−1, 31−5; the reference to the scribes coming down from Jerusalem (3:22); the charge that βεελζεβοὺλ ἔχει, recalling 3:21 (3:22); the reference to Jesus speaking 'in parables' (3:23); the question in 3:23b which precedes the maxims; the formulation of 3:26; and possibly the sayings about blasphemy against the Spirit in 3:28−9, followed by direct reference to the opponents' charge in 3:30. See also J. D. Crossan, 'Relatives', 82−98; and, in dialogue with Crossan, J. Lambrecht, 'Relatives', 241−58; and E. Best, 'Mark iii. 20, 21, 31−35', 309−19.
118 W. G. Kümmel, *Promise*, 109; see also E. Schweizer, *Mark*, 86; H. Anderson, *Mark*, 72, 123.
119 A. Jacobson ('Christology', 161−2) observes that the scribal accusation in Mk 3:22 consists of *two* charges, the first corresponding to the judgement of the family that he is a demoniac (Mk 3:30) and the second that Jesus acted in the power of the *archon* of demons to cast out demons (3:28−9). See also J. D. Crossan, 'Relatives', 92−6; E. Best, 'Mark iii. 20, 21, 31−35', 316; and J. Lambrecht, 'Relatives', 248−9.
120 The similarities between Matthew and Mark are numerous, but Luke's version in Lk 11:21−2 is quite different. R. Laufen, *Doppelüberlieferungen*, 84, 130−1, accepts that Luke derived his formulation from Q because Matthew and Luke locate the 'strong man' saying at the same point in the Beelzebul pericope. Also

cf. R. Bultmann, *Tradition*, 13–14; T. W. Manson, *Sayings*, 85 (with some hesitation); A. Polag, *Fragmenta*, 52–3; J. D. Crossan, 'Relatives', 92; E. Käsemann, 'Lukas 11,14–28', 245. Doubting inclusion in Q are D. Lührmann, *Redaktion*, 33; S. Schulz, *Q*, 203 n. 200; A. Jacobson, 'Christology', 163.

121 On Satan's kingdom, see H. Kruse, 'Reich', 29–61.

122 N. Perrin, *Language*, 53, even referred to Mk 3:24–6 as 'a form of proclamation of the kingdom of God', but this is stronger in the double-tradition version. For a parallel to this proverb, see Cicero, *Pro Ligario*, 11.33, which describes the attitudes of two opposing sides in a civil war (so A. E. Harvey, 'Workman', 210).

123 On this saying and its original formulation, see W. G. Kümmel, *Promise*, 105–8; S. Schulz, *Q*, 205, 209–12. Supporting (against most) the originality of 'Spirit' in Mt 12:28 are P. D. Meyer, 'Community', 71–2; and J.-M. van Cangh, 'L'esprit', 337–42, who also cites recent bibliography of the discussion.

124 See D. Lührmann, *Redaktion*, 34; W. D. Davies, *Setting*, 458. Also cf. J. L. Houlden, 'Meaning', 251–9, who leaves open the question of Q and refers differences between Mk 9:40 and Mt 12:30 to differences in the general perspectives of the two evangelists. The function of Mt 12:30 par in its immediate context, though, deserves more attention.

125 *Promise*, 105–6. See also E. Käsemann, 'Lukas 11, 14–28', 243–4, who, however, ultimately wants to see the exorcisms as a basis for belief even though this is not strictly reflected in the initial argument. For a brief review of views on this passage, see A. Jacobson, 'Christology', 164, which rightly rejects attempts to see in Jesus' exorcisms alone an eschatological significance (Schulz, E. Percy, W. Grundmann) or only Jesus knowing *why* the demons are subject to him and to other Jewish exorcists (B. Noack).

126 See R. A. Edwards, *Sign*, 65: 'Mark seems to be more interested in defining the nature of Jesus – his is a christological statement, and not primarily a definition of discipleship.' Cf. also D. Zeller ('Redaktionsprozesse', 406), who rightly rejects J. Wanke's view ('Kommentarworte', 218–20) that Lk 11:20 is a *Kommentarwort* pointing to the special nature of Jesus over against the Jewish exorcists.

127 R. Laufen (*Doppelüberlieferungen*, 146–7) accepts the presence of a 'strong man' saying like Lk 11:21–2 in Q, but rightly sees that the nucleus of Lk 11:20–6 in Q is found in verses 20 and 23. He argues, then, that each saying is elaborated by a parable (21–2, 24–6). Lk 11:20–2 'sich noch mit dem Vorwurf des Teufelsbündnisses auseinandersetzt und ihn "positiv" widerlegt' (*ibid.*, 147). Verse 20, though, does more than this: it prepares for the contrast on which verse 23 depends. E. Käsemann ('Lukas 11, 14–28', 245) also observes rightly that in the Lukan/Q sequence a 'christologische Deutung in strengen Sinn (Christus – der Stärkere) ist also wiederum nicht berechtigt'. Käsemann sees it as expressing that only by overcoming the strong man can one intrude upon his sphere of power, in reference to the binding of demons.

128 See R. Laufen (*Doppelüberlieferungen*, 139-40, 441 n. 117), citing many other scholars in support. Less certain are S. Schulz, *Q*, 478-9; E. Käsemann, 'Lukas 11, 14-28', 246.

129 *Doppelüberlieferungen*, 139-49.

130 *Ibid.*, 146-7. Cf. also D. Zeller, 'Redaktionsprozesse', 407.

131 See D. Lührmann, *Redaktion*, 24ff.

132 A. Jacobson's theory ('Christology', 172-9) that Lk 11:24-6 polemically uses the idea of 'a demonic counterpart of Sophia' which leaves its 'home', seeks a place to 'rest', and finds a ready welcome runs into problems of detail. Its finding a welcome is actually a 'return' (with others). If it is used polemically against 'this generation', in what sense has this demonic Sophia ever 'left home'?

133 Its value for Christians therefore goes beyond hypothetical debates between the early church and Judaism over the church's exorcisms (as R. A. Edwards, *Sign*, 65).

134 See M. J. Suggs, *Wisdom*, 33-48; D. Lührmann, *Redaktion*, 24-31.

135 The 'parable' of the children's game in Mt 11:16-17 par is not included here (despite the Arabic proverb quoted by R. Bultmann, *Tradition*, 202 n. 1), because it is expressly used as a similitude in this context and is more in the style of a 'poem' than of an aphoristic observation or insight. H. Schürmann (*Lukas*, I, 425) is therefore sceptical about any actual proverbial reference, but a contrasting view is taken by D. Zeller ('Bildlogik', 252-7), who examines various interpretations of the parable in the light of the 'proverbial' background. While no very precise parallels can be found, Zeller does cite the ancient midrashim on Prov 29:9 (R. Papa, *c.* late fourth century, Sanh. 103) and on Prov 25:20 (R. Berekhja, *c.* AD 340), which draw on ideas of the 'fool' and the 'obdurate son' and fit remarkably well into the context of an unresponsive Israel which then is to be contrasted with the 'children of Wisdom'. Also on the 'parable', with rather different conclusions, see O. Linton, 'Game', 159-79.

136 C. Daniel, 'Esséniens', 261-77: the men in fine clothing refer to the Essenes, and the king's houses to Masada and to Herod's winter palace at Jericho. Unconvinced is J. Fitzmyer, *Luke*, I, 674.

137 N. Krieger, 'Kleidern', 228-30; R. Gundry, *Matthew*, 207.

138 K. Stendahl, 'Matthew', 783; disputed by E. Schweizer, *Matthew*, 260.

139 I. H. Marshall, *Luke*, 294.

140 F. W. Beare, *Matthew*, 259.

141 *Geschick*; see also below, pp. 166-70.

142 On the form of this saying, see below, pp. 168-9.

143 *Redaktion*, 29. See also H. Schürmann, *Lukas*, I, 428.

144 See D. Lührmann, *Redaktion*, 31; M. J. Suggs, *Wisdom*, 48, 54-5; R. Hamerton-Kelly, *Pre-Existence*, 30-1; S. Schulz, *Q*, 386; A. Jacobson, 'Christology', 89; M. Hengel, 'Lehrer', 155; W. Wink, *John*, 23.

145 Another interesting, but subtle, correspondence between the series

of sayings which the Beelzebul controversy introduces (Lk 11:14–23, 24–6, 29–32 par) and the series in Lk 7:18–35 par is that in the first the affirmation of Jesus' validity as a representative of God leads ultimately to the declaration that in Jesus is one 'greater than Jonah'/'greater than Solomon', and in the second John is ultimately portrayed as 'more than a prophet'. Notice also the charge against John in Lk 7:33 par: δαιμόνιον ἔχει.

146 The independence of the 'lamp on a stand' saying is shown in Mk 4:21 and GThom 33, as well as in Matthew, but not apparently in TeachSilv 99:16–20. See also F. Hahn, 'Licht', 107–8; M. Krämer, 'Salz', 143.

147 On the textual problem in Lk 11:33 (οὐδὲ ὑπὸ τὸν μόδιον), see C. E. Carlston (*Parables*, 90 n. 3), who also discusses Lk 8:16 (*ibid.*, 91–2). Speculating on the background of the Hanukkah lamp, see J. D. M. Derrett, 'Light', 18.

148 These include (i) ἀλλ' ἐπὶ τὴν λυχνίαν in both Mt 5:15 and Lk 11:33; (ii) the common absence of Mark's ἢ ὑπὸ τὴν κλίνην; and (iii) the common inclusion of a concluding phrase (in different words) about all who enter (or are inside) benefiting from the light. The difference in the concluding phrase is attributed to architecture (and missionary interest) by J. Jeremias, *Parables*, 66, and 'Lampe', 238–9; but to theology by C. E. Carlston, *Parables*, 90. See also M. Steinhauser, *Doppelbildworte*, 353–9. Opting for separate traditions is H.-T. Wrege, *Bergpredigt*, 32–3.

149 S. Schulz, *Q*, 474–5; G. Schneider, 'Lampe', 184–6 (who also considers Matthew's form the oldest in the synoptics); E. Sjöberg, 'Licht', 89; R. Schnackenburg, 'Salz', 183–4; M. Steinhauser, *Doppelbildworte*, 356–9; J. Gnilka, *Matthäusevangelium*, I, 133–4.

150 F. Hahn, 'Licht', 115–17, 129–34, argues, though, for Lk 11:36a as part of the Q tradition (partly through the common εἰ οὖν formulation and through its antithetical relationship to Mt 6:23b). He also suggests 11:36b may have been pre-Lukan and used to join 11:33 and 11:34–36a in Q, or just conceivably to join 11:29–32 with 11:33, 34–36a. Also including 11:36 in a Q-version are D. Lührmann, *Redaktion*, 44, 84; A. Polag, *Fragmenta*, 54–5; U. Luz, *Matthäus*, I, 356; J. Gnilka, *Matthäusevangelium*, I, 241; I.H. Marshall, *Luke*, 488–9. Against inclusion, see S. Schulz, *Q*, 469; J. Amstutz, 'ΑΠΛΟΤΗΣ, 97.

151 See above, pp. 96–9; so also F. Hahn, 'Licht', 124–7.

152 Cf. H. Betz, 'Matthew vi. 22f', 54–5.

153 See D. Hill, *Matthew*, 142; F. Hahn, 'Licht', 125–6; F. W. Beare, *Matthew*, 183; M. Goulder, *Midrash*, 264, 302. Hill and Hahn derive the meaning of ἁπλοῦς here from the Hebrew *tām* or the Aramaic *šᵉlîm*, referring to health. J. Amstutz ('ΑΠΛΟΤΗΣ, 100–1) insists that one distinguish between generosity in giving (so Cadbury, 'Eye', 70) and ἁπλοῦς as 'ungrudging' in itself, with the latter being the true sense here.

154 I. H. Marshall, *Luke*, 487–90; W. Grundmann, *Lukas*, 243–4; E. Klostermann, *Lukas*, 129.

155 See above, n. 151; also J. Dupont, 'Marc 4, 21–25', 211, 227. E. Schweizer (*Matthew*, 99–100) acknowledges that Matthew himself brought together the salt and lamp sayings in Mt 5 and added the 'You are ...' introductions, but he believes the lamp saying was already joined to the 'city on the hill' logion on account of the awkward disruption between 5:14a and 5:15. See also M. Krämer, 'Salz', 145–6. There is no evidence, however, that the 'city on the hill' saying was known to Luke or part of the common underlying tradition.

156 'Marc 4, 21–25', 211–12. F. Hahn ('Licht', 129–30) argues for the conjunction on different grounds, but also attributes Lk 11:36b to Q (see above n. 150). The reference to λύχνος in Lk 11:34 is taken to be 'the light of the body', which does introduce a different idea from 11:33, but still prepares a transition. Less certain of the combination in Q is R. Edwards, *Theology*, 115, and *Sign*, 66.

157 *Untersuchungen*, 276. W. Schenk, *Synopse*, 73, ascribes the addition of the 'eye/light' saying to the 'lamp' saying as 'Q-Redaktion'; see also J. Wanke, 'Kommentarworte', 221–2.

158 This is not apparently recognized by R. Edwards, *Sign*, 66, 88–9, 91–3. However, cf. the theory of development by M. Steinhauser, *Doppelbildworte*, 371–7.

159 F. Hahn, 'Licht', 133–4, sees a christological function for Lk 11:33 and 36b which derives ultimately from Q in connection with the 'Sign of Jonah' pericope; see also M. Steinhauser, *Doppelbildworte*, 376–7; J. Wanke, 'Kommentarworte', 222. But doubtful of such a christological interpretation in Q is J. Dupont ('Marc 4, 21–25', 228–9), whose ground for hesitation is the uncertain connection with Lk 11:29–32. G. Schneider ('Lampe', 208–9) understands a development whereby the lamp saying originally referred to Jesus (Lk 11:33; Q), later to his message (Mk 4:21; Lk 8:16; GThom 33), and finally to discipleship (Mt 5:15).

160 So S. Schulz, *Q*, 470. This interpretation does not depend on inclusion of Lk 11:36.

161 So A. Jacobson, 'Christology', 182, who also believes the 'eye' refers to leaders of a community (here Jewish); he cites Is 29:10.

162 J. Amstutz, 'ΑΠΛΟΤΗΣ, 98, relying on Matthew's formulation, outlines the argument as presenting a thesis (6:22a, the eye is the lamp of the body), an elucidation (6:22b–23a, the light–dark contrast), and a final application (6:23b). However, M. Steinhauser (*Doppelbildworte*, 376–7) significantly considers Lk 11:35 as secondarily introduced into the sequence 11:33, 34, 36, and considers that in this warning 'erreicht der Abschnitt einen paränetischen Höhepunkt'.

163 Again, A. Jacobson, 'Christology', 181–2.

164 So, rightly, S. Schulz, *Q*, 470; A. Jacobson, 'Christology', 182.

165 So H. Kee, *Jesus in History*, 91; E. Sjöberg, 'Licht', 104–5.

166 See also, rightly, D. Zeller, 'Redaktionsprozesse', 407.

167 'Matthew vi. 22f', 56.

168 See S. Schulz, *Q*, 428–30.

169 The address 'Lord, Lord' may be a polite address to a teacher, though, according to O. Cullmann, 'Christology', 202−5; C. F. D. Moule, *Origin*, 35; A. Jacobson, 'Christology', 64.

170 Cf. above, p. 115. On Lk 14:34−5, see also Appendix.

171 See T. W. Manson, *Sayings*, 132; S. Schulz, *Q*, 470−1; A. Polag, *Fragmenta*, 72−3; J. Fitzmyer, *Luke*, II, 1067; R. Edwards, *Theology*, 135−6; W. Schenk, *Synopse*, 112. Matthew's introduction ('You are the salt of the earth') seems secondary, however (cf. Mt 5:14a). Against a common source for Matthew and Luke here, see M. Lattke, 'Salz', 47.

172 See I. H. Marshall, *Luke*, 595; J. Latham, *Salt*, 196−200. One resolution of the problem is to trace the double meaning to the Hebrew root *tpl*: see J. Jeremias, *Parables*, 168; M. Black, *Aramaic*, 166−7; J. Fitzmyer, *Luke*, II, 1068−9. Yet the choice of the Greek μωρανθῇ in the double tradition is still significant!

173 See W. Nauck, 'Salt', 165−78; J. Latham, *Salt*, 125, 147, 169−73. Further discussion is found in U. Luz, *Matthäus*, I, 222 n. 22.

174 See, e.g., I. H. Marshall, *Luke*, 595−7; J. Jeremias, *Parables*, 168−9; O. Cullmann, 'Salz', 193−4; J. Latham, *Salt*, 200−1.

175 See E. Sjöberg, 'Licht', 104, who recognizes this connection of thought.

176 For the sapiential connotations of light, see H. Conzelmann, 'φῶς', esp. 322−3.

177 See S. Schulz, *Q*, 472; M. Krämer, 'Salz', 138−9, 148. T. W. Manson (*Sayings*, 132) cites in favour of this interpretation the anecdote of R. Joshua ben Chananiah (*c.* AD 70), which seems to mock this saying. Accepting its application to disciples in the early Christian tradition are I. H. Marshall, *Luke*, 597 [who also cites J. Dupont, 'Renoncer', 576−9, and somewhat questionably J. Jeremias, *Parables*, 168]; O. Cullmann, 'Salz', 196−7, 200−1, who applies it to the sacrifice, suffering and self-denial required of disciples; M. Steinhauser, *Doppelbildworte*, 347−8.

178 See above, pp. 39−42.

179 See J. Jeremias, *Sprache*, 146. But R. Riesner (*Lehrer*, 258) insists on trying to trace it back to the Aramaic.

180 *Q*, 450. He admits that the verb appears only here in Luke, but notes that it derives from 'literarische Sprache' (so also W. Grundmann, *Lukas*, 153; H. Schürmann, *Lukas*, I, 369 n. 175; M. Steinhauser, *Doppelbildworte*, 188).

181 But Jn 13:16 has a parallel clause using ἀπόστολος − ὁ πέμψας αὐτόν. Interestingly, references to κύριος and διδάσκαλος appear together in the preceding verses, 13:13−14.

182 *Q*, 449. So also R. Bultmann, *Tradition*, 93, 99; J. Ernst, *Lukas*, 233; J. Crossan, *Fragments*, 86; W. Schmithals, *Lukas*, 87−8; against R. Riesner, *Lehrer*, 257−8; J. Wanke, 'Kommentarworte', 214; A. Zimmermann, *Lehrer*, 191−2.

183 Cf. E. Schweizer, *Matthew*, 242.

184 The presence of the final clause about a disciple being *as* his teacher, or servant *as* his master, is not a feature of the Johannine sayings.

It characterizes the versions in Matthew and Luke (and DialSav 139:11; b.Ber. 58b: see C. Tuckett, *Nag Hammadi*, 129–30).
185 See E. Schweizer, *Matthew*, 244. The same must be considered for Jn 13:16: see R.E. Brown, *John*, II, 569.
186 So S. Schulz, *Q*, 450–1.
187 See *ibid.*, 451.
188 *Lukas*, I, 370. More generally, see J.D.M. Derrett, 'Mt 23, 8–10', 384: 'it is good rabbinical law that a teacher must not give instruction in the presence of his own teacher, some say even in the latter's lifetime without his permission' (b.Ber. 31b; Erub. 63a). R. Riesner (*Lehrer*, 259) argues further that the master of a house had a teaching function in Palestinian Judaism.
189 See M. Boring, *Sayings*, 78–80, and below pp. 161–2.
190 J. Wanke, 'Kommentarworte', 213–14, attempts to make this an anti-Pharisaic saying (or possibly against Christians who hold still to such traditions), by showing the fallacy of the Pharisaic principle of gaining understanding through passing on tradition. But he is unable to take account of the δοῦλος – κύριος parallelism or its independence from Lk 6:39/Mt 15:14. Matthew, whom one might expect to be most familiar with scribal practice, also apparently misses this significance by splitting the saying from Mt 15:14 and applying it as an example for Christians in general, as the early Christian tradition consistently does. J. Fitzmyer, *Luke*, I, 642, states that even for Luke this saying and Lk 6:39 'undoubtedly refer to instruction in the Christian community'.
191 S. Schulz, *Q*, 410–19; P. Hoffmann, *Studien*, 288–9, 291–2, 302–4; H. Schürmann, *Untersuchungen*, 145–8; A. Jacobson, 'Christology', 134–5; F. Hahn, *Mission*, 42–6; R. Laufen, *Doppelüberlieferungen*, 286–7.
192 On the secondary location in Matthew, see P. Hoffmann, *Studien*, 256; R. Laufen (*Doppelüberlieferungen*, 205, 493 n.32), who cites other scholars.
193 See P. Hoffmann, *Studien*, 290–2 (resisting the attempts of Lührmann and Bornkamm to see the image referring to *Gentile* mission); S. Schulz, *Q*, 410 (citing also 4 Ezra 4:28ff., 9:17, 31; 2 Bar 70:2): F. Hauck, 'θερισμός', 133.
194 'Wisdom', 109, 112; he sees the eschatological overtones of the saying supplied only by the context, not the inherent form of the saying. See also H.-J. Venetz, 'Bittet', 149–52; A. Polag, *Christologie*, 71.
195 A.E. Harvey, 'Workman', 209, sees Lk 10:2a par as a basic economic law (*ibid.*, 211). Both parts of Lk 10:2 are considered originally independent of the missionary instructions by R. Laufen, *Doppelüberlieferungen*, 270. Note also GThom 73.
196 So, rightly, H.-J. Venetz, 'Bittet', 152–3; I.H. Marshall, *Luke*, 416; A. Polag, *Christologie*, 71.
197 *Redaktion*, 60.
198 *Studien*, 290–2; followed by S. Schulz, *Q*, 410.
199 'Christology', 150 n.30; followed by J. Crossan, *Fragments*, 270.

200 See P. Hoffmann, *Studien*, 294—5, on the reversal here of a traditional image and the implicit reference to persecution.

201 For the closeness of Lk 10:2 and 10:7b, see P. Hoffmann, *Studien*, 301; D. Zeller, 'Redaktionsprozesse', 404; A. Jacobson, 'Unity', 421.

202 For the view that Matthew altered μισθός for τροφή, probably on account of the instructions about eating and drinking, see R. Laufen, *Doppelüberlieferungen*, 219. See also P., Hoffmann, *Studien*, 274; S. Schulz, *Q*, 406 n. 21; A. Polag, *Fragmenta*, 44—5; W. Schenk, *Synopse*, 53.

203 Contrast Lk 10:4, 5—7a par. Yet, even there the pattern of conduct should not be overstressed: cf. A. Jacobson, 'Christology', 134.

204 *Studien*, 298. See also F. Hahn, *Mission*, 42, 46; R. Laufen, *Doppelüberlieferungen*, 288.

205 *Studien*, 302.

206 Also in the later tradition, see 1 Tim 5:18; Did 13:1—2; DialSav 139:10; and further in A. Harvey, 'Workman', 209—21.

207 Matthew actually brings the two closer together in Mt 10:9—10. For a discussion of other tensions, see I. H. Marshall, *Luke*, 420—1.

208 'Workman', 215.

209 J. Gnilka (*Markus*, II, 192) also speculates about its application to the Neronian persecution.

210 See J. Ernst, *Markus*, 431.

211 See H. C. Kee, *Community*, 161.

212 For Mk 8:34b, 35—6, see Appendix.

213 But W. Nauck ('Salt', 165—78) still would see a sapiential motif in the Markan version.

214 See, amongst others, J. Dupont, 'Marc 4, 21—25', 201—9.

215 For the maxims on greatness (e.g. Mk 9:35), see above pp. 115—16.

216 As a secondary addition to the parable, see J. Jeremias, *Parables*, 106—7, 111; E. Schweizer, *Matthew*, 421; F. Beare, *Matthew*, 437.

217 On the tension between this saying and Mt 15:1ff., see F. Beare, *Matthew*, 448; E. Schweizer, *Matthew*, 437.

218 Cf. above, p. 118.

219 Uncertain about whether this last saying belonged to Q is A. Polag (*Fragmenta*, 86—7), who notes that most scholars are against this attribution.

220 See H. Hollander, *Joseph*, esp. 6—7, 12—13, 93.

221 See G. Nickelsburg ('1 Enoch 92—105', 310—12, 317—18) who notes the prominence of the beatitude or woe forms.

222 'Wisdom', 199, 204.

223 Cf. J. Crenshaw, 'Questions', 19—23, esp. 28—9.

224 See also Amos 3:3—6a, 8a. R. B. Y. Scott, *Proverbs*, xxviii, also gives examples of other types of proverbs used by the prophets.

225 Cf. W. McKane, *Prophets*; J. Fichtner, 'Isaiah', 429—38; S. Terrien, 'Amos', 448—55; and articles by H. W. Wolff, W. Brueggemann, W. McKane, J. M. Ward and G. M. Landes in J. G. Gammie *et al* (eds.), *Israelite Wisdom*, 75—158.

226 See R. B. Y. Scott, *Proverbs*, 5.

227 See above on Mt 6:21 par; also M. Goulder (*Midrash*, 78), who lists other 'aetics', all of which are double-tradition except Mt 18:20.

228 Supporting the greater originality of Matthew's πτῶμα and συνάγειν, see S. Schulz, *Q*, 280–1; A. Polag, *Fragmenta*, 76; W. Schenk, *Synopse*, 120; I.H. Marshall, *Luke*, 669; M. Steinhauser, *Doppelbildworte*, 299–300.

229 T.W. Manson (*Sayings*, 146–7) considered this the last saying in Q, but more recent studies of Q allow for some later material: see A. Polag, *Fragmenta*, 78–82; W. Schenk, *Synopse*, 123–30; and esp. E. Bammel, 'Ende', 39–50.

230 Also Lk 17:31–2, 33/Mt 24:17–18; 10:39. Cf. D. Lührmann, *Redaktion*, 72.

231 See S. Schulz, *Q*, 280; D. Lührmann, *Redaktion*, 72; A. Polag, *Fragmenta*, 76; J. Fitzmyer, *Luke*, II, 1173; W. Schenk, *Synopse*, 120–1. For a contrasting view, see R. Schnackenburg, 'Lk 17, 20–37', 225–6, who would, however, attribute 17:37a to Luke, thereby running into difficulties in explaining the Lukan reformulation (so J. Zmijewski, *Eschatologiereden*, 507 n. 5); C. Tuckett, *Revival*, 168–75; J. Crossan, *Fragments*, 178.

232 Cf. I.H. Marshall, *Luke*, 668–9; J. Fitzmyer, *Luke*, II, 1173; W. Schmithals, *Lukas*, 178; J. Zmijewski, *Eschatologiereden*, 351, 506–7; C. Tuckett, *Revival*, 175 (who also has doubts that spatial considerations apply in Lk 17:23–4 (*ibid.*, 172)).

233 *St Luke*, 221; also, more recently, J. Zmijewski, *Eschatologiereden*, 508.

234 H. Conzelmann, *St Luke*, 120–5; and, with some differences, E. Franklin, *Christ*, 16–19.

235 C. Tuckett, *Revival*, 173, 224 n.33.

236 Yet Tuckett (*ibid.*, 172), following W. Grundmann, would also see a christological interpretation by Luke 'so that Jesus himself appears to radiate lightning'.

237 See also Lk 19:11.

238 D. Lührmann, *Redaktion*, 73; S. Schulz, *Q*, 279; C. Tuckett, *Revival*, 169.

239 Considering these secondary is C. Tuckett, *Revival*, 170. But P. Hoffmann, *Studien*, 206 n. 71, and esp. 'Versuchungsgeschichte', 207–23, relates these warnings to the refusal of Jesus to perform miracles in the Q temptation narrative (Mt 4:2–11/Lk 4:2–12).

240 For various interpretations as to who these were for Matthew, see D. Hill, 'False Prophets', 327–33; A. Denaux, 'Wegen', 310–12; F. Burnett, *Testament*, 234ff. See also Mt 7:15–20, 22–3, 24:11–12.

241 C. Tuckett, *Revival*, 170–1, sees a tension between Mt 24:23–5 ('wrong people appearing in the right way') and 24:26–8 ('people appearing in the wrong way'). The question of recognition, though, is common to both, and in both cases it is presumably the 'wrong people' who appear.

242 So, rightly, C. Tuckett, *Revival*, 170; F. Burnett, *Testament*, 264–7;

E. Schweizer, *Matthew*, 454–5; D. Hill, *Matthew*, 322; F. Beare, *Matthew*, 470.

243 J. Jeremias (*Parables*, 162 n.46) prefers 'vultures', tracing ἀετοί to an Aramaic mistranslation; see also T. W. Manson, *Sayings*, 147.

244 S. Schulz, *Q*, 277–8; R. Bultmann, *Tradition*, 122; also A. Polag, *Fragmenta*, 76; W. Schenk, *Synopse*, 120–1; P. Hoffmann, *Studien*, 206 n.71.

245 Favouring inclusion of the 'Lot' pericope in Q are W. Schenk, *Synopse*, 122; T. W. Manson, *Sayings*, 143; A. J. B. Higgins, *Son of Man*, 62; R. Schnackenburg, 'Lk 17, 20–37', 223 (who considers such double sayings often original); C. Tuckett, *Revival*, 172–5. Against are S. Schulz, *Q*, 278; D. Lührmann, *Redaktion*, 72; R. Bultmann, *Tradition*, 117. On Lk 17:25, see also the discussion of C. Tuckett, *Revival*, 173–4. On Lk 17:31–33, see below, n.259.

246 Debating with P. Vielhauer over whether the titles 'Messiah' and 'Son of Man' are to be identified in these sayings is H.-E. Tödt, *Son of Man*, 337–8.

247 For useful reviews of the interpretations of this unit, see J. Zmijewski, *Eschatologiereden*, 513–18; C. Tuckett, *Revival*, 170, 223 n.16.

248 *Q*, 283.

249 Recently arguing for its coming as 'self-authenticating', 'inescapable' and 'imminent', see A. J. B. Higgins, *Son of Man*, 72.

250 *Redaktion*, 72.

251 *Revival*, 172–5.

252 *Ibid.*, 172.

253 R. A. Edwards, 'Correlative', 17, would also see a threat here to those outside the church, but both Matthew and Luke treat this as a problem for followers.

254 R. A. Edwards, *Theology*, 41, and 'Correlative', 9–20; but cf. J. Crossan, *Fragments*, 176–8.

255 Rightly against such attempts is J. Zmijewski, *Eschatologiereden*, 511–12. For a recent attempt to find allusions in Mt 24:28 to the temple ruin and Roman standards, see S. Brown, 'Apocalypse', 12. The general popularity of the eagle imagery, though, can be found as early as Archilochus' tale of the fox and the eagle: see M. West, *Hesiod*, 29.

256 *Redaktion*, 98–9 (also 75–83). Lührmann notes similar examples in Sir 16:7–8; WisSol 10:4, 6; TNaph 3:4–5; etc. The aphorism itself can be compared to some OT texts: e.g., Job 39:30 LXX, which is a clearer parallel than 4 Ezra 13, cited by Tödt and Schulz.

257 But P. Gächter (*Matthäus*, 781) suggests that the aphorism itself expresses a judgement motif: the corpse = evil men, vultures = means of judgement.

258 See D. Lührmann, *Redaktion*, 73; A. J. B. Higgins, *Son of Man*, 65, 72.

259 See C. Tuckett, *Revival*, 174; and see below, pp. 151–3.

260 Namely, Lk 17:24 par, 26–7 par, 28ff. par; cf. R. A. Edwards, 'Correlative', 12, 16–18; J. Crossan, *Fragments*, 176–9.

261 Some scholars, however, still see the section as encouraging watch-fulness, despite this remarkable difference from Mk 13: see R. Schnackenburg, 'Lk 17, 20–37', 229; D. Zeller, 'Zusammenhang', 75–6.

262 See S. Schulz, *Q*, 370–8; D. Lührmann, *Redaktion*, 31; A. Polag, *Christologie*, 154–6; A. Jacobson, 'Christology', 30–2; P. Hoffmann, *Studien*, 26–8.

263 The entire passage is preserved with only slight differences of wording in Matthew and Luke: see S. Schulz, *Q*, 366–7.

264 S. Schulz, *Q*, 375 n. 345, quoting Klostermann, describes these as 'Präsentia der apodiktischen Gewissheit, nicht des gewohnheits-mässigen Geschehens'; and H. Schürmann (*Lukas*, I, 166 n. 36) argues that they represent 'das Bevorstehende sehr lebhaft'. Certainly the present tense is suited to the imminence with which the events are viewed, but this should not obscure the extent to which these verbs depict also a normal practice (contrast with Lk 3:17 par). Cf. I. H. Marshall, *Luke*, 141.

265 The use of the passive as a Semitic circumlocution for God is well known (see J. Jeremias, *Theology*, I, 10–11), but what is significant here is the careful ambiguity of agency, which permits both a divine and a more general reference.

266 So, rightly, J. Fitzmyer, *Luke*, I, 469. S. Schulz (*Q*, 376 n. 347) presents the evidence in the OT and intertestamental literature for fire as a symbol of judgement; and C. Maurer ('ῥίζα', 988) sees here an allusion to Mal 4:1 in particular, but the anarthrous use is significant. Ideas of divine judgement may be triggered by the imagery of the saying (including that of the 'tree': see H. Schür-mann, *Lukas*, I, 166 n. 37), but the actual formulation does nothing to highlight such allusions at the expense of the saying's general validity.

267 On its proverbial formulation, see R. Bultmann, *Tradition*, 168.

268 See above, n. 266.

269 A. Jacobson, 'Christology', 31, observes that because Lk 3:8b (the 'Abraham as our father' saying) interrupts the flow of thought and imagery between Lk 3:8a and 9, and because it is more specifically levelled against Jewish *leaders*, it is a sign of Q-redaction. The flow of imagery does suggest this, although the thought is in harmony with Lk 3:9b par.

270 Contrast this with R. Bultmann's affirmation (*Jesus*, 68) that man's decision of faith is not made 'on the basis of any past experience or rational deductions, but directly from the immediate situation'.

271 E.g., J. Jeremias, *Parables*, 166; C. H. Dodd, *Parables*, 109–10; S. Schulz, *Q*, 288ff.; A. Weiser, *Knechtsgleichnisse*, 226ff.

272 E.g., J. Jeremias, *Parables*, 62–3.

273 *Questions*, 98–9: 'there has been a transition here from the gnomic future to the eschatological' (p. 98); so also S. Schulz, *Q*, 297.

274 So S. Schulz, *Q*, 288ff.; D. Lührmann, *Redaktion*, 70–1 (who sees also a rough parallel in Mk 13:33–7 but with different concerns); P. Hoffmann, *Studien*, 42–3, 48–9; A. Polag, *Fragmenta*, 80–3;

W. Schenk, *Synopse*, 125—9; E. Schweizer, *Matthew*, 472—3. See J. Dupont, 'Talents', 377 n.1 for a list of scholars who have held that these were originally two distinct parables; and also note the helpful discussion of J. Fitzmyer, *Luke*, II, 1230—1, who ultimately accepts a Q form roughly in line with Matthew's version.

275 I.H. Marshall, *Luke*, 701—2; A. Weiser, *Knechtsgleichnisse*, 227—58. While Marshall will refer to different recensions of Q, Weiser attempts to argue that the common origin of the versions was independent of Q altogether.

276 See esp. S. Schulz, *Q*, 288—93; also W. Resenhöfft ('Talenten', 318—24), who doubts, though, that the evangelists had an early Greek translation of the parable.

277 So J. Jeremias, *Parables*, 58—9 (reflecting Archelaus' journey to Rome); M. Zerwick, 'Thronanwärter', 654—74 (surveying earlier studies); L. McGaughy, 'Fear', 236—7; J. Dupont, 'Talents', 377—8; J. Crossan, *In Parables*, 100, 103; F. Weinert, 'Claimant', 505—14; W. Resenhöfft, 'Talenten', 327—31 (who also identifies a third related parable, that of the wedding invitation). An alternative is to attribute verses 12, 14, 15a, 27 to Lukan redaction: see J. Fitzmyer, *Luke*, II, 1231.

278 'Fear', 241. See also S. Schulz, *Q*, 293; J. Dupont, 'Talents', 377—8. But A. Polag (*Fragmenta*, 80—3) and W. Schenk (*Synopse*, 123—8) prefer Luke's sequence for the story after omission of the 'throne claimant' material. This mainly affects the 'Development' section of McGaughy.

279 The words καὶ περισσευθήσεται in Matthew are widely accepted as a Matthean addition, particularly since the same redactional addition is observed in Mt 13:12/Mk 4:25. On this and the textual tradition , see G. Lindeskog, 'Logia', 134—40, who also discusses the possible development of the proverb (*ibid.*, 145—8).

280 Cf. L. McGaughy, 'Fear', 235—6.

281 So, rightly, L. McGaughy, 'Fear', 243; J. Jeremias, *Parables*, 61.

282 'Fear', 235—45.

283 See Lk 11:23 par for similar imagery.

284 J. Jeremias, *Parables*, 62; E. Schweizer, *Matthew*, 473; J. Crossan, *Fragments*, 199—202; J. Dupont, 'Talents', 384; S. Schulz, *Q*, 292—3; W. Schenk, *Synopse*, 126—7; L. McGaughy, 'Fear', 239—40. A. Weiser (*Knechtsgleichnisse*, 244) admits that this is one of the strongest arguments for attributing the parable to the double tradition. Its occurrence in Mk 4:25/Mt 13:12/Lk 8:18 also indicates that it was an independent saying. See also GThom 41; ApPet 83:27 — 84:6 (the latter argued to be dependent on Matthew by C. Tuckett, *Nag Hammadi*, 123).

285 *Synopse*, 126—7.

286 Yet Matthew's fuller form of the saying is supported by S. Schulz, *Q*, 291; A. Polag, *Fragmenta*, 80—1.

287 See S. Schulz, *Q*, 291; I.H. Marshall, *Luke*, 706; H. Seesemann, 'ὀλίγος', 172.

288 *Q*, 292–3. See also the reconstructions by A. Polag, *Fragmenta*, 82–3; W. Schenk, *Synopse*, 126.

289 *Matthew*, 470.

290 The use of the aphorisms as generalizing conclusions for parables is even doubtful for other double-tradition parables. S. Schulz, *Q*, 292 n. 226, cites Mt 18:13 and Lk 14:24, but neither of these is a proverb in form. J. Crossan, *Fragments*, 200–2, suggests that Mt 25:29 par is an aphoristic conclusion added at a 'pre-Q' stage of tradition, and in Q the concluding verse became Lk 19:27 when the parable was conflated with that of the throne claimant. It is our contention, however, that the aphorism in Mt 25:29 par plays a more integral role in the parable (once it has been added) than simply serving as a 'generalizing conclusion'.

291 See J. Jeremias, *Parables*, 62, who, however, draws a different conclusion from this observation.

292 Although textually uncertain, this is usually assigned either to Luke (S. Schulz, *Q*, 292) or to pre-Lukan tradition (A. Weiser, *Knechtsgleichnisse*, 251–2). But J. Crossan (*Fragments*, 201) considers 'Luke 19:25 to be most likely original' and 'a presumably pre-Q smoothing of the linkage between parable and aphoristic conclusion'.

293 S. Schulz (*Q*, 293) considers the λέγω ὑμῖν introduction to the aphorism in Lk to represent Q and illustrate the transition from the story to addressing the community. But F. Neirynck ('Developments', 63, 67) attributes it to Lukan redaction.

294 See J. Jeremias, *Parables*, 62 n. 60; J. D. M. Derrett, 'Talents', 194–5.

295 'Talents', 194–5.

296 For parallels to the principle from outside the business sphere, see G. Lindeskog, 'Logia', 148–50.

297 The future passives of the maxim may lend themselves to interpretation as divine passives, although this is not demanded: see J. Jeremias, *Parables*, 62 n. 58.

298 See J. Dupont, 'Talents', 385, and 'Marc 4, 21–25', 234.

299 So D. Lührmann, *Redaktion*, 71; S. Schulz (*Q*, 293–4), who argues, though, that the delay of the parousia is not the central feature of the parable. A. Polag, *Christologie*, 16, 165, detects a correspondence to the imminent expectation of judgement in the Baptist material at the opening of Q.

300 Yet J. Jeremias (*Parables*, 61) claims that in Luke's version he does act irresponsibly. Contrast with the version in the Gospel to the Nazaraeans 18 where the condemned servant 'squandered his master's substance with harlots and flute-girls'.

301 So, rightly, E. Schweizer, *Matthew*, 472–3.

302 His fault was not that he had little (for in Matthew the initial trust is in differing amounts), but that he did not commit what he had to investment.

303 See J. Jeremias, *Parables*, 61–2; J. Dupont, 'Talents', 388–9; C. H. Dodd, *Parables*, 112–13; L. McGaughy, 'Fear', 241–5; E. Kamlah,

'Kritik', 34−8; others are listed by A. Weiser, *Knechtsgleichnisse*, 260−1.

304 For the different emphases in Matthew and Luke, however, see J. Jeremias, *Parables*, 58−60; J. Dupont, 'Talents', 379−84, and 'Marc 4, 21−25', 233; L. McGaughy, 'Fear', 238−9.

305 Luke has the 'enemies', not the third servant, condemned, which provides a rather different emphasis. J. Crossan, *Fragments*, 203, observes: 'As a Q composition, the double parable of The Pounds/Throne Claimant, with its double emphasis on servants and citizens, served to give the Q community's history of salvation. It contained both a warning to those within (servants) and a judgment on those without (citizens).'

306 *Tradition*, 105.

307 'Wahrheiten', 248.

308 *Ethics*, 118.

309 *Ibid.*, 117 n.3 (citing only 'C.H. Kraeling, ms. note').

310 *Rhetoric*, 71−88; 'Speech-Modes', 22−7.

311 'Wisdom Tradition', 236−9.

312 'Uses', 65−72; *Criticism*, 39−41.

313 'Uses', 66−9; *Criticism*, 34−41. This tendency is reduced, however, in the use of proverbs in GThom: see W. Beardslee, 'Thomas', 101−3.

314 *Criticism*, 36. But the assignment of a sapiential background for the Q-beatitudes is brought into question by R. Guelich, 'Beatitudes', 416−21.

315 'Uses', 72; *Criticism*, 40−1; 'Saving', 58−9.

316 Most recently in *Language*, 48−54.

317 These are alleged to 'shatter the form of proverbial saying altogether' (*Language*, 51).

318 A fourth category, 'the parenetical sayings', is concerned with response rather than proclamation (*Language*, 53−4).

319 'Suche', 567.

320 'Saving', 58−72.

321 *Raid*, esp. 69−72.

322 'Biblical Hermeneutics', esp. 112−14.

323 See a similar qualification earlier by A. Wilder, *Rhetoric*, 125.

324 *Questions*, 98−9. Yet in Käsemann's article on 'sentences of holy law' (*ibid.*, 66−81) mention is not made of these reversal sayings, since reversal rather than reciprocity does not fit exactly the model which he describes. Against Käsemann's classification of this reversal saying, see K. Berger, 'Sätzen', 22−3. More generally on Käsemann's 'sentences of holy law', see above pp.59−60 and Chapter 2 n.252.

325 *Q*, 451−2, on Mt 23:12/Lk 14:11, 18:14.

326 Cf. Job 22:29; Prov 11:2, 16:18, 18:12, 29:23, Ezk 21:26; Jas 4:10; 1 Pet 5:6; TJos 17:8; TeachSilv 104:21−4; IntKnow 10:27−30; LevR 1:5; Erub 13b.

327 See also GThom 4; PistSoph 52, 87 (discussed by J. Crossan, *Fragments*, 45−6, 267−8); OxyP 654.4.2.

328 *Doppelüberlieferungen*, 86, 315ff. See also D. Zeller, *Kommentar*, 50.

329 *Doppelüberlieferungen*, 315–18, where he specifically attempts to counter the arguments of J. Zmijewski (*Eschatologiereden*, 480–2) that Lk 17:33 is derived from Mark.

330 So also J. Lambrecht, 'Q-Influence', 294; S. Schulz, *Q*, 445; W. Schmithals, *Lukas*, 177; J. Wanke, 'Kommentarworte', 224–5; but against R. Schnackenburg, 'Lk 17, 20–37', 224–5 (who attaches it to Lk 17:29); A Polag, *Christologie*, 6, 12 (who sees it following Lk 17:31–2 in Q).

331 *Doppelüberlieferungen*, 318–21. See also H. Schürmann, *Lukas*, I, 544; S. Schulz, *Q*, 447; J. Lambrecht, 'Q-Influence', 295.

332 *Doppelüberlieferungen*, 332–4. S. Schulz (*Q*, 445–6), however, argues that the ἕνεκεν ἐμοῦ was original to the saying, and therefore it is an 'I-saying' and a much sharper and more direct call to discipleship within a context of martyrdom and eschatological expectation. The inclusion of the ἕνεκεν ἐμοῦ would call into question the gnomic character of the saying; yet arguing for the absence of the phrase from Q is J. D. Crossan, *Fragments*, 91.

333 'Developments', 50–1.

334 *Ibid.*, 51; also J. Zmijewski, *Eschatologiereden*, 481–2.

335 'Developments', 50; also J. Zmijewski, *Eschatologiereden*, 407–8, 419 (referring also to Mk 9:12). It also must be stated that the verbal correspondence between Mt 10:39 and Lk 17:33 is slight (cf. F. Neirynck, 'Developments', 51 n. 94), which is often explained by Luke's having 'conflated' with Mk 8:35 (cf. even J. Lambrecht, 'Q-Influence', 283–4).

336 Mt 23:8–10 was very probably aimed by Matthew at the Christian church specifically; see e.g., F. Beare, *Matthew*, 450; E. Schweizer, *Matthew*, 431–2.

337 For extensive parallels, see above, n. 326.

338 'Uses', 66–7.

339 So J. Jeremias, *Parables*, 107, 192, citing a rabbinic parallel to Lk 14:11 attributed to Hillel. That this logion was found in Q is questioned by A. Polag, *Fragmenta*, 86–7; H. Schürmann, *Untersuchungen*, 275–8, 286.

340 J. Jeremias, *Parables*, 192–3.

341 See above, p. 118; see also E. Franklin, *Christ*, 165, who argues that ethical teaching is not in itself a concern of Luke: 'He is not out to edify the Church by equipping it for a continuing role, but by giving a description of its origins, to recall the Christian community to the true nature of its being.'

342 On Lk 17:32, see I. H. Marshall, *Luke*, 665; R. Schnackenburg, 'Lk 17, 20–37', 224, 230; J. Zmijewski, *Eschatologiereden*, 482–9.

343 See R. Laufen, *Doppelüberlieferungen*, 88 (uncertain); S. Schulz, *Q* (omits); D. Lührmann, *Redaktion* (omits); P. Hoffmann, 'Lk 13, 22–30', 192, 211 ('Wanderlogion'); H. Schürmann, 'Zeugnis', 160–1 (uncertain), 167 n. 206 (arguing that both Mt 19:30 and Mt 20:16 derive from Mk 10:31, and for Lk 13:30 as a Lukan addition);

D. Zeller, *Kommentar* (omits); J. Fitzmyer, *Luke*, II, 1022 (assigning it to 'L'). Assigning it to Q are W. Schenk, *Synopse*, 104; A. Polag, *Fragmenta*, 68–9; R. A. Edwards, *Theology*, 131 (parallel to Mt 19:30).

344   On the interpretation of the parable and its ending, see E. Schweizer, *Matthew*, 395; J. Jeremias, *Parables*, 33–6, 136–9. Jeremias also discusses the textual question raised by this verse.

345   See H. Schürmann, 'Zeugnis', 167 n. 206; I. H. Marshall, *Luke*, 568; W. Schmithals, *Lukas*, 154 (who applies this also to Q, given Lk 13:29).

346   See RSV, and J. Fitzmyer, *Luke*, II, 1027.

347   See P. Hoffmann, 'Lc 13. 22–30', 211. J. Crossan (*Fragments*, 45) also notes how the last/first//first/last formulation is not in harmony with the Jews/Gentiles context.

348   *Q*, 444–6, 451–2.

349   See D. Zeller, *Mahnsprüche*, 124–6, who compares here the formulation of Jas 5:12.

350   See *ibid.*, 93–4.

351   See Prov 16:5, and J. Fitzmyer, *Luke*, II, 1112–12. I. H. Marshall (*Luke*, 626), however, describes this as 'a threat of judgement'.

352   R. Bultmann, *Tradition*, 105, places it with Lk 14:11 as a probable genuine saying of Jesus on humility and exaltation. Yet W. Schmithals, *Lukas*, 168, considers it a redactional formulation from other bits of the gospel such as Lk 1:51–3, 13:30, 14:11, 18:14b (the last three being future reversal sayings).

353   *Jesus*, 58.

4. The place of aphoristic wisdom in the sapiential traditions of the double tradition

1   A 'circle' or 'sapiential activity' will be referred to rather than an individual, but without prejudice to the latter possibility.

2   *Sayings*, 78–80. See also D. Hill, 'Christian Prophets', 108–30; J. D. G. Dunn, *Jesus*, 186, 237, 282–4; H. Schürmann, 'Lehrer', 107–47.

3   Boring (*Sayings*, 78–80) believes that the author of James comes closest to the 'office' of teacher. See also A. Zimmerman, *Lehrer*, esp. 92ff.; and on the prophetic–sapiential teacher, see W. Grundmann, 'Weisheit', 175–6.

4   *Sayings*, 79–80.

5   One can only make selections from a vast bibliography, some of which has also been recently considered by J. D. G. Dunn, *Christology*, 168–76. Dunn persuasively argues for Sophia as a personification of Yahweh's wise creative activity and purposes rather than as a Near Eastern hypostatization; also R. Marcus, 'Hypostases', 157–71; R. Whybray, *Wisdom in Proverbs*, 76–104; H. Jaeger, 'Conception', 93–4 (esp. 93 n. 3 for other literature); and possibly for Jewish writings prior to WisSol, G. von Rad, *Wisdom*, 144–76. Preferring to refer to 'reflective mythology' in Jewish

traditions are H. Conzelmann, 'Mother', 230–42; E. Fiorenza, 'Mythology', 26–33. Other views, which include taking Sophia as a hypostasis similar to Astarte or Isis and involving *religions-geschichtliche* analyses, have been expressed by H. Ringgren, *Word*; H. Schmid, *Wesen*; B. Mack, *Logos*, and 'Wisdom Myth', 46–60; C. Kayatz, *Studien*, 86–119; F. Christ, *Jesus*, 13–60; C. Larcher, *Etudes*, 298–414; M. Hengel, *Judaism*, I, 153–75; P. Bonnard, 'Sagesse', 117–49; M. Küchler, *Frühjüdische*, esp. 31–113. Recently B. Lang (*Frau Weisheit*, esp. 147–84) has argued that the teacher in the scribal school is the model for divine Sophia's activity. The relation of a Jewish Wisdom figure to a (proto-) gnostic-syncretistic Sophia myth has also been of interest to the *religions-geschichtliche Schule* (see citations in H. Jaeger, 'Conception', 91–2) and is discussed by R. Bultmann, 'Hintergrund', 10–35, and 'Bedeutung', 55–104; U. Wilckens, *Weisheit*, 97–213, and 'σοφία', 509–14; P. Perkins, 'Gnostic', 590–606.

6 *Frühjüdische*, 110.

7 See above, Chapter 1, n. 22; also C. Larcher, *Etudes*, 343–8; and G. Schimanowski, *Weisheit*, 56–8. An earlier fusion of wisdom and law in Deut 4:6–8 is noted by R. Murphy, 'Assumptions', 415; E. Schnabel, *Law*, 84.

8 For uncertainty about Wisdom as a later gloss in 1 Bar 3:34 – 4:1a, see R. Pfeiffer, *History*, 417–21. M. Hengel, *Judaism*, I, 170, sees the passage as dependent on Sir 24; but cf. G. Sheppard, *Construct*, 84–119; E. Schnabel, *Law*, 95–9.

9 See, e.g., M. Hengel, *Judaism* I, 169–75; M. Küchler, *Frühjüdische*, 54–7.

10 J. Reese, *Influence*, esp. 36–50; E. Schnabel, *Law*, 130–4; B. Mack, *Wisdom*, esp. 139–71; J. Blenkinsopp, *Wisdom*, 146–50. For the association of wisdom and spirit in WisSol 7:22 – 8:1, see G. Schimanowski, *Weisheit*, 74–85 (who also discusses Wisdom's role in creation and the 'sending' of Wisdom in WisSol 9:1–18).

11 See above, Chapter 1, n. 23. On Philo, see B. Mack, *Logos*, 108–95; J. Laporte, 'Philo', 103–41; G. Schimanowksi, *Weisheit*, 85–94.

12 2 En and 2 Bar show little interest in a divine Sophia-figure, although wisdom and law are combined in a few texts in 2 Bar: see E. Schnabel, *Law*, 152–62; M. Küchler, *Frühjüdische*, 76–7. Speculation about Sophia was also limited at Qumran despite a keen interest in wisdom as revelation. Two important texts, though, are 11 QPs[a] col. 18 and 4Q 184 ('Wiles of the Wicked Woman'): see *ibid.*, 102–5; M. Hengel, *Judaism*, I, 176; J. Sanders, *Psalms Scroll*, 68–9, and 'Psalms', 57–75; J. Lebram, 'Chokmah', 202–21; D. Lührmann, 'Weisheitspsalm', 87–98. J. Worrell ('Wisdom', esp. 230–6) conjectures that Qumran had its own agency of interpretative revelation, so that Sophia would have undermined their separatist stance. More generally, see G. Schimanowski, *Weisheit*, 95–104; E. Schnabel, *Law*, 190–226.

13 'Lehrer', 166–77; see also C. Larcher, *Etudes*, 329ff.; G. Schiman-owski, *Weisheit*, 305–8; J. Rylaarsdam, *Revelation*, 99–118.

J. Robinson ('Shifts', 83) refers to Q as 'a book of the acts of the Spirit Sophia'; see also R. Hamerton-Kelly, *Pre-Existence*, 24.

14 Cf. 1 En 48:2, 7, 10; 52:4–5; 49:1–3. Outside chs. 37–71, only occasional references to Wisdom occur which may suggest a Sophia-figure: see 1 En 84:3; 91:10; 94:5.

15 *Christology*, 176.

16 'Background', 88.

17 M. Hengel, 'Lehrer', 148–9; M. Johnson, 'Reflections', 45–53; R. Fuller/P. Perkins, *Christ*, 55; J. Kloppenborg, 'Wisdom', 129–30, 147; even M. J. Suggs, *Wisdom*, 42 n. 18 (but cf. 44). For a Pauline Wisdom Christology, see the works listed in the bibliographical note of J. Kloppenborg, 'Wisdom', 130 n. 5; J. Dunn, *Christology*, 176–96; and J. Davis, *Wisdom*, 65ff. For GThom, see recently S. Davies, *Thomas*, 81–99; and, for Nag Hammadi documents more generally, see R. Arthur, *Goddess*.

18 'Matthew 11:28–30', 3–8; also, along different lines, M. Johnson, 'Reflections', 60–1. This contrasts with T. Arvedson, *Mysterium*, 158ff.; M.J. Suggs, *Wisdom*, 95–7; followed by J.D.G. Dunn, *Christology*, 200–1.

19 Note particularly J. Dunn, *Christology*, 196–206; M. J. Suggs, *Wisdom*, 5ff.; R. Hamerton-Kelly, *Pre-Existence*, 22–47; A. Jacobson, 'Christology'; C. Tuckett, *Revival*, 148–66; M. Hengel, 'Lehrer', 149–60; D.W. Smith, *Christology*, 15–78; F. Christ, *Jesus*, 61ff.; J.M. Robinson, 'Jesus', 1–16; U. Wilckens, 'σοφία', 514–17; F. Burnett, *Testament*, 30–112; G. Stanton, 'Christology', esp. 36–42; J. Kloppenborg, 'Christology', 129–47.

20 *Wisdom*, 97, 127; followed by J. Dunn, *Christology*, 197–206; R. Hamerton-Kelly, *Pre-Existence*, 67–83; see also M. Hengel, 'Lehrer', 149–62. The identification of Jesus as Wisdom may also be found in GThom: see S. Davies, *Thomas*, 97–9.

21 *Revival*, 148–62. Tuckett uses these observations against the Griesbach hypothesis.

22 *Wisdom*, 67.

23 *Revival*, 162–3; also B. Lindars, *Apologetic*, 172–3; F. Burnett, *Testament*, 77; D. Garland, *Intention*, 205–6.

24 Supported by R. Bultmann, *Tradition*, 114–15; M.J. Suggs, *Wisdom*, 64–6; D. Lührmann, *Redaktion*, 48; J. Robinson, 'Jesus', 13; W. Schenk, *Synopse*, 80–1. Doubts, though, are expressed by A. Jacobson, 'Christology', 210–11; D. Garland, *Intention*, 188–97; O. Steck, *Geschick*, 47–8; A. Polag, *Fragmenta*, 66. There is little, however, to commend F. Christ's doubts (*Jesus*, 136) about assigning Lk 13:34–5 to double tradition; on the common vocabulary, see F. Weinert, 'Luke', 72.

25 Cf. Strack-Billerbeck I, 927, 943 ('bringing him under the wings of the Shekinah': LevR 2.134b), cited in Suggs, *Wisdom*, 66. It has been argued that Wisdom and Shekinah are parallel figures, on the basis of passages such as Sir 24:8–10 and 11QPs^a 18:20 (F. Christ, *Jesus*, 141; F. Burnett, *Testament*, 68–75; H. Jaeger,

'Conception', 93—8), but this is challenged by E. Urbach, *Sages*, 64—5. See also Deut 32:11 for another background.

26 F. Christ, *Jesus*, 138; R. Bultmann, *Tradition*, 114.

27 C. Tuckett, *Revival*, 162. This suggests that the Sophia motif applies to Lk 13:35 as well as 13:34; but contrast E. Haenchen, 'Matthäus 23', 57. On 'not finding' Sophia, see also GThom 38 in the light of Prov 1:28 (so S. Davies, *Thomas*, 95). For other background texts without sapiential motifs (e.g., Jer 22:5), see J. Fitzmyer, *Luke*, II, 1036—7.

28 See R. Hamerton-Kelly, *Pre-Existence*, 33, contra Suggs.

29 *Christology*, 203—4; see also P. Hoffmann, *Studien*, 173—4; D. Garland, *Intention*, 196; I. H. Marshall, *Luke*, 574. D. Smith, *Christology*, 77—8, would apparently go further and question the Sophia motif here altogether.

30 Dunn argues that the 'how often' need only express Jesus' frustration with the religious authorities (*Christology*, 203); see also P. Hoffmann, *Studien*, 173; J. Fitzmyer, *Luke*, II, 1034, 1036.

31 Other sayings have occasionally been considered. D. W. Smith (*Christology*, 79—83) briefly examines Lk 12:11—12, 4:16—30, 4:31—7; Mt 18:20; but he doubts any Sophia allusion in Lk 9:41 and Mt 8:17. On Mt 18:20, see also M. J. Suggs, *Wisdom*, 120—1; F. Burnett, *Testament*, 68—70, 242—3 (who associates it with Shekinah—Torah). A Jacobson ('Christology', 228) sees Sophia's vain search for a dwelling-place behind Lk 11:24—6 par, although it is the antithesis of Wisdom (Unrighteousness as in 1 En 42:3) who is specifically seen as the unclean spirit who returns (*ibid.*, 177—8). Yet this may strain the sense of 'rest', and it leaves unexplained the seven other spirits or the motif of the spirit returning to the place it has left. Jacobson sees an invitation by Wisdom to the simple in Lk 14:15—24 par (*ibid.*, 228); see also P. D. Meyer, *Community*, 21; T. Arvedson, *Mysterium*, 212—14. F. Christ (*Jesus*, 61—2) adds for consideration Lk 2:40—52; Mt 2:1—12; Mk 6:2; but these hardly amount to an interest in a Sophia-figure.

32 Cf. other double-tradition texts which draw lessons from Israel's salvation-history as a warning against judgement: Lk 17:26—7 par, 10:12—14 par, 11:51 par.

33 The term κήρυγμα appears only here in the gospels. On the juxtaposition with σοφία, see J. M. Robinson, 'Kerygma', 42; A. Jacobson, 'Christology', 170—1; M. Hengel, 'Lehrer', 151—2.

34 *Sign*, 83—9, and 'Correlative', 9—20; see also D. Lührmann, *Redaktion*, 41.

35 A. Jacobson, 'Christology', 170. The phenomenon of a double saying is not wholly unexpected (see A. J. B. Higgins, *Son of Man*, 102), but this in itself does not explain the place of σοφία in the pericope.

36 J. Fitzmyer (*Luke*, II, 937) observes: 'The phraseology recalls that of 7:35.'

37 T. Arvedson, *Mysterium*, 210—11 n.9; R. Hamerton-Kelly, *Pre-Existence*, 29; P. Hoffmann, *Studien*, 181—2; M. Hengel, 'Lehrer',

165; A. Jacobson, 'Christology', 131–2; J. Crossan, *Fragments*, 240; J. Gnilka, *Matthäusevangelium*, I, 311–12. Jacobson, 'Christology', 131–2, notes the unusual κατασκήνωσις for 'nest', which can be used of a dwelling-place for God. He also draws attention to the image of 'resting' in the 'Son of Man' clause, but it is only GThom 86 that actually includes the words 'and rest'.

38 H.-E. Tödt, *Son of Man*, 121. R. Hamerton-Kelly, *Pre-Existence*, 43, only finds 'concealment' in this saying by importing it from Lk 12:10 par.

39 Epictetus, *Diss.* 3.22.45–69; see also G. Theissen, *Followers*, 14–15; H. Fischel, 'Transformation', 78. Doubting the application of homelessness to rabbis is M. Hengel, 'Lehrer', 165, and *Leader*, 54–5 (also 27–33). But J. Neusner (*Judaism*, 99) observes a change in the ideal from the upper-class intellectual, such as Ben Sira, to the poor sage in early rabbinic times.

40 *Tradition*, 28, 98, 102 (citing Plutarch, *Vita Tiberii Gracchi* 9 [828c]); also W. Grundmann, *Lukas*, 204; but doubted by R. Otto, *Kingdom*, 234 n.1.

41 The precise dating of 1 En 37–71 may not itself be a difficulty if it is assumed that 1 En 42 testifies to tradition roughly contemporary with the early gospel tradition. For a first-century AD date (contra Milik), cf. M. Knibb, 'Date', 345–59; J. Greenfield/M. Stone, 'Pentateuch', 51–65; and, recently, M. Black, *Enoch*, 181–8.

42 *Fragmenta*, 42; see also V. Taylor, 'The Order', 29, and 'Original Order', 265–6; W. Schenk, *Synopse*, 45–9. On the form and context of GThom 86, see J. Crossan, *Fragments*, 241–2.

43 'Christology', 132 (also 24–8, 127–8); see also T.W. Manson, *Sayings*, 67–73.

44 The last 'Sophia' pericope appears to be Lk 13:34–5 par.

45 No apparent attempt to find an allusion to Sophia here is made by F. Christ, *Jesus*; M.J. Suggs, *Wisdom*; J.M. Robinson, 'Jesus'; J. Dunn, *Christology*.

46 *Geschick*, 50ff., 222ff.

47 *Ibid.*, 20ff., 257ff.; see also P. Hoffmann, *Studien*, 182. Regarding the transitional nature of this beatitude in Q, see R. Guelich, 'Beatitudes', 420–1, 432.

48 *Geschick*, 269ff.

49 F. Christ, *Jesus*, 120–52; J. Robinson, 'Jesus', 13; D. Lührmann, *Redaktion*, 45–8; S. Schulz, *Q*, 343–4, 350–1; J. Dunn, *Christology*, 201–4 (on Lk 11:49–51 par).

50 *Revival*, esp. 164–6.

51 'Christology', esp. 228–30.

52 *Ibid.*, 225. See also D. Lührmann's discussion (*Redaktion*, 24ff.) of 'Jesus und dieses Geschlecht'.

53 'Christology', 132; see also R. Hamerton-Kelly, *Pre-Existence*, 29 n.2 (against Tödt); H. Conzelmann, *Outline*, 133–4; C.-H. Hunzinger, 'Unbekannte Gleichnisse', 214. For the view that 'following after' Jesus is particularly concerned in this saying with sharing the perils and uncertainties faced by him see also M. Hengel,

Leader, 54. Lk 9:57/Mt 8:19 is responsible for extending the application to disciples, and may anticipate the 'rejection' motif in the 'missionary' logia of Lk 10:6b, 10–12 par.

54 See Prov 27:8; Sir 36:31 (26), 29:21–8; and R. Tannehill, *Sword*, 161–2.

55 It is far from clear that Prov 1:20 can be used to explain the presence of the reference to Sophia in Lk 7:35 par.

56 On Lk 7:35 par as a concluding addition, see J. Wanke, *Kommentarworte*, 36–9.

57 The example of non-Jews (see also Lk 10:13–15 par, 13:28–9 par; 7:1–10 par) shows an openness to the Gentile world, but need not imply the complete abandonment of Israel. The Gentiles were an obvious foil against which to demonstrate Israel's shameful history of rejection, and the very strength of the polemic suggests that a dialogue with Judaism may here be continuing: see P. Meyer, 'Mission', 405–17; O. Steck, *Geschick*, 286–8, A. Jacobson, 'Christology', 200 n. 44; against D. Lührmann, *Redaktion*, 86–8.

58 *Wisdom*, 24–9, 38–48, 66–7, 89–95.

59 T. Arvedson, *Mysterium*, esp. 209–11 (on Lk 11:49 par and 13:34 par); U. Wilckens, *Weisheit*, 197–200, and 'σοφία', 515–16; F. Christ, *Jesus*, especially 74–5, 153–4; A. Feuillet, 'Jésus', 161–96, and *Christ*, 386–7 (but not specifically regarding Q). For reservations, see W. Beardslee, 'Wisdom Tradition', 236–7; the earlier study of J.M. Robinson, 'Shifts', 83–5, has subsequently been modified in 'Jesus', 1–16.

60 D. Smith, *Christology*, esp. 119–22 (independent of Suggs); S. Schulz, *Q*, *passim*; D. Lührmann, *Redaktion*, 99; M. Hengel, 'Lehrer', 159–60; R. Hamerton-Kelly, *Pre-Existence*, 25–36; G. Stanton, 'Christology', 36–8; J. Dunn, *Christology*, 197–206; C. Tuckett, *Revival*, 148–66; J. Kloppenborg, 'Wisdom', 129–47. Noting some ambiguity in role, however, are W. Grundmann, 'Weisheit', 180–3; A. Jacobson, 'Christology', esp. 230.

61 M.J. Suggs, *Wisdom*, 60–1, 97, 106–8, 130; J. Dunn, *Christology*, 197–206; R. Hamerton-Kelly, *Pre-Existence*, 67–83; F. Burnett, *Testament*, esp. 33–50. Against Suggs, see M. Johnson, 'Reflections', 44–64.

62 M.J. Suggs, *Wisdom*, 37, 56–7; J. Dunn, *Christology*, 197; F. Christ, *Jesus*, 75–6; D. Lührmann, *Redaktion*, 29–3. M. Goulder, *Midrash*, 358; S. Schulz, *Q*, 380 n. 18; G. Stanton, 'Christology', 36; C. Tuckett, *Revival*, 150. O. Linton ('Game', 164) rightly rejects the idea of translation variants.

63 J. Fitzmyer, *Luke*, I, 679; E. Schweizer, *Luke*, 136–7; I.H. Marshall, *Luke*, 303–4. On the special use of δικαιόω, see T.W. Manson, *Sayings*, 70; G. Schrenk, 'δικαιόω', 214–15; C. Tuckett, *Revival*, 149. O. Linton's attempt ('Game', 177–8) to take ἀπό as 'against' and τέκνα as 'sons of the kingdom who will be cast out' fails to accept the parallel between 7:35 and 7:29. Linton himself notes that the use of ἀπό for ὑπό was no problem for Greek readers.

64 *Wisdom*, 35.

65 M. Hengel, 'Lehrer', 154–6. Hengel also draws attention to the adversative καί with which the logion begins.

66 J. Dunn, *Christology*, 198.

67 M. Hengel, 'Lehrer', 155; F. Mussner, 'Kairos', 610 n.2; D. Catchpole, 'Tradition History', 169, 179 n.16; C. Tuckett, *Revival*, 148–51.

68 C. Tuckett, *Revival*, 164–5; see also (*contra* Suggs) M.D. Johnson, 'Reflections', 43–53; A. Jacobson, 'Unity' (*JBL*), 387. M.J. Suggs (*Wisdom*, 39–44) argues for a pre-Christian motif of Sophia sending prophets and messengers, indebted in part to R. Bultmann, 'Hintergrund', 18. The text most often cited is WisSol 7:22 – 8:1. Also arguing on these lines is R. Hamerton-Kelly (*Pre-Existence*, 36), who further cites D. Georgi, 'Hymnus', 263–93.

69 Favouring the originality of the Sophia oracle in Luke to the 'I' saying in Matthew are R. Bultmann, *Tradition*, 114; E. Haenchen, 'Matthäus 23', 53; D.R.A. Hare, *Theme*, 92; O. Steck, *Geschick*, 29; D. Lührmann, *Redaktion*, 46; P. Hoffmann, *Studien*, 164; S. Schulz, *Q*, 336; M. Suggs, *Wisdom*, 14; C. Tuckett, *Revival*, 160; J. Dunn, *Christology*, 201; D. Garland, *Intention*, 172–3. For a contrary view, see W. Kümmel, *Promise*, 80. The absence of a marked interest in Sophia on Luke's part is decisive. For other differences between Matthew and Luke in this pericope, see S. Schulz, *Q*, 336–9; C. Tuckett, *Revival*, 157–62; both emphasize the secondary nature of Matthew's formulation.

70 Both Matthew's σοφοὺς καὶ γραμματεῖς and Luke's ἀποστόλους may be secondary. On Matthew, see Mt 13:52, and cf. J. Dunn, *Christology*, 202; R. Hummel, *Auseinandersetzung*, 27; D. Hill, 'Δίκαιοι', 296–7; O. Steck, *Geschick*, 29–30; G. Strecker, *Weg*, 37–40; S. Schulz, *Q*, 336–7. On Luke, see R. Bultmann, *Tradition*, 114 n.1; E. Haenchen, 'Matthäus 23', 53; G. Klein, 'Verfolgung', 113–24. But ἀπόστολος can be taken in a less specific sense as ἀπεσταλμένος (cf. Mt 23:37 par): see F. Christ, *Jesus*, 122–6; O.J.F. Seitz, 'Commission', 239; O. Steck, *Geschick*, 30–1; S. Schulz, *Q*, 336–7; M. Hengel, 'Lehrer', 157.

71 On Lk 11:49–51 par as an oracle of a Christian prophet, see E.E. Ellis, 'Luke xi.49–51', 157–8. Some identify 'Zechariah' (Lk 11:51; Mt 23:35 adds υἱοῦ Βαραχίου) with Josephus' 'Zechariah son of Βαρεις', murdered by the Zealots before the fall of Jerusalem (*Bell.*, 4:334–44): see the discussion in D. Garland, *Intention*, 182 n.69; O. Steck, *Geschick*, 39–40.

72 If Jesus was the speaker of the lament in the underlying tradition, then it may still be as the representative of Sophia (so Dunn: see above, n.29), but his relationship to Sophia is then even less explicit and he appears to express the expectation of a future figure (the Son of Man?).

73 B. Lindars, *Jesus*, 40; I.H. Marshall, *Luke*, 486–7; J. Wanke, *Kommentarworte*, 59. But the connection with Lk 11:30 par may provide a christological reference.

74 'Christology', 35.

75 *Redaktion*, 24–48.
76 See above, n. 52.
77 *Kommentarworte*, 35ff., 40ff., 56ff.
78 M. Hengel, 'Lehrer', 157. This may be indicated also by the reference to 'Son of Man' in the context of several 'Sophia' logia (cf. Lk 7:34 par, 11:30 par, 9:58 par, and possibly ὁ ἐρχόμενος in 13:35 par). Yet Lk 11:49 par lacks any such reference, and there is little evidence of christological speculation on the relationship between the Son of Man and the representative of Sophia in any of the passages.
79 On the reconstruction of the text, and against an original connection with Mt 11:28–30, see J. Kloppenborg, 'Christology', 132–5.
80 'Christology', 140–3.
81 On the 'Johannine' nature of the passage, see recently, M. Sabbe, 'Mt 11, 27', 363–71. The *religionsgeschichtliche* investigations of Mt 11:27 par have also encompassed a wide variety of explanations for the sayings: e.g., as a Hellenistic revelation saying (R. Bultmann, *Tradition*, 159–60; M. Dibelius, *Tradition*, 279–83; E. Haenchen, 'Gnosis', II, 1653); as comparable to Qumran views of 'knowledge' (W. D. Davies, 'Knowledge', 118–39); as reflecting ideas from Jewish apocalyptic (P. Hoffmann, 'Offenbarung', 270–88, and *Studien*, 118–31, 139–42); as reflecting 'Hellenistic – Jewish' speculation about Sophia (J. Kloppenborg, 'Christology', 145–6). See also the recent investigations of J. Dunn (*Christology*, esp. 200), J. Fitzmyer (*Luke*, II, 867–70), and M. Hengel (*Son of God*, 41ff.), who doubt that 'Son of God' must be a late Hellenistic creation.
82 'Christology', 155 n. 54.
83 See also 1 QH 2:8–10.
84 See M. Hengel, *Judaism*, I, 80, 176–7; J. Kloppenborg, 'Christology', 139 n. 72. For the 'humble' being receptive to wisdom, see Sir 3:17–20; Prov 26:12. WisSol 10:21; 1 En 5:8; 1QS 11:6–7. But it is not usual to find wisdom restricted to the humble and set in stark contrast to the wise.
85 Some parallelism of thought may also exist with Lk 13:35 par. In the time just preceding the Messiah's advent even moral evil would worsen (4 Ezra 6:24, 9:3–4, 5:2).
86 M. Dibelius, *Tradition*, 281; J. Kloppenborg, 'Christology', 135–6.
87 So, rightly, D. Smith, *Christology*, 33; *contra* F. Christ, *Jesus*, 89–90; J. M. Robinson, 'Jesus', 9; J. Crossan, *Fragments*, 196. P. Hoffmann ('Offenbarung', 286) notes: 'bei Philo wird die Weisheit als Sohn bezeichnet'; see also M. Hengel, *Son of God*, 51–6, 57 n. 109. But the fact that various terms may be used in Philo does not relieve one of the necessity of explaining why a particular term appears in a particular context.
88 *Contra* P. Hoffmann, 'Offenbarung', 273–4.
89 *Contra* J. Jeremias, *Theology*, I, 57–61, and possibly I. H. Marshall, *Luke*, 436; A. Polag, *Christologie*, 161–2. M. Hengel (*Son of God*, 63 n. 116) accepts the filial relationship, but criticizes as one-sided K. Berger's attempt ('Hintergrund', 422ff.) to derive

Lk 10:22 par from sapiential understandings of 'teacher' and 'pupil'.
Cf. also W. Grundmann, 'Weisheit', 185—6.

90 Against the view that this phrase is an interpolation, see M. J. Suggs, *Wisdom*, 71—7.

91 *Christology*, 199; M. J. Suggs, *Wisdom*, 91—5.

92 M. Johnson, 'Reflections', 50—2. Dunn, *Christology*, 199, also appeals to the Isaianic servant tradition for such a mediatorial function: Is 42:6, 43:10, 49:6, 45:1, 6.

93 *Christology*, 200. This is also emphasized in Luke by the presence of the beatitude in Lk 10:23—4/Mt 13:16—17: see W. Grundmann, 'Weisheit', 187. In favour of the originality of this conjunction of sayings, see W. Schenk, *Synopse*, 59; A. Polag, *Fragmenta*, 48, and *Christologie*, 162; V. Taylor, 'The Order', 29—30; I. H. Marshall, *Luke*, 431. More hesitant are A. Jacobson, 'Christology', 130; D. Lührmann, *Redaktion*, 61; P. Hoffmann, *Studien*, 287.

94 *Constraints*, 159—68.

95 On the didactic tone of lines 2—4 in Lk 10:22 par, see J. Wanke *Kommentarworte*, 49—50, who considers this the comment of a Christian teacher. But cf. above, n. 89.

96 *Constraints*, 165.

97 See also, recently, J. Kloppenborg, 'Christology', 147.

98 *Ibid.*, 142—3; see also P. Hoffmann, 'Offenbarung', 275; D. Lührmann, *Redaktion*, 65—8, 97, 99; J. Crossan, *Fragments*, 196 ('the emphasis moves from Son/Father towards the believer in Q'); *contra* J. Wanke, *Kommentarworte*, 49—51.

99 A. Jacobson ('Christology', 232—3) also assigns Lk 11:2—4 par, 11:9—13 par, 12:22—34 par, 17:5—6 par, and 4:1—12 par to this 'later' perspective.

100 *Frühjüdische*, esp. 547—52.

101 M. Küchler, *Frühjüdische*, 52—61; M. Hengel, *Judaism*, I, 161—2, 169—75; J. Davis, *Wisdom*; 10—26, 50—4, 60—2.

102 See H. Hübner, *Gesetz*, 212—13. Lk 11:42 par may come near the 'Sophia' saying in Lk 11:49—51 par in the underlying tradition, but it is difficult to conclude that this represents speculation about Torah and Sophia. R. Banks (*Law*, 247 n. 1) refers to a lack of reflection on the Torah in Q. A. Jacobson ('Christology', 187) and S. Schulz (*Q*, 99) argue that the validity of the Law is assumed.

103 S. Schulz (*Q*, 94—116, 169—70) speaks of 'die charismatisch— eschatologische Torahverschärfung' of the earlier Q-community; but see our discussions of the relevant passages.

104 J. Rylaarsdam (*Revelation*, 187—8) speculates that in the NT generally Wisdom appears as Spirit rather than Law because the former preserves the contemporaneity of Wisdom as a living personality coming directly into human experience.

105 W. Grundmann ('Weisheit', esp. 176, 180) argues that Jesus is Wisdom's envoy not with respect to the Law, but rather 'im Horizont des Reiches Gottes', again emphasizing the link with prophetic eschatology.

106 See, e.g., R. Bultmann, 'Wahrheiten', 244ff.; D. Zeller, 'Überlieferung', esp. 94—5, 109; G. von Rad, *Wisdom*, 317 (who describes this in terms of the historical movement from the old wisdom to a later wisdom which attempted to bring man and the world 'back once again into the centre of God's sphere of activity').

107 'Logoi Sophōn', 105.

108 See, e.g., H.-M. Schenke, 'Tendenz', 351—72.

109 On Lk 9:58 par, cf. n. 40, although even Plutarch's somewhat similar saying is not aphoristic in form: see J. Fitzmyer, *Luke*, I, 835. On Lk 7:35 par, see D. Lührmann, *Redaktion*, 29; and see above pp. 125—6. Also on Mt 11:27/Lk 10:22, see J. Jeremias, *Theology*, 60; J. Crossan, *Fragments*, 191—7 (who considers it an 'aphoristic conclusion' to Jesus' prayer in Lk 10:21 par).

110 It is absent, e.g., from the comprehensive treatment of J. Crossan, *Fragments*.

111 B. Lindars (*Jesus Son of Man*, 30) notes that it 'is manifestly untrue of people in general'. This particularly applies if an eschatological function for the Son of Man here is recognized (see S. Schulz, *Q*, 438—9), but it equally applies the more the saying is recognized as a statement specifically about Jesus (A. Jacobson, 'Christology', 132) or about Jesus and those who share his vocation (B. Lindars, *Jesus Son of Man*, 30—1).

112 *Redaktion*, 97, 99.

113 *Q*, 316ff., 461ff.

114 *Christologie*, 127, 137—9, 145.

115 'Christology', 233—4, and his 'Unity' (*JBL*), 382—9.

116 'Christology', 55—6, 62—3.

117 *Ibid.*, 56—8, 62—3.

118 *Ibid.*, 60—5.

119 *Ibid.*, 215—22 (*contra* Schulz, who considers these early).

120 'Lehrer', 160, 163—6; M. Küchler, *Frühjüdische*, 583—6; *contra* D. Lührmann (*Redaktion*, 86—8), who sees them mainly as deriving from Hellenistic Christianity.

121 See above, pp. 51—61.

122 On the latter, see D. Seccombe, *Possessions*, 151—2.

123 See above, pp. 107—10, 121—4, 127—30, 144—9.

124 See also Lk 12:10, 11—12 par.

125 E.g., R. Bultmann, *Jesus*, 48—97, and 'Wahrheiten', 244—54; A. Wilder, *Ethics*; R. Jeske, 'Wisdom'; H. Bald, 'Ethics', 133—53; D. Zeller, 'Überlieferung', 94—111; W. Beardslee, 'Koan', 151—77.

126 D. Lührmann, 'Verweis', especially 188, 195—6; C. Carlston, 'Proverbs', 87—105.

127 'Weisheit', 175—99.

128 *Ibid.*, 183—8.

129 On the mercy of God, see Lk 6:36, at the end of the collection on love of enemy (W. Grundmann, 'Weisheit', 190—1). See also D. Lührmann, 'Verweis', 192, 195—6; H. Bald, 'Ethics', 141, 151—2; D. Zeller, 'Überlieferung', 99—103; but, in contrast, see W. Beardslee, 'Koan', esp. 157—9.

130 'Weisheit', 191–3.
131 *Ibid.*, 195–6.
132 *Ibid.*, 197.
133 'Verweis', 192–6; see also D. Zeller, 'Überlieferung', 94–111.
134 Lührmann ('Verweis', 194) explicitly denies that persuasion was significant. However, D. Zeller ('Überlieferung', 101) does give greater attention to how such sayings may serve to create a feeling of certainty in the hearers.
135 H. Bald ('Ethics', 151–2) argues that for Jesus 'God's activity in creation is not deduced from his eschatological activity, but the certainty of his present and future activity is derived from his creative activity (Matt 6:25ff.)'. Even if this should be true for Jesus, the later bearers of the tradition could not but have been influenced by Jesus' proclamation of God's eschatological rule. It is true, though, that the 'certainty' of this may be reinforced by reference to God's creative activity.
136 G. von Rad, *Wisdom*, 124–7; see also above, p. 22.
137 See above, p. 22.
138 Perhaps also found in Lk 16:9–12; Mt 6:19–20 par.
139 J. Rylaarsdam, *Revelation*, 72.
140 'Koan', esp. 156–9, 170–2.
141 Beardslee does consider the question of Q-sayings, though, in 'Wisdom Tradition', 236–8.
142 Cf. D. Zeller, 'Überlieferung', 102–5, who would however see a more radical tone in Mt 10:28 par. In so far as eschatology is not just concerned with the reversal of this age, but with the fulfilment of promises, the future hope is not purely concerned with future events: see also J. Collins, 'Apocalyptic', 41–3. Regarding the understanding of time in Q, see K. Woschitz, 'Reflexionen', 78–9.
143 The present life is thereby understood as 'responsible': see W. Grundmann, 'Weisheit', 197. R. Jeske, 'Wisdom', 154–5, concludes that in the Jesus-tradition 'wisdom' stresses the present as all that one has access to, and in this sense is a corrective to Jewish apocalyptic.
144 *Redaktion*, 98–9.
145 D. Lührmann, 'Verweis', 188, and *Redaktion*, 98–9, 75–83 (where he draws parallels with the use of OT history in Sir,T12P and other literature).
146 This is noted for Mt 5:39–42 par by C. H. Dodd, *Gospel*, 52–3; J. Piper, *Love*, 100–33, and esp. 136–9. Questioning a catechetical interest in the gospels, see F. V. Filson, 'Teacher', 328; J. P. Brown, 'Parallels', 46; and more specifically against a catechetical interpretation of Q, see W. D. Davies, 'Setting', 366–86, 460–1; H.-E. Tödt, *Son of Man*, 235–53.
147 *Mahnsprüche*, 198. A. Jacobson ('Christology', 134) notes that even the so-called missionary instructions in Q are more an errand of judgement against Israel than actual instructions for missionaries.
148 Perhaps also see Mt 5:25–6 par.
149 See above, p. 177.

150 See above, pp. 172–3.

151 See above, p. 171. There is no other clear reference to σοφοί in the double tradition (but cf. Mt 23:34 (diff Lk 11:49)). The word φρόνιμος does appear, though, in a positive sense in Mt 7:24 (diff Lk 6:48) and particularly in the parable of the prudent and faithful servant in Lk 12:42/Mt 24:45 (also see Lk 16:8b).

152 Questioning the older theory of an 'Antioch source' behind Acts 6:1 – 8:4, see J. Lienhard, 'Acts 6:1–6', 228–30; also N. Walter, 'Anfänge', 388 n. 12. For recent reviews of the entire question of Stephen, the Seven and the Hellenists, see H.-W. Neudorfer, *Stephanuskreis*; G. N. Stanton, 'Stephen', 345–6; M. Hengel, 'Between', 1–29. Calling into question theories of a direct theological affinity between Samaria and the group around Stephen is G. Schneider ('Stephanus', 215ff.), although he does not deny that the mission of the Hellenists may have extended to Samaria; see also E. Richard, 'Acts 7', 190–208.

153 So M. Hengel, 'Between', 13.

154 M. Simón, *St Stephen*, 5, suggests a deeper cause of dissension than food alone; also G. Schneider, 'Stephanus', 237. N. Walter, 'Anfänge', 374–6, suggests that the conflict extended beyond Christian circles in Jerusalem to the Jewish community there.

155 J. Lienhard, 'Acts 6:1–6', 231, who also argues that mentioning the dispute goes against Luke's intent in writing Acts; see also E. Haenchen, *Acts*, 83–4, 268; N. Walter, 'Anfänge', 372–3.

156 E. Haenchen, *Acts*, 266; M. Hengel, 'Between', 13. G. Stanton, 'Stephen', 357, notes that even so the Hellenists are not shown as moving out immediately into Gentile areas (cf. Acts 11:19); see also T. Boman, *Jesus-Überlieferung*, 115; H. Koester, 'GNOMAI', 120.

157 *Geschick*, 265–9, 274–9. Steck considers that Acts 7:51–3 reflects a tradition formulated prior to Luke himself; *contra* E. Haenchen, *Acts*, 289. G. Schneider agrees that the polemical parts of these sayings must precede Luke ('Stephanus', 233–5), and sees Luke's hand mainly in Acts 7:42b–43, 48b–50 and perhaps 22b. He argues also that the Deuteronomistic imagery derives 'aus der Diaspora stammende Judenchristen – möglicherweise die Hellenisten' (234). B. Lindars (*Apologetic*, 20–1) notes: 'it is remarkable that v. 52 is closer to the developed Matthean form of the Q passage than to the Lucan' (referring to Mt 23:35).

158 M. Sabbe, 'Son of Man', 249. Sabbe only cites *one* comparable passage outside the Q-passages of Lk: namely, Acts 3:13–15; but this only refers to the murder of 'the Holy and Righteous One', not to the Deuteronomistic tradition.

159 'Wisdom' is also joined with πνεῦμα in Lk 21:15: see below. See also J. Zmijewski, *Eschatologiereden*, 136–7; E. Haenchen, *Acts*, 271; J. Kilgallen, *Stephen*, 137.

160 J. Lienhard ('Acts 6:1–6', 231–5) has little comment on these words in his analysis of Acts 6:2–4, which he considers largely redactional. He accepts 6:5, however, as 'a received tradition' (*ibid.*, 236).

161 On χάρις, see J. Kilgallen, *Stephen*, 137. R. Morgenthaler (*Statistik*, 90, 132–3, 155) cites for πίστις: 11 times Luke, 15 times Acts; for χάρις: 8 times Luke, 17 times Acts; for πνεῦμα: 36 times Luke, 70 times Acts; for δύναμις: 15 times Luke, 10 times Acts.

162 M. Hengel, 'Between', 18–19; J. Kilgallen, *Stephen*, 49–50. But E. Haenchen (*Acts*, 262) considers that in Acts 6:3 σοφία may mean 'worldly prudence'.

163 E. Richard, *Acts 6:1–8:4*, 348. M. Hengel, 'Between', 12–13, observes that Stephen and the others of the Seven appear more in the role of preachers or missionaries than simply of ones who look after the poor.

164 G. N. Stanton, 'Stephen', 345ff. For a wider review of the study of the speeches in Acts, and especially Acts 6–8, see E. Richard, *Acts 6:1–8:4*, 9–26, 248–54, who also cites other relevant works.

165 All three (Abraham being the third) were depicted as responding to God 'outside' of Palestine, but this may reflect Lukan interests. Note also the comparison with *Pseudo-Jonathan*, cited by E. Richard, *Acts 6:1–8:4*, 350.

166 G. Stanton, 'Stephen', 352.

167 See also J. Kilgallen, *Stephen*, 63–4, 147–8. E. Richard, *Acts 6:1–8:4*, 323 n.183, rather oddly suggests that the proverbial wisdom of Egypt, possessed by Moses and Joseph, is confounded by the higher wisdom/spirit of Stephen. But he himself is aware that the polemical element is not directed against Moses or Joseph but rather against the people's response to them (*ibid.*, 325); nor is there any polemic againt Egypt (*ibid.*, 326).

168 M. Hengel, *Judaism*, I, 129. The growth of 'Solomonic' writings from Proverbs and Qoheleth to PssSol, WisSol, OdesSol and TSol testifies to the importance and breadth of the Solomonic traditions. See also the useful surveys of D. Duling, 'Testament', 944–51, 956–7; L. Feldman, 'Josephus', 68–98; S. Shimoff, *Legends*, 212–310.

169 Occurrences in Jn 10:23; Acts 3:11, 5:12 refer only to the στοά of Solomon.

170 Also G. Stanton, 'Stephen', 352. J. Kilgallen, *Stephen*, 89–90, attempts to differentiate between criticism of the Temple and the attitude towards Solomon.

171 J. Kilgallen, *Stephen*, esp. 97, argues that, although Christ is only mentioned directly in 7:52, Joseph and Moses are used as 'types' of Christ earlier. But the emphasis seems to lie with showing Jesus as the climax to the history of rejected leaders of Israel rather than with any explicit typology; see also E. Haenchen, *Acts*, 286–9. A. Hanson (*Jesus Christ*, 103–4) interestingly suggests that, rather than Moses depicted as a type of Christ in Acts 7:25, 35, we find 'Christ acting as ruler and redeemer through Moses'. Again, we would suggest that the consistent pattern of revelation and response is more emphasized than the work of Christ himself.

172 M. Sabbe, 'Son of Man', 260ff., argues for assimilation by Luke to Lk 22:69.

173 See also Acts 3:14; Lk 23:47. For a possible Messianic background, see E. Haenchen, *Acts*, 206. But J. Kilgallen, *Stephen*, 98–100, points to the idea of ὁ δίκαιος in the wisdom literature, esp. WisSol 2:12–20. M. Simón concludes 'that those who called Jesus "the Righteous One" had no feeling that there was any substantial difference between him and the other righteous ... Thus, the speech of Stephen does not in itself show any sign of a very evolved Christology' (*St Stephen*, 65).

174 M. Scharlemann draws attention to how Stephen's interpretation of the OT differs from the rest of Acts, and to the christological reserve shown in Stephen's speech (*Stephen*, 29); see also M. Simon, *St Stephen*, 43ff.

175 M. Sabbe ('Son of Man', 245) observes regarding Stephen's speech that 'the most widely spread position is that Lk has inserted a previous source on the history of Israel, adapting it to his own perspective'. Sabbe's own view seems to put more emphasis on the speech as a product of Luke, although perhaps using doctrinal themes from the Hellenists (*ibid.*, 247–9).

176 On a historical nucleus to the Hebrews – Hellenists problem, see M. Hengel, *Acts*, 71. On Stephen's speech, see M. Dibelius, *Studies*, 184 (referring to an authentic 'echo' of Stephen's own position); E. Richard, *Acts 6:1–8:4*, 267 (who argues that 'what the author thought Stephen did or would have said is no doubt what one finds in Acts 7'). It is our contention only that this holds particularly for distinctive themes in the speeches which are not typical of Lukan redaction elsewhere. See also M. Scharlemann, *Stephen*, 22–30, who, however, doubts that Stephen was a Hellenist, at least of an anti-Jewish kind (*ibid.*, 52–6).

177 Attempts to link Q with 1 Corinthians have recently come under careful attack by C. Tuckett, '1 Corinthians', 607–19, who also considers sapiential terminology. For a recent attempt to link 1 Cor 1–4 with Lk 10:21–4 par, see P. Richardson, 'Thunderbolt', 91–111. Richardson, though, states: 'This is not to suggest that either Apollos or Paul had any hand in collecting Q-materials!' (*ibid.*, 109).

178 Accepting some possible connection between Q and the Hellenists, see M. Hengel, 'Lehrer', 150, and *Acts*, 72. See also T. Boman, *Jesus-Überlieferung*, 105–20. But Hengel's view that Hellenist theology also involved radical criticism of the Law and the Temple has recently been questioned in F. Watson, *Paul*, 25–6.

Conclusion

1 The greatest disruption is found in Mt 10:26–33 par, which appears to have been extended or re-worked in the early tradition.

2 Cf. R. Riesner, *Lehrer*; G. Theissen, *Biblical Faith*, 93–5, 98–9.

3 'Lehrer', 163–6, 180–8.

4 N. Perrin, *Language*, 48–54, and 'Wisdom', 543–72; W. Beardslee, 'Wisdom Tradition', 238–9; 'Koan', 151–77; 'Saving', 57–72. See

also on wisdom admonitions D. Zeller, *Mahnsprüche*, 147–84, and, more generally, his 'Überlieferung', 94–111. On wisdom and Jesus' eschatology, see R. Jeske, 'Structure'.
5 'Proverbs', 104–5.

Appendix

1 See also Mk 3:23–7, 10:23–31, in which sayings of an aphoristic nature are scattered.
2 Cf. E. Trocmé, *Formation*, 38. On Mk 4:21–5, see also V. Taylor, *St Mark*, 262–3; but, more recently, finding a coherent composition, is J. Dupont, 'Marc 4, 21–25', 201–9. On Mk 2:19–22, see E. Schweizer, *Mark*, 67.
3 R. Bultmann, *Tradition*, 149–50; V. Taylor, *St Mark*, 408–10; E. Schweizer, *Mark*, 196–7; but, for reservations about a previously existing catechism, see H.-W. Kuhn, *Sammlungen*, 32–6; R. Schnackenburg, 'Markus 9, 33–50', 142–3, 148–50; H. Fleddermann, 'Discipleship', 57–75.
4 On cross-bearing, see E. Dinkler, 'Kreuzsymbols', 148–72, and 'Kreuztagen', 110–29, who sees it as a familiar, almost semi-proverbial symbol denoting devout service. But, against this theory, see D. Seccombe, *Possessions*, 109, who states that 'no evidence of such an image exists prior to the gospels'; and J. Griffiths ('Cross', 358–64), who sees a more specific reference to crucifixion, possibly alluding to non-violent political resistance to Rome.
5 W. Beardslee ('Saving', 61–4) describes the background evidence for the motif of gaining one's life by losing it: it was used as an encouragement in war (Xenophon and the Syriac *Sayings of the Wise Menander*), as sacrifice to a principle (Socrates), as a response to a divine command (Epictetus), or as a loyalty between two persons (Pindar, Euripides).
6 E. Best, *Following*, 42; J. Lambrecht, 'Q-Influence', 288–9.
7 V. Taylor, *St Mark*, 380; E. Best, *Following*, 37. The indications of persecution are the command to 'take up his cross' (8:34b) and the sayings about forfeiting one's life (8:35, 36–7). G. Schwarz ('ἀπαρνησάσθω', 109–12) interestingly suggests 'deny' meant originally 'consider as a foreigner', referring to rejection by Jews.
8 The ἐμοῦ καί (8:35b) is likely to be in the Markan text despite its absence in p[45], D, 28, and other MSS; see R. Pesch, *Markus*, II, 57; B. Metzger, *Commentary*, 99.
9 D. Zeller, *Mahnsprüche*, 52. R. Bultmann (*Tradition*, 111) classifies Mk 8:35 as an 'I' saying.
10 E. Best, 'Collection', 11, suggests Mark may have been responsible for the conditional formulation of 8:34, changing it from a relative clause (R-form) to place the hearer more firmly in the position of making a response. See also Lk 14:26 par.
11 Among others, W. Marxsen, *Mark*, 125; E. Schweizer, *Mark*, 176; J. Gnilka, *Markus*, II, 22. There is less consensus regarding the words ἕνεκεν ἐμοῦ, which do not appear in Lk 17:33; Jn 12:25. But

W. Beardslee ('Saving', 66) argues that some relational element, 'for something', is essential to the saying if self-interest is not to be dominant.

12 H. C. Kee, *Community*, 140–4, seems to consider this saying in connection with the 'sentences of holy law' classified by Käsemann; but cf. E. Best, *Following*, 50 n. 70. Best argues also that Mk 8:38 is less 'juridical' than 'missionary' (*ibid.*, 43).

13 J. Crossan, *Fragments*, 167–8, argues that the structure of the collection is chiastic, which may also show the difference between this and the double-tradition collections.

14 J. Lambrecht, 'Q-Influence', 289. The use of γάρ in 8:35, 36, 37, 38 emphasizes also the close connection of these sayings, but it is not certain how far these are due to Mark himself: see, recently, E. Pryke, *Style*, 126–35.

15 F. Neirynck, *Duality*, 125–6.

16 E. Best, *Following*, 41, interprets ψυχή as 'the real or essential person', and not just 'physical life'; against E. Haenchen, *Weg*, 298. See also G. Dautzenberg, *Leben*, 13–48, 51–82; K.-G. Reploh, *Markus*, 132–7; E. Schweizer, 'ψυχή', 642; J. Gnilka, *Markus*, II, 24–5.

17 B. Lindars (*Jesus Son of Man*, 51) notes that this phrase is 'more characteristic of Q than of Mark and therefore probably added in the pre-Markan stage'; see also E. Best, *Following*, 43, *contra* Horstmann. W. Schenk ('Einfluss', 143) would attribute this and almost all other differences to Markan redaction of Q-material; so also for Mk 8:34 relative to Mt 10:38 par (*ibid.*, 156–8).

18 Warning against too firm a distinction, however, is A. J. B. Higgins, *Son of Man*, 82.

19 M. Casey, *Son of Man*, 162–4, sees the reference to ἔλθη as particularly significant; see also H.-E. Tödt, *Son of Man*, 44–5. The reference to angels is shared with Lk 12:9 but not Mt 10:33.

20 R. Pesch ('Autorität', 36–7) disputes Kümmel's view that Mark's 'ashamed of' is more original than the Q 'deny', especially since the pairing of 'deny' with 'confess' is better than with 'ashamed', and because 'ashamed' is closely bound with the addition καὶ τοὺς ἐμοὺς λόγους (see below n. 21). B. Lindars (*Jesus Son of Man*, 51), however, prefers to argue for translation variants; see also his 'Advocate', 484–8.

21 This is probably a secondary addition, matching the reference to 'gospel' in 8:35: see J. Gnilka, *Markus*, II, 22–3; E. Best, *Following*, 43; R. Pesch, 'Autorität', 37–9 (who nonetheless sees it as pre-Markan); W. Schmithals, 'Menschensohn', 442.

22 N. Perrin, 'Mark ix 1', 67–70, views 9:1 as produced by Mark 'as the promise antithetical to the warning contained in viii 38'. Even if it is not a Markan creation, it does serve this function.

23 For καὶ ἔλεγεν αὐτοῖς as a typical Markan linking phrase, see J. Jeremias, *Parables*, 14; E. Best, *Following*, 31, 44–5.

24 So, e.g., J. Gnilka, *Markus*, II, 21–9; R. Pesch, *Markus*, II, 57–68; E. Haenchen, 'Komposition', 96 (who sees Mk 8:27–9:1 as 'eine Komposition des Evangelisten'); H. Anderson, *Mark*, 217–22.

25 So, e.g., R. Pesch, 'Autorität', 26–39; S. Schulz, *Q*, 66–7; A.J.B. Higgins, *Son of Man*, 80–4; H.-E. Tödt, *Son of Man*, 40–7; M.D. Hooker, *Son of Man*, 119; W. Schenk, 'Einfluss', 143–4, 146–7. See also the review by C.K. Barrett, 'Ashamed', 24–8; and the analysis by W.G. Kümmel (*Promise*, 44–6) who states, however, that the original wording of the saying cannot be reconstructed.

26 *Following*, 31.

27 'Q-Influence', 297–8. Uncertainty continues, e.g., on whether Mark used catchwords himself in compiling 4:21–5 (see H. Anderson, *Mark*, 135; J. Gnilka, *Markus*, I, 178) and 9:42–9, 50 (see J. Gnilka, *Markus*, II, 67; R. Pesch, *Markus*, II, 113).

28 J. Lambrecht, 'Q-Influence', 297–8, surmises that Mark himself brought together a 'double Q-context, that of a group of sayings ('Relatives', 'Cross' and 'Life', uncertain place in Q) and that of the 'Ashamed-of' saying (presumably part of the 'No fear'-section in Q; cf. Lk 12:2–12)'. He has more difficulty, however, in fitting in 8: 36–7, which he attempts to relate to another Q-unit, Lk 12:22–34, containing the term ψυχή and a double τί-question (*ibid.*, 301–2). Lambrecht in effect supposes an extensive use of different sections of Q by Mark, which goes considerably beyond our own hypothesis below.

29 *Son of Man*, 117.

30 *Studien*, 34.

31 *Formation*, 123 n.1.

32 *Markus*, II, 57.

33 *Markus*, 174–8.

34 H. Anderson, *Mark*, 217; W.L. Knox, *Sources*, I, 63–5.

35 See also above, pp. 151–2. Noting the similarity between the structure of this group of sayings and the aphoristic collections of the double tradition adds a new dimension to the debate about whether the doublets represent a double-tradition formulation.

36 Further development may also have occurred in the double tradition, such as the combination with the saying in Mt 10:39 (cf. Lk 17:33; but also ἔτι τε καὶ τὴν ψυχὴν ἑαυτοῦ in 14:26!). It is doubtful whether such a grouping included all of Mt 10:26–39, though: see R. Laufen, *Doppelüberlieferungen*, 332–3.

37 For such doublets, see esp. R. Laufen, *Doppelüberlieferungen*.

38 E. Best, 'Collection', 15–16; R. Laufen, *Doppelüberlieferungen*, 385–6. Contrast W. Schenk, 'Einfluss', esp. 161–3, who speculates that Mark's limited use of Q is due to dislike of the Sophia-christology of the Q-redaction (*ibid.*, 162).

39 For other changes, see E. Haenchen, 'Komposition', 96–109; J. Fitzmyer, *Luke*, I, 783–90; R. Gundry, *Matthew*, 339–41.

40 Assigned to Q by S. Schulz, *Q*, 430–3, 446–9; W. Schmithals, *Lukas*, 161; J. Fitzmyer, *Luke*, II, 1060; A. Polag, *Fragmenta*, 70–1; I.H. Marshall, *Luke*, 591. Less certain are W. Grundmann, *Lukas*, 301; D. Seccombe, *Possessions*, 100.

41 But cf. the conjecture of E. Hirsch (noted by W. Grundmann, *Lukas*, 301–2) that Lk 14:28–32 was in the expanded version of Q used by Luke (which he designated Lu I).

42 R. Bultmann, *Tradition*, 194–5; J. Jeremias, *Parables*, 90–2. Bultmann cites Mk 3:24–5; Mt 13:31–3, 44–6; Lk 15:4–11 as other examples of double similitudes in the tradition, of which Mk 3:24–5 and Lk 14:28–32 are considered 'original' connections. Also cf. Lk 15:4–10, which is formulated in rhetorical questions.

43 A third parable of a similar kind is found in GThom 98.

44 The Lukan form of the 'salt' saying seems to draw heavily on a double-tradition variant of Mk 9:49–50, except for the opening clause 'salt is good': see S. Schulz, *Q*, 470–1; R. Schnackenburg, 'Salz', 180. D. Seccombe, *Possessions*, 116, describes verses 34–5 as 'loosely attached' to vv. 26–33, but does consider them as concluding sayings brought here by Luke.

45 O. Cullmann, 'Salz', 197; J. Latham, *Salt*, 212–14; M. Krämer, 'Ihr seid', 137–8 (who sees a double conclusion); I. H. Marshall, *Luke*, 591; E. Schweizer, *Lukas*, 159–60.

46 R. Bultmann, *Tradition*, 160, 170–1; J. Dupont, 'Renoncer', 568–70; F. Horn, *Glaube*, 195; W. Schmithals, *Lukas*, 161–2; W. Grundmann, *Lukas*, 303; R. Karris, 'Poor', 121; H.-J. Degenhardt, *Lukas*, 111 (with reservations); I. H. Marshall, *Luke*, 591 ('an editorial composition, based on Q'). For an attempt to relate it more to tradition, see D. Mealand, *Poverty*, 30–1, 57–8, 114 n. 51.

47 The absence of a supporting clause in Lk 14:26–7 can also be contrasted with Matthew's Q-version, where a maxim in Mt 10:39 follows the exhortations in Mt 10:37–8. On the original form of these sayings, see J. Gnilka, 'Martyriumsparänese', 232–4, who generally favours Luke's version, except for the conditional formulation of Lk 14:26 and the interesting inclusion of 'and even his own life' in Lk 14:26. Gnilka views the sharp, negative formulation as unique: 'Diese Form der Martyriumsparänese besitzt nichts Vergleichbares in der Umwelt' (*ibid.*, 234). D. Seccombe, *Possessions*, 102–3, rejects Degenhardt's view that this applies mainly to church office-bearers in Luke.

48 The view that the 'parables' in Lk 14:28–32 refer to *God's* having calculated correctly (thus assuring those facing difficulties) is put by C.-H. Hunzinger, 'Unbekannte Gleichnisse', 211–17; J. D. M. Derrett, 'Nisi Dominus', 241–61. Unlike the others, Derrett specifically accepts this interpretation for the Lukan context. More prevalent opinion, though, is that all the sayings in their Lukan context of 14:26ff. refer to the actions of disciples or would-be disciples: see J. Dupont, 'Renoncer', 572–4; F. Horn, *Glaube*, 199–201; R. Schnackenburg, 'Salz', 182; R. Karris, 'Poor', 120–1; W. Schmithals, *Lukas*, 161–2. Attempts to see a primary reference in Luke to Jewish leaders is rightly rejected in O. Cullmann, 'Salz', 196; C. E. Carlston, *Parables*, 87–9; J. Latham, *Salt*, 213.

49 J. Jeremias, *Parables*, 106. C.-H. Hunzinger, 'Unbekannte Gleichnisse', 214, draws attention to a similar mixing of themes in Lk 9:
57–62.
50 See the efforts of J. Dupont, 'Renoncer', 561–82; F. Horn, *Glaube*,
194–201.
51 For the opinion that it was a Lukan compilation, see J. Lambrecht,
'Q-Influence', 296.

BIBLIOGRAPHY

Amstutz, Joseph, 'ΑΠΛΟΤΗΣ. *Eine begriffsgeschichtliche Studie zum jüdisch–christlichen Griechisch*, Theoph. 19 (Bonn, 1968)

Anderson, Hugh, *The Gospel of Mark*, NCeB (London, 1976)

Arthur, Rose Horman, *The Wisdom Goddess. Feminine Motifs in Eight Nag Hammadi Documents* (Lanham/New York/London, 1984)

Arvedson, Tomas, *Das Mysterium Christi. Eine Studie zu Mt 11.25–30*, AMNSU 7 (Leipzig/Uppsala, 1937)

Bailey, Kenneth E., *Poet and Peasant. A Literary Cultural Approach to the Parables in Luke* (Grand Rapids, Mich., 1976)

Bald, Hans, 'Eschatological or Theocentric Ethics? Notes on the Relationship between Eschatology and Ethics in Jesus' Preaching', in B. Chilton (ed.), *The Kingdom of God in the Teaching of Jesus* (London, 1984), 133–53.

Bammel, Ernst, 'Das Ende von Q', in O. Böcher und K. Haacker (eds.), *Verborum Veritas. Festschrift für Gustav Stählin zum 70. Geburtstag* (Wuppertal, 1970), 39–50

Banks, Robert, *Jesus and the Law in the Synoptic Tradition*, MSSNTS 28 (Cambridge, 1975)

Barrett, C.K., 'I Am Not Ashamed of the Gospel', in *Foi et salut selon S. Paul (Épître aux Romains 1,16). Colloque Oecuménique à l'Abbaye de S. Paul, Hors les Murs, 16–21 Avril 1968*, AnBib 42 (Rome, 1970), 19–41.

Barth, Gerhard, 'Auseinandersetzungen um die Kirchenzucht im Umkreis des Matthäusevangeliums', *ZNW*, 69 (1978), 158–77

'Matthew's Understanding of the Law', in G. Bornkamm, G. Barth and H.J. Held (eds.), *Tradition and Interpretation in Matthew*, 2nd edn (London, 1982), 58–164

Barth, Markus, 'The Dishonest Steward and His Lord: Reflections on Luke 16:1–13', in D.Y. Hadidian (ed.), *From Faith to Faith. Essays in Honor of Donald G. Miller on his Seventieth Birthday*, Pittsburgh Theological Monograph Series 31 (Pittsburgh, Pa, 1979), 65–73

Bartsch, H.-W., 'Traditionsgeschichtliches zur goldenen Regel und zum Aposteldekret', *ZNW*, 75 (1984), 128–32

Bauer, Johannes B., '"Wer sein Leben retten will ..." Mk 8,35 Parr.', in J. Blinzler, O. Kuss, F. Mussner (eds.), *Neutestamentliche Aufsätze. Festschrift für Prof. Josef Schmid zum 70. Geburtstag* (Regensburg, 1963), 7–10

Beardslee, William A., *Literary Criticism of the New Testament*, Guides to Biblical Scholarship (Philadelphia, 1971)

'Parable, Proverb, and Koan', in his *The Poetics of Faith. Essays offered to Amos Niven Wilder*, Part I: *Rhetoric, Eschatology and Ethics in the New Testament*, Semeia 12 (Missoula, Mont., 1978), 151–77

'Proverbs in the Gospel of Thomas', in D. E. Aune (ed.), *Studies in New Testament and Early Christian Literature: Essays in Honor of Allen P. Wikgren*, NT.S 33 (Leiden, 1972), 92–103

'Saving One's Life By Losing It', *JAAR*, 47 (1979), 57–72

'The Wisdom Tradition and the Synoptic Gospels', *JAAR*, 35 (1967), 231–40

'Uses of the Proverb in the Synoptic Gospels ', *Interp.*, 24 (1970), 61–73

Beare, Francis Wright, *The Gospel according to Matthew. A Commentary* (Oxford, 1981)

Berger, Klaus, 'Materialien zu Form und Überlieferungsgeschichte neutestamentlicher Gleichnisse', *NT*, 15 (1973), 1–37

'Zu den sogenannten Sätzen heiligen Rechts', *NTS*, 17 (1970), 10–40

'Zum traditionsgeschichtlichen Hintergrund christologischer Hoheitstitel', *NTS*, 17 (1971), 391–425

Best, Ernest, 'An Early Sayings Collection', *NT*, 18 (1976), 1–16

Following Jesus. Discipleship in the Gospel of Mark, JSNT Supplement Series 4 (Sheffield, 1981)

'Mark iii.20, 21, 31–35', *NTS*, 22 (1976), 309–19

Betz, Hans Dieter, 'Matthew vi.22f and Ancient Greek Theories of Vision', in Ernest Best, R. McL. Wilson (eds.), *Text and Interpretation. Studies in the New Testament Presented to Matthew Black* (Cambridge, 1979), 43–56

Plutarch's Theological Writings and Early Christian Literature, SCHNT 3 (Leiden, 1975)

'The Logion of the Easy Yoke and of Rest (Matt 11:28–30)' in *JBL*, 86 (1967), 10–24

Biguzzi, Giancarlo, 'Mc. 11,23–25 e il Pater', *RivBib*, 27 (1979), 57–68

Black, Matthew, *An Aramaic Approach to the Gospels and Acts*, with an Appendix on 'The Son of Man' by Geza Vermes, 3rd edn (Oxford, 1967)

The Book of Enoch or 1 Enoch. A New English Edition, SVTP 7 (Leiden, 1985)

Blenkinsopp, Joseph, *Wisdom and Law in the Old Testament. The Ordering of Life in Israel and Early Judaism* (Oxford, 1983)

Boman, Thorleif, *Die Jesus-Überlieferung im Lichte der neueren Volkskunde* (Göttingen, 1967)

Bonnard, P.-É., 'De la Sagesse personnifiée dans l'Ancien Testament à la Sagesse en personne dans le Nouveau', in M. Gilbert (ed.), *La Sagesse de l'Ancien Testament*, BEThL 51 (Louvain, 1979), 117–49

La Sagesse en Personne annoncée et venue: Jésus Christ, LeDiv 44 (Paris, 1966)

Boring, M. Eugene, 'How May We Identify Oracles of Christian Prophets in the Synoptic Tradition? Mark 3:28–29 as a Test Case', *JBL*, 91 (1972), 501–21

Sayings of the Risen Jesus. Christian Prophecy in the Synoptic Tradition, MSSNTS 46 (Cambridge, 1982)

Bornkamm, Günther, 'Der Aufbau der Bergpredigt', *NTS*, 24 (1978), 419–32
'End-Expectation and Church in Matthew', in G. Bornkamm, G. Barth, H. J. Held (eds.), *Tradition and Interpretation in Matthew* (London, 1963), 15–57

Braun, Herbert, *Qumran und das neue Testament*, 2 vols. (Tübingen, 1966) *Spätjüdisch-häretischer und frühchristlicher Radikalismus. Jesus von Nazareth und die essenische Qumransekte*, II: *Die Synoptiker*, 2nd edn (Tübingen, 1969)

Broer, Ingo, 'Die Antithesen und der Evangelist Mattäus. Versuch eine alte These zu revidieren', *BZ*, 19 (1975), 50–63

Brown, John Pairman, 'Synoptic Parallels in the Epistles and Form-History', *NTS*, 10 (1963), 27–48

Brown, Raymond E., *The Gospel according to John*, 2 vols., AncB 29, 29A (London/Dublin/Melbourne, 1966–72)

Brown, Schuyler, 'The Matthean Apocalypse', *JSNT*, 4 (1979), 2–27
'The Mission to Israel in Matthew's Central Section (Mt 9.35–11.1)', *ZNW*, 69 (1978), 73–90

Brox, Norbert, 'Suchen und Finden. Zur Nachgeschichte von Mt 7,7b/Lk 11,9b', in P. Hoffmann *et al.* (eds.), *Orientierung an Jesus. Zur Theologie der Synoptiker. Für Josef Schmid* (Freiburg/Basle/Vienna, 1973), 17–36

Bryce, Glendon E., '"Better"-Proverbs: An Historical and Structural Study' in L. C. McGaughy (ed.), *The Society of Biblical Literature 1972 Proceedings [108th Annual Meeting, 1–5 September 1972, Los Angeles]. Book of Seminar Papers*, Vol. II (1972), 343–54
'Book Review: *The Intellectual Tradition in the Old Testament* by R. N. Whybray', *JBL*, 94 (1975), 596–8

Bultmann, Rudolf, 'Allgemeine Wahrheiten und christliche Verkündigung. Friedrich Gogarten zum 70. Geburtstag', *ZThK*, 54 (1957), 244–54 (= 'General Truths and Christian Proclamation', in his *History and Hermeneutic*, JTC 4 (1967), 153–162)
'Der religionsgeschichtliche Hintergrund des Prologs zum Johannes-Evangelium', in E. Dinkler (ed.), *Exegetica. Aufsätze zur Erforschung des Neuen Testaments* (Tübingen, 1967), 10–35
'Die Bedeutung der neuerschlossenen mandäischen und manichäischen Quellen für das Verständnis des Johannesevangeliums', in E. Dinkler (ed.), *Exegetica. Aufsätze zur Erforschung des Neuen Testaments* (Tübingen, 1967), 55–104
Die Geschichte der synoptischen Tradition, FRLANT NF 12, 3rd edn (Göttingen, 1957) (= *The History of the Synoptic Tradition*, trans. J. Marsh, 2nd edn (Oxford, 1972))
Jesus and the Word (London/Glasgow, 1958)
'The Study of the Synoptic Gospels', in F. C. Grant (ed.), *Form Criticism: A New Method of New Testament Research* (Chicago/New York, 1934)

Burnett, Fred W., *The Testament of Jesus–Sophia. A Redaction-Critical Study of the Eschatological Discourse in Matthew* (Washington DC, 1981)

Cadbury, Henry J., *Jesus. What Manner of Man?*, Shaffer Lectures for 1946 (New York, 1948)

The Making of Luke–Acts (London, 1961)

'The Single Eye', *HThR*, 47 (1954), 69–74

The Style and Literary Method of Luke, HThS 6 (Cambridge, MA/ London, 1920)

Caird, George B., 'Expounding the Parables: I. The Defendant (Matthew 5:25f.; Luke 12:58f.)', *ET*, 77 (1965), 36–9

The Gospel of St Luke, PGC (London, 1968)

Cangh, J.-M. van, 'Par l'esprit de Dieu – par le doigt de Dieu. Mt 12,28 par. Lc 11,20', in J. Delobel (ed.), *Logia. Les Paroles de Jésus – The Sayings of Jesus. Mémorial Joseph Coppens*, BEThL 59 (Louvain, 1982), 337–42

Carlston, Charles E., 'Proverbs, Maxims, and the Historical Jesus', *JBL*, 99 (1980), 87–105

'Reviews: *Die Überlieferungsgeschichte der Bergpredigt.* By Hans-Theo Wrege', *JAAR*, 38 (1970), 104–6

The Parables of the Triple Tradition (Philadelphia, Pa, 1975)

'Wisdom and Eschatology in Q', in J. Delobel (ed.), *Logia. Les Paroles de Jésus – The Sayings of Jesus. Mémorial Joseph Coppens*, BEThL 59 (Louvain, 1982), 101–19

Carrington, Philip, *The Primitive Christian Catechism. A Study in the Epistles* (Cambridge, 1940)

Casey, Maurice, *Son of Man. The Interpretation and Influence of Daniel 7* (London, 1979)

Catchpole, David R., 'Jesus and the Community of Israel. The Inaugural Discourse in Q', *JRLB*, 68 (1986), 296–316

'Q and "The Friend at Midnight" (Luke xi.5–8/9)', *JThS*, n.s. 34 (1983), 407–24

'Reproof and Reconciliation in the Q Community. A Study in the Tradition history of Mt 18, 15–17.21–22/Lk 17, 3–4', *Studien zum Neuen Testament und seiner Umwelt*, 8 (1983), 79–90

'The Angelic Son of Man in Luke 12:8', *NT*, 24 (1982), 255–65

'The Ravens, the Lilies and the Q Hypothesis. A Form-Critical Perspective on the Source-Critical Problem', *Studien zum Neuen Testament und seiner Umwelt*, 6–7 (1981–2), 77–87

'Tradition History', in I. Howard Marshall (ed.), *New Testament Interpretation. Essays on Principles and Methods* (Exeter, 1977), 165–80

Charlesworth, James H., *The Old Testament Pseudepigrapha*, I: *Apocalyptic Literature and Testaments* (London, 1983)

Christ, Felix, *Jesus Sophia. Die Sophia-Christologie bei den Synoptikern*, AThANT 57 (Zürich, 1970)

Clark, Donald Lemen, *Rhetoric in Greco-Roman Education* (New York, 1957)

Clark, Kenneth W., 'Worship in the Jerusalem Temple after A.D. 70', *NTS*, 6 (1960), 269–80

Clarke, M. L., *Higher Education in the Ancient World* (London, 1971)

Collins, John J., 'Apocalyptic Eschatology as the Transcendence of Death', *CBQ*, 36 (1974), 21–43

'Proverbial Wisdom and the Yahwist Vision', in J. D. Crossan (ed.), *Gnomic Wisdom*, Semeia 17 (Chico, Calif., 1980), 1–18

Conzelmann, Hans, *An Outline of the Theology of the New Testament* (London, 1969)

1 Corinthians, trans. J. Leitch, Hermeneia (Philadelphia, Pa, 1975)

'Paulus und die Weisheit', *NTS*, 12 (1965–6), 231–44

'φῶς, κτλ.', in *TDNT* IX, 310–58

'The Mother of Wisdom', in James M. Robinson (ed.), *The Future of Our Religious Past. Essays in Honour of Rudolf Bultmann* (London, 1971), 230–43

The Theology of St Luke (London, 1960)

Couroyer, B., 'De la mesure dont vous mesurez il vous sera mesuré', *RB*, 77 (1970), 366–70

Creed, John M., *The Gospel according to St Luke. The Greek Text with Introduction, Notes and Indices* (London, 1930)

Crenshaw, James L., 'Impossible Questions, Sayings, and Tasks', in J. D. Crossan (ed.), *Gnomic Wisdom*, Semeia 17 (Chico, Calif., 1980), 19–34

'Method in Determining Wisdom Influence upon "Historical" Literature', *JBL*, 88 (1969), 129–42

Old Testament Wisdom: An Introduction (London, 1982)

'Prolegomenon', in James L. Crenshaw (ed.), *Studies in Ancient Israelite Wisdom*, LBS (New York, 1976), 1–45

'Wisdom', in John H. Hayes (ed.), *Old Testament Form Criticism* (San Antonio, Tex., 1974), 225–64

'Wisdom and Authority: Sapiential Rhetoric and Its Warrants', in J. A. Emerton (ed.), *Congress Volume: Vienna 1980*, VT.S 32 (Leiden, 1981), 10–29

Crossan, John Dominic, *A Fragile Craft. The Work of Amos Niven Wilder*, SBL Biblical Scholarship in North America 3 (Chico, Calif., 1981)

In Fragments. The Aphorisms of Jesus (San Francisco, Calif., 1983)

In Parables. The Challenge of the Historical Jesus (New York, 1973)

'Kingdom and Children. A Study in the Aphoristic Tradition', in K. H. Richards (ed.), *SBL 1982 Seminar Papers*, SBL Seminar Papers 21 (Chico, Calif., 1982), 63–80

'Mark and the Relatives of Jesus', *NT*, 15 (1973), 81–113

(ed.), *Paul Ricoeur on Biblical Hermeneutics*, Semeia 4 (Missoula, Mont., 1975)

Raid on the Articulate. Comic Eschatology in Jesus and Borges (New York, 1976)

Cullmann, Oscar, 'Das Gleichnis vom Salz. Zur frühesten Kommentierung eines Herrenworts durch die Evangelisten', in K. Fröhlich (ed.), *Oscar Cullmann: Vorträge und Aufsätze 1925–1962* (Tübingen/Zürich, 1966), 192–201

The Christology of the New Testament, NTLi, 2nd edn (London, 1967)

Dalman, Gustav, *Jesus–Jeschua. Die drei Sprachen Jesu: Jesus in der Synagogue, auf dem Berge, beim Passahmahl, am Kreuz* (Leipzig, 1922)

Daniel, Constantin, 'Les Esséniens et "Ceux qui sont dans les maisons des rois" (Matthieu 11,7–8 et Luc 7,24–25)', *RdQ*, 6 (1967), 261–77

Dautzenberg, Gerhard, *Sein Leben Bewahren. Ψυχή in den Herrenworten der Evangelien*, StANT 14 (Munich, 1966)

Davies, Stevan L., *The Gospel of Thomas and Christian Wisdom* (New York, 1983)

Davies, W. D., '"Knowledge" in the Dead Sea Scrolls and Matthew 11: 25–30', *HThR*, 46 (1953), 113–39

Paul and Rabbinic Judaism. Some Rabbinic Elements in Pauline Theology, rev. edn (New York/Evanston, 1967)

The Setting of the Sermon on the Mount (Cambridge, 1966)

Davis, James A., *Wisdom and Spirit. An Investigation of 1 Corinthians 1.18 – 3.20 against the Background of Jewish Sapiential Traditions in the Greco-Roman Period* (Lanham/New York/London, 1984)

Degenhardt, Hans-Joachim, *Lukas. Evangelist der Armen. Besitz und Besitzverzicht in den lukanischen Schriften. Eine traditions- und redaktionsgeschichtliche Untersuchung* (Stuttgart, 1965)

Deissner, Kurt, 'μέτρον, κτλ.', in *TDNT*, IV, 632–4

Denaux, A., 'Der Spruch von den zwei Wegen im Rahmen des Epilogs der Bergpredigt (Mt 7,13–14 par. Lk 13,23–24). Tradition und Redaktion', in J. Delobel (ed.), *Logia. Les Paroles de Jésus – The Sayings of Jesus. Mémorial Joseph Coppens*, BEThL 59 (Louvain, 1982), 305–35

Derrett, J. Duncan M., 'Fresh Light on St Luke xvi: I. The Parable of the Unjust Steward', *NTS*, 7 (1961), 198–219

'Law in the New Testament: The Parable of the Talents and Two Logia', *ZNW*, 61 (1965), 184–95

'Mt 23,8–10 a Midrash on Is 54,13 and Jer 31,33–34', *Bib.*, 62 (1981), 372–86

'Nisi Dominus Aedificaverit Domum: Towers and Wars (Lk XIV 28–32)', *NT*, 19 (1977), 241–61

'Salted with Fire. Studies in Texts: Mark 9:42–50', *Theol.*, 76 (1973), 364–8

'"Take Thy Bond ... and Write Fifty" (Luke xvi.6). The Nature of the Bond', *JThS*, n.s. 23 (1972), 438–40

'The Light under a Bushel: The Hanukkah Lamp?', *ET*, 78 (1966), 18

'The Merits of the Narrow Gate (Mt. 7:13–14, Lk. 13:24)', *JSNT*, 15 (1982), 20–9

'"You Build the Tombs of the Prophets" (Lk. 11,47–51, Mt. 23,29–31)', in F. L. Cross (ed.), *StEv IV: Papers Presented to the Third International Congress on New Testament Studies Held at Christ Church Oxford 1965*, Part I: *The New Testament Scriptures* (= TU 102 (Berlin, 1968)), 187–93

Descamps, A., 'La Composition littéraire de Luc XVI 9–13', *NT*, 1 (1956), 47–53

Devisch, M., 'La relation entre l'évangile de Marc et le document Q', in M. Sabbe (ed.), *L'Evangile selon Marc. Tradition et rédaction*, BEThL 34 (Louvain, 1974), 59–91

'Le document Q, source de Matthieu. Problématique actuelle', in M. Didier (ed.), *L'Evangile selon Matthieu: Rédaction et théologie*, BEThL 29 (Gembloux, 1972), 71–97

Dibelius, Martin, *Die Formgeschichte des Evangeliums*, 5th edn (Tübingen, 1966) (= *From Tradition to Gospel*, Library of Theological Translations (Cambridge/London, 1971))

Dihle, Albrecht, *Die Goldene Regel. Eine Einführung in die Geschichte der antiken und frühchristlichen Vulgärethik*, SAW 7 (Göttingen, 1962)

Dinkler, Erich, 'Jesu Wort vom Kreuztragen', in W. Eltester (ed.), *Neutestamentliche Studien für Rudolf Bultmann zu seinem siebzigsten Geburtstag am 20. August 1954*, BZNW 21, 2nd edn (Berlin, 1957), 110–29

'Zur Geschichte des Kreuzsymbols', *ZThK*, 48 (1951), 148–72

Dodd, C. H., *Gospel and Law. The Relation of Faith and Ethics in Early Christianity*, BLA 3 (Cambridge, 1951)

Parables of the Kingdom (Glasgow, 1978)

Drury, John, *Tradition and Design in Luke's Gospel. A Study in Early Christian Historiography* (London, 1976)

Duling, Dennis C., 'Testament of Solomon', in James H. Charlesworth (ed.), *The Old Testament Pseudepigrapha*, I: *Apocalyptic Literature and Testaments* (London, 1983), 935–88

Dundas, Alan (ed.), *The Evil Eye. A Folklore Casebook* (New York/London, 1981)

Dunn, James D. G., *Christology in the Making. A New Testament Inquiry into the Origins of the Doctrine of the Incarnation* (London, 1980)

Jesus and the Spirit. A Study of the Religious and Charismatic Experience of Jesus and the First Christians as Reflected in the New Testament (London, 1975)

'Prophetic "I"-Sayings and the Jesus Tradition: The Importance of Testing Prophetic Utterances within Early Christianity', *NTS*, 24 (1977/78), 175–98

Dupont, Jacques, 'La Parabole des Talents (Mat. 25:14–30) ou des Mines (Luc. 19:12–27)', *RThPh*, 19 (1969), 376–91

'La Transmission des paroles de Jésus sur la lampe et la mesure dans Marc 4, 21–25 et dans la tradition Q', in J. Delobel (ed.), *Logia. Les Paroles de Jésus − The Sayings of Jesus. Mémorial Joseph Coppens*, BEThL 59 (Louvain, 1982), 201–36

Les Béatitudes, I: *Le Problème Littéraire. Les deux versions du sermon sur la montagne et des Béatitudes*, 2nd edn (Paris, 1969)

'Renoncer à tous ses biens (Luc 14,33)', *NRTh*, 93 (1971), 561–82

Edlund, Conny, *Das Auge der Einfalt. Eine Untersuchung zu Matth. 6, 22–23 und Luk. 11,34–35*, ASNU 19 (Copenhagen/Lund, 1952)

Edwards, Richard Alan, *A Theology of Q. Eschatology, Prophecy, and Wisdom* (Philadelphia, Pa, 1976)

'Book Review: Q. Die Spruchquelle der Evangelisten by Siegfried Schulz', *JBL*, 94 (1975), 609–12

'The Eschatological Correlative as a *Gattung* in the New Testament', *ZNW*, 60 (1969), 9–20

'Matthew's Use of Q in Chapter Eleven', in J. Delobel (ed.), *Logia. Les Paroles de Jésus − The Sayings of Jesus. Mémorial Joseph Coppens*, BEThL 59 (Louvain, 1982), 257–75

The Sign of Jonah. In the Theology of the Evangelists and Q, SBT 2. ser. 18 (London, 1971)

Ehrhardt, Arnold A. T., 'Greek Proverbs in the Gospel', *HThR*, 46 (1953), 59–77

Eissfeldt, Otto, *The Old Testament. An Introduction including the Apocrypha and Pseudepigrapha, and also the Works of Similar Type from Qumran. The History of the Formation of the Old Testament*, trans. P. R. Ackroyd (Oxford, 1965)

Elliott, John H., 'Ministry and Church Order in the NT: A Traditio-Historical Analysis (1 Pt 5,1–5 & plls.)', *CBQ*, 32 (1970), 367–91

Ellis, E. Earle, 'Luke xi.49–51: An Oracle of a Christian Prophet?', *ET*, 74 (1963), 157–8

Ernst, Josef, *Das Evangelium nach Lukas*, RNT (Regensburg, 1977)
Das Evangelium nach Markus, RNT (Regensburg, 1981)

Farmer, William Reuben, 'A Fresh Approach to Q', in Jacob Neusner (ed.), *Christianity, Judaism and Other Greco-Roman Cults. Studies for Morton Smith at Sixty*, Part I: *New Testament*, SJLA 12 (Leiden, 1975), 39–50
The Synoptic Problem. A Critical Analysis (Macon, Ga., 1976)

Farrer, Austin, 'On Dispensing with Q', in Dennis E. Nineham (ed.), *Studies in the Gospels. Essays in Memory of R. H. Lightfoot* (Oxford, 1955), 55–88

Feldman, Louis H., 'Josephus as an Apologist of the Greco-Roman World: His Portrait of Solomon', in E. S. Fiorenza (ed.), *Aspects of Religious Propaganda in Judaism and Early Christianity*, University of Notre Dame Center for the Study of Judaism and Christianity in Antiquity 2 (Notre Dame/London, 1976), 68–98

Fenton, J. C., 'Inclusio and Chiasmus in Matthew', in K. Aland, F. L. Cross, J. Daniélou, H. Riesenfeld, W. C. van Unnik (eds.), *StEv* I: *Papers Presented to the International Congress on 'The Four Gospels in 1957' held at Christ Church Oxford 1957* (= TU 73) (Berlin, 1959), 174–9

Feuillet, André, 'Jésus et la Sagesse Divine d'après les Évangiles Synoptiques', *RB*, 62 (1955), 161–76
Le Christ Sagesse de Dieu d'après les Épîtres Pauliniennes, EtB (Paris, 1966)
'Le Fils de l'Homme de Daniel et la tradition biblique', *RB*, 60 (1953), 321–46
'Les Riches intendants du Christ (Luc XVI,1–13)', *RSR*, 34 (1947), 30–54

Fichtner, Johannes, 'Isaiah among the Wise', in J. L. Crenshaw (ed.), *Studies in Ancient Israelite Wisdom*, LBS (New York, 1976), 429–38

Filson, Floyd V., 'The Christian Teacher in the First Century', *JBL*, 60 (1941), 317–28

Fiorenza, Elisabeth Schüssler, 'Wisdom Mythology and the Christological Hymns of the New Testament', in R. L. Wilken (ed.), *Aspects of Wisdom in Judaism and Early Christianity*, University of Notre Dame Center for the Study of Judaism and Christianity in Antiquity 1 (Notre Dame/London, 1975), 17–41

Fischel, Henry A., *Rabbinic Literature and Greco-Roman Philosophy. A Study of Epicurea and Rhetorica in Early Midrashic Writings*, StPB 21 (Leiden, 1973)
'The Transformation of Wisdom in the World of Midrash', in R. L. Wilken (ed.), *Aspects of Wisdom in Judaism and Early Christianity*, University of Notre Dame Center for the Study of Judaism and Christianity in Antiquity 1 (Notre Dame/London, 1975), 67–101

Fitzgerald, John T., and White, L. Michael (eds.), *The Tabula of Cebes*,

SBLTT 24/Greco-Roman Religion Series 7 (Chico, Calif., 1983)

Fitzmyer, Joseph A., *Essays on the Semitic Background of the New Testament* (London, 1971)

The Gospel According to Luke, 2 vols., AncB 28, 28A (New York, 1981–5)

'The Priority of Mark and the "Q" Source in Luke', in Donald G. Miller (ed.), *Jesus and Man's Hope*, Vol. I, Perspective (Pittsburgh, 1970), 131–70

Fleddermann, Harry, 'The Discipleship Discourse (Mark 9,33–50)', *CBQ*, 43 (1981), 57–75

Flender, Helmut, *Heil und Geschichte in der Theologie des Lukas*, BEvTh 41 (Munich, 1965)

Fletcher, Donald R., 'The Riddle of the Unjust Steward: Is Irony the Key?', *JBL*, 82 (1963), 15–30

Franklin, Eric, *Christ the Lord. A Study in the Purpose and Theology of Luke–Acts* (London, 1975)

Fuchs, Eric, 'L'Evangile et l'Argent. La Parabole de l'intendant intelligent', *Bulletin du Centre Protestant d'Etudes*, 30 (1978), 3–14

Fuller, Reginald H., and Perkins, Pheme, *Who Is This Christ? Gospel Christology and Contemporary Faith* (Philadelphia, Pa., 1983)

Funk, Robert W., 'The Parables: A Fragmentary Agenda', in Donald G. Miller, Dikran Y. Hadidian (eds.), *Jesus and Man's Hope*, Vol. II, Perspective (Pittsburgh, Pa., 1971), 287–303

Funk, Wolf-Peter, *Die zweite Apokalypse des Jakobus aus Nag-Hammadi-Codex V*, TU 119 (Berlin, 1976)

Furnish, Victor Paul, *The Love Command in the New Testament* (London, 1973)

Theology and Ethics in Paul (Nashville/New York, 1968)

Gächter, Paul, 'The Parable of the Dishonest Steward after Oriental Conceptions', *CBQ*, 12 (1950), 121–31

Galot, J., 'Qu'il soit pour toi comme le païen et le publicain', *NRTh*, 96 (1974), 1009–30

Gammie, John G., Brueggemann, Walter A., Humphreys, W. Lee, Ward, James M. (eds.), *Israelite Wisdom. Theological and Literary Essays in Honor of Samuel Terrien* (Missoula, Mont., 1978)

Garland, David E., *The Intention of Matthew 23*, NT.S 52 (Leiden, 1979)

Gaston, Lloyd, *No Stone on Another. Studies in the Significance of the Fall of Jerusalem on the Synoptic Gospels*, NT.S 23 (Leiden, 1970)

Georgi, Dieter, 'Der vorpaulinische Hymnus Phil 2,6–11', in E. Dinkler (ed.), *Zeit und Geschichte. Dankesgabe an Rudolf Bultmann zum 80. Geburtstag* (Tübingen, 1964), 263–93

Die Geschichte der Kollekte des Paulus für Jerusalem, ThF 38 (Hamburg, 1965)

'The Records of Jesus in the Light of Ancient Accounts of Revered Men', in Lane C. McGaughy (ed.), *The SBL 1972 Proceedings [108th Annual Meeting, 1–5 September 1972, Los Angeles] Book of Seminar Papers*, Vol. II (Missoula, Mont., 1972), 527–42

Gnilka, Joachim, *Das Evangelium nach Markus*, 2 vols., EKK II.1,2 (Zürich/Einsiedeln/Köln/Neukirchen-Vluyn, 1978–9)

Das Matthäusevangelium, I: *Kommentar zu Kap. 1,1 – 13,58*, HThK I.1 (Freiburg/Basle/Vienna, 1986)

'Martyriumsparänese und Sühnetod in synoptischen und jüdischen Traditionen', in R. Schnackenburg, J. Ernst, J. Wanke (eds.), *Die Kirche des Anfangs. Für Heinz Schürmann* (Freiburg/Basle/Vienna, 1978), 223–46

Gordis, Robert, 'Quotations in Wisdom Literature', *JQR*, 30 (1939–40), 123–47

Goulder, Michael, 'Farrer on Q', *Theol.*, 83 (1980), 190–5

'Mark XVI.1–8 and Parallels', *NTS*, 24 (1977–8), 235–40

Midrash and Lection In Matthew, Speaker's Lectures in Biblical Studies 1969–71 (London, 1974)

'On Putting Q to the Test', *NTS*, 24 (1977–8), 218–34

'The Composition of the Lord's Prayer', *JThS*, n.s. 14 (1963), 32–45

The Evangelists' Calendar. A Lectionary Explanation of the Development of Scripture, Speaker's Lectures in Biblical Studies 1972 (London, 1978)

'The Order of a Crank', in C. M. Tuckett (ed.), *Synoptic Studies. The Ampleforth Conferences of 1982 and 1983*, JSNT Supplement Series 7 (Sheffield, 1984), 111–30

Grant, Robert M., *A Historical Introduction to the New Testament* (London, 1963)

Green, H. Benedict, 'The Credibility of Luke's Transformation of Matthew', in C. M. Tuckett (ed.), *Synoptic Studies. The Ampleforth Conferences of 1982 and 1983*, JSNT Supplement Studies 7 (Sheffield, 1984), 131–55

Greenfield, Jones C. and Stone, Michael E., 'The Enochic Pentateuch and the Date of the Similitudes', *HThR*, 70 (1977), 51–65

Greeven, Heinrich, 'Wer unter euch ...?', *WuD*, NF 3 (1952), 86–101

'ζητέω, κτλ.', in *TDNT*, II, 892–6

Griffiths, J. Gwyn, 'The Disciple's Cross', *NTS*, 16 (1970), 358–64

Grundmann, Walter, *Das Evangelium nach Lukas*, 9th edn, ThHK 3 (Berlin, 1981)

Das Evangelium nach Markus, 2nd edn, ThHK 2 (Berlin, n.d.)

'Weisheit im Horizont des Reiches Gottes. Eine Studie zur Verkündigung Jesu nach der Spruchüberlieferung Q', in R. Schnackenburg, J. Ernst, J. Wanke (eds.), *Die Kirche des Anfangs. Für Heinz Schürmann* (Freiburg/Basle/Vienna, 1978), 175–99

Guelich, Robert A., 'The Antitheses of Matthew v. 21–48: Traditional and/or Redactional?', *NTS*, 22 (1976), 444–57

'The Matthean Beatitudes: "Entrance-Requirements" or Eschatological Blessings?', *JBL*, 95 (1976), 415–34

Gundry, Robert H., *Matthew. A Commentary on his Literary and Theological Art* (Grand Rapids, Mich., 1982)

Haenchen, Ernst, 'Die Komposition von Mk viii 27 – ix 1 und par.', *NT*, 6 (1963), 81–109

'II. Gnosis und NT', in *RGG*³ II, 1652–6

'Matthäus 23', *ZThK*, 48 (1951), 38–63

The Acts of the Apostles. A Commentary, trans. revised by R. McL. Wilson (Oxford, 1971)

Hahn, Ferdinand, 'Die Worte vom Licht Lk 11,33–36', in P. Hoffmann *et al.* (eds.), *Orientierung an Jesus. Zur Theologie der Synoptiker. Für Josef Schmid* (Freiburg/Basle/Vienna, 1973), 107–38

Mission in the New Testament, SBT 47 (London, 1965)

The Titles of Jesus in Christology. Their History in Early Christianity (London, 1969)

Hamerton-Kelly, R. G., *Pre-Existence, Wisdom, and the Son of Man. A Study of the Idea of Pre-Existence in the New Testament*, MSSNTS 21 (Cambridge, 1973)

Hanson, Anthony Tyrrell, *Jesus Christ in the Old Testament* (London, 1965)

Hare, Douglas R. A., *The Theme of Jewish Persecution of Christians in the Gospel According to St Matthew*, MSSNTS 6 (Cambridge, 1967)

Harnack, Adolf, *The Sayings of Jesus: The Second Source of St. Matthew and St. Luke*, Crown Theological Library 23, New Testament Studies 2 (London, 1908)

Harvey, A. E., *Jesus and the Constraints of History* (London, 1982)

' "The Workman is Worthy of His Hire": Fortunes of a Proverb in the Early Church', *NT*, 24 (1982), 209–21

Hasler, Victor, *Amen. Redaktionsgeschichtliche Untersuchung zur Einführungsformel der Herrenworte 'Wahrlich ich sage euch'* (Zürich/Stuttgart, 1969)

Hauck, Friedrich, 'θερισμός', in *TDNT*, III, 133

'Μαμωνᾶς', in *TDNT*, IV, 388–90

'παραβολή', in *TDNT*, V, 744–61

'παροιμία', in *TDNT*, V, 854–6

Havener, Ivan, *Q. The Sayings of Jesus*, with a Reconstruction of Q by A. Polag, Good News Studies 19 (Wilmington, Del., 1987)

Hengel, Martin, *Acts and the History of Earliest Christianity*, trans. J. Bowden (London, 1979)

'Between Jesus and Paul', in his *Between Jesus and Paul. Studies in the Earliest History of Christianity*, trans. J. Bowden (London, 1983), 1–29 (= 'Zwischen Jesus und Paulus', *ZThK*, 72 (1975), 151–206)

'Book Review: Th. Middendorp, *Die Stellung Jesu ben Siras zwischen Judentum und Hellenismus'*, *JSJ*, 5 (1974), 83–7

'Jesus als messianischer Lehrer der Weisheit und die Anfänge der Christologie', in *Sagesse et Religion. Colloque de Strasbourg, octobre 1976*, Bibliothèque des Centres d'Études Supérieures Spécialisés (Paris, 1979), 147–88

Judaism and Hellenism: Studies in Their Encounter in Palestine during the Early Hellenistic Period, trans. J. Bowden, 2 vols. (London, 1974)

Property and Riches in the Early Church. Aspects of a Social History of Early Christianity, trans. J. Bowden (London, 1974)

The Charismatic Leader and His Followers (Edinburgh, 1981)

The Son of God. The Origin of Christology and the History of Jewish–Hellenistic Religion (London, 1976)

War Jesus Revolutionär?, CwH 110 (Stuttgart, 1970)

Hermisson, Hans-Jürgen, *Studien zur israelitischen Spruchweisheit*, WMANT 28 (Neukirchen-Vluyn, 1968)

Hiers, Richard H., 'Friends by Unrighteous Mammon: The Eschatological Proletariat (Luke 16:9)', *JAAR*, 38 (1970), 30–6

Higgins, Angus J. B., ' "Menschensohn" oder "ich" in Q: Lk 12,8–9/Mt 10,32–33?', in R. Pesch, R. Schnackenburg (eds.), *Jesus und der Menschensohn. Für Anton Vögtle* (Freiburg/Basle/Vienna, 1975), 117–23

The Son of Man in the Teaching of Jesus, MSSNTS 39 (Cambridge, 1980)

Highet, Gilbert, 'Anthology', in *OCD*^{2} (1970), 67–8

Hill, David, 'Christian Prophets as Teachers or Instructors in the Church', in J. Panagopoulos (ed.), *Prophetic Vocation in the New Testament and Today*, NT.S 45 (Leiden, 1977), 108–30

'Δίκαιοι as a Quasi-Technical Term', *NTS*, 11 (1965), 296–302

'False Prophets and Charismatics: Structure and Interpretation in Matthew 7,15–23', *Bib.*, 57 (1976), 327–48

'On the Evidence for the Creative Role of Christian Prophets', *NTS*, 20 (1974), 262–74

The Gospel of Matthew, NCeB (London, 1978)

Hoffmann, Paul, 'Die Offenbarung des Sohnes. Die apokalyptischen Voraussetzungen und ihre Verarbeitung im Q-Logion Mt 11,27 par Lk 10,22', *Kairos*, 12 (1970), 270–88

'Die Versuchungsgeschichte in der Logienquelle. Zur Auseinandersetzung der Judenchristen mit dem politischen Messianismus', *BZ*, NF 13 (1969), 207–23

'Neutestamentliche Rezensionen: Siegfried Schulz, *Q. Die Spruchquelle der Evangelisten*', *BZ*, NF 19 (1975), 104–15

'Πάντες ἐργάται ἀδικίας. Redaktion und Tradition in Lc 13.22–30', *ZNW*, 58 (1967), 188–214

Studien zur Theologie der Logienquelle, NTA n.s. 8 (Münster, 1972)

Hollander, Harm W., *Joseph as an Ethical Model in the Testaments of the Twelve Patriarchs*, SVTP 6 (Leiden, 1981)

Honeyman, A. M., 'The Etymology of *Mammon*', *ArLg*, 4 (1952), 60–5

Hooker, Morna D., *The Son of Man in Mark. A Study of the Background of the Term 'Son of Man' and its Use in St Mark's Gospel* (London, 1967)

Horn, Friedrich Wilhelm, *Glaube und Handeln in der Theologie des Lukas*, GTA 26 (Göttingen, 1983)

Horsley, Richard A., 'Wisdom of Word and Words of Wisdom in Corinth', *CBQ*, 39 (1977), 224–39

Horstmann, Maria, *Studien zur markinischen Christologie. Mk 8,27–9,13 als Zugang zum Christusbild des zweiten Evangeliums*, NTA n.s. 6 (Münster, 1969)

Houlden, J. L., 'The Development of Meaning', *Theol.*, 82 (1979), 251–9

Hübner, Hans, *Das Gesetz in der synoptischen Tradition. Studien zur These einer progressiven Qumranisierung und Judaisierung innerhalb der synoptischen Tradition* (Witten, 1973)

Hultgård, Anders, *L'Eschatologie des Testaments des Douze Patriarches*, II: *Composition de l'ouvrage textes et traductions*, HR[U] 7 (Uppsala, 1982)

Hummel, Reinhart, *Die Auseinandersetzung zwischen Kirche und Judentum im Matthäusevangelium*, BEvTh 33 (Munich, 1963)

Hunzinger, C.-H., 'Unbekannte Gleichnisse Jesu aus dem Thomas-Evangelium', in W. Eltester (ed.), *Judentum, Urchristentum, Kirche. FS für Joachim Jeremias*, BZNW 26 (Berlin, 1960), 209–20

Jacobson, Arland D., 'The Literary Unity of Q', *JBL*, 101 (1982), 365–89

'The Literary Unity of Q. Lc 10,2–16 and Parallels as a Test Case', in J. Delobel (ed.), *Logia. Les Paroles de Jésus – The Sayings of Jesus*. *Mémorial Joseph Coppens*, BEThL 59 (Louvain, 1982), 419–23

'Wisdom Christology in Q' (dissertation, Claremont Graduate School, 1978)

Jaeger, H., 'The Patristic Conception of Wisdom in the Light of Biblical and Rabbinical Research', in F.L. Cross (ed.), *StPatr* IV: *Papers Presented to the Third International Conference on Patristic Studies Held at Christ Church Oxford, 1959*, Part II: *Biblica, Patres Apostolici, Historica* (= TU 79) (Berlin, 1961), 90–106

Jeremias, Joachim, 'Die Lampe unter dem Scheffel', *ZNW*, 39 (1940), 237–40

Die Sprache des Lukasevangeliums. Redaktion und Tradition im Nicht-Markusstoff des dritten Evangeliums, KEK Sonderband (Göttingen, 1980)

Jerusalem in the Time of Jesus. An Investigation into Economic and Social Conditions during the New Testament Period, trans. F. and C. Cave (London, 1969)

New Testament Theology, I: *The Proclamation of Jesus* (London, 1975)

'πύλη, πυλῶν', in *TDNT*, VI, 921–8

The Parables of Jesus, 3rd edn (London, 1975)

The Prayers of Jesus, SBT 2. Ser. 6 (London, 1967)

'θύρα' in *TDNT*, III, 173–80

Unknown Sayings of Jesus, 2nd edn (London, 1964)

'Zur Hypothese einer schriftlichen Logienquelle Q', *ZNW*, 29 (1930), 147–9

Jeske, Richard L., 'The Wisdom Structure of Jesus' Eschatology' (dissertation, Ruprecht-Karl Universität Heidelberg, 1969)

Johnson, A.R., ' מָשָׁל ', in M. Noth, D. Winton Thomas (eds.), *Wisdom in Israel and in the Ancient Near East. Presented to Professor Harold Henry Rowley by the Society for Old Testament Study in Association with the Editorial Board of Vetus Testamentum in Celebration of his Sixty-fifth Birthday, 24 March 1955*, VT.S 3 (Leiden, 1955), 162–9

Johnson, Luke T., *The Literary Function of Possessions in Luke – Acts*, SBLDS 39 (Missoula, Mont., 1977)

Johnson, Marshall D., 'Reflections on a Wisdom Approach to Matthew's Christology', *CBQ*, 36 (1974), 44–64

Judge, Edwin A., 'St Paul and Classical Society', *JAC*, 15 (1972), 19–36

Jülicher, Adolf, *Die Gleichnisreden Jesu*, II: *Auslegung der Gleichnisreden der drei ersten Evangelien* (Freiburg i. B./Leipzig/Tübingen, 1899)

Käsemann, Ernst, *Essays on New Testament Themes*, trans. W.J. Montague, SBT 41 (London, 1964)

'Lukas 11,14–28', in his *Exegetische Versuche und Besinnungen*, 3rd edn, Vol. I (Göttingen, 1964), 242–8

New Testament Questions of Today (London, 1969)

Kamlah, Ehrhard, 'Die Parabel vom ungerechten Verwalter (Luk. 16,1ff) im Rahmen der Knechtsgleichnisse', in O. Betz, M. Hengel, P. Schmidt (eds.), *Abraham unser Vater. Juden und Christen im Gespräch über die Bibel. Festschrift für Otto Michel zum 60. Geburtstag*, AGSU 5 (Leiden/Cologne, 1963), 276–94

'Kritik und Interpretation der Parabel von den anvertrauten Geldern. Mt. 25,14ff; Lk. 19,12ff', *KuD*, 14 (1968), 28–38

Karris, Robert J., 'Poor and Rich: The Lukan *Sitz im Leben*', in C. H. Talbert (ed.), *Perspectives on Luke – Acts* (Edinburgh/Danville, 1978), 112–25

Kayatz, C., *Studien zu Proverbien 1–9. Eine form- und motivgeschichtliche Untersuchung unter Einbeziehung ägyptischen Vergleichsmaterials*, WMANT 22 (Neukirchen, 1966)

Kee, Howard Clark, *Community of the New Age. Studies in Mark's Gospel*, NTLi (London, 1977)

Jesus in History. An Approach to the Study of the Gospels, 2nd edn (New York, 1977)

Kilgallen, John, *The Stephen Speech. A Literary and Redactional Study of Acts 7,2–53*, AnBib 67 (Rome, 1976)

Klassen, William, 'Coals of Fire: Sign of Repentance or Revenge?', *NTS*, 9 (1962–3), 337–50

Klein, Günter, 'Die Verfolgung der Apostel, Luk 11,49', in H. Baltensweiler, B. Reicke (eds.), *Neues Testament und Geschichte. Historisches Geschehen und Deutung im Neuen Testament. Oscar Cullmann zum 70. Geburtstag* (Zürich/Tübingen, 1972), 113–24

Kloppenborg, John S., 'Tradition and Redaction in the Synoptic Sayings Source', *CBQ*, 46 (1984), 34–62

'Wisdom Christology in Q', *LTP*, 34 (1978), 129–47

Klostermann, Erich, *Das Lukasevangelium*, 3rd edn, HNT 5 (Tübingen, 1975)

Das Matthäusevangelium, 2nd edn, HNT 4 (Tübingen, 1927)

Knibb, Michael A., 'Apocalyptic and Wisdom in 4Ezra', *JSJ*, 13 (1982), 56–74

'The Date of the Parables of Enoch: A Critical Review', *NTS*, 25 (1979), 345–59

Knox, Wilfred L., *The Sources of the Synoptic Gospels*, 2 vols. (Cambridge, 1953–7)

Koester, Helmut, 'GNOMAI DIAPHOROI: The Origin and Nature of Diversification in the History of Early Christianity', in J. M. Robinson, H. Koester (eds.), *Trajectories through Early Christianity* (Philadelphia, Pa., 1971), 114–57

'Gnostic Writings as Witnesses for the Development of the Sayings Tradition', in B. Layton (ed.), *The Rediscovery of Gnosticism. Proceedings of the International Conference on Gnosticism at Yale, New Haven, Connecticut, March 28–31, 1978, I: The School of Valentinus*, Numen Suppl. SHR 41 (Leiden, 1980), 238–61

'Mark 9:43–47 and Quintilian 8.3.75', *HThR*, 71 (1978), 151–3

Kosmala, Hans, 'The Parable of the Unjust Steward in the Light of Qumran', *ASTI*, 3 (1964), 114–21

Krämer, Michael, *Das Rätsel der Parabel vom ungerechten Verwalter. Lk 16,1–13. Auslegungsgeschichte – Umfang – Sinn. Eine Diskussion der Probleme und Lösungsvorschläge der Verwalterparabel von den Vätern bis Heute*, BSRel 5 (Zürich, 1972)

'Hütet euch vor den falschen Propheten. Eine überlieferungsgeschichtliche Untersuchung zu Mt 7,15–23/Lk 6,43–46/Mt 12,33–37' in *Bib.*, 57 (1976), 349–377

'Ihr seid das Salz der Erde ... Ihr seid das Licht der Welt: Die vielgestaltige Wirkkraft des Gotteswortes der Heiligen Schrift für das Leben der Kirche aufgezeigt am Beispiel Mt 5,13–16', *MThZ*, 28 (1977), 133–57

Krieger, Norbert, 'Ein Mensch in weichen Kleidern', *NT*, 1 (1956), 228–30

Kruse, Heinz, 'Das Reich Satans', *Bib.*, 58 (1977), 29–61

Küchler, Max, *Frühjüdische Weisheitstraditionen. Zum Fortgang weisheitlichen Denkens im Bereich des frühjüdischen Jahweglaubens*, OBO 26 (Freiburg/Göttingen, 1979)

Kümmel, Werner Georg, 'Das Verhalten Jesus gegenüber und das Verhalten des Menschensohns. Markus 8,38 par und Lukas 12,3f [*sic*] par Mattäus 10,32f', in R. Pesch, R. Schnackenburg (eds.), *Jesus und der Menschensohn. Für Anton Vögtle* (Freiburg/Basle/Vienna, 1975), 210–24

Introduction to the New Testament, rev. edn, trans. H. Kee (London, 1975)

Promise and Fulfilment. The Eschatological Message of Jesus, SBT 23 (London, 1974)

Kuhn, Heinz-Wolfgang, *Ältere Sammlungen im Markusevangelium*, StUNT 8 (Göttingen, 1971)

Lambrecht, Jan, 'Q-Influence on Mark 8,34–9,1' in J. Delobel (ed.), *Logia. Les Paroles de Jésus – The Sayings of Jesus. Mémorial Joseph Coppens*, BEThL 59 (Louvain, 1982), 277–304

'The Relatives of Jesus in Mark', *NT*, 16 (1974), 241–58

Lang, Bernhard, *Frau Weisheit. Deutung einer biblischen Gestalt* (Düsseldorf, 1975)

Laporte, Jean, 'Philo in the Tradition of Biblical Wisdom Literature', in R. L. Wilken (ed.), *Aspects of Wisdom in Judaism and Early Christianity*, University of Notre Dame Center for the Study of Judaism and Christianity in Antiquity 1 (Notre Dame/London, 1975), 103–41

Larcher, C., *Études sur le Livre de la Sagesse*, EtB (Paris, 1969)

Latham, James E., *The Religious Symbolism of Salt*, ThH 64 (Paris, 1982)

Lattke, Michael, 'Salz der Freundschaft in Mk 9.50c', *ZNW*, 75 (1984), 44–59

Laufen, Rudolf, *Die Doppelüberlieferungen der Logienquelle und des Markusevangeliums*, BBB 54 (Bonn, 1980)

Lebram, Jürgen C., 'Die Theologie der späten Chokma und häretisches Judentum', *ZAW*, 77 (1965), 202–11

Lienhard, Joseph T., 'Acts 6:1–6. A Redactional View', *CBQ*, 37 (1975), 228–36

Lindars, Barnabas, 'Jesus as Advocate: A Contribution to the Christology Debate', *JRLB*, 62 (1980), 476–97

Jesus Son of Man. A Fresh Examination of the Son of Man Sayings in the Gospels in the Light of Recent Research (London, 1983)

New Testament Apologetic: The Doctrinal Significance of the Old Testament Quotations (London, 1961)

'Salvation Proclaimed VII. Mark 10.45: A Ransom for Many', *ET*, 93 (1982), 292–5

Lindblom, Johannes, 'Wisdom in the Old Testament Prophets', in M. Noth, D. W. Thomas (eds.), *Wisdom in Israel and in the Ancient Near East. Presented to Professor Harold Henry Rowley by the Society for Old Testament Study in Association with the Editorial Board of Vetus*

Testamentum in Celebration of his Sixty-Fifth Birthday, 24 March 1955, VT.S 3 (Leiden, 1955), 192–204

Lindeskog, Gösta, 'Logia-Studien', *StTh*, 4 (1952), 129–89

Linton, Olof, 'The Parable of the Children's Game. Baptist and Son of Man (Matt. XI.16–19 = Luke VII.31–5): A Synoptic, Text-Critical, Structural and Exegetical Investigation', *NTS*, 22 (1975–6), 159–79

Lohse, Edward, '"Ich aber sage euch"', in E. Lohse (ed.), *Der Ruf Jesu und die Antwort der Gemeinde. Exegetische Untersuchungen Joachim Jeremias zum 70. Geburtstag gewidmet von seinen Schülern* (Göttingen, 1970), 189–203

Lührmann, Dieter, *Das Offenbarungsverständnis bei Paulus und in paulinischen Gemeinden*, WMANT 16 (Neukirchen-Vluyn, 1965)

'Der Verweis auf die Erfahrung und die Frage nach der Gerechtigkeit', in G. Strecker (ed.), *Jesus Christus in Histoire und Theologie. Neutestamentliche Festschrift für Hans Conzelmann zum 60. Geburtstag* (Tübingen, 1975), 185–96

Die Redaktion der Logienquelle, WMANT 33 (Neukirchen-Vluyn, 1969)

'Ein Weisheitspsalm aus Qumran (11Q Ps^a XVIII)', *ZAW*, 80 (1968), 87–98

'Liebet euer Feinde (Lk 6,27–36/Mt 5,39–48)', *ZThK*, 69 (1972), 412–38

'Wrege, Hans-Theo, *Die Überlieferungsgeschichte der Bergpredigt*', *ThLZ*, 95 (1970), 199–200

Lunt, Ronald G., 'Expounding the Parables III: The Parable of the Unjust Steward (Luke 16.1–15)', *ET*, 77 (1966), 132–6

Luz, Ulrich, *Das Evangelium nach Matthäus*, I: *Mt 1–7*, EKK 1.1 (Zürich/Einsiedeln/Cologne/Neukirchen-Vluyn, 1985)

'Die wiederentdeckte Logienquelle', *EvTh*, 33 (1973), 527–33

McGaughy, Lane C., 'The Fear of Yahweh and the Mission of Judaism: A Postexilic Maxim and its Early Christian Expansion in the Parable of the Talents', *JBL*, 94 (1975), 235–45

McKane, William, *Prophets and Wise Men*, SBT 44 (London, 1965)

Proverbs. A New Approach, OTL (London, 1970)

McKenna, Margaret Mary, '"The Two Ways" in Jewish and Christian Writings of the Greco-Roman Period. A Study of the Form of Repentance Parenesis' (dissertation, University of Pennsylvania, 1981)

McKenzie, John L., 'Reflections on Wisdom', *JBL*, 86 (1967), 1–9

McNeile, Alan Hugh, *The Gospel According to St Matthew. The Greek Text with Introduction, Notes, and Indices* (London, 1915)

Mack, Burton L., *Logos und Sophia. Untersuchungen zur Weisheitstheologie im hellenistischen Judentum*, StUNT 10 (Göttingen, 1973)

Wisdom and the Hebrew Epic. Ben Sira's Hymn in Praise of the Fathers, Chicago Studies in the History of Judaism (Chicago/London, 1985)

'Wisdom Myth and Mytho-logy: An Essay in Understanding a Theological Tradition', *Interp.*, 24 (1970), 46–60

Macrae, George W., 'The Jewish Background of the Gnostic Sophia Myth', *NT*, 12 (1970), 86–101

Manson, T. W., *The Sayings of Jesus, as Recorded in the Gospels according to St. Matthew and St. Luke Arranged with Introduction and Commentary* (London, 1964)

The Teaching of Jesus. Studies of its Form and Content, 2nd edn (Cambridge, 1955)

Marböck, Johann, *Weisheit im Wandel. Untersuchungen zur Weisheitstheologie bei Ben Sira*, BBB 37 (Bonn, 1971)

Marcus, Ralph, 'On Biblical Hypostases of Wisdom', *HUCA*, 23 (1950–1), 157–71

Marshall, I. Howard, 'How to Solve the Synoptic Problem: Lk 11:43 and Parallels', in W. C. Weinrich (ed.), *The New Testament Age. Essays in Honor of Bo Reicke*, Vol. II (Macon, Ga., 1984), 313–25

'Luke xvi.8 – Who Commended the Unjust Steward?', *JThS*, n.s. 19 (1968), 617–19

The Gospel of Luke. A Commentary on the Greek Text, NIGTC (Exeter, 1978)

'Uncomfortable Words VI. "Fear him who can destroy both soul and body in hell" (Mt 10:28 R.S.V.)', *ET*, 81 (1970), 276–80

Martin, James D., 'Ben Sira – A Child of his Time', in James D. Martin, Philip R. Davies (eds.), *A Word in Season. Essays in Honour of William McKane*, JSOT Supplement Series 42 (Sheffield, 1986), 141–61

'Ben Sira's Hymn to the Fathers. A Messianic Perspective', *OTS*, 24 (1986), 107–23

Marxsen, Willi, *Mark the Evangelist. Studies on the Redaction History of the Gospel*, trans. J. Boyce *et al.* (Nashville, Tenn., 1969)

Mattill, A. J., Jr, 'The Way of Tribulation', *JBL*, 98 (1979), 531–46

Maurer, Christian, ῥίζα', in *TDNT*, VI, 985–91

Mealand, David L., '"Paradisial" Elements in the Teaching of Jesus', in E. A. Livingstone (ed.), *Studia Biblica 1978*, II: *Papers on the Gospels. Sixth International Congress on Biblical Studies. Oxford 3–7 April 1978*, JSNT Supplement Series 2 (Sheffield, 1980), 179–84

Poverty and Expectation in the Gospels (London, 1980)

Merkelbach, R., 'Über das Gleichnis vom ungerechten Haushalter (Lukas 16,9–13)', *VigChr*, 33 (1979), 180–1

Metzger, Bruce M., *A Textual Commentary on the Greek New Testament. A Companion Volume to the United Bible Societies' Greek New Testament (third edition)* (London/New York, 1971)

Meyer, Paul D., 'The Community of Q' (dissertation, University of Iowa, 1967)

'The Gentile Mission in Q' *JBL*, 89 (1970), 405–17

Michaelis, Wilhelm, 'ὁδός', in *TDNT*, V, 42–114

Middendorp, Th., *Die Stellung Jesu ben Siras zwischen Judentum und Hellenismus* (Leiden, 1973)

Milik, J. T., *The Books of Enoch: Aramaic Fragments of Qumran Cave 4* (Oxford, 1976)

Minear, Paul S., *Commands of Christ* (Nashville/New York, 1972)

Molina, Jean-Pierre, 'Luc 16/1 à 13: L'injuste *Mamon*', *ETR*, 53 (1978), 371–5

Molitor, Joseph, 'Zur Übersetzung von μετεωρίζεσθε Lk 12,29' *BZ*, 10 (1966), 107–8

Montefiore, Hugh, 'A Comparison of the Parables of the Gospel according to Thomas and of the Synoptic Gospels', *NTS*, 7 (1960–1), 220–48

Morgan, Donn F., *Wisdom in the Old Testament Traditions* (Atlanta, Ga, 1981)

Morgenthaler, Robert, *Statistik des neutestamentlichen Wortschatzes* (Zürich/Frankfurt am Main, 1958)

Statistische Synopse (Zürich/Stuttgart, 1971)

Moule, C. F. D., *The Origin of Christology* (Cambridge, 1977)

Murphy, Roland E., 'A Consideration of the Classification "Wisdom Psalms"', in *Congress Volume: Bonn 1962*, VT.S 9 (Leiden, 1963), 156–67

'Assumptions and Problems in Old Testament Wisdom Research', *CBQ*, 29 (1967), 407–18

'Form Criticism and Wisdom Literature', *CBQ*, 31 (1969), 475–83

Mussner, Franz, 'Der nicht erkannte Kairos (Mt 11,16–19 = Lk 7,31–35)', *Bib.*, 40 (1959), 599–612

Nauck, Wolfgang, 'Salt as a Metaphor in Instructions for Discipleship', *StTh*, 6 (1953), 165–78

Neirynck, Frans, *Duality in Mark. Contributions to the Study of Markan Redaction*, BEThL 31 (Louvain, 1972)

'Minor Agreements Matthew–Luke in the Transfiguration Story', in his *Evangelica. Gospel Studies – Etudes d'Evangile. Collected Essays*, ed. by F. van Segbroeck, BEThL 60 (Louvain, 1982), 797–810

'Recent Developments in the Study of Q', in J. Delobel (ed.), *Logia. Les Paroles de Jésus – The Sayings of Jesus. Mémorial Joseph Coppens*, BEThL 59 (Louvain, 1982), 29–75

'Studies on Q since 1972', *EThL*, 56 (1980), 409–13

The Minor Agreements of Matthew and Luke against Mark, with a Cumulative List, BEThL 37 (Louvain, 1974)

Nel, Philip Johannes, *The Structure and Ethos of the Wisdom Admonitions in Proverbs*, BZAW 158 (Berlin/New York, 1982)

Nestle, Eb., 'Mammon', in *EB(C)*, III, 2912–15

Neudorfer, Heinz-Werner, *Der Stephanuskreis in der Forschungsgeschichte seit F. C. Baur* (Giessen/Basle, 1983)

Neuhäusler, Englebert, 'Mit welchem Masstab misst Gott die Menschen?', *BiLe*, 11 (1970), 104–13

Neusner, Jacob, *Early Rabbinic Judaism. Historical Studies in Religion, Literature and Art*, SJLA 13 (Leiden, 1975)

First-Century Judaism in Crisis. Yohanan ben Zakkai and the Renaissance of Torah (Nashville/New York, 1975)

The Rabbinic Traditions about the Pharisees before 70, Part I: *The Masters* (Leiden, 1971)

Nicklesburg, George W. E., 'The Apocalyptic Message of 1 Enoch 92–105', *CBQ*, 39 (1977), 309–28

Nötscher, Friedrich, *Gotteswege und Menschenwege in der Bibel und in Qumran*, BBB 15 (Bonn, 1958)

Norden, Eduard, *Agnostos Theos. Untersuchungen zur Formengeschichte religiöser Rede* (Leipzig/Berlin, 1913)

Orchard, Bernard, *Matthew, Luke & Mark*, The Griesbach Solution to the Synoptic Question 1 (Manchester, 1976)

Ott, Wilhelm, *Gebet und Heil. Die Bedeutung der Gebetsparänese in der lukanischen Theologie*, StANT 12 (Munich, 1965)

Otto, Rudolph, *The Kingdom of God and the Son of Man. A Study in the History of Religion* (London, 1938)

Paul, Geoffrey, 'Studies in Texts: The Unjust Steward and the Interpretation of Luke 16.9', *Theol.*, 61 (1958), 189–93

Pearson, Birger A., 'Hellenistic–Jewish Wisdom Speculation and Paul', in R.L. Wilken (ed.), *Aspects of Wisdom in Judaism and Early Christianity*, University of Notre Dame Center for the Study of Judaism and Christianity in Antiquity 1 (Notre Dame/London, 1975), 43–66

Percy, Ernst, *Die Botschaft Jesu. Eine traditionskritische und exegetische Untersuchung*, Lunds Universitets Årsskrift. NF Avd 1 Bd 49 Nr 5 (Lund, 1953)

Perkins, Pheme, 'Gnostic Christologies and the New Testament', *CBQ*, 43 (1981), 590–606

Love Commands in the New Testament (New York, 1982)

Perrin, Norman, *Jesus and the Language of the Kingdom. Symbol and Metaphor in New Testament Interpretation* (London, 1976)

'The Christology of Mark: A Study in Methodology', in his *A Modern Pilgrimmage in New Testament Christology* (Philadelphia, Pa., 1974), 104–21 (= *JR*, 51 (1971), 173–87)

'The Composition of Mark ix 1', *NT*, 11 (1969), 67–70

'Wisdom and Apocalyptic in the Message of Jesus', in L.C. McGaughy (ed.), *The SBL 1972 Proceedings [108th Annual Meeting, 1–5 September 1972, Los Angeles]. Book of Seminar Papers*, Vol. II (Missoula, Mont., 1972), 543–72

Pesch, Rudolf, *Das Markusevangelium*, 2 vols., HThK II.1,2 (Freiburg/ Basle/Vienna, 1976–7)

'Über die Autorität Jesus. Eine Rückfrage anhand des Bekenner- und Verleugnerspruchs Lk 12,8f. par.', in R. Schnackenburg, J. Ernst, J. Wanke (eds.), *Die Kirche des Anfangs. Für Heinz Schürmann* (Freiburg/ Basle/Vienna, 1978), 25–56

Pesch, W., 'Zur Exegese von Mt 6,19–21 und Lk 12,33–34', *Bib.*, 41 (1960), 356–78

Pfeiffer, Robert H., *History of New Testament Times. With an Introduction to the Apocrypha* (New York, 1949)

Piper, John, *'Love Your Enemies': Jesus' Love Command in the Synoptic Gospels and the Early Christian Paraenesis*, MSSNTS 38 (Cambridge, 1979)

Piper, Ronald A., 'Matthew 7,7–11 par. Luke 11,9–13: Evidence of Design and Argument in the Collection of Jesus' Sayings', in J. Delobel (ed.), *Logia. Les Paroles de Jésus – The Sayings of Jesus. Mémorial Joseph Coppens*, BEThL 59 (Louvain, 1982), 411–18

Pokorný, P., 'Die Worte Jesu nach der Logienquelle im Licht des zeitgenössischen Judentums', *Kairos*, 11 (1969), 172–80

Polag, Athanasius, *Die Christologie der Logienquelle*, WMANT 45 (Neukirchen-Vluyn, 1977)

'Die theologische Mitte der Logienquelle', in P. Stuhlmacher (ed.), *Das Evangelium und die Evangelien. Vorträge vom Tübinger Symposium 1982*, WUNT 28 (Tübingen, 1983), 103–11

Fragmenta Q. Textheft zur Logienquelle (Neukirchen-Vluyn, 1979)

'Zu den Stufen der Christologie in Q', in F. L. Cross (ed.), *StEv* IV: *Papers Presented to the Third International Congress on New Testament Studies Held at Christ Church Oxford 1965*, Part I: *The New Testament Scriptures* (= TU 102) (Berlin, 1968), 72–4

Preisker, Herbert, 'Lukas 16,1–7', *ThLZ*, 74 (1949), 85–92

'Sind die jüdischen Apokalypsen in den drei ersten kanonischen Evangelien literarisch verarbeitet?', *ZNW*, 20 (1921), 199–205

Pryke, E. J., *Redactional Style in the Marcan Gospel. A Study of Syntax and Vocabulary as Guides to Redaction in Mark*, MSSNTS 33 (Cambridge, 1978)

Przybylski, Benno, *Righteousness in Matthew and his World of Thought*, MSSNTS 41 (Cambridge, 1980)

Quesnell, Quentin, *The Mind of Mark. Interpretation and Method through the Exegesis of Mark 6,52*, AnBib 38 (Rome, 1969)

Rad, Gerhard von, *Wisdom in Israel*, trans. J. D. Martin (London, 1975)

Reese, James M., *Hellenistic Influence on the Book of Wisdom and its Consequences*, AnBib 41 (Rome, 1970)

Reicke, Bo, 'Official and Pietistic Elements of Jewish Apocalypticism', *JBL*, 79 (1960), 137–50

'πᾶς, ἅπας', in *TDNT*, V, 886–96

Rengstorf, Karl Heinrich, 'δοῦλος,κτλ.', in *TDNT*, II, 261–80

Reploh, Karl-Georg, *Markus-Lehrer der Gemeinde. Eine redaktionsgeschichtliche Studie zu den Jüngerperikopen des Markus-Evangeliums*, SBM 9 (Stuttgart, 1969)

Resenhöfft, Wilhelm, 'Jesu Gleichnis von den Talenten, ergänzt durch die Lukas-Fassung', *NTS*, 26 (1980), 318–31

Richard, Earl, *Acts 6:1 – 8:4. The Author's Method of Composition*, SBLDS 41 (Missoula, Mont., 1978)

'Acts 7: An Investigation of the Samaritan Evidence', *CBQ*, 39 (1977), 190–208

Richardson, Peter, 'The Thunderbolt in Q and the Wise Man in Corinth', in P. Richardson and J. C. Hurd (eds.), *From Jesus to Paul. Studies in Honour of Francis Wright Beare* (Waterloo, Ont., 1984), 91–112

Rickenbacher, Otto, *Weisheitsperikopen bei Ben Sira*, OBO 1 (Freiburg/ Göttingen, 1973)

Ricoeur, Paul, 'Biblical Hermeneutics', in J. D. Crossan (ed.), *Paul Ricoeur on Biblical Hermeneutics*, Semeia 4 (Missoula, Mont., 1975), 29–148

Riesenfeld, Harald, 'Vom Schätzesammeln und Sorgen – ein Thema urchristlicher Paränese. Zu Mt. VI 19–34', in *Neotestamentica et Patristica. Eine Freundesgabe, Herrn Professor Dr. Oscar Cullmann zu seinem 60. Geburtstag überreicht*, NT.S 6 (Leiden, 1962), 47–58

Riesner, Rainer, *Jesus als Lehrer. Eine Untersuchung zum Ursprung der Evangelien-Überlieferung*, WUNT 2. Ser. 7 (Tübingen, 1981)

Ringgren, Helmer, *Word and Wisdom. Studies in the Hypostatization of Divine Qualities and Functions in the Ancient Near East* (Lund, 1947)

Robbins, Vernon, *Jesus the Teacher. A Socio-Rhetorical Interpretation of Mark* (Philadelphia, Pa., 1984)

Robinson, James M., 'Basic Shifts in German Theology', *Interp.*, 16 (1962), 76–97

'Die Hodajot-Formel in Gebet und Hymnus des Frühchristentums', in W. Eltester, F. H. Kettler (eds.), *Apophoreta. Festschrift für Ernst Haenchen zu seinem siebzigsten Geburtstag am 10. Dezember 1964*, BZNW 30 (Berlin, 1964), 194–235

'Jesus as Sophos and Sophia: Wisdom Tradition and the Gospels', in R. L. Wilken (ed.), *Aspects of Wisdom in Judaism and Early Christianity*, University of Notre Dame Center for the Study of Judaism and Christianity in Antiquity 1 (Notre Dame/London, 1975), 1–16

'Logoi Sophon: On the *Gattung* of Q', in J. M. Robinson, H. Koester (eds.), *Trajectories through Early Christianity* (Philadelphia, Pa., 1971), 71–113

The Nag Hammadi Library in English (San Francisco/New York/Leiden, 1977)

Roloff, Jürgen, 'Anfänge der soteriologischen Deutung des Todes Jesu (Mk. x.45 and Lk. xxii.27)', *NTS*, 19 (1972), 38–64

'Auf der Suche nach einem neuen Jesusbild. Tendenzen und Aspekte der gegenwärtigen Diskussion', *ThLZ*, 98 (1973), 561–72

Roon, A. van, 'The Relation between Christ and the Wisdom of God according to Paul', *NT*, 16 (1974), 207–39

Rordorf, W., 'Un Chapitre d'éthique judéo-chrétienne: les deux voies', *RSR*, 60 (1972), 109–28

Roth, Wolfgang, 'On the Gnomic-Discursive Wisdom of Jesus ben Sirach', in J. D. Crossan (ed.), *Gnomic Wisdom*, Semeia 17 (Chico, Calif., 1980), 59–79

Rüger, Hans Peter, 'Aramäisch: II. Im Neuen Testament' in *TRE*, III, 602–10

'Μαμωνᾶς', *ZNW*, 64 (1973), 127–31

Rylaarsdam, J. Coert, *Revelation in Jewish Wisdom Literature* (Chicago, 1946)

Sabbe, Maurits, 'Can Mt 11,27 and Lk 10,22 be called a Johannine Logion?', in J. Delobel (ed.), *Logia. Les Paroles de Jésus – The Sayings of Jesus. Mémorial Joseph Coppens*, BEThL 59 (Louvain, 1982), 363–71

'The Son of Man Saying in Acts 7,56', in J. Kremer (ed.), *Les Actes des Apôtres. Traditions, Rédaction, Théologie*, BEThL 48 (Louvain, 1979), 241–79

Safrai, Shmuel, 'Education and the Study of the Torah', in *CRI*, Section I: *The Jewish People in the First Century. Historical Geography, Political History, Social, Cultural and Religious Life and Institutions*, Vol. II (Assen/Amsterdam, 1976), 945–70

Safrai, Shmuel, and Flusser, David, 'The Slave of Two Masters', *Imm.*, 6 (1976), 30–3

Sahlin, Harald, 'Traditionskritische Bemerkungen zu zwei Evangelienperikopen', *StTh*, 33 (1979), 69–84

Sanders, Jack T., *Ben Sira and Demotic Wisdom*, SBL Monograph Series 28 (Chico, Calif., 1983)

Sanders, James A., *The Psalms Scroll of Qumran Cave 11 (11Q Psᵃ)*, DJD 4 (Oxford, 1965)

'Two Non-Canonical Psalms in 11Q Ps^a', *ZAW*, 76 (1964), 57–75

Scharlemann, Martin H., *Stephen. A Singular Saint*, AnBib 34 (Rome, 1968)

Schenk, Wolfgang, 'Der Einfluss der Logienquelle auf das Markusevangelium', *ZNW*, 70 (1979), 141–65

Synopse zur Redenquelle der Evangelien. Q-Synopse and Rekonstruktion in deutscher Übersetzung mit kurzen Erläuterungen (Düsseldorf, 1981)

Schenke, Hans-Martin, 'Die Tendenz der Weisheit zur Gnosis', in B. Aland (ed.), *Gnosis. Festschrift für Hans Jonas* (Göttingen, 1978), 351–72

Schenke, Hans-Martin, and Fischer, Karl Martin, *Einleitung in die Schriften des Neuen Testaments*, II: *Die Evangelien und die anderen neutestamentlichen Schriften* (Berlin, 1979)

Schimanowski, Gottfried, *Weisheit und Messias. Die jüdischen Voraussetzungen der urchristlichen Präexistenzchristologie*, WUNT 2.17 (Tübingen, 1985)

Schmid, Hans Heinrich, *Wesen und Geschichte der Weisheit. Eine Untersuchung zur altorientalischen und israelitischen Weisheitsliteratur*, BZAW 101 (Berlin, 1966)

Schmidt, Daryl, 'The LXX *Gattung* "Prophetic Correlative"', *JBL*, 96 (1977), 517–22

Schmithals, Walter, *Das Evangelium nach Lukas*, ZBK NT 3.1 (Zürich, 1980)

'Die Worte vom leidenden Menschensohn. Ein Schlüssel zur Lösung des Menschensohn-Problems', in C. Andresen, G. Klein (eds.), *Theologia Crucis – Signum Crucis. Festschrift für Erich Dinkler zum 70. Geburtstag* (Tübingen, 1979), 417–45

Schnabel, Eckhard J., *Law and Wisdom from Ben Sira to Paul. A Tradition Historical Enquiry into the Relation of Law, Wisdom and Ethics*, WUNT 2.16 (Tübingen, 1985)

Schnackenburg, Rudolf, 'Der eschatologische Abschnitt Lk 17,20–37', in A. Descamps, A. de Halleux (eds.), *Mélanges bibliques en hommage au R. P. Béda Rigaux* (Gembloux, 1970), 213–34

'Die Bergpredigt', in R. Schnackenburg (ed.), *Die Bergpredigt. Utopische Vision oder Handlungsanweisung?*, Schriften der katholischen Akademie in Bayern 107 (Düsseldorf, 1982), 13–59

'"Ihr seid das Salz der Erde, das Licht der Welt"', in his *Schriften zum Neuen Testament. Exegese in Fortschritt und Wandel* (Munich, 1971), 177–200

'Markus 9,33–50', in his *Schriften zum Neuen Testament. Exegese in Fortschritt und Wandel* (Munich, 1971), 129–54

Schneider, Gerhard, 'Das Bildwort von der Lampe. Zur Traditionsgeschichte eines Jesus-Wortes', *ZNW*, 61 (1970), 183–209

'Stephanus, die Hellenisten und Samaria', in J. Kremer (ed.), *Les Actes des Apôtres. Traditions, Rédaction, Théologie*, BEThL 48 (Louvain, 1979), 215–40

Schottroff, Luise, 'Gewaltverzicht und Feindesliebe in der urchristlichen Jesustradition: Mt 5,38–48; Lk 6,27–36', in G. Strecker (ed.), *Jesus Christus in Historie und Theologie. Neutestamentliche Festschrift für Hans Conzelmann zum 60. Geburtstag* (Tübingen, 1975), 197–221 (= 'Non-Violence and the Love of One's Enemies', in L. Schottroff *et al., Essays on the Love Commandment* (Philadelphia, Pa, 1978), 9–39)

Schottroff, Luise and Stegemann, Wolfgang, *Jesus von Nazareth – Hoffnung der Armen*, Urban-Taschenbücher T-Reihe 639 (Stuttgart/Berlin/Cologne/Mainz, 1978)

Schrage, Wolfgang, *Das Verhältnis des Thomas-Evangeliums zur synoptischen Tradition und zu den koptischen Evangelienübersetzungen. Zugleich ein Beitrag zur gnostischen Synoptikerdeutung*, BZNW 29 (Berlin, 1964)

'τυφλός', in *TDNT*, VII, 270–94

Schrenk, Gottlob, 'δικαιόω' in *TDNT*, II, 211–19

Schürer, Emil, *The History of the Jewish People in the Age of Jesus Christ (175B.C. – A.D. 135)*, II, rev. G. Vermes, F. Millar, M. Black (Edinburgh, 1979)

Schürmann, Heinz, 'Beobachtungen zum Menschensohn-Titel in der Redenquelle. Sein Vorkommen in Abschluss- und Einleitungswendungen' in R. Pesch, R. Schnackenburg (eds.), *Jesus und der Menschensohn. Für Anton Vögtle* (Freiburg/Basle/Vienna, 1975), 124–47

Das Lukasevangelium, I: *Kommentar zu Kap. 1,1–9,50*, HThK 3 (Freiburg/Basle/Vienna, 1969)

'Das Zeugnis der Redenquelle für die Basileia-Verkündigung Jesu' in J. Delobel (ed.), *Logia. Les Paroles de Jésus – The Sayings of Jesus. Mémorial Joseph Coppens*, BEThL 59 (Louvain, 1982), 121–200

'Sprachliche Reminiszenzen an abgeänderte oder ausgelassene Bestandteile der Spruchsammlung im Lukas- und Matthäusevangelium', *NTS*, 6 (1960), 193–210

Traditionsgeschichtliche Untersuchungen zu den synoptischen Evangelien, KBANT (Düsseldorf, 1968)

'"… und Lehrer". Die geistliche Eigenart des Lehrdienstes und sein Verhältnis zu anderen geistlichen Diensten im neutestamentlichen Zeitalter', in W. Ernst, K. Feiereis, F. Hoffmann (eds.), *Dienst der Vermittlung. Festschrift zum 25-jährigen Bestehen des philosophisch-theologischen Studiums im Priesterseminar Erfurt*, EThSt 37 (Leipzig, 1977), 107–47

Schulz, Siegfried, 'Die Anfänge urchristlicher Verkündigung. Zur Traditions- und Theologiegeschichte der ältesten Christenheit', in U. Luz, H. Weder (eds.), *Die Mitte des Neuen Testaments. Einheit und Vielfalt neutestamentlicher Theologie. FS für Eduard Schweizer zum siebzigsten Geburtstag* (Göttingen, 1983), 254–71

'Die neue Frage nach dem historischen Jesus', in H. Baltensweiler, B. Reicke (eds.), *Neues Testament und Geschichte. Historisches Geschehen und Deutung im Neuen Testament. Oscar Cullmann zum 70. Geburtstag* (Zürich/Tübingen, 1972), 33–42

Q. Die Spruchquelle der Evangelisten (Zürich, 1972)

Schwarz, Günther, '"… ἀπαρνησάσθω ἑαυτὸν …"'? (Markus viii 34 Parr.)' *NT*, 17 (1975), 109–12

'"… lobte den betrügerischen Verwalter"?', *BZ*, 18 (1974), 94–5

'Matthäus vii 13a. Ein Alarmruf angesichts höchster Gefahr', *NT*, 12 (1970), 229–32

Schweizer, Eduard, *Das Evangelium nach Lukas*, NTD 3 (Göttingen, 1982) (= *The Good News According to Luke*, trans. D. E. Green (London, 1984))

'Der Menschensohn (Zur eschatologischen Erwartung Jesu)', *ZNW*, 50 (1959), 185–209

Matthäus und seine Gemeinde, SBS 71 (Stuttgart, 1974)

'Observance of the Law and Charismatic Activity in Matthew', *NTS*, 16 (1970), 213–30

'ψυχή, κτλ.', in *TDNT*, IX, 637–56

The Good News According to Mark. A Commentary on the Gospel (London, 1978)

The Good News According to Matthew, trans. D. E. Green (London, 1978)

'Zum religionsgeschichtlichen Hintergrund der "Sendungsformel" Gal 4,4f. Rom 8,3f. Joh 3,16f. 1 Joh 4,9', *ZNW*, 57 (1966), 199–210

Scott, R. B. Y., 'Folk Proverbs of the Ancient Near East', *Transactions of the Royal Society of Canada*, 55 (1961), 47–56 (= J. L. Crenshaw (ed.), *Studies in Ancient Israelite Wisdom* (New York, 1976), 417–26)

Proverbs–Ecclesiastes, AncB 18 (New York, 1965)

The Way of Wisdom in the Old Testament (New York, 1971)

Seccombe, David Peter, *Possessions and the Poor in Luke–Acts*, Studien zum Neuen Testament und seiner Umwelt. Serie B Band 6 (Linz, 1982)

Seesemann, Heinrich, 'ὀλίγος', in *TDNT*, V, 171–3

Seitz, O. J. F., 'Love Your Enemies', *NTS*, 16 (1969), 39–54

'The Commission of Prophets and "Apostles": A Re-Examination of Matthew 23,34 with Lk 11,49', in F. L. Cross (ed.), *StEv*, IV: *Papers Presented to the Third International Congress on New Testament Studies Held at Christ Church Oxford 1965*, Part I: *The New Testament Scriptures* (= TU 102) (Berlin, 1968), 236–40

Selwyn, Edward Gordon, 'Miscellanea. Studies in Texts: St Luke xii. 27,28', *Theol.*, 16 (1928), 163–4

The First Epistle of St Peter. The Greek Text with Introduction, Notes and Essays (London, 1947)

Sheppard, Gerald T., *Wisdom as a Hermeneutical Construct. A Study in the Sapientializing of the Old Testament*, BZAW 151 (Berlin/New York, 1980)

Shimoff, Sandra R., 'Rabbinic Legends of Saul, Solomon, and David: Political and Social Implications of Aggada' (dissertation, St Mary's Seminary and University Ecumenical Institute, 1981)

Sider, John W., 'The Meaning of *Parabole* in the Usage of the Synoptic Evangelists', *Bib.*, 62 (1981), 453–70

Simón, Marcel, *St Stephen and the Hellenists in the Primitive Church* (London/New York/Toronto, 1958)

Simons, E., *Hat der dritte Evangelist den kanonischen Matthäus benutzt?* (Bonn, 1880)

Sjöberg, Erik, 'Das Licht in dir. Zur Deutung von Matth. 6,22f Par.', *StTh*, 5 (1952), 89–105

Smith, David W., *Wisdom Christology in the Synoptic Gospels*, Pontificia Studiorum Universitas a S. Thoma Aq. in Urbe (Rome, 1970)

Stadelmann, Helge, *Ben Sira als Schriftgelehrter. Eine Untersuchung zum Berufsbild des vor-makkabäischen Söfer unter Berücksichtigung seines Verhältnisses zu Priester-, Propheten- und Weisheitslehrertum*, WUNT 2. Ser. 6 (Tübingen, 1980)

Stanton, Graham N., 'On the Christology of Q', in B. Lindars, S. S. Smalley (eds.), *Christ and Spirit in the New Testament* (Cambridge, 1973), 27–42

'Salvation Proclaimed: X. Matthew 11:28–30: Comfortable Words?', *ET*, 94 (1982), 3–9

'Stephen in Lucan Perspective', in E. A. Livingstone (ed.), *Studia Biblica 1978: Sixth International Congress on Biblical Studies, Oxford, 3–7 April 1978, III: Papers on Paul and Other New Testament Authors*, JSNT Supplement Series 3 (Sheffield, 1980), 345–60

Steck, Odil Hannes, *Israel und das gewaltsame Geschick der Propheten. Untersuchungen zur Überlieferung des deuteronomistischen Geschichtsbildes im Alten Testament, Spätjudentum und Urchristentum*, WMANT 23 (Neukirchen-Vluyn, 1967)

Steinhauser, Michael G., *Doppelbildworte in den synoptischen Evangelien. Eine Form- und Traditions-kritische Studie*, FzB 44 (Stuttgart, 1981)

Stendahl, Krister, 'Hate, Non-Retaliation, and Love: 1QS X,17–20 and Rom. 12:19–21', *HThR*, 55 (1962), 343–55

'Matthew', in M. Black, H. H. Rowley (eds.), *PCB* (London, 1962), 769–98

The School of St. Matthew and its Use of the Old Testament, ASNU 20 (Uppsala/Lund/Copenhagen, 1954)

Strecker, Georg, *Der Bergpredigt. Ein exegetischer Kommentar* (Göttingen, 1984)

Der Weg der Gerechtigkeit. Untersuchung zur Theologie des Matthäus, FRLANT 82 (Göttingen, 1962)

'Die Antithesen der Bergpredigt (Mt 5.21–48 par)', *ZNW*, 69 (1978), 36–72

'Die Makarismen der Bergpredigt', *NTS*, 17 (1971), 255–75

Suggs, M. Jack, 'The Antitheses as Redactional Products', in G. Strecker (ed.), *Jesus Christus in Historie und Theologie. Neutestamentliche Festschrift für Hans Conzelmann zum 60. Geburtstag* (Tübingen, 1975), 433–44

'The Christian Two Ways Tradition: Its Antiquity, Form, and Function', in D. E. Aune (ed.), *Studies in New Testament and Early Christian Literature. Essays in Honor of Allen P. Wikgren*, NT.S 33 (Leiden, 1972), 60–74

Wisdom, Christology, and Law in Matthew's Gospel (Cambridge, Mass., 1970)

Tannehill, Robert C., *The Sword of His Mouth*, SBL Semeia Supplement 1 (Philadelphia/Missoula, 1975)

Taylor, Archer, *The Proverb* (Cambridge, Mass., 1931)

Taylor, Vincent, *The Gospel According to St Mark. The Greek Text with Introduction, Notes and Indexes*, 2nd edn (London, 1972)

'The Order of Q', *JThS*, n.s. 4 (1953), 27–31

'The Original Order of Q', in A. J. B. Higgins (ed.), *New Testament Essays: Studies in Memory of Thomas Walter Manson 1893–1958* (Manchester, 1959), 246–69

Telford, William R., *The Barren Temple and the Withered Tree. A Redaction-Critical Analysis of the Cursing of the Fig-Tree Pericope in Mark's Gospel and its Relation to the Cleansing of the Temple Tradition*, JSNT Supplement Series 1 (Sheffield, 1980)

Terrien, Samuel, 'Amos and Wisdom', in J.L. Crenshaw (ed.), *Studies in Ancient Israelite Wisdom* (New York, 1976), 448–55

Theissen, Gerd, *Biblical Faith. An Evolutionary Approach*, trans. J. Bowden (London, 1984)

Studien zur Soziologie des Urchristentums, WUNT 19 (Tübingen, 1979)

The First Followers of Jesus. A Sociological Analysis of the Earliest Christianity (London, 1978)

Thompson, John Mark, *The Form and Function of Proverbs in Ancient Israel*, Studia Judaica 1 (The Hague/Paris, 1974)

Tilborg, S. van, 'A Form-Criticism of the Lord's Prayer', *NT*, 14 (1972), 94–105

Tödt, Heinz Eduard, *The Son of Man in the Synoptic Tradition* (London, 1965)

Topel, L. John, 'On the Injustice of the Unjust Steward: Lk 16:1–13', *CBQ*, 37 (1975), 216–27

Trilling, Wolfgang, *Das wahre Israel. Studien zur Theologie des Matthäus-Evangeliums*, 3rd edn, StANT 10 (Munich, 1964)

Trocmé, Étienne, *The Formation of the Gospel according to Mark* (London, 1975)

Tuckett, Christopher M., 'Arguments from Order: Definition and Evaluation', in C.M. Tuckett (ed.), *Synoptic Studies. The Ampleforth Conferences of 1982 and 1983*, JSNT Supplement Series 7 (Sheffield, 1984), 197–219

'1 Corinthians and Q', *JBL*, 102 (1983), 607–19

Nag Hammadi and the Gospel Tradition. Synoptic Tradition in the Nag Hammadi Library (Edinburgh, 1986)

'On the Relationship between Matthew and Luke', *NTS*, 30 (1984), 130–42

The Revival of the Griesbach Hypothesis. An Analysis and Appraisal, MSSNTS 44 (Cambridge, 1983)

Unnik, W.C. van, 'Die Motivierung der Feindesliebe in Lukas vi 32–35', *NT*, 8 (1966), 284–300

Urbach, Ephraim E., *The Sages. Their Concepts and Beliefs*, 2 vols. (Jerusalem, 1975)

Venetz, Hermann-Josef, 'Bittet den Herrn der Ernte. Überlegungen zu Lk 10, 2//Mt 9,37', *Diakonia*, 11 (1980), 148–61

Vielhauer, Philipp, 'Jesus und der Menschensohn. Zur Diskussion mit Heinz Eduard Tödt und Eduard Schweizer', *ZThK*, 60 (1963), 133–77

Walker, William O., 'Jesus and the Tax Collectors', *JBL*, 97 (1978), 221–38

Walter, Nikolaus, 'Apostelgeschichte 6.1 und die Anfänge der Urgemeinde in Jerusalem', *NTS*, 29 (1983), 370–93

Wanke, Joachim, *'Bezugs- und Kommentarworte' in den synoptischen Evangelien. Beobachtungen zur Interpretationsgeschichte der Herren-worte in der vorevangelischen Überlieferung*, EThSt 44 (Leipzig, 1981)

'Die urchristlichen Lehrer nach dem Zeugnis des Jakobusbriefes', in R. Schnackenburg, J. Ernst, J. Wanke, (eds.), *Die Kirche des Anfangs. Für Heinz Schürmann* (Freiburg/Basle/Vienna, 1978), 489–511

'"Kommentarworte". Älteste Kommentierungen von Herrenworten', *BZ*, n.s. 24 (1980), 208–33

Watson, Francis, *Paul, Judaism and the Gentiles. A Sociological Approach*, MSSNTS 56 (Cambridge, 1986)

Watt, William S., 'Sententia' in *OCD²* (1970), 977–8

Wedderburn, A. J. M., 'ἐν τῇ σοφίᾳ τοῦ θεοῦ – 1 Kor 1.21', *ZNW*, 64 (1973), 132–4

Weeden, Theodore J., *Mark. Traditions in Conflict* (Philadelphia, Pa., 1971)

Weinert, Francis D., 'Luke, the Temple and Jesus' Saying about Jerusalem's Abandoned House (Luke 13:34–35)', *CBQ*, 44 (1982), 68–76

'The Parable of the Throne Claimant (Luke 19:12, 14–15a, 27) Reconsidered', *CBQ*, 39 (1977), 505–14

Weiser, Alfons, *Die Knechtsgleichnisse der synoptischen Evangelien*, StANT 29 (Munich, 1971)

West, M.L., *Hesiod's Works & Days* (Oxford, 1978)

Whybray, R. N., *The Intellectual Tradition in the Old Testament*, BZAW 135 (Berlin/New York, 1974)

Wisdom in Proverbs. The Concept of Wisdom in Proverbs 1–9, SBT 45 (London, 1965)

Wilckens, Ulrich, 'σοφία, σοφός, σοφίζω', in *TDNT*, VII, 465–76, 496–528

Weisheit und Torheit. Eine exegetisch-religionsgeschichtliche Untersuchung zu 1.Kor. 1 und 2, BHTh 26 (Tübingen, 1959)

'Zu 1 Kor 2, 1–6', in C. Andresen, G. Klein (eds.), *Theologia Crucis – Signum Crucis. Festschrift für Erich Dinkler zum 70. Geburtstag* (Tübingen, 1979), 501–37

Wilder, Amos Niven, *Early Christian Rhetoric. The Language of the Gospel* (Cambridge, Mass., 1971)

Eschatology and Ethics in the Teaching of Jesus, 2nd edn (New York, 1950)

'Eschatology and the Speech-Modes of the Gospel', in E. Dinkler (ed.), *Zeit und Geschichte. Dankesgabe an Rudolf Bultmann zum 80. Geburtstag* (Tübingen, 1964), 19–30

Williams, Francis E., 'Is Almsgiving the Point of the "Unjust Steward"?', *JBL*, 83 (1964), 293–7

Williams, James G., *Those Who Ponder Proverbs. Aphoristic Thinking and Biblical Literature*, Bible and Literature Series 2 (Sheffield, 1981)

Wilson, R. McL., 'Gnosis at Corinth', in M. D. Hooker, S. G. Wilson (eds.), *Paul and Paulinism. Essays in Honour of C. K. Barrett* (London, 1982), 102–14

Studies in the Gospel of Thomas (London, 1960)

Windisch, Hans, *The Meaning of the Sermon on the Mount. A Contribution to the Historical Understanding of the Gospels and to the Problem of their True Exegesis* (Philadelphia, Pa., 1951)

Wink, Walter, *John the Baptist in the Gospel Tradition*, MSSNTS 7 (Cambridge, 1968)

Winter, Paul, 'Ben Sira and the Teaching of "Two Ways"', *VT*, 5 (1955), 315–18

'Matthew xi 27 and Luke x 22 from the First to the Fifth Century. Reflections on the Development of the Text', *NT*, 1 (1956), 112–48

Worrell, John Edward, 'Concepts of Wisdom in the Dead Sea Scrolls' (dissertation, Claremont Graduate School, 1968)

Woschitz, Karl, 'Reflexionen zum Zeitverständnis in der Spruchquelle "Q"', *ZKTh*, 97 (1975), 72–9

Wrege, Hans-Theo, *Die Überlieferungsgeschichte der Bergpredigt*, WUNT 9 (Tübingen, 1968)

Yamauchi, E.M., 'The "Daily Bread" Motif in Antiquity', *WThJ*, 28 (1966), 145–56

Zeller, Dieter, 'Der Zusammenhang der Eschatologie in der Logienquelle', in R. Fiedler, D. Zeller (eds.), *Gegenwart und kommendes Reich: Schülergabe Anton Vögtle zum 65. Geburtstag*, SBB (Stuttgart, 1975) 67–77

'Die Bildlogik des Gleichnisses Mt 11, 16f./Lk 7, 31f.', *ZNW*, 68 (1977), 252–7

Die weisheitlichen Mahnsprüche bei den Synoptikern, FzB 17 (Würzburg, 1977)

Kommentar zur Logienquelle, Stuttgarter Kleiner Kommentar NT 21 (Stuttgart, 1984)

'Redaktionsprozesse und wechselnder "Sitz im Leben" beim Q-Material', in J. Delobel (ed.), *Logia. Les Paroles de Jésus – The Sayings of Jesus. Mémorial Joseph Coppens*, BEThL 59 (Louvain, 1982), 395–409

'Weisheitliche Überlieferung in der Predigt Jesu', in W. Strolz (ed.), *Religiöse Grunderfahrungen. Quellen und Gestalten*, Veröffentlichungen der Stiftung Oratio Dominica (Freiburg/Basle/Vienna, 1977), 94–111

Zerwick, M., 'Die Parabel vom Thronanwärter', *Bib.*, 40 (1959), 654–74

Zimmermann, Alfred F., *Die urchristlichen Lehrer. Studien zum Tradentenkreis der διδάσκαλοι im frühen Urchristentum*, WUNT 2. Ser. 12 (Tübingen, 1984)

Zmijewski, Josef, *Die Eschatologiereden des Lukas-Evangeliums. Eine traditions- und redaktionsgeschichtliche Untersuchung zu Lk 21, 5–36 und Lk 17, 20–37*, BBB 40 (Bonn, 1972)

INDEX OF SELECTED BIBLICAL AND RELATED WORKS

INDEX OF AUTHORS